VICTORY AT FALAISE

The Soldiers' Story

Brigadier-General Denis Whitaker,
DSO *and* BAR, CM, ED, CD, LD'H, COC

Shelagh Whitaker

with
Terry Copp

HarperCollins*PublishersLtd*

VICTORY AT FALAISE:
THE SOLDIERS' STORY
Copyright © 2000 by Denis Whitaker
and Shelagh Whitaker.

www.harpercanada.com

HarperCollins books may be purchased for
educational, business, or sales promotional use.
For information please write:
Special Markets Department,
HarperCollins Canada,
55 Avenue Road, Suite 2900,
Toronto, Ontario, Canada M5R 3L2

First HarperCollins hardcover ed.
  ISBN 0-00-200017-2
First HarperCollins trade paper ed.
  ISBN 0-00-638498-6

Canadian Cataloguing in Publication Data

Whitaker, W. Denis
Victory at Falaise : the soldiers' story

ISBN 0-00-200017-2

  1. Falaise Gap, Battle of, 1944.
  2. World War, 1939–1945 – Campaigns –
     France – Normandy.
  I. Whitaker, Shelagh.
  II. Copp, Terry, 1938– .
  III. Title.

D756.5.F34W44 2000   940.54'21422   C00-930092-9

00 01 02 03 04 HC 6 5 4 3 2 1

Printed and bound in the United States
Set in Times

There is something refreshingly clear and right
about fighting for what you believe in,
with men you respect.

Col. James Moore Dunwoody,
DSO, DCM, ED, CD, FCA

CONTENTS

Normandy Key Maps

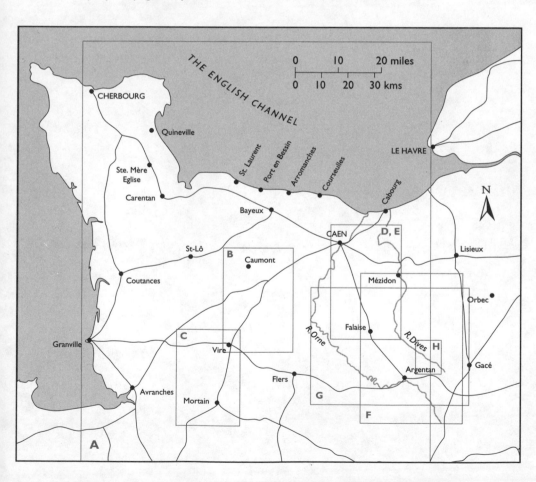

PROLOGUE
YOUNG INTEREST
IN OLD WARS

A fifteen-year-old lad, Stephen Campbell, picks up a book in a Toronto library. On the cover is a photograph that rivets the boy's attention, and continues to absorb him for the next twenty-five years.

At first he thinks it's his English dad's war in Burma, 1941. Then he recognizes Canadians: an officer, pistol in hand, is taking German infantry troops as prisoners of war. The picture is that of Major David Currie, a tank squadron commander fighting at St. Lambert-sur-Dives in 1944 in Normandy. The caption, written by Canada's official historian Colonel Charles Stacey, reads: "This is as close as we are ever likely to come to a photograph of a man winning the Victoria Cross."

With a boy's innocent curiosity, Campbell starts to read, to probe. What special qualities does it take for a man to stand on a field of battle and confront an enemy who is intent on killing him?

As the boy matures, his casual interest turns into an intense absorption, focused on this one man, David Currie. Campbell's research takes him to Normandy, where he walks the battlefield where Currie fought, and to England, where he locates the man who shot that famous news photograph. He seeks out veterans who fought with Currie—his friends, his widow, his son. He hunts records in the archives of Ottawa and London. After several decades, Campbell has amassed seventeen large books of data, all on Major David Currie and the battle of St. Lambert in August, 1944, where Currie was awarded the Victoria Cross for exceptional courage and leadership.

We met Stephen Campbell in 1998 and were intrigued. Why would this forty-five-year-old man from Manotick, Ontario—a father of four, a dedicated coach of junior soccer, an accountant with a brilliant and demanding career—pursue this hobby so single-mindedly? And why is this whole-hearted admiration and respect for the men who fought in Normandy not reflected in the writings of so many military historians and armchair generals?

In the epilogue of this book, historian Terry Copp has written a powerful rebuttal to all the nay-sayers of the past half-century, the revisionist historians who have belittled the superb achievements of the Allied soldiers by failing to analyse the battle in light of the actual conditions and circumstances of August 1944. As well, many historians have focused on the "battle of the generals." Few have tried to portray the "soldiers' story": the battle from the point of view of the fighting men. Yet with no experience in actual combat, it is difficult for anyone to fairly assess the efforts of men at the sharp end whose very lives are at risk each and every day, or even every minute.

In *Victory at Falaise: The Soldiers' Story*, we have let the soldiers tell their own stories.

I fought with the men of Normandy until I was wounded, and I rejoined them to fight for seven more months through Belgium, Holland, and Germany. I believe they were damned good soldiers. We weren't fighting a war of individuals; we fought in cohesive, disciplined, well-trained units that pulled together to take objectives.

This book was inspired by—and is dedicated to—Stephen Campbell, and to the growing number of young men and women like him who are currently pioneering a fresh groundswell of interest in World War II, not so much in weapons used or battles won, but in the human experience of war.

These young, amateur historians share a passion to understand how men and women—the ages of teenagers and young adults—could have found the physical courage and mental stamina to put their lives and futures in peril: the unborn child they will never see, the wife with whom they will never grow old, the profession they will never pursue. They try to imagine, and cannot, what it is like to hold the shattered body of their closest friend, to wake each morning knowing that in just minutes, hours, or days they, too, could be dead.

This very personal identification with those who fought in the Second World War provokes and deserves new answers.

We hope our book will help a new generation find them.

Denis and Shelagh Whitaker   *Oakville, Ontario, June 2000*

I
THE CLASS OF '26

The Class of '26 crouched in their slit trenches, faces glowering skywards.

"Sons of bitches," they muttered to themselves as Allied fighters and bombers screamed overhead. "We'll get them yet."

The Class of '26, now incorporated into the élite 12th SS Hitler-jugend, had been in action almost since 6 June 1944—D-Day. For forty-four days and forty-four nights, the Hitler Youth had struggled ceaselessly to keep the Allied forces from breaking out beyond Caen, holding their defensive positions despite every action the enemy had mounted against them. They believed in their destiny: they were invincible. Hitler had said so.

The Nazi party had created the Hitler Youth to provide a steady supply of young *soldaten* committed to the cause of the Third Reich. The "Class of 1926," some 800,000 ten-year-olds, formed the base of the movement when they were enrolled in the Jungvolk movement on the date of Hitler's forty-seventh birthday—20 April 1936. As junior members of the Hitler Youth, they took an oath to be repeated on the same date every year, promising "to do my duty at all times in love and faithfulness to help the Fuhrer."[1]

With membership in the Hitlerjugend (HJ) compulsory for all boys between the ages of ten and eighteen, the numbers burgeoned in the next years and by 1939 over five million lads were being methodically indoctrinated and manipulated to accept the Nazi doctrine.

It was carefully staged. At first the lads eagerly participated in competitive sports activities at the youth camps. Through athletics, they learned unquestioning discipline, teamwork and obedience. Gradually, the principles of Nazism were introduced. The youths learned to despise Jews and communists; to focus their loyalty on the state rather than on family and church; and, above all, to dedicate their lives to the Nazi credo that war is noble.

By 1939 Hitler had forged a generation to his Aryan ideal: youth that were "slim and strong, swift as greyhounds, tough as leather and hard as Krupp steel."[2]

After the outbreak of war, German youth between the ages of sixteen and eighteen received training in weapons and basic tactics. By 1942, combat veterans were brought in to intensify the training in special camps. The teenage graduates of these camps—numbering in the tens of thousands—would join Hitler's élite units, especially the Waffen-SS.

A decision to form a separate Hitler Youth Division, drawn from the best of the Class of 1926, was made after Germany's disastrous defeat at Stalingrad in 1943. Twenty thousand youths, just seventeen years old, were selected from among the most physically fit and ordered to report for duty. Proudly wearing their trademark camouflage suits, the boys were given specialized combat training at the platoon and company level in tanks, artillery, anti-tank and machine guns, trucks and motorcycles, engineering, mine laying, and reconnaissance. The Hitlerjugend trained under officers from the Führer's personal security guard, the 1st SS (Leibstandarte Adolf Hitler or LAH). These black-uniformed LAH were battle-hardened troops who had fought a relentless war on the eastern front.

The youngsters were treated as equals of the older recruits, but there were two provisos: they were denied visits to the local pub and to the local brothel. Relationships with girls were prohibited for those under eighteen. The "Baby Division," as some Americans later dubbed it, was given sweets instead.

Some babies.

In a single generation, Hitler had created in 12th SS Hitlerjugend Division a killing machine: the meanest, toughest fighting unit Germany had ever produced. They had been brilliantly trained, with the best equipment and most dedicated instructors; and they had been systematically brainwashed to be unshakably loyal to Hitler and the National Socialist Party.

When the Hitlerjugend troops—now numbering 20,540—were en route to Normandy in the spring of 1944, members of the French Resistance made a brave but futile effort to derail their ninety-car transport train in Ascq, near Lille. The SS commander in charge immediately had the entire male population between the ages of seventeen and fifty in the area rounded up. In "L'Affaire d'Ascq," as the tragedy is known, the 12th SS executed at least seventy-seven Frenchmen.[3]

The 25th Panzer Grenadier Regiment of the Hitlerjugend, commanded by SS Standartenführer (Colonel) Kurt Meyer, reached Caen on 7 June 1944 (D-plus-1). On 14 June, when the 12th SS commander, Brigadeführer (Brigadier-General) Fritz Witt, was hit and killed by a 16-inch shell from a naval gun, Kurt Meyer immediately took command. At thirty-three, he became the youngest divisional commander in the German or any other army in Normandy.[4] He was determined to throw the British and Canadian "little fish" back into the sea.

Meyer's unorthodox battle tactics, daring motorcycle feats (which had caused him no fewer than eighteen fractures and four concussions), and charismatic, swaggering demeanour (a rumpled camouflage suit being his habitual garb), all endeared him to the impressionable young Hitlerjugend. They called him "Panzermeyer" or, at times, *der schnelle Meyer*. He ordered reckless attacks, sacrificing hundreds of men and precious Panther tanks in fruitless efforts to destroy the Allied beachhead.

After the bitter confrontation with Canadian troops, the frustrated Hitler Youth became engaged in an orgy of violence, murdering over one hundred Canadian prisoners of war. The conduct of the officers was the most reprehensible. They not only killed in the heat of battle; they conducted the mass murder of nineteen Canadian prisoners of war in cold blood. One by one they led each prisoner into the walled garden of the Abbaye d'Ardenne, where Kurt Meyer had his headquarters, and put a bullet in the back of his head.

Twenty-one-year-old Gerhard Lemcke, a Hitlerjugend commander, justified the fanatical fighting. "One is told 'soldiers are murderers.' But that wasn't what it was about; it was about trying to weaken our enemy so that we would not be pushed back quickly. It was simplest to say 'Führer's orders,' and then no one was allowed to question it."[6]

There was ongoing rivalry and resentment between the National Socialist police force (the SS), which was newly created under Hitler's direct control, and the traditional, centuries-old Wehrmacht commanded by the German High Command (OKW). The Wehrmacht commanders, many of whom had little confidence in Hitler's military judgment and that of his neophyte subordinates, were furious when Hitler gave SS-Oberstgruppenführer (General) Paul Hausser command of the Seventh Army—the first SS general officer to head up a German army.

The rivalry was felt even down to the front-line forces. Hitler pampered all of the SS divisions, supplying them with the best weapons and recruits. Wehrmacht soldiers often resented and feared the young élitists for their arrogance and ruthlessness, envied them for their fine equipment and preferential treatment, and tried to distance themselves from the taint of Nazism.

"Our infantry was non-political," one Wehrmacht obersturmführer (lieutenant) insisted. "We did not get along with the Nazis. Our Panzer Lehr Wehrmacht Division always behaved in a 'correct' and soldierly manner."[8] His pride was understandable. So skilfully trained were that division's troops that the German tank expert General Guderian told its commander, General Bayerlein, "With this division alone you will throw the Anglo-Americans back into the sea."[9] Guderian's reckoning did not take into account the American air forces that were to decimate the élite division in a few hours' time in late July 1944.

Wenzel Borgert, a twenty-two-year-old lieutenant in 116th Panzer Division, was one of the millions drafted into the German army. When he was posted to Normandy, he went to great pains to explain to the French villagers that, despite the similarity of dress—the black uniform, with its skull emblem—he was not SS. "We were Catholics [so we] went to church with them. Suddenly we were no longer Nazis; we were German soldiers."

He got a special kick when the Americans started calling them "Jerries" instead of "Nazis."[10]

Before the invasion of Normandy, the troops posted there had enjoyed a peaceful and pleasant occupation, with bountiful food from the lush farming regions. Lieutenant Hans-Heinrich Dibbern remembers the friendly reception from the French populace at large.

"The French lived quietly with us. The women did our laundry, the farmers gave us food when we needed it, or sold us cider. It was an excellent relationship."[11]

A 2nd Panzer Division corporal recounted how "the farmers still had everything: milk, butter, eggs. The pastor's wife made a big meal for us, cooking eggs in a pan and so forth. She told us, "My son is a guest worker in Germany. I do not know where he is. I have no news from him. But I hope that a German mother gives him something like I now offer to you."[12]

Although the Germans introduced universal conscription in 1933, their propaganda made the pretense that many of the Wehrmacht and SS soldiers signed up on their own. "Naturally, my entire class registered as 'volunteers.' There was no other category," Friedrich Bertenrath, a signaller with the 2nd Panzer Division, recalled sardonically of the propaganda pretense.[13]

"[Some] were not asked as to whether they wanted to join a SS Division. [They] were given the SS uniform to put on and told where to go," agreed Adolf Rogosch, a private in the 353rd Infantry Division.[14]

Some of the troops—Poles, Alsacians, Russians, and even Koreans—had been captured by the Germans and forced into service. Ten thousand troops were anti-Soviet "volunteers"— Russians, Georgians, Cossacks, Turcomans, Tartars, and Caucasians—who were fighting in the German army in Normandy under the badges of their respective countries, but in German uniform.[15] They received distinctive treatment, even as far as having separate casualty lists and paybooks in their national currencies. (The Polish volunteers fighting in Normandy with their Canadian and British allies kept spare uniforms handy in case a captured enemy soldier turned out to be a fellow Pole who would be able to rejoin his countrymen.)

Yet as historian John Keegan notes, "The German army had always taken the greatest care to see that its units were formed of men from the same province or city, that replacements for casualties also came from the same places, and that returned wounded went back to the units with which they started."[16] Bonds of camaraderie were strong.

"In our unit, we would never abandon each other," Corporal Bertenrath concurred. "We had fought in Russia together. We were comrades, and always came to the rescue. We protected our comrades so they could go home to their wives, children and parents. That was our motivation. The idea that we would conquer the world had fallen long ago."[17]

As the Normandy campaign progressed, to the destruction of so many German units, this policy of bonding became almost impossible to facilitate.

Gradually, many of the Wehrmacht troops like Corporal Bertenrath were becoming disenchanted. Earlier they had been, in the words of one of their generals, "doped" by propaganda, but "the effects did not easily wear off."[18]

"German propaganda? We believed it all. We knew nothing else," Wenzel Borgert said bitterly. "We were the dogs of war, fighting on the front, so we didn't hear much of anything."[19]

With the D-Day landings, a new realism was setting in. A 21st Army Group Intelligence Report stated at the time that only 5 per cent of German troops believed in the possibility of ultimate victory.[20]

Hans-Heinrich Dibbern recalled his moment of disillusionment: "I went through a village, Bretteville. It had a church steeple, a typical Norman one that came to a sharp point with a belfry. [From the top] I could see the coast. I could see nothing but masses of material and weapons—it was such an experience for me. I thought, 'The war is lost. We don't stand a chance.' "[21]

"We were trained to believe that the final victory would be ours," Günter Materne, an artillery officer, said. "But during the fighting, many of us came to have a certain scepticism. The American weapon superiority was so great, I told my second-in-command that we'd be knocked back to the Siegfried Line. But of course we had to be very careful about saying this; one could be court-martialed for being a defeatist.

"The worst part was seeing comrades, whom I had been with for a long time, suddenly dying from some enemy action.

"I said, 'Man, is it worth this costly price in human life to go on? Is it not incredible?' But one did not say this out loud."[22]

Walter Padberg admitted that "as officers we were expected to do our duty. One cannot desert; one cannot simply throw away one's grenades. One can only . . . survive by doing one's duty. Duty, honour, and custom—that's how we came out of this shitty war."[23]

"[At first] we were quite confident that we could throw them back into the sea," SS-Sturmbannführer (Major) Helmut Ritgen of the Panzer Lehr Division said. "We learned on the third day that this was a dream. Rommel did not include the naval guns in his evaluation. If you have ever heard the detonation of a big naval gun—this is an unforgettable experience. It was impossible to fight a new war with just the ground forces alone. You can't do without a navy and an air force."[24]

Perhaps because of their own shortages, the enormous amount of *matériel* that flooded the Allied beachhead awed the Germans: "We had never seen the way a rich man fights the war," 12th SS Hitlerjugend commander Gerhard Lemcke observed bitterly. "The Americans could fire day and night; they had an unlimited supply of shells."[25]

Of all the troops, the 12th SS generally maintained the highest morale in the weeks following the Allied invasion of Normandy. While they had not been able to drive the Allies back into the sea, they had at least kept them from surging out of the beachhead. Their confidence was unshaken, even after weeks of heavy casualties and growing shortages of reinforcements and ammunition.

As one small measure the Germans adopted to prevent their heavy casualties from further demoralizing the troops was a strange practice first noticed by a Gordon Highlander: "One very seldom sees German graves; it is said that they are not thought good for morale so the Hun usually cheats, burying half a dozen in each individual grave."[26]

The Germans remained confident that Hitler's miracle weapons would destroy the enemy. The V-1 rocket ("buzz bomb") was launched just a few weeks after D-Day. The German troops were told of the horror of tens of thousands of Londoners, helpless as they watched the pilotless aircraft silently dive to the ground, killing and maiming scores of civilians.

Letters the German soldiers got from home reported that the round-the-clock Royal Air Force (RAF) bombings over Germany had eased, because the Allies had shifted their air power to support the invasion. The German populace at large, like its forces on the western front, had little idea of the seriousness of Hitler's plight.

7

On 20 July, the German troops heard via a radio broadcast of the attempted assassination of Adolf Hitler at the Führer's headquarters, "Wolfschanze," in Rastenburg in East Prussia.

Hitler's enemies, who had arranged to place a bomb at Hitler's feet during a briefing conference, were identified as senior officers of the Wehrmacht. Although the culprits were not immediately named, Walter Kaspers, adjutant with the 116th (Greyhound) Division, recalls the impact the news had on one highly placed officer.

"The son of General Guderian was on our division staff. He had just heard the news of the attempt on Hitler, and left quickly to make a phone call. When he returned he was completely pale. Later, he made another phone call and returned looking rather relieved. He had probably heard that his father was not in danger, though General Guderian and Hitler had an uneasy relationship."[27]

It was a near miss. Wehrmacht general Walter Warlimont described the map room as a "scene of stampede and destruction. There was nothing but wounded men groaning, and the acrid smell of burning and charred fragments of maps and papers fluttering in the wind."[28] Although injured, Hitler survived and was able to address his Nazi supporters by radio within a few hours. He quickly squashed the uprising and executed hundreds of people he suspected of plotting against him.

The members of the Hitlerjugend in particular were angered by and bewildered at the assassination attempt. This was the ultimate betrayal of their leader. How could the army attempt a coup against their supreme military leadership while the SS were themselves involved in a bitter defensive fight to the death?

"We considered those who had taken part in it as traitors," said Herbert Meier, a nineteen-year-old signaller with the Panzer Lehr Division. "They were pulling out just when the going was getting tough. It was sabotage, changing sides like that. The Führer was 'The Man' to us until the end."[29]

By D-plus-44, the Germans had two armies totalling some 700,000 men—forty-three divisions—to block the advance of a million and a half Allied troops. Ten of these forty-three divisions were powerful tank (panzer) divisions, on whom the Germans rested "all hopes of successful defence."

The Allies were by now established firmly on a beachhead stretching fifty miles along the Normandy coastline between Caen and Carentan. In places, though, they were contained in a narrow perimeter of just five or six miles of French soil. Their forty-four-day struggle had been an attempt, so far futile, to break through the enemy's defensive ring of steel and fire.

Normally in battle, the attacking side opposite a strong enemy requires five times the strength of the defender. In Normandy, the Allies' mere two-to-one ratio would challenge every ounce of their skill.

The defender, the German, had two main advantages: control and knowledge of the ground, and superiority of weapons, especially of armour and anti-tank guns.

After they were driven back from the beaches, the Germans built field fortifications, creating a new defensive line on the high ground just a few miles behind the coast. Hitler would not permit withdrawal beyond the range of the enemy's naval guns, so the soldiers, Wehrmacht and SS, learned to dig in and to disperse.

In the Caen sector, the successful German tactic was to hold their forward positions lightly, keeping back their strongest reserves in constant readiness to counter-attack against any Allied penetration. "We were [known as] the fire brigades," panzer corporal Friedrich Bertenrath explained. "Anywhere something was happening—a breakthrough or whatever—we were sent there to repel it as much as possible, a difficult task that we could not always do in those days. Luckily, we were quickly replaced by the infantry. Then it was off to the next place. Our mobility was still good in Normandy. The tiny dirt roads and the large hedges everywhere provided good cover from air attacks."[30]

German infantry companies, lacking motorized equipment or fuel, often marched all night or even bicycled twenty or thirty miles with full pack, not even stopping to rest or eat. Their transport was largely horse-drawn. Arriving at the front line, they would be flung immediately into battle. "The infantry was the real miracle arm of Hitler," Major Ritgen believed.[31]

Mortars and rockets were the weapons of choice. The 81mm mortar needed a crew of just two men. A small-weapons pit was easy to camouflage, and if two or three alternative positions were dug, the crew could fire off a dozen rounds and then move away before Allied counter-mortar batteries could locate them.

The Nebelwerfer, a six-barrelled heavy mortar, was not as easy to hide as an 81mm, but its range meant it could be sited on reverse slopes a long way from the forward lines. The mortar was fired in groups of six, the first screaming out its message, to be joined in rapid succession by the others. The effect was "a spine-chilling inharmonious screech,"[32] terrifying because the soldier on the ground was convinced a rocket was heading straight for him. Allied troops called the Nebelwerfer the "Moaning Minnie" because of the eerie sound it made. The French called it *la vache*—the cow. In either language it spelled death to anyone above ground. In turn, both mortar and Nebelwerfer fire could be registered by the Allies, so that any movement by German infantry prompted an accurate, almost instant, response.

The Germans also possessed the vaunted 88mm anti-tank gun, capable of destroying the thinly armoured Allied Sherman tanks almost at will. As well, the MG-42 German machine gun fired 1,200 rounds per minute. No Allied nation had weaponry anything like it.

When the British and Canadians mounted a serious attack with armour, the enemy's enormous advantage of being on the defensive with superior weapons was quickly evident. At Villers Bocage, a lone Tiger commanded by Michael Wittmann, the SS ace of aces, had in five minutes single-handedly destroyed twenty-five tanks and self-propelled guns (SPs) of the 3rd County of London Yeomanry (British 22nd Armoured Brigade), leaving behind "a trail of wrecked and burning vehicles."[33]

During *Operation Goodwood*, launched on 18 July, the Allies gained a pitifully few miles at the cost of more than two hundred tanks, despite an immense effort by the RAF and the concentrated weight of nine armoured regiments.[34]

Where the Allies' superiority lay was chiefly in its total supremacy at sea and in the air.

"In June we thought we still had a chance," Major Ritgen of the Panzer Lehr Regiment explained. "Then came the rockets." The relentless rocket attacks by fighter-bombers of the Allied Tactical Airforce (Typhoons and P-47 Thunderbolts) brought daytime movement by German troops almost to a standstill.

"We were constantly attacked by Jabos [Jäger bombers or fighter-bombers] during our march," recorded Private Meier. "Those who brought the ammunition forward lived a dangerous life. [Quite] a few were blown into the air along with their cargo."[35]

Günter Materne, an artillery lieutenant, still shudders at the recollection: "The march toward Caen was already a catastrophe. We could only march at night because of air superiority. The worst part was, sometimes the aerial observers would drop Christmas trees [clusters of lights], which would light up the area. They photographed us, our march direction, how many vehicles and of what type . . . then they were prepared for their next day's bombing attack."[36]

That knowledge of enemy troop positions could also be attributed to the huge advantage the Allies had in intelligence: Ultra. The code breakers at Bletchley Park, north of London, could intercept and decipher all of the wireless signals the Germans transmitted through their Enigma machines. The Germans thought their coding system could never be broken. The resulting decodes were entrusted to a small handpicked group of senior Allied military personnel, their key staff officers, and heads of state, who were cleared for Ultra intelligence.

On the ground, however, soldiers cared nothing about wireless signals. Life day to day was about survival. The old adage that war is hell took on new meaning. An infantryman's world, German or Allied, became a deep, cold muddy trench. He ate and slept and cowered there like some four-legged creature, as shells crashed around him without let-up. The most terrifying times came when he was ordered to emerge from his slimy haven and charge, gun at ready, into a solid curtain of fire. He might exchange a word with a buddy one moment and then witness the man's unspeakable mutilation the next.

At great cost, painfully, through these long weeks of battle, British and Canadian attackers still managed to achieve their prime objective: to keep the seven powerful panzer divisions in the Caen area pinned down. Strategists on both sides knew that an Allied breakthrough into the open country on the Caen–Falaise Road would quickly end the Normandy battle.

Hitler had taken direct control of his western armies. Since the attack on his life, he appointed only loyal Nazi officers to all-important commands. He did not trust the professional General Staff of the Wehrmacht. One of the first to be fired was the old war-horse Field Marshal Gerd von Rundstedt, who resented the interference and was reputed to have been sacked twenty-four hours after he shouted on the telephone to the army chiefs: "Make peace, you fools! What else can you do?" before he slammed down the receiver.[37]

Hitler's senior commanders disagreed with their leader, but dared not defy him in case they, too, were accused of plotting against him. The newly appointed Commander-in-Chief West, sixty-one-year-old Field Marshal Günther Hans von Kluge, warned Hitler that the tide of battle was turning against them.

"Der kluge Hans," or "Clever Hans" as he was nicknamed, quoted from the now-doomed Field Marshal Rommel's situation report (sitrep) of 15 July: "We have lost 97,000 men, including 2,360 officers. We have received up till now 10,000 men as replacements."

As well, Kluge reminded Hitler that constant Allied air strikes were crippling their rail lines, resulting in a severe loss of arms and equipment, especially radio equipment, artillery, cannon, and machine guns. "The enemy are daily providing new forces and masses of materials for the front; the enemy supply lines are not challenged by the Luftwaffe and enemy pressure is continually increasing. The German reserves are dwindling.

"The moment is fast approaching when this overtaxed front line is bound to break up."[38]

Hitler insisted that he would not, under any circumstances, consider withdrawal.

No military leader was brave enough to bring up the subject of surrender again, but many Wehrmacht front-line troops were having sober thoughts about the folly of continuing this seemingly futile struggle. Their fight was for their Fatherland, not their leader. Conditional surrender was becoming a secret option for some. Lieutenant Wenzel Borgert felt personally that "if the Allies had said, get rid of the Nazis, no one would have objected to that. But none of the Allies said that."[39]

Fortunately for the Allies, the Führer continued to be convinced that Montgomery was planning a massive attack through the Pas de Calais with a fresh U.S. army under Lieutenant-General George Patton. Hitler was stubbornly holding the entire Fifteenth German Army in the northeast sector of France against such an attack.

But there was a mystery. *Where was Patton*? Was he still held in disgrace after his clash with his superiors in Sicily, the infamous slapping incident when he accused a soldier of malingering? Or was he, as the Wehrmacht spies insisted, waiting in the wings in Kent?

And when would Armee Gruppe Patton launch the main Allied assault on the Pas de Calais?

OPERATION FORTITUDE

Adolf Hitler would have been surprised to learn that the elusive Lieutenant-General George Patton was, at D-plus-44, sitting in a Normandy orchard in the warm July sunshine, munching on an apple and venting his frustrations to his headquarters staff: "My destiny in this war," he growled, "is to sit here on my ass and watch the cider apples grow."[1] The staff remained silent. The only response was the energetic tail-wagging of Patton's white English bull terrier, Willie, a canny pooch whose original owner had been shot down over Germany.

Patton had arrived secretly in France on 6 July. For two weeks since, the tall and spirited tank commander had been languishing at Nehou, a rural village in the interior of the Cotentin Peninsula. As he had only a paper army, a minuscule tented Third Army headquarters, and no orders, his frustration grew and festered. It seemed that while everyone else was doing the fighting, George Patton was left waiting in the wings prior to taking centre stage. It was not a role he accepted easily. At fifty-nine years of age, he was afraid a younger man would take over his command. Slightly tongue-in-cheek, Patton had offered General Dwight D. Eisenhower one thousand dollars for each week by which Ike would hasten his operational command.[2]

In the winter months prior to D-Day, Ike had privately assigned command of Third U.S. Army to Patton. But the army could not become operational in Normandy until First U.S. Army achieved its breakout at Avranches, at the base of the Cherbourg Peninsula. Meanwhile, elements of Third U.S. Army were gradually and surreptitiously being moved into Nehou. Patton had been unable to resist making his unauthorized appearance there.

His impatience stemmed from the fact that by the third week of July he seemed not much closer to fulfilling his command. For almost two months, the Americans and British had been mired in a desperate and costly battle of attrition while struggling to get through the twenty-mile-deep belt of swamp and hedgerow country.

For Patton, the breakout of Third U.S. Army was tantalizingly close.

For security purposes, Eisenhower had issued a media ban concerning Patton, so there was no general knowledge of Patton's appointment as commander of Third U.S. Army in Normandy. Press interviews and quotes were forbidden. This was particularly hard on a man who so relished publicity. And the media loved Patton because he was good copy. Eisenhower, who was his boss and close friend, said he had a "genius for explosive statements."[3] In truth, he shot from the mouth with the same flair as he carried his famed ivory-handled pistols: indiscreetly and for effect.

Patton's impulsive "Top Secret" arrival on 6 July was a case in point: a crowd of soldiers cheering "Georgie!" met him, along with an inquisitive press who had somehow deduced his plans. They pestered him with questions.

The performance was typical of the Patton paradox: he was feared by the troops yet adored by them; admired by his commanders and associates as a skilled tank strategist but in constant hot water with them. He was the most quotable of all the Allied generals but, under an official press secrecy ban, was unquotable.

Eisenhower was unsure of his army commander. All the world knew Patton was in disgrace, and very nearly fired, for slapping a shell-shocked soldier in a hospital ward in Sicily. How far, Eisenhower wondered, could he be trusted again?

All things considered, there never was a less suitable candidate to be the focus of a conspiracy hatched at the top echelon of British intelligence, one of World War II's most elaborate deceptions, known as *Operation Fortitude*.

Fortitude was the brainchild of XX (Twenty) Committee. In 1942, British intelligence became aware of reports being passed to Berlin, allegedly by a German agent in Portugal. The reports, full of inaccuracies and absurdities, intrigued the committee sufficiently that they tracked down the author, one Juan Pujol Garcia, a twenty-nine-year-old Spaniard of a good family. Garcia, it transpired, loathed the German regime, and had been feeding German intelligence gross misinformation under the guise of serving as a German agent. His research resources were almost as ludicrous as the reports that stemmed from them: "a map of the United Kingdom, a *Blue Guide* to England, a Portuguese study of the British Fleet and an Anglo-French dictionary of military terms."[4]

Working from Lisbon, Garcia had for the previous ten months been concocting reports of troop movements of non-existent British regiments, the sailing of imaginary convoys, and lurid details of drunken orgies of Glasgow dock workers. XX Committee lost no time in recruiting this enterprising young Spaniard as a double agent and relocated him to Great Britain. "Garbo" was born.

The objective of XX Committee was not only to pass misinformation convincingly to the enemy, but also to persuade the Abwehr (German foreign and counter intelligence) to eventually act on it. This was the challenge XX Committee faced in the months leading up to the 1944 invasion of France. It was pointless to cover up the fact that an assault was being planned; the massing of troops, tanks, and landing craft would make that obvious. Its intention, therefore, became one of deceiving the enemy as to the time, strength, and location of the attack.

As plans for the D-Day invasion took shape, it became apparent to the Allies that they would have enormous difficulties landing a small force on the open beaches of the Normandy coast against a large force of well-entrenched defenders. The Germans had to be convinced somehow that the main thrust of the D-Day landing would take place elsewhere. Thus would the strength of the German defenders be reduced.

Enter "Garbo." Comfortably settled in England by his new employers, and cheerfully banking the generous pay of his old ones, he set about convincing the Abwehr that a non-existent 1st U.S. Army Group (FUSAG) was massing in strength in Kent, in southeastern England. This army group would form the main invasion force, striking at the Pas de Calais after General Montgomery's secondary 21st Army Group had established a lodgement farther west in Normandy.

Described by the dean of British intelligence, Michael Howard, as "perhaps the most complex and successful deception operation in the entire history of the war," *Fortitude* established its credibility with the Abwehr through an intricate weave of lies and half-truths, laced with just enough facts to make the deception plausible. To command this army group, XX Committee made the inspired selection of Lieutenant-General George Patton, who was deemed "temporarily unemployable" following his disgraceful loss of temper in Sicily. The committee relied on his notorious exhibitionism to attract attention to the force.[5]

FUSAG had (notionally) two real armies under command—First Canadian Army and Third U.S. Army—with a feigned headquarters established in eastern England for this imaginary force of 150,000 men. To reinforce the fiction, a radio network was set up to handle the busy administrative and operational functions. XX Committee arranged that all of Montgomery's 21st Army Group signals to his armies in France, emanating from Portsmouth, be rerouted via Dover. The Royal Air Force (RAF) cooperated by flying twice as many air missions and dropping twice as many bombs over the Pas de Calais as it did over Normandy.

"Garbo" worked with extreme dedication for two years to establish the deception. He flooded German intelligence with manufactured data. Writing with secret ink, and hiding his communications under innocent messages written with real ink, he wrote no fewer than 315 letters, each averaging two thousand words, in the first year. Via shortwave radio, he sent five or six transmissions each day—1,200 in all—dedicated to persuading the Abwehr to divert some of their divisions to the Pas de Calais. He had built up an imaginary network of more than two dozen agents that fed him information from across Britain. His favourites were the team of "Donny, Dick, and Derrick."[6]

In the months leading up to D-Day, XX Committee spared no effort to convince the German High Command of its "invasion plan." To his credit, Patton tried to go along with the plan. He obediently spent some time at the bogus army headquarters in Kent, where, in fact, components of his Third Army divisions were being trained for a landing—but not for the contrived assault that Hitler determinedly believed would be laid on by Armee Gruppe Patton from Dover to the Pas de Calais, a mere twenty miles across the English Channel.

At 0300 hours on 6 June 1944—D-Day—"Garbo" sent an urgent

dispatch to his control in Madrid that the invasion was imminent. The message, of course, was carefully timed to be just too late to have any value. There was no response from the Germans, and it wasn't until 0608 hours that he finally got through. Later that day "Garbo" complained, with mock indignation, to his German control about their lack of efficiency. "This makes me question your seriousness and sense of responsibility," he told them sternly. "I therefore demand a clarification immediately as to what has occurred." The next morning, after a "sleepless" night, he made contact again. "I am very disgusted as in this struggle for life and death I cannot accept excuses or negligence," he berated his unfortunate employers. "Were it not for my ideals and faith I would abandon this work as having proved myself a failure."[7]

The German agent apologized profusely: "I wish to stress in the clearest terms that your work over the last few weeks has made it possible for our command to be completely forewarned and prepared."[8]

Throughout the next few weeks, "Garbo" continued his extraordinary charade, and German intelligence continued to believe that an American army was at Dover, ready to launch a second invasion. By Hitler's direct order, the German Fifteenth Army—whose mobile panzer and infantry divisions were urgently needed by his armies fighting for their lives on the Normandy beaches—was still positioned north of the Seine River, awaiting an invasion that would never come. Even Rommel, the astute field marshal, "expected a second landing on both sides of the [Seine] river." An extract from his weekly report read: "In England, another 67 formations are standing to, of which 57 at the very least can be employed for a large-scale operation."[9]

Problems arose, however, when the irrepressible Patton's surreptitious visits to his army headquarters in France began to draw attention. It seemed just a matter of time before the media leaked Patton's movements. The planners dreaded the moment when the Germans realized they had been the victims of a hoax. "When the moment came," American historian Carlo D'Este wrote, " there would be a massive and immediate enemy reinforcement of Normandy."[10]

It was imperative that a new front for *Operation Fortitude* be devised.

Again, XX Committee went to work, persuading highly regarded Lieutenant-General Lesley McNair in Washington to assume nominal command of the bogus army. They reckoned that McNair, chief of Army Ground Forces, had the credibility to convince the Germans that he was replacing the once-again "demoted" perennial bad boy, Patton.

The greatest hoax of World War II continued to be played out. Armee Gruppe McNair was often referred to as an invasion force in German intelligence as late as August, and fifteen German divisions enjoyed peaceful seaside postings during June and July at the Pas de Calais.[11]

As for "Garbo," a grateful Abwehr agent informed him in July that the "Führer had been graciously pleased to bestow on him the Order of the Iron Cross, Class II."[12]

3

THE BOCAGE:
A LAND SO EVIL

Normandy: D-Plus-44

After five weeks of desperate and costly fighting, the Allied forces were still penned in the anteroom of Normandy. Access to the broad Norman plains remained firmly blocked by the weight of firepower of a desperate enemy.

The original 176,000 Allied invaders had now burgeoned into a multinational force of more than 1 million men, all still contained within this narrow stretch of land some fifty miles long backing onto the English Channel. The deepest penetration inland was twenty-five to thirty miles; in many places it was a mere five or six miles.

Crammed in with them was undoubtedly the largest assembly of *matériel* in the history of modern warfare: tanks, armoured vehicles, fuel, weapons, ammunition, materials for bridging and for building airstrips; food, water, and medical supplies for the troops. And it was growing by the day. Traffic jams of immense proportions were the norm.

General Bernard Montgomery's break-in plan was twofold. The Canadians and British at Caen, at the eastern end of the lodgement, would use all their resources to pin down and keep pinned down the might of seven of the nine German panzer tank divisions in Normandy. The illusion of a further attack by the mythical Armee Gruppe Patton at the Pas de Calais continued to immobilize still more German divisions east of the Seine River.

The Americans at the western end of the confined area could therefore exert their ever-growing power to force an entry into the interior of Normandy against minimal panzer opposition. The build-up of American forces and *matériel* to achieve this was essential.

But by D-plus-44 the reality seemed to be that Monty's plan was not working. After the fall of Cherbourg on 26 June, the Americans had turned the full weight of their army south. As they penetrated the enemy-held territory, they found the battleground to be as formidable as the enemy. The area between the U.S. sector on the coast south to St-Lô—the area the Allies had to penetrate if they were to achieve a breakout—was twenty miles of dense, hilly hedgerow country. This was the *bocage*.

The Germans were ready for them. They knew that the *bocage* was some of the most difficult fighting terrain in France, and the German troops and defences had been skilfully prepared. Seventh SS Army general Paul Hausser felt secure that in reinforcing his infantry battalions with just two powerful armoured divisions—Panzer Lehr and 2nd SS Panzer—he could control the advancing American army.

There was never a land more evil for men to fight over than the *bocage*.

The Norman farmers had done their work diligently over the centuries to enclose their small patches of green pasture and apple orchard, and protect their livestock. A single twelve-mile tract might have as many as four thousand of these small enclosed fields, each surrounded on four sides by imposing, impenetrable hedgerows.

Steep high banks, their soil compacted by centuries of rain and sun, and thick with roots, rose like ridges on a monstrous waffle around each tiny field. Tall, thickly entwined hedges surmounted each bank. Their branches sometimes reached a height of twenty feet and formed a canopy over the narrow, sunken lanes that hugged the perimeters of the fields. Sharp ditches on both sides made the roads too narrow for military vehicles to navigate and too deep for man to traverse.

Typically, each enclosure had just one entrance. It was at these narrow openings that the Germans set up killing zones. Troops or tanks attacking through these gaps were caught in cross-fire of the *bur-rup bur-rup* of Schmeissers and MG-2 machine guns, capable of firing 1,200 rounds a minute. Allied troops would face the well-camouflaged and securely dug-in 88mm anti-tank gun. This gun was far superior to any weaponry the Allies had. Designed as an anti-aircraft gun, to be manned by the Luftwaffe (and still under its command), the 88mm was without rival as an anti-tank weapon and also as an anti-personnel gun used in a ground role.

The Nebelwerfer mortars were capable of inflicting terrible wounds. Lieutenant Barney Danson of the Queen's Own Rifles has lasting memories of a "whining, whistling, groaning, ear-splitting roar that I mistook for dive-bombing aircraft . . . The noise was followed by exploding bombs all around us."[1] Danson was lucky. When you can hear the noise, the bomb is not dangerously close. Not hearing the bomb has deadly consequences.

German snipers sometimes tied themselves in branches of trees so as to have full use of their arms. They would pick off the Allied infantrymen with ease. German anti-tank and anti-personnel mines shattered the Allied troops. Booby-traps, even on lifeless German soldiers, were rigged with explosives.

War correspondent Ernie Pyle filed this account of German tactics in the *bocage*:

> The Germans dig deep trenches behind hedgerows and cover them with timber, so that it is almost impossible for artillery to get at them. Sometimes they will prop up machine guns with strings attached so they can fire [on fixed lines] over the hedge without getting out of their holes. They even cut out a section of the hedgerow and hide a big gun or tank in it, covering it with brush. Also they tunnel under the hedgerows from the back to make the opening on the forward side just large enough to stick a machine gun through.[2]

Each of these thousands of fields must be attacked, one by one. The Allies had no conception of the ruggedness of the country, nor had they the appropriate equipment or special training to assure them hope of success in this close-quarter fighting.

The unhappy reality was that the Allied planners had focused so single-mindedly on the massive problems of landing two armies on the D-Day beaches that they hadn't really thought beyond them. The troops were trained exhaustively for an amphibious assault, but not for the deadly ground to follow.

Certainly the planners were familiar with *bocage* country. Field Marshal Alan Brooke (professional head of the British army and

Montgomery's boss) had vacationed there often; Patton had spent his honeymoon in the region. But no one had envisioned that the Germans would create a new defensive line in its interior. The Allies had not factored in the enormous difficulties of being the aggressors in *bocage* warfare, where the large-scale armoured operations they had trained for just didn't work.

Tactics and weaponry had to be improvised as the Allied troops advanced, but as historian Russell Weigley summed up, "It was too bad that these revelations had to wait upon experience."[3]

It was a well-known fact before D-Day that the Sherman tanks were handicapped by the height of their sixteen-foot turrets. German tank guns could shoot off the turrets of Sherman tanks that poked up among the branches of apple trees at will. So, asked tank trooper Ken Tout, "why did we have months of training on the Salisbury Plain? Why not in the craggy terrain and orchards of Herfordshire or Wales?"[4]

A platoon commander from 4th Somerset Light Infantry (43rd Wessex Division), Lieutenant Sydney Jary, reflected that "too little time had been spent training the [infantry] in stimulating their imagination, initiative, and individual resourcefulness." If the armour and artillery weren't there to back them up, he noted, the infantrymen felt alone and helpless. They had never been encouraged to "probe, draw conclusions, infiltrate and exploit weakness in the enemy's dispositions."[5]

Not so the Germans. Private Adolf Rogosch of the German 353rd Infantry Division, one of Hitler's "miracle" infantrymen, was seventeen years old when he was thrust into *bocage* fighting. After months of practice in Brittany, he could rely on his own skills and not be dependent on other combat units. "We knew that if the American attack came, we'd probably be cut off from one another. So we learned to fight as individuals.

"Our division was being trained for the close combat that was sure to occur because of the hedgerows-specialized training. So we dug in among the hedges. Coming within thirty meters of the enemy was what we meant by close combat. We trained rather hard almost every day, throwing hand grenades and so forth."[6]

The Allies tried to give themselves some protection by laying on heavy-artillery barrages designed to keep the defenders' heads down. In this way they hoped to rush the enemy position at the last moment. But the Germans were canny. They nullified the effect with devastating counter-barrages of their own.

"They could do nothing," Private Adolf Rogosch scoffed. "We had figured out the tactics of the Americans. When the Americans pulled back, we pushed forward and threw them back into the open. And when they came back, we hit them again. We caused them heavy losses there, because they had to come out always . . . toward us. They could not deploy their tanks because of all the hedges. We got our first bazookas about then, and then we really got started. We would shoot their tanks, and that scared the others."[7]

The German soldiers had poor opinions of the calibre of the Allied infantry and tankers' equipment. They had been assured that the American GIs and the Canadian foot soldiers were rank amateurs, that the British were worn down, that their weaponry was crude.

The massive German tanks and self-propelled guns, dug-in and well concealed, were ideally suited to fighting in this terrain. The Panthers were almost immune to frontal attack because shells would glance off their sloping armour. With turrets closed, the German panzers could survive heavy shelling from enemy artillery.

Lieutenant Jary observed that the Allies were "hopelessly outgunned by the German Mark IV, Mark V (Panther) and Mark VI (Tiger) tanks. The German 75mm and 88mm anti-tank guns also wreaked a terrible havoc."[8]

These guns had a high velocity and penetrating power, and could knock out a Sherman tank at two thousand yards. The Sherman's guns—also 75mm but without the range or penetrating power—could only pierce German artillery at *two hundred* yards.

In any tank firefight—the Sherman nose to nose with a Tiger—it was clearly no contest. In fact, one 1st Northamptonshire Yeoman described his 75mm shots as bouncing off German armour plating "like tennis balls."[9]

The cumbersome, ungainly British Churchills, and the flimsier British and American Shermans, which had been designed as swift, mobile pursuit tanks, were at a disadvantage in *bocage* fighting.

An exception was the Firefly: a Sherman armed with a 17-pounder gun that had the equivalent striking power of the German 88mm. Incredibly, the 17-pounder was first produced in 1941. But the idea of installing them on the lightly armoured Sherman, thereby creating the powerful "Firefly," was not thought of until just prior to D-Day. It was by then too late to produce enough of these guns for every Sherman tank. They were in such short supply that there was only one Firefly for each British or Canadian troop of four tanks (though none, apparently, for the Americans).

But by then there was no time for gunners to practise on them and to work out the inevitable kinks—some quite complex and treacherous—before being battle-ready. It also never occurred to British planners to give their armoured forces extra clout by putting four Fireflies together in a single, powerful troop, modelling what the Germans did with their troops of Tigers.

British historian and veteran tank gunner Ken Tout commented wryly on "the folly of Britain's armaments program which organized tank design and gun design as two different functions in two different establishments."[10]

The one advantage the Allies had was that the Shermans were produced in huge numbers. They had to be. The general expectation was to lose three to five Shermans for every German tank destroyed. But whereas Allied losses, however immense, could be replaced in a day, the German tanks were virtually irreplaceable. They depended on their efficient workshops located just behind the front lines to "cannibalize and cobble together" refurbished armour overnight.[11]

The Wehrmacht troops had little respect for the Shermans. "Swiss cheese!" they would sneer, or "Ronson lighters"—references to how vulnerable they were to being pierced by shells and how swiftly they torched. The tanks powered by gasoline caught fire more quickly than those with diesel. Just a flick and then . . . [12]

Tankers trapped in what they themselves called a "mobile crematorium" had just two escape hatches in the event they were hit and their tank began to "brew." But escape was a long shot. The turret hatch might be obstructed by the body of the tank's commander, or the gun could block the opening. The floor's escape hatch might not yield if the tank was stuck in soft soil.

The enemy knew these medium tanks were incapable of cutting through the dense *bocage* hedges and steep banks, and that they would not be able to negotiate the narrow rutted farm lanes that zigzagged around the fields.

Any attempts by the Allies to go around the end met with almost inevitable annihilation by mines, by panzerfausts (portable, throw-away, one-shot guns), or by the lethal 88s. The tanks had to try to climb over the hedgerows. The Germans would wait until the tank had mounted the summit of the bank when its exposed undercarriage became an easy target for an armour-piercing shell.

"To add to these perils," Lieutenant Jary noted, "the German infantry had by far the most effective short-range anti-tank weapons." The panzerfaust could knock out a Sherman at fifty yards. It was probably the best-conceived weapon of its type in any army. "Lurking in woods and hedgerows, German infantry armed with this weapon exacted a heavy toll on any of our tanks that strayed from the immediate protection of our rifle sections."[13]

As General Bernard Montgomery's campaign continued on through July, there was growing talk of stalemate in the United Kingdom and the United States, conjuring up the horrors of the battle of attrition in France in World War I. Britons were shuddering at memories of the dreadful toll in the 1917 deadlock.

Since the U.S. First Army had turned its energies away from Cherbourg and moved south, it had advanced just twenty-four miles, with heavy losses. British VIII Corps on their left gained just over six miles in twelve days. It seemed an impossible task for the Allies to force their way through the dense maze of banks and hedges. The *bocage* still remained essentially an infantry battle, "dogged dough-boy fighting at its worst."[14] The casualties—90 per cent of them infantry—attested to this. Second Lieutenant J. Kussman, of U.S. 115th Infantry, 29th Division, noted: "Advances were made one hedgerow at a time." He cited a single day, 9 July, when, in progressing just two hedgerows, they had suffered eight casualties: "one officer and seven men in our company. . . . We were held up by German paratroop fire, rifle, automatic weapons and 88s and quite a few mortars."[15]

Monty's problems were exacerbated by the British and American press. Normandy abounded with newspaper and broadcast journalists from the United States, Britain, and Canada. Someone quipped that "practically every newspaper in the U.S. sent a correspondent except *Dog World*."[16] The U.S. media were not only overabundant; they were frustrated. The D-Day landings had provided the action for dynamic articles, with the pace and sizzle that sold newspapers and delighted editors. Now the correspondents found the war of attrition, with gains (or losses) of a few hundred yards, pretty dull stuff.

Front-line troops read in same-day or day-old English newspapers or heard on live BBC broadcasts detailed accounts of every action— often infuriatingly dismal. Yet when Monty did give statements, as he did following the failed *Operation Goodwood,* it was with a bravado that exaggerated the British and Canadian successes.

The Americans smouldered. Here they were (they thought) doing most of the work and suffering the bulk of the casualties while the British were getting all the credit.

"Now comes the trouble," Field Marshal Alan Brooke noted in his diary. "The Press chip in and we hear that the British are doing nothing and suffering no casualties whilst the Americans are bearing all the brunt of the war."[17]

A groundswell of antagonism arose among a small but vocal band of conspirators from Supreme Headquarters of the Allied Expeditionary Force (SHAEF). Thus influenced, Eisenhower complained to British prime minister Winston Churchill that Montgomery's tentativeness was stalling the war effort. Brooke was able to defuse the crisis, but he could not solve the controversy.

There was really nothing Montgomery and General Omar Bradley, commander of U.S. First Army, could do to counter the accusations. Had 21st Army Group revealed the exact numbers of troops of both nations in combat it would have been evident that, percentage-wise, there was little difference. Of 591,000 British and Canadians on the ground, 49,000, or 8.29 per cent, were casualties by 26 July. U.S. troops, from a fighting strength of 770,000, had sustained 73,000, or 9.5 per cent, casualties.[18]

But this was intelligence that would only help the enemy.

The high British casualties worried Montgomery for another reason. He was running out of manpower. There were no replacements. Within a few weeks he would be forced to disband one entire division in order to resupply the others with reinforcements.

So severe had the casualties been through the war, especially among junior officers, that Britain had turned to Canada for help. In 1943, Canadian officers were asked to volunteer to fill the shortfall of lieutenants with British battalions. Six hundred and seventy-three Canadians volunteered as "Canloan" officers. They served in almost every British division and fought in every major battle in Northwest Europe. Many of them took reductions in rank to do so.[19]

It was the media that finally stirred up the tank-design controversy. A CBS broadcast by correspondent Edward Murrow had members of Congress on their feet, posing passionate questions. "How can we send our boys to war with such inferior equipment?"[20]

In hindsight, Eisenhower's response of immediately initiating an investigation appears more politically motivated than practical. He had known for some time that Sherman guns were ineffective against German armour. But Eisenhower's boss, U.S. Army chief of staff General George C. Marshall, had deliberately chosen quantity over quality and size. The Sherman tank, at thirty-two tons, was lighter and faster than the Wehrmacht's forty-three-ton Panther and the fifty-six-ton Tiger. And tanks, he proclaimed, should not fight other tanks. Theirs was a breakout role.[21]

The men in the *bocage* found little comfort in that proclamation as they struggled frantically out of a flaming tank after being hit at long range.

In Britain there was a similar commotion. Major Martin Lindsay of the Gordon Highlanders noted in his battle diary that "[Labour MP Richard] Stokes raised the matter in Parliament and was always snubbed."[22]

In a savage attack against the government, Stokes was contemptuous. "We are just as far behind the Germans as we were in 1940. . . . This is a disgraceful state of affairs." Parliament's mocking response, recorded by Hansard, was laughter.

"It is all very well for the honourable members to laugh," Stokes rejoined, "but these men are dying." He quoted from a letter sent him by a tank crewman from Normandy, suggesting that the Secretary of State for war should go out and fight "with one of these ruddy things." The government's response was to censure Stokes for using rude language in the House.

British historian Max Hastings, who chronicled this encounter, wrote "the government lied systematically, until the very end of the war, about the Allies' tragic failure to produce tanks capable of matching those of the Germans."[23] Another English journalist despaired, "One can only hope the scandal of British tank manufacture will come out."[24]

In Normandy, even Montgomery finally forbade his senior commanders from speaking of it. We have the right tank, he assured them—but in the wrong place. Just wait until the breakout, when the little Sherman can show off its speed and manoeuvrability.

Desperation generates solutions. The resourcefulness of tankers in the field finally provided life-saving answers.

Sergeant Curtis Culin, a twenty-nine-year-old cab driver from Chicago, demonstrated both resourcefulness and mechanical ability. He came up with an ingenious device for cutting through hedgerows to confound the Wehrmacht's *bocage* defence tactics.

Culin borrowed the idea from the burrowing antics of a rhinoceros. He collected steel blades from abandoned beach defences and welded them to the front of his tank, enabling the Sherman to cut through thick hedgerows. This was an instant success and a huge morale booster for the troops. Impressed, the division gave immediate priority to producing as many "Rhino tanks" as possible, and the Sherman's effectiveness was restored.[25]

As they encountered the hazards of armoured combat in the *bocage*, other American and British tankers became equally innovative. Captain John McCoy of U.S. 743rd Tank Battalion rammed holes in the banks and then stuffed them with dynamite charges to blast his way through. Soon, tankers from all Allied countries were welding tracks from knocked-out tanks and pieces of steel from the hulls of landing craft onto the bodies of their Shermans to add armoured protection.

Flame-throwing Crocodile tanks, some of the "Funnies" devised by British 79th Division, were brought in. These fired a thick black liquid into the hedges that was quickly ignited into a fire that could not be extinguished. This flushed out many terrorized enemy infantry, as did the white phosphorus "snow" that was used with equally frightening effect.

Another chronic problem that had dogged the armour—communication between tank and infantryman—was solved by American improvisation. The rifleman's job was to protect the armour by warning its crew of impending danger. The only way he could do this was to hammer on the tank with his rifle butt or entrenching tool—all the while being ripe pickings for a German sniper. Alternatively the tank commander had to stick his head out the turret— more appetizers for the sniper.

The Americans, as historian Stephen Ambrose noted, were "learning by doing." In this case, trial and error led them to the solution of installing an interphone box on the tank, into which the infantryman could plug a radio handset. The handset's long cord enabled him to crouch for cover as he communicated any dangers to the men in the tank.[26]

Unspeakable weather made conditions in the *bocage* area between the coast and St-Lô even more unbearable. France was having the wettest July in forty years. The troops—Allied and foe—lived like moles in deep, mud-filled holes, never dry, never clean.

A soldier would lower himself gingerly, or on occasion would have to dive, into what often seemed a tomb of slop: six feet long, four feet deep, dug while mortar and artillery shells exploded around him and snipers' bullets searched for their mark. Any movement invited a sniper's bullet. When the sun did come out, the trenches became sweltering prisons.

"From time to time," rifleman J.J. How recalled, "there would be a diversion: the snout of a long 88mm gun would appear . . . and the turret of the Tiger tank that owned it would come slowly into view. A couple of rounds would swoosh past, leaving a vacuum that took the breath away and threatened to collapse the lungs."[27]

It was only at night that they could stir. Food came in fourteen-man packs that were distributed nightly. How remembers: "We tossed the tins from one trench to another, counted out the cigarettes and sweets, and looked thoughtfully at the sheets of toilet paper also provided, hoping that it would be only in the dark that the urge came to use it."[28]

Despite the truckloads of chlorinated water hauled up to the troops each day, dysentery became the inevitable by-product of countryside littered with thousands of dead cows and horses. "One could never get used to that appalling sweet sickly stench," Alan Moorehead wrote. "There was only one thing worse—the sweet smell of dead men."[29]

Mosquitoes buzzed around in huge swarms, taking (as one British tank soldier grimly recalls) "sadistic delight in sinking the teeth into skin, veins, cheeks, ears, arms, ankles, out of sheer rabid animosity towards mankind. No escape with darkness and no escape with daylight."[30]

They were newsworthy enough that the *Yorkshire Pud*, a newssheet published at the front for 7th Battalion, The Duke of Wellington's regiment, even ran this headline: "The Battalion was attacked by hordes of mosquitoes."[31]

One Scottish officer tried incinerating them. "Every time you get out of your dug-out it gets full of mosquitoes, and once more I had to go through the drill of burning them up with a torch of paper; then, after singeing my eyebrows and almost setting my bedding alight, I closed the trap-door and went round again with a torch, swatting a few hardy survivors."[32]

"They delight in catching us on the latrine," lamented one corporal, attributing increasing illness to the pests. "They are enough to drive a man mad."[33]

Wasps, the French summer plague, were so vicious there were times a soldier could not open his mouth to take a bite of food without being stung by one—or swallowing it. A hasty gulp of Compo tea, tasting sour from the fumes of a Tommy Cooker, had to suffice.

The bad weather in July brought another element of ill fortune for the Allies: no air support. Because of persistent rain and fog, one U.S. Marauder unit—323 Group—had seventeen straight missions scrubbed. Others fared little better; 50 per cent of all missions for all planes in England and France were washed out.[34]

Weather permitting, the Allied photo reconnaissance Mustangs identified enemy targets from the air and radioed the positions in the *bocage* to ground artillery. A captured German report confirms that "the enemy overcomes the difficulty of hedgerow country by employment of artillery air observers. They fly over the battle zone in regular reliefs and their reconnaissance is followed by strong, short bursts of fire with considerable ammunition expenditure. In sectors where there are only a few AA guns, these planes sweep down to a low level in order to direct the fire to picked targets."

The report goes on to note that "artillery is distinguished by accuracy of fire and manoeuvrability. Employment of fire and phosphorus bombs as well as HE ammunition . . . has been frequently observed [causing] stomach trouble and headaches."[35]

German lieutenant Walter Padberg crouched behind a hedgerow, wondering where the Americans were and why they were silent. He cautiously peered through the brush but could see nothing. So he decided it was time to get a look. He leaped over the hedge and landed almost directly upon the Americans' front line. "I had landed with my legs spread and in a panic the American lying there shot through my legs. I jumped back over the hedge and allowed us both to recover from the shock." Padberg received the Close Combat Medal for what he sardonically called his "greatest heroic deed. It was given to those who had stared the enemy in the eyes."[36]

A platoon of some American infantry lads—"Doughboys," or "Dogfaces" as they preferred to be called—retaliated with a strange and frightening ruse. A snake had slithered into their slit. They caught it with a forked stick and tossed it into a German machine gun nest. "Immediately there were screams and a great commotion," Private Kenneth Russell recalled with a chortle. "Very shortly there were three or four hand grenades lobbed over the hedge." The Germans were routed.[37]

Bocage fighting had no shortcuts, "no dramatic charges across open fields," as Ernie Pyle put it. The men soon learned it was to be a "slow and cautious business, and there's nothing very dashing about it. They go in tiny groups, a squad or less, moving yards apart and sticking close to the hedgerows on either side of the field. They creep a few yards, squat, wait, then creep again.

"This hedgerow business is a series of little skirmishes . . . . thousands and thousands of little skirmishes. No single one of them is very big. But add them all up over the days and weeks and you've got a man-sized war, with thousands on both sides being killed."[38]

Hitler's order to Hauser's Seventh Army to "hold fast" was causing grave casualties to the German defenders as well. They learned a healthy respect for the determined Tommies and Doughboys. Their price for delaying the Allied advance was described by their own corps commander as "one tremendous bloodbath, such as I have never seen in eleven years of war."[39]

By D-plus-44, 80,000 of the 700,000 Wehrmacht soldiers committed to fighting in Normandy had become prisoners of war and the same number had been killed and wounded.[40]

It seemed as though the agonizing weeks, overcoming one wretched hedgerow, only to be met by another and another, would never end. Would they ever get through this hellhole?

But suddenly they did. Before dawn on 17 July, Major-General Charles Gerhardt's 29th Division broke through into the outskirts of St-Lô and seized the high ground, gazing in wonder and relief at the objective so long denied.

Eleven thousand young Americans had already become casualties in this evil land.[41] The 29th Division's rifle companies were close to 100 per cent replacements. Using pain relief as a yardstick for the agonies of *bocage* combat, the medics reckoned that they injected an average of thirty-two grains of morphine per hedgerow.[42]

"It was the same on both sides," German private Adolf Rogosch said, "because the Americans were also only nineteen or twenty, the same as us. One wounded man told our commander, 'We'll send them back to their mothers.'

"You can't imagine what happened there. It was a 'munitions battle,' with fifteen hours of continuous shelling a day. The banging was everywhere. We thought the world was going to end."[43]

One final hurdle for 29th Division was a fiercely fought battle to seize St-Lô. Casualties exceeded those on Omaha Beach on D-Day, when two thousand young Americans were killed, wounded, or taken prisoner. But for 29th Division, the Battle of the Hedgerows was over.

4
BLESS 'EM ALL

I marched away
To the glorious trumpets of war, the haunting horns of
Ambition, the laughing trombones of youthfulness, the
Pounding tubas of discipline.

I limped back home
To the shivering violins of fear, the moaning violas of pain,
The sombre cellos of self-knowledge, the stumbling basses
Of self-doubt.

Only later did I discover
that I was my own composer and my own conductor.[1]

The meadow stretches as far as the eye can see. In a moment of
sanity—the last moment before the battle begins, or before you are
hit by an enemy's bullet—you might think: it's like the one at home,
behind my farm. Looking around, you see hundreds or even thousands of guys like yourself, moving up on the attack. Young fit men
in their twenties. Toughened by training, hardened to their mission
to kill. Or be killed. Some of the tough ones are smooth-faced lads
in their teens.

It could be a college rally or a high school track meet. It could be
harvest time back home, or the outpouring of shop workers, like
yourself, from the local factory.

But this is war, and you are attacking the enemy. Your objective
is to reach the enemy positions beyond that meadow and kill its
defenders.

Most times, you are too terrified to think nostalgically of the green
meadows of home. But you sure as hell will often think: "Oh God, I
wish I were there."

35

Or maybe you're anguishing: can I do this? Can I make myself go out on that field and take that objective? Can I help my buddies, not let them see how scared I am? And a fervent P.S.: Please let me do my job well, or I'll never again believe in myself.

Your insides scream, oh God, I'm too young. You look around for a leader, a sergeant, a lieutenant or captain to carve the way for you.

The first shots are fired and the cacophony of the shrill sounds of war takes over. You hear your own artillery shells shrieking over-head as you move forward. Your guns offer a temporary canopy of safety. You hope their fire will keep the enemy's heads down long enough for you to move up and overrun their position. You know you have to stay as close as you dare to where the support shells explode because that's your only hope of survival.

Machine guns are cracking nearby; mortar bombs whistle over-head, making a nightmarish noise. The enemy wakes up; now you're sure to get it. German shells are landing all around you, cratering massive holes in the ground. But it's the ones you don't hear that bring a message of terror; death comes silently with mortars' direct hits.

German 88mms scream by. Snipers are shooting at you from ahead and from the right and the left of your position. Shrapnel shells explode, piercing young bodies with lethal bits of fiery metal. MG-42s firing twenty rounds per second make a loud *brrrrp* noise. Now there's the sinister ghostly moan of the aptly named "Moanin' Minnie," firing six bombs in succession. And the screams of men wounded, gutted, limbs amputated by the shells . . . suffering, dying.

You know that no matter what your age or your training, once a shell or bomb or bullet hits you, you become just another body on the field . . . a body screaming in pain, calling desperately for stretcher-bearers to get you out of this hellhole . . . calling for your mother or your God.

Help came swiftly on the battlefield.

Stretcher-bearers were the first to arrive, either moving up in the wake of the infantry attack, or having been sent out by the medical officer (MO) when casualties were observed. Driving their jeep ambulances through the turmoil of fire, ducking sniper cross-fire and enemy shells, they braved the battlefield to rescue the fallen soldier.

Many regimental padres, although not required to, made a point of going out with them to help bring in the wounded. Thirty-year-old honorary captain Padre Jock Anderson of the Highland Light Infantry (HLI) could not bring himself to abandon those young men.

"Those fellows, they were lying out there wounded and they were being mortared. And shelled. A lot of them just had a leg wound but they were lying there unable to move and were being killed. I thought, hey, I've got to get those poor devils out of there. I made all kinds of trips and brought them out. I had shell dressings, morphine, and ether, but most times I never bothered with first aid. When they're being shelled and mortared you just grab them and shove them on a stretcher and off you go. No one ever talks about these ordinary stretcher-bearers, but they were utterly fantastic. Many were volunteers."[2] Some were conscientious objectors who refused to carry arms but worked magnificently to save lives.

"The jeeps were just going in, getting their casualties on and going like a bat out of hell," the Royal Canadian Army Medical Corps (RCAMC) history reports. "It wasn't the best way to drive with casualties, but it was either do that or get them out dead. The jeeps suffered a lot, coming in with four flat tires and holes through them from shrapnel. . . . The jeep ambulances and orderlies have always done a marvelous job."[3]

One such stretcher-bearer was Corporal Wes Burrows of the Royal Hamilton Light Infantry (RHLI). For a while, Burrows had been having an easy time of it, spending much of his pre-D-Day service investigating Britain's pubs while officially listed as the commanding officer's driver. On the side, he played a pretty hot trumpet with his own dance band.

Given the sack for overzealous "research," Burrows volunteered as a stretcher-bearer, transferring his energies into driving a stretcher-jeep onto shell-pocked fields to pick up casualties.

"I got out two hundred, easy, and sometimes I'd help out others as they ran into problems too—like, with another company that couldn't get the casualties out, I'd go in and get them. It got a little hairy at times. I lost four jeeps from mortar and shellfire, and once a mine blew my jeep up.

"You knew the job had to be done. There were chaps to be picked up. You got a little scared maybe when you were on your own out there, but at the time that you were taking them back, you had it in your head to get them out as fast as you could. Those mortars—the faster you'd drive, the closer they'd keep coming. You'd swear they were just trying to catch you. I had the Red Cross flag on the jeep, but it was drawing fire. I took the flag down."

Burrows's bravery was rewarded with the Military Medal (MM). On his way home, after his five years of overseas service, he reflected on his experience: "I thought I had been some help. I had no other training to do anything else."

But on the troop ship, rifle drill was called and Burrows, clumsily wrestling with the gun bolt, was hauled up by a sergeant major. "What do you think you're doing? Hold your head up! What a pitiful sight you are!"

"I guess there were some people who thought I wasn't much of a soldier without a gun," Burrows concluded sadly.[4]

Anderson, as did many padres and medics, shunned carrying the Red Cross banner on his jeep. It made them stand out and attracted too much enemy fire. A favourite SS trick was to camouflage their troop-carrying or weapon-carrying transport with a large Red Cross. They knew the Allies would never target them.

"Sometimes the German would respect the Red Cross and sometimes he would show such utter disregard for it that he would actually concentrate on the stretcher-bearers and ambulances," Royal Winnipeg Rifles captain Cliff Chadderton wrote, recounting with some bitterness a tragic incident. Their stretcher-bearers had been working since dusk, bringing in wounded Winnipeggers. "As night set in, but while there was still enough light to distinguish the Red Cross, the Germans swept the field with bullets. Milnes, the driver, was killed, and Mercer, the stretcher-bearer, died of his wounds. Both had been murdered while doing their duty under the protection of the International Red Cross."[5]

Sometimes the German mortaring was so intensive that it wasn't even possible to drive the ambulance-jeep into the bomb-pounded battleground. The war diary of 11th Canadian Field Ambulance noted that, "during a night action, cases unable to walk or crawl are often not picked up until morning. This applies especially to casualties occurring in the standing wheat, or where our troops had passed on and had not been able to notify stretcher-bearers of the location of the wounded."[6]

Dr. Art Stevenson (noted Winnipeg Blue Bomber quarterback) recalled that, on occasion, the stretcher-bearers would crawl out on their bellies to the battlefield, heave the wounded man on their shoulders, and crawl back to the Regimental Aid Post (RAP) or Field Surgical Unit. "These guys were—man!—they were just great. They didn't scare at all."[7]

The function of a Field Surgical Unit was to deal with those casualties too severely wounded to travel to the rear. The surgeons, regardless of how complex the surgical challenge, would have to conduct intricate surgery in the crudest of facilities. They would often operate with shells bursting around them or snipers firing at them, with rain lashing in the tent flaps and lights flickering from unreliable generators. Supplies of medicines depended on the courage and determination of the transport men braving enemy fire to bring them forward. Despite these difficulties, the surgeons became so proficient at their jobs that casualties were known to reach the casualty clearing station (CCS) one-half hour after being wounded.

"I was the first medical officer to help each of these guys who were wounded, the only doctor out there," Dr. Stevenson said. "I had to deal with first-stage resuscitation, keeping their blood pressure up with fluids and quickly getting them out of there down to the advanced field dressing station or the casualty clearing station by ambulance, where we could get medication into them. I did all the emergency surgical stuff, even a few amputations because of bleeding. We didn't have any blood. What we had to use was not even good plasma."[8]

One of the incoming casualties, South Alberta Regiment captain John Redden, had been riddled with bullets and had a tag "condition poor" pinned on him at the RAP. He tells this story: "I passed out, to be awakened by Dr. John King Kelly, who knew me from Winnipeg as a kid. He looked at the card that said 'condition poor,' called out 'silly bastard!' and wrote 'condition good.' It probably saved my life."[9]

Redden was experiencing the "triage" approach to combat medicine, which essentially sorted out casualties according to the seriousness of their injuries. Treatment priority was given to those with the least severe wounds. The badly wounded who could be saved were rushed to hospital. Those with lighter wounds were stabilized by medics and transferred later to CCS. But the hopeless ones, men like Redden with a "condition poor" tag, immediately received painkillers but were last in line for treatment.[10]

Major Don Campbell, MD, describes his role at CCS: "We were a fully operating hospital with full surgical, X-ray and blood bank facilities for as many as two hundred patients. There were two casualty stations side by each. One would be receiving and assessing all the emergencies, and the other would be operating. Then we'd switch.

"Our staff was small: eight nurses, two surgeons, three physicians and a medical blood bank specialist—with more surgical teams available as we needed them.

"There were so many shattered arms and legs from land mines. A man would step on a mine and his foot would be blown off. So then we had to amputate. The army public-health manual ordered what they called an 'operating pit' to be built, which was just a hole in the ground six feet by six feet by nine feet. We filled it—just with arms and legs. Then we had to dig another one. That's how busy we were."[11]

The surgeons had a gruelling schedule—eight hours in the operating room, then eight hours off, and eight hours back on. In the first seven weeks of the Normandy battle, Allied doctors used 18,000 pints of blood, 15,000 pints of plasma, and 2,400 mega units of penicillin, the wonder drug of the Second World War.[12]

It was tough, grisly, heart-rending work.

Shrapnel from shell, gunshot, and mortar wounds accounted for many injuries. Blast wounds saw men brought in concussed but without a mark on them. It was discovered that, by being too close to a mortar explosion, a soldier could be knocked out, lung-damaged, or killed.

One man was admitted, his right foot thickly bandaged. He'd stepped on a Schü-mine.

"It's a mess," he said bitterly to the surgeon. "Try to save as much as you can. Got a boy ten years old. Hate like hell to have him see the old man on crutches with one leg. God! If I could only walk down that gangplank."

The surgeon stared at a mass of torn tissue and fractured bones. He was right: it *was* a mess. But there might be a chance of saving the foot—at least until he walked down that gangplank. Hours of repairing tissue and resetting bone followed. In the morning, the reward was seeing the toes, pink and warm—and the soldier weeping silently. "There is no joy to compare to that."[13]

A tanker heard of a Canadian soldier that medics had found, barely alive, on the field. "Wasps [were] swarming on the bloody flesh of his leg, maggots already emerging, the medic saying: 'Best chance is bandage the wasps [and] maggots all into the leg—provide some leeching.' "[14]

Nursing Officer Brenda McBryde of 75th British General Hospital recalled her first view of the Resuscitation Department where she would spend so many hours of each day in the coming weeks. The whole medical facility was under canvas, dug in to a depth of about eighteen inches. It was floored with a heavy tarpaulin groundsheet, slippery with muddy trickles of rainwater.

Trestles supported the stretchers of wounded as they arrived from the ambulances. Here the men were given intensive treatment for shock until they were sufficiently restored to undergo operations, after which they passed straight from the theatre to the wards.

At the entrance to Resus. (Resuscitation) was a crudely erected treatment area. Trays of instruments, syringes, and sterilizers were laid out on trestle tables covered by sheets. Shelves were improvised from up-ended wooden boxes. Large wooden chests contained transfusion apparatus.

McBryde felt keenly the tragedy of war as she recorded the names and units of the casualties into the Admission Book, so many from famous British regiments: the Staffordshire Yeomanry, 4th Wilts, Dorsets, Green Howards, and East Yorks, men of 7th Armoured and 50th Northumbrian Divisions.

"Most of their proud uniforms, stiff with blood and caked in mud, had to be cut from them. We sliced the tough boots with razors to release shattered feet." McBryde reports having thought, "Hard-won stripes and pips and crowns, sewn on by proud moms and wives and girlfriends . . . it was all the same now. The field incinerator smoked all night."

The stream of wounded seemed never to end. The tent became so cramped that there was barely room to put a foot down or kneel between the stretchers.

Nurse McBryde recalls, "The surgeon kept up a running commentary: 'Stomach here: Put him in number one. Quarter of morphia, Sister. Straight away. Two pints of blood, one of plasma . . .' Gunshot, mortar blast, mines, incendiaries. Limbs, eyes, abdomen, chest. The surgeon would chew his pencil. Who had priority? Of all these desperately wounded men, whose need was the most urgent?"[15]

But as one surgeon expressed it, they all had to learn to "turn off the emotional taps"—the only way they could handle shattered and torn bodies day after day. They soon became war-wise veterans.

"We saw the tragic sights from which we were never to be free: men with heads shattered and grey, dirty brains oozing out from the jagged margins of skull bones. Youngsters with holes in their chests fighting for air and breathing with a ghastly sucking noise. Soldiers with intestines draining faeces onto their belly walls and with their guts churned into a bloody mess by high explosives. Legs that were dead and stinking—but that still wore muddy shoes.

"Operating floors that had to be scrubbed with Lysol to rid the operating theatre of the stench of dead flesh. Red blood that flowed and spilled over while life held on by the slender thread of time. Boys who came to you with a smile and died on the operating table. Boys who lived long enough for you to learn their name and then were carried away in trucks piled high with the dead.

"We learned to work with heavy guns rocking and blasting the thin walls of our tent. We learned to keep our tent ropes slack so that anti-aircraft fragments would rain down harmlessly and bounce off the canvas."[16]

One Canadian casualty, speaking for many, called the nurses "angels of mercy." Regaining consciousness in a British field hospital near Bayeux, with one eye reduced to pulp, and his head and mouth pierced by a large hunk of jagged shrapnel, Lieutenant Barney Danson saw a nursing sister "in a blue uniform with gold accoutrements and a flowing white veil," comforting him with offers of food and water. To him, she was an angel.[17]

Major John Connors, Royal Canadian Army Medical Corps (RCAMC), writes in his autobiography, *The Story of an Unremarkable Canadian*, of being shaken awake on his first night at the front by his second-in-command, Dr. Don McCrimmon, and told to move up to Verson, a hamlet outside Caen. "They're having severe casualties there; a number of our men have been killed," McCrimmon said. Within twenty minutes, Connors was navigating his way through the darkness to Verson, where he joined the doctors at the CCS, who were already dealing with victims of the enemy mortars.

The twenty-nine-year-old commanding officer of the Royal Hamilton Light Infantry, Lieutenant-Colonel Denis Whitaker, co-author of this book, was Major Connors's first patient. The RHLI, in a defensive position, had been continually mortared and shelled by the enemy for three days and three nights. No one had any sleep. Finally, the demolition platoon fashioned Whitaker a small dugout (using several grenades), large and deep enough to hold his camp cot. In went the cot; in went the officer, stretching his full length on a cot for the first time in three nights. The platoon covered the dugout with a sheet of galvanized iron and soil.

Two sounds followed each other in minutes: "Ahhh," said the relaxing CO. And shortly after—Whaaaam! A shell came directly through the roof into the trench, exploding in Whitaker's face and knocking him unconscious. He was taken to a CCS, where he was treated by two Canadian doctors, Major Connors and an old football buddy, Captain Turney Williams, who played for the University of Toronto.[18]

The shrapnel gashes in his face were repaired and after several days he was air-evacuated to England. His eyes were bandaged tight for three weeks. He learned to knit, to keep his mind from dwelling on the possibility of being blind for the rest of his life. Happily, he was one of the 93 per cent of Normandy's wounded who recovered. Whitaker rejoined his battalion in France six weeks later.

In addition to Canadian, British, and American troops, the hospital treated several other nationalities. "We were very impressed with the Poles. They were a great gang," Dr. Stevenson reported. "But we had trouble with quite a few German prisoners. We treated them as we did our own, but they were all scared stiff. They took far more narcotics than our boys took. They were quite chicken-hearted, I would say."[19]

One German was far from chicken-hearted. For two days he had clung to his post, sniping at his enemy, holding his ruptured belly with guts spilling out all the while. When they brought him in he was still defiantly wearing his jacket with its SS insignia. The orderly tried to give him a transfusion. "No! No English blood!" he snarled, and spat at the orderly.[20]

As the casualty rates mounted, so did the strain on the medical personnel. Fortunately, rigorous pre-invasion training in Britain had hardened them to some extent to primitive life in field conditions in tents. A basic training course taught them the use of small arms and vehicle training, first aid, and basic survival. This was known as the DDPP course: doctors, dentists, padres, and paymasters—a curious mixture.

Medical orderlies practised pitching large hospital tents (thirty feet by fifteen feet) in all kinds of weather, and in the blackest of nights, in as fast a time as possible and without the use of flashlights. They had to lug in a 900–pound generator and be able to repair and service it, so it could supply power to 120 electric bulbs. They rehearsed sterilizing instruments in the dark.

The nursing sisters in particular found the British field training out in the open to be an exhilarating experience and a pleasant change from routine duties under a roof. One nurse recalled that "training was strenuous, but time could generally be found for relaxation. We marched over the moors all day, and we marched to the pubs at night."

All nurses had been issued battle dress and field kit. But a problem arose over sisters wearing the large packs. One account relates wryly that "it was found that the position of the supporting straps over the chest had not been designed with the female anatomy in mind. A decision to try discarding the pack in favour of hand luggage produced an assortment of suitcases of varied size, shape and colour purchased by the nurses. When one bag burst during an exercise, spilling its contents across the muddy path, the reviewing commander said in disgust, "I can only liken this to the retreat from Moscow!"[21]

American women serving with the Army Nurse Corps (ANC) rolled up their pant legs and waded ashore on the Normandy beaches and, like their British counterparts, were catapulted immediately into around-the-clock, mind-numbing efforts to keep shattered young bodies alive. One nurse, Lieutenant Aileen Hogan, recalled the challenges of making the penicillin rounds—sixty patients to a tent—especially at night. "Not a glimmer of light anywhere; the tents are just a vague silhouette against the darkness, ropes and tent pins a constant menace, syringes and precious medications balanced precariously on one arm."

In volunteering for the ANC, these women soon earned the highest respect and became the vanguard for an eventual ANC force in Europe numbering 17,345.[22]

Evacuation to English hospitals was smoothly managed by sea or air in a few days. The post-operative abdominal cases had to be retained a little longer; if they were moved too soon, they wouldn't survive.

In the early days of the Normandy battle, the majority of evacuations took place in Landing Ship Tanks (LSTs). As soon as an LST had unloaded the tanks carried in its voyage from England to Normandy, the medical party would let down the folding stretcher racks, fitted in tiers along the ship's sides, to accommodate 350 stretcher cases.

An operating room was set up in the stern. Amphibian vessels could bring as many as twenty-five casualties right into the bowels of the ship, where treatment would begin immediately. In this way the wounded men reached hospital in the United Kingdom in the best possible condition, very different in appearance from the mud-covered and bloodstained casualties that had landed in England after the Dieppe raid in 1942.

An impressed British surgeon noted that the Normandy casualties "were in good heart; their dressings were immaculate and it was difficult to believe that the careful notes which accompanied them had been made out on a shell-torn beach."[23] By early August, the evacuation process had been streamlined. Besides sea evacuation (in somewhat more comfortable hospital ships), six air flights a day, each carrying twenty passengers, had been put in place.

But by now, after two months in Normandy, the hospital staff was worn out. In the crowded tents, doctors, nursing sisters, and orderlies worked long, exhausting shifts, often sixteen hours in every twenty-four. And to make matters worse, after the incessant rains of July, the August weather was hot and sultry. The dry spell created clouds of dust that penetrated clothes, inflamed eyes, and permeated skin and even food. Mosquitoes and wasps increased their relentless attacks. Water was scarce. Much of the water supply had been sabotaged by the Germans, or polluted by decaying corpses of farm animals. Until the engineers repaired it, everyone was down to a tight ration transported under dangerous conditions by the Service Corps personnel.

"I have never worked so hard in my life," Nurse Hogan remembers. "I can't call it nursing. The boys get in, get emergency treatment . . . and are out again. It is beyond words."[24]

5

IT ALL SEEMED
SO HOPELESS —
AND THEN . . .

How do you, as a commander, convince citizen soldiers—many of them teenagers untried in war—that they should plunge blindly into a battle they have little or no hope of winning? How can you maintain their confidence in their leaders, who seem to be constantly ordering them into no-win situations?

This was one of General Bernard Montgomery's dilemmas on D-plus-50.

Monty could hardly reassure his British and Canadian troops that their seemingly futile attempts to break the German line at Caen, with so many men killed and wounded, were in reality achieving exactly what he had planned and hoped for.

Seven German panzer divisions had been pinned down on the Caen front for almost two months. Only two opposed the Americans, who could take advantage of the Germans' dilemma and who were now on the brink of a momentous breakout. As Eisenhower himself wrote to Monty on 28 July, "Am delighted that your basic plan has begun brilliantly to unfold with Bradley's initial success."[1]

Montgomery urged 21st Army Group army commanders that "along the whole front now held by the First Canadian and Second British Armies it was essential that the enemy be attacked to the greatest degree possible."

In the same directive he admitted candidly that, while the Anglo-Canadians must persist in fighting and incurring heavy casualties, they had little possibility of success. "[The enemy] is so strong

47

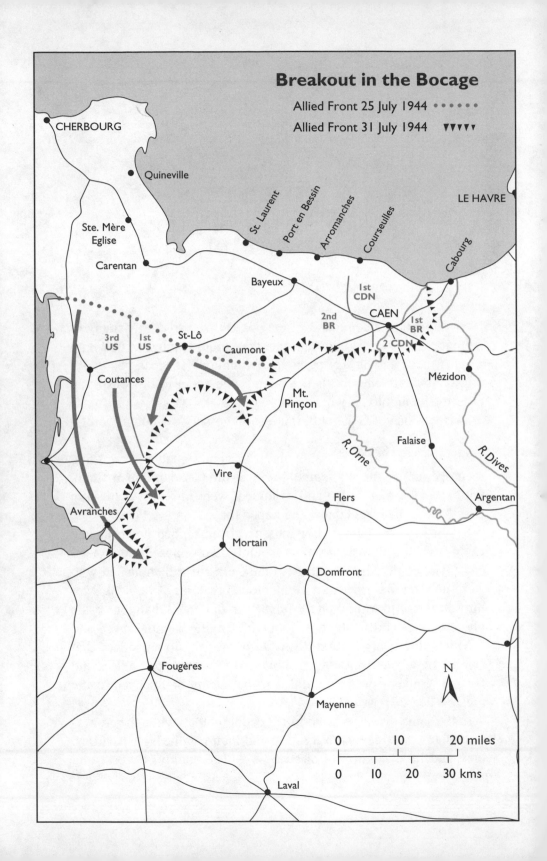

Breakout in the Bocage

Allied Front 25 July 1944 ••••••
Allied Front 31 July 1944 ▼▼▼▼▼

CHERBOURG

Quineville

Ste. Mère
Eglise

Carentan

LE HAVRE

St. Laurent

Port en Bessin

Arromanches

Courseulles

Cabourg

Bayeux

1st
CDN

2nd
BR

CAEN

1st
BR

3rd
US

1st
US

St-Lô

Caumont

2 CDN

Coutances

Mt.
Pinçon

Mézidon

Vire

Falaise

R. Orne

R. Dives

Flers

Argentan

Avranches

Mortain

Domfront

Fougères

N

Mayenne

0   10   20 miles

0   10   20   30 kms

Laval

[south of Caen] that any large-scale operations by us in that area are definitely unlikely to succeed."[2]

Indeed, in late July, Monty made no pretense to his senior army commanders, Lieutenant-General Miles Dempsey and Lieutenant-General Harry Crerar, that their role was anything but as a decoy to lure panzer divisions from the American front. They accepted their roles, but it was a tough sell to the young volunteers and recruits at the sharp end. Montgomery's chief of intelligence, Bill Williams, brutally summed up the dilemma of his waning credibility: "He'd got to be overconfident in order to get the people to be willing to be killed [on the Caen front]."[3]

It was on the Caen front that British and Canadian troops were not only struggling against much of the fiercest opposition, at an enormous sacrifice of lives; they—and Monty—were getting nothing but biting criticism in return. SHAEF commanders, the media, and, later, historians all denounced 21 Army Group as "slow," its performance "feeble," its "enthusiasm waning."[4]

Reflecting the sometimes negative press coverage they had been receiving, a Canadian war diary noted wryly: "The enemy is not giving ground as easily as one would gather from reading the London papers."[5]

Sadly, though, the criticism—absolutely unwarranted and without justification—has been perpetuated to this day by historians, including Canada's own official military historian C.P. Stacey, who have unrealistic conceptions of the field of battle. That the forces at Caen succeeded in operations where they were "definitely unlikely to succeed" is a huge tribute to the citizen soldiers of both nations.

Dempsey's Second Army was still tackling the miserable *bocage* and hill fighting in the *Suisse Normande* that the American troops had endured for seven weeks through June and July. Not in jest, a non-commisioned officer (NCO) of 6th Battalion King's Own Scottish Borderers asked his commanding officer, Lieutenant-Colonel Charles Richardson, "if it was the high command's intention to wipe out all the British and finish the war with the Americans."[6]

The weeks of intense fighting throughout July had exhausted the British troops to a point almost beyond combat effectiveness. Their morale sank with the huge casualties and scant hope of replenishment, and with the apparent lack of progress and the increasingly vocal criticism from their countrymen. It all seemed hopeless. Fifty days and nights of little sleep, wretched weather, and constant fear were taking their toll. As the men saw their buddies horribly maimed or killed, they wondered would it be their turn next?

"There was no escape—except being buried or taken out on a stretcher," one young corporal said.[7] Men going into an attack would have the unnerving experience of seeing white crosses piled up, ready for use, and ambulances lined up waiting. Makeshift graves were everywhere.

A young private soldier in the Durham Light Infantry spoke for many when he said, "I thought that if by some fluke I survived and went back to England there would be no young men walking about at all because they were all being killed and wounded in Normandy."[8]

On D-plus-49, 25 July, the sun finally came out.

Operation Cobra, Bradley's long-planned air-cum-artillery attack to open the way for Patton's Third Army, postponed for some days because of poor weather, was finally launched. Despite short bombing that caused 600 American casualties, the subsequent bomber assault, with 2,500 planes dropping 16,000 tons of bombs, shattered the Germans.

An observer, press correspondent A.J. Liebling, watched the barrage from an artillery headquarters, an upstairs window of a Normandy farm house. "Some of the men, watching the bombardment from the sloping ground under my window, rolled on the grass with unsportsmanlike glee. Their emotion was crude but understandable. 'The more bombs we drop, the less fight there'll be left in them.'"[9]

One division, the Wehrmacht's highly regarded Panzer Lehr, was virtually decimated. Major-General Fritz Bayerlein, its commander, said: "My front lines looked like the face of the moon and at least 70 per cent of my troops were out of action—dead, wounded, crazed or numbed."[10] The French civilians, fortunately, had by then fled the area to escape the mutilation of their gentle Norman homeland.

One tragic American casualty was General Lesley McNair. Just a few days before, this man had given up his name and his chances of taking a front-line command to help maintain the myth that an American army was still in England, poised for a major invasion on the Pas de Calais.

General McNair was killed while observing the bombing raid. To perpetuate the charade of Armee Gruppe McNair, the ever-vigilant XX Committee arranged for a quiet burial in the field, and informed his wife merely, and in a sense accurately, that he was a casualty of war.

Within a week of *Cobra*, U.S. Major-General Troy Middleton's VIII Corps had fought its way down the Atlantic coast, capturing the strategic town of Avranches.

On 1 August, at 1200 hours, Third U.S. Army was finally on the move. The moment it became operational, General Patton's pent-up energies were unleashed. On his feet, yelling and brandishing his revolver, Patton urged his eighteen divisions headlong down a two-mile-wide corridor that led from Avranches to the plains of Brittany and southern Normandy. More than 100,000 men and 15,000 vehicles had to get through that bottleneck before they could drive out in three directions across France.

Lapping on the right flank of this narrow passage were the Atlantic swells. Ahead, at the end of the Avranches corridor, was Pontaubault Bridge, the last obstacle before his breakout cork escaped the bottle. But, on his left flank, determined German infantry and an awakened Luftwaffe tried, for seventy-two hours non-stop, to hit and destroy the bridge and the American troops crossing it.

It was a dangerous gamble—one of the most daring offensive strikes of the war. But nothing could stop George Patton: not the enemy, not his own startled Allies, not even his own capricious nature.

British Breakout: Operation Bluecoat

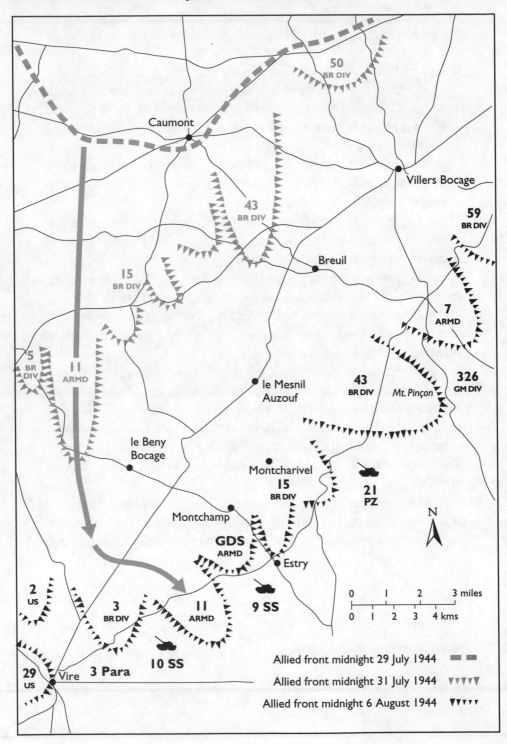

50 BR DIV

Caumont

Villers Bocage

59 BR DIV

43 BR DIV

Breuil

7 ARMD

15 BR DIV

5 BR DIV

11 ARMD

le Mesnil Auzouf

43 BR DIV

Mt. Pinçon

326 GM DIV

le Beny Bocage

Montcharivel

15 BR DIV

21 PZ

Montchamp

GDS ARMD

Estry

9 SS

N

2 US

3 BR DIV

11 ARMD

0   1   2   3 miles

0 1 2 3 4 kms

29 US

Vire

3 Para

10 SS

Allied front midnight 29 July 1944

Allied front midnight 31 July 1944

Allied front midnight 6 August 1944

6

THE BRITISH BREAKOUT

The moment of American triumph came at a time of heightened British despair.

On 30 July, Montgomery launched the Second British Army's *Operation Bluecoat*, the most powerful Allied push to date. He abruptly shifted almost all of the British troops from the Caen front west to Caumont to support the Americans in their breakout. Three entire corps—some 200,000 men of armoured and infantry divisions—were committed.

Lieutenant-General Richard O'Connor's British VIII Corps was the spearhead, drawing the start position of the far right flank next to the U.S. First Army. "O'Connor is the only general who makes me nervous," Rommel is reported to have said, following O'Connor's audacious victory in the North African desert. When he was subsequently taken prisoner by a German patrol, Churchill (it is rumoured) offered any six Italian generals to get him back. He escaped—on the second attempt—in time to command the "White Knight" Division of VIII Corps in Normandy.

As a British historian describes them, O'Connor's "White Knight" divisions were made up predominantly of peacetime weekend soldiers. These territorial troops were "closely knit local groups: men of Scotland in regiments like the Ayrshire Yeomanry, Cameronians and Glasgow Highlanders; men from the Welsh border counties of Shropshire, Herefordshire and Monmouthshire; men of Wessex in the Hampshires, Wiltshires, Somerset Light Infantry and other famous west country regiments; there were Cockneys with the Rifle Brigade and men of the Midlands in the Northamptonshire Yeomanry.

The years of training had turned them into professionals: at heart they had remained civilians."[1]

O'Connor's lead division was the 11th Armoured, commanded by Major-General G.P.B. "Pip" Roberts.

In Pip Roberts, Monty had a man of superlatives. He was, at thirty-seven, the youngest divisional commander in the British Army. He was one of the most experienced, having fought his way through the war from the rank of captain in the western desert. He was the smallest and shortest by stature; the most boyish and benign by appearance, but the toughest by performance. He led a winning team and everyone knew it—especially Roberts. "In the unblooded 11th Armoured, I found everyone raring to go."[2]

"Step on the gas for Vire," Monty had said. Pip's similarly diminutive and tough-minded corps commander, Richard O'Connor, ordered him into what proved to be a seventy-two-hour marathon to achieve this.

Vire, the capital of *bocage* country, was a key hub for seven major roads and in effect marked the junction, then unmanned, of two German armies: Eberbach's Panzer Group West and Hausser's Seventh Army. Vire was the home of the *andouille*, a sausage of pigs' intestines. It was *not*, as of 30 July, a home to any Germans. It lay unoccupied, waiting.

Roberts stepped on the gas. His marathon began with an all-night cross-country march just to reach his start-line. He wheeled his 3,000 armoured and transport vehicles and 12,000 men of his division in an incredible cross-country sweep over inferior roads, cutting across the supply lines of some 90,000 men in two other corps. "It was a scramble, but just worked," Roberts said in typical understatement.[3]

For Trooper John Thorpe, 2nd Fife and Forfar Yeomanry, it wasn't just a scramble. As he drove his tank over steep hills and through valleys, all the while kicking up dense dust, he kept himself awake by smoking between sixty and eighty cigarettes a day and singing his favourite song, "As Time Goes By." As his diary reveals, it was a night of total misery:

> *July 29: It was hell trying to see and follow the tank in front of us in this sand storm in the dark. The dirt was beginning to accumulate in the corners of my eyes, but I dared not touch my eyes or face or it would have made them water and would have blinded me. A wet dew mist rose during the night and my face became encased with a thick mask.*

The temptation to drop off to sleep through the noise, fatigue and tiredness was terrific and I could only keep awake by twisting up my ear till it hurt or singing at the top of my voice which could not be heard by anyone over the overall noise. To go off to sleep would have been to lose consciousness and perhaps our lives.[4]

The division reached the start-line south of Caumont just in time to launch immediately into a heavy day's fighting in the worst of *bocage* country. Roberts had reorganized his two brigades into two forces so each had infantry and armour as mutual support. It proved a magic formula. Riflemen went into battle clinging to tanks—"quick lift," it was called—and the attack surged forward.

From Trooper Thorpe's diary:

July 30: We had not gone a couple of hundred yards when a number of our tanks went up on mines each side of us. Met heavy shellfire—theirs or ours? Poor bloody infantry going over like ninepins. They were advancing and there was no cover nor the chance to dig in through heavy mortar fire.

The plan is for the infantry to lead us in this now heavy wooded area and our job is to clear away machine gun nests.[5]

After a gruelling twenty-four hours, General Roberts noted that all were "yearning to call it a day as the sun went down." Instead, he received orders from an insistent corps commander—Dick O'Connor—to seize the next road.

Doggedly he ordered an exhausted and mildly protesting 4th Battalion KSLI (Kings Shropshire Light Infantry) to clear a steep, heavily mined wooded trail and then plunge single file into its depth. The Shropshires gamely set off into the moonless night on a three-mile trek. The only way any of them could keep his bearings was to grope for the shoulder of the rifleman in front. Finally they reached their crossroads objective, luckily with no enemy opposition.

"Within seconds—I had just time to take my boots off and blow on my red hot feet—another order group," KSLI captain Clayton groaned. "This time the news was electrifying—the finding of an unguarded bridge."[6]

No one realized that five soldiers in two scout cars from the Household Cavalry (better recognized in peacetime guarding Buckingham Palace) had already leapfrogged ahead, blindly unaware that they were traversing the actual boundary between the two German armies. ("Though neither army had thought to guard it," Roberts added, with a grin.)[7]

Soon the men came upon an intact bridge—*the* unguarded bridge—that was the key to the capture of Bény-Bocage ridge overlooking Vire. Lieutenant "Dickie" Powle sent three men across while he covered them in the armoured car.

Corporal Bland describes the adventure: "After quickly dismounting, we (myself and Trooper Read) slipped up behind a German sentry and quietly finished him off. We had to dispose of any such visitors, otherwise we were sunk as there was no hope of holding any numbers off with only two cars."[8]

The five men hid, camouflaging the cars. They were at the limit of effective radio range and had lost contact. Corporal Staples, the operator, eventually got a faint response and sent the following message: "At 1030 hours the bridge at 6374432 is clear of enemy and still intact. I say again, at 1030 hours the bridge at 6374432 is clear of enemy and still intact."

The regimental headquarters of the Household Cavalry picked up this faint message through the static. The map reference was plotted. It was the bridge over the Souleuvre River, five miles into enemy territory. There must be some mistake. A repeat was requested.[9]

It was no mistake. When the message was passed to 11th Armoured headquarters, there was great excitement. "Cavalry Bridge" (as it was immediately dubbed by the exuberant liberators of the Household Cavalry) opened the way to Vire—and beyond.

Pip Roberts saw his chance and seized it. In seventy-two hours the 11th Armoured Division had spearheaded a spectacular breakout five miles behind the German lines. Vire was just eight miles away.[10]

On 1 August, Roberts' 11th Armoured was on the verge of the breakout Montgomery had demanded. "Throw all caution overboard; step on the gas for Vire," he had said on 30 July.

However, squabbling among the Allies over boundary lines spoiled this moment of triumph—the seizing of Cavalry Bridge behind enemy lines. These lines were established by Montgomery to avoid any Allied army colliding with its neighbour. They became, too often during the Normandy campaign, a source of rivalry and dissension among army commanders. The Germans managed to turn this to their advantage on several occasions.

General Leonard Gerow, commander of U.S. V Corps, was miffed to learn of the British success in driving a wedge deep into enemy-held territory at Vire, threatening to split the German Seventh Army and Panzer Group West.

"I don't like the British walking out front taking objectives," he complained.

"What are you British doing in our sector?" echoed an infantry sergeant from U.S. 5th Division.[11]

The troops didn't care a bit about boundaries. Men of the British Rifle Brigade snatching a few minutes' rest watched with sympathy as the GIs plodded by them, down the narrow road, "quite expressionless, sallow with fatigue, one and all masticating gum and silent in their rubber-studded top boots."[12] Learning that the Americans had had nothing to eat for forty-eight hours, the riflemen tossed them packets of biscuits. The Yanks tossed back chewing gum.

At the rear, U.S. and British echelons officers traded veiled insults about whose bridge it was. Finally, after an interminable delay the issue was solved—amicably—by sharing the bridge.

Unaccountably, Monty then queered the act for Roberts. On 1 August, two days after he had demanded that Pip seize Vire, he changed the boundaries to allot the task of Vire's liberation to the Americans. It is reasonable to speculate that Gerow's complaints, probably lodged at higher levels, influenced Montgomery's decision-making.

The German High Command could not so easily be calmed. "The British are trying to cut us off [from the] north," signalled General Meindl frantically. "Once again we are threatened with encirclement."[13]

"The capture of Vire would have made sense, and we could have done that," a disappointed Roberts acknowledged.[14] Had this objective not been abruptly snatched from their grasp, British forces could have taken an undefended Vire "with nothing more than a skirmish."[15]

Reacting swiftly to the imminent danger, three panzer divisions—

9th SS, 10th SS, and 21st Panzer—and elements of 12th SS and 116th Panzer were ordered to plug the hole at Vire and demolish the British attackers. At dawn on 2 August, more than one hundred Tiger and Panther tanks were poised to attack. By the time five divisions of American troops reached Vire on 6 August, it had been heavily fortified. More than three thousand GIs were casualties in the renewed battle for an objective that could have been snapped up in a skirmish on 1 August.

Pip Roberts' outstanding offensive on the right flank of the *Bluecoat* attack—a crackling twelve-mile advance through enemy lines in less than thirty-six hours—only highlighted the dismal efforts of 30th Corps on its left.

"Get going or get out!" was General Dempsey's final cry of frustration. Their lack of progress was so tortuous that Montgomery ruthlessly fired 30th Corps' commander, Lieutenant-General G.C. Bucknall, on the third day of the assault.

"I have ordered that General Bucknall be removed from command," Montgomery wrote peevishly. "He is nearly always twenty-four hours too late, and the enemy profits thereby."

Next to be sacked was the commander of 7th Armoured Division—the famed Desert Rats. "Major-General Erskine is stale: he needs a rest, and a change of employment," Monty stated.[16]

"I request that Major-General Horrocks be appointed to command 30th Corps."[17]

In those early August days of frustration and lack of achievement, more than one hundred officers and men in 30th Corps were transferred to other posts. They were all veterans of fighting in North Africa, Italy, and Normandy.

In truth, *bocage* fighting had taken some of the starch out of the veteran 7th Armoured "desert warriors." Dilution, staleness, and war weariness had set in.[18] As Monty put it, "The old desert divisions are apt to look over their shoulder and wonder if it is all okay behind, or if the flanks are secure. . . . 7th Armoured Division is like that. They want a new general, who will drive them headlong into, and through, gaps torn in the enemy defence."[19]

They had proven themselves in vast stretches of open country in

North Africa, in a desert war that stretched on for three years. Then just a year later, on D-plus-1, they had been flung almost directly into this dangerous and strange new form of close warfare in the *bocage*.

German snipers hiding in the thick hedgerows easily picked off tank commanders accustomed in the desert to going into battle standing in their turrets.[20] Their Churchill tanks, no match for the German Panthers and Tigers, became tombs for young British tank crews. They were "Tiger shy"—with good reason. There were 645 enemy tanks—Tigers, Panthers, and Mark IVs—facing the British front; a mere 190 faced the U.S. First Army. Monty's strategy was working, but at what a price.[21]

The infantry were exhausted, punch-drunk from fighting in continuous action for seven weeks. Conditions for the tankers were unspeakable. Temperatures inside the tanks soared as they crashed through *bocage* hedges and over banks. The driver could see little and the tank commander had to stand up to guide him while struggling with the branches to keep the other tanks in view. The stench of five unwashed men caged together in a hot metal box for hours was heightened with the sour smell of rotting green apples that had fallen into the high turrets of the Shermans.

"We were all black and blue from the jumps we had been over," one British officer recalled of the rough terrain. "And quite a number of men, including my signal officer in my own tank, had been knocked senseless."[22]

Most of all, the men had been fighting too long. They were stale. They reckoned they'd made it through four years' worth of fighting and, now that the war was being won, they wanted to get safely home. "Why would I stick my blinking neck out and get killed when the 'effing war may be over before Christmas?" the Tommies grumbled.[23]

"Jorrocks"—General Brian Horrocks, Roberts' old friend—was the incoming commander of 30th Corps, and a seasoned desert fighter. He recognized the symptoms of mass battle fatigue. The "gloss was gone," as he put it. Within days, troops became accustomed to the comfortable sight of the tall, white-haired leader casually dressed in corduroys mingling in their midst.

Horrocks first set himself the task of making a "whistle-stop tour" to his units. He explained to the frustrated and battle-weary officers and men how well the battle was really going and how close they were to breaking out of the bridgehead and swanning off across France.[24]

"He was very good, and made us feel quite cheerful," a tank wireless-operator from 4th/7th Royal Dragoon Guards said. "We [had] all thought that we should have to fight for every field all the way to Germany."[25]

A trooper from 8th Hussars termed him "a very warm man, exuding confidence and determination but one who cared for the welfare and safety of his troops."[26]

The prime objective of 30th Corps was the capture of Mont Pinçon, the steep-sided, 1,200-foot-high hill that dominated the *Suisse Normande*. Montgomery had had his eye on this feature from the beginning. You could see for miles in every direction from its summit—and call down artillery fire at a considerable distance on all sides.

There were only two possible approach roads, each cutting through typical *bocage* fields with thick hedgerows on each side. The Germans were heavily dug in at two stone villages on the sides of the mountain, and had a full view of any attacker. On a swelteringly hot 6 August, two infantry battalions from 43rd Wessex and their supporting armour, 13th/18th Hussars, fought their way to a small river at the base of the mountain. Casualties had cut their ranks in half. Fourth Battalion Somerset Light Infantry came under what platoon commander Lieutenant Sydney Jary described as "concentrated Spandau fire from the front and both flanks. There must have been twelve machine guns fired at one time. This devastating display of firepower stopped the battalion dead in its tracks. There was no way forward or round it and no way to retire."[27]

On their right, their sister battalion, 5th Wiltshires, was equally pinned down by heavy fire. The commanding officer, Lieutenant-Colonel "Pop" Pearson, knew that his men needed some special boost to attack the heavily defended position. Tucking a red rose in his steel helmet and swinging his walking stick, he strode calmly towards the bridge. He was shot dead by a sniper in a tree. But his display of courage inspired the surviving men of his battalion to swarm across the river and overrun the enemy position.

At 1800, an armoured patrol from 13th/18th Hussars, led by its commander, Captain R. Denny, discovered a narrow track winding up the hill, apparently undefended. The track was so tight that one tank toppled over into an abandoned gravel pit; another had its track blown off. The remaining seven tanks pushed steadily upwards, clinging to the rim of the sheer cliff until they reached the summit. Fog settled on the heights, and the small band of tankers heard German voices all around them. The troop leader radioed to headquarters that they felt "rather lonely."[28]

Later, startled infantry below glimpsed the tanks silhouetted against the sky. Fourth Wiltshire was ordered to follow them up. Though exhausted from forty-eight hours of fighting, the battalion gamely set off single file up the steep thorny slopes, and struggled to the top. By nightfall, Mont Pinçon had been secured, with many casualties to the 43rd Wessex Division. But their emblem, the golden Wyvern—a double-winged dragon with clawed feet and arrow-tipped tail—flew above its summit.

If there were moments when the troops fighting in *Bluecoat* lost hope, or were discounted by their peers, there were many more times when they shone with courage.

"Basher" Bates, a corporal with 1st Royal Norfolk, was such a man. Basher—aka Sidney—Bates was a product of London's East End. His father was a street peddler—a "rag and bone" man, as the Cockneys termed it. When Basher was asked his civilian occupation at the recruiting office he just scratched his head, perplexed.

On 6 August, Corporal Bates and his depleted section of five or six men ran into a strongly defended German position. Heavy and accurate artillery and mortar fire poured down on the British. As the enemy position strengthened in the area occupied by Sidney's section, about fifty to sixty Germans, supported by machine guns and mortars, assembled in the steeper dead ground beyond an opposite hedge. Bates realized that he and his handful of men were all that stood between the Germans and his battalion headquarters. He reckoned he could better counter the enemy thrust if he could get through the hedge and confront the enemy.

At that moment, little "Tojo" Tomlin, an eighteen-year-old section

Bren gunner from Bethnal Green, was wounded. Sidney Bates picked him up and was holding him as they made for cover. Tomlin was then killed outright by a bullet to his head. He died in Bates' arms. Seeing that the situation was becoming desperate, Bates took Tomlin's Bren gun and charged the enemy, moving forward through a hail of bullets and splinters, firing the gun from his hip.

"Basher" Bates' one-man charge "repulsed a force of fanatical panzergrenadiers, thereby preventing the overrunning and destruction of his unit. Corporal Bates advanced alone, to meet and rout his enemy." Bates was wounded three times, in the throat and abdomen, and died two days later.

"Basher did a really good job on them," his buddy Private Bill Holden remembered. "There were dead Germans all over [the] field. And I know there were dead Germans on the other side of the hedge because I picked them up myself the next day."[29]

The Cockney corporal from London's East End was given the highest award for valour of the British Empire: a posthumous Victoria Cross. The Royal Norfolk Regiment won five VCs in World War II, more than any other British or Commonwealth regiment. (Captain David Jamieson, who led his company in repulsing seven enemy counter-attacks on the Orne, won the fourth the next day.)

Montgomery's overriding mandate to all his divisions in *Operation Bluecoat* had been to "push on, regardless of casualties." The order had certainly been heeded. In the last two weeks of July, 7th Armoured Division had 400 casualties and, in the first week of August, 523 more.

On 8 August, Trooper John Yorke, 2nd Fife and Forfar Yeomanry, wriggled his toes with relish. For the first time in twelve days, he had a chance to take off his socks and boots. "This was the battle that really won the war," he exulted with his buddies.[30]

However, a tank officer from 7th Armoured noted bitterly: "I read how we 'lost our dash' or how the infantry went to ground rather than pressing on. Where, I wonder, were the people who wrote this? Do they realize . . . just what the British Army went through?"[31]

7
HITLER'S GAMBLE

At "Wolfschanze," the Führer's headquarters in East Prussia, the atmosphere of the map room was electric. It was 2 August 1944, the day after Patton's breakout through the Avranches corridor. The supreme commander of the Wehrmacht, Adolf Hitler, was intently studying that narrow strip of land leading to the Pontaubault Bridge. Once across the bridge, the Allies would spill out into the wide-open countryside of Brittany.

But Hitler had a bold scheme. He telephoned Field-Marshal Günther Hans von Kluge, commander-in-chief of his armies in Normandy, to command him to move immediately eight of the nine panzer divisions in Normandy to mount a counter-attack against the Americans through the town of Mortain and advance west twenty miles to Avranches, to cut off all Patton's forces from his supply line.

Hitler went on to assure his C-in-C that he would find Mortain only lightly defended. In the Führer's view, the U.S. Third Army was running in four directions; Patton hadn't enough strength in any one place to repel us. Once you have retaken Avranches, you will be in a position to annihilate the Third Army and drive Bradley's First Army back into the *bocage*—or into the sea.

Avranches is the key!

The Führer then dictated the entire battle plan. He called it *Operation Lüttich,* named for a great German victory thirty years earlier, when the Kaiser broke through to the Belgian city of Liege/Lüttich. He personally worked out every detail: the units, the sectors for each, specific objectives—and the date of the attack: 8 August, six days hence. He pointedly did not ask for advice from his military commanders.

Kluge was astounded. If he used all the available panzer strength in this one attack, the entire Normandy front could collapse. Two of

63

his nine divisions were already heavily engaged in holding back the British offensive at Caumont. The 1st and 12th SS were fighting the Canadians at Caen. Ninth Panzer Division had not yet arrived from the south of France. The American bombing at St-Lô had shattered another division, the Panzer Lehr. Only remnants were left.

By the simplest of mathematics, that left only four panzer divisions for Hitler's ambitious counter-attack, not the eight he demanded. The alternative was to denude the Caumont front, a sure-fire invitation for the British to complete their breakout.

Kluge's own latest weekly report, sent to the High Command (OKW) on 30 July, informed Hitler that "our losses in men and material were so high because of the enemy's superiority in artillery and the air that it was not possible to build up a new defence front quickly."[1]

"Madness!" Kluge thought. "Does he not read his own intelligence? If he insists on this business, he will force the entire Seventh and Fifth Armies into a trap—100,000 men. We *must* withdraw our armies to the Seine before they are completely encircled and destroyed."

Kluge decided the only hope was to stage the attack as quickly as possible before the Allies, who now encircled them on three sides, closed in. He dared not wait another six days until the 9th Panzer Division, ordered from the south of France by Hitler, arrived at the front. He would simply have to limit the counter-attack to the four panzer divisions available.

Of these, casualties had reduced two divisions, 2nd SS Panzer Das Reich and von Luttwitz's 2nd Panzer, to 60 per cent combat efficiency. The third division, the élite 1st Leibstandarte-SS Adolf Hitler Division (the LAH), would have to be disengaged from combat near Caen and replaced by a fresh German unit: the 89th Infantry Division. This division was just now moving into the Caen front. It was known as the "Horseshoe Division" for its reliance on horses for its transportation. However, the soldiers had nicknamed it the "Wheelbarrow Division" because of the primitive nature of some of its equipment.[2] The transition would be slower than if it were mechanized, therefore taking several days. Daytime troop movement was also limited by Allied air superiority.

The fourth division ordered to the Mortain front was a relative newcomer to the Normandy scene. The 116th Panzer Division was a powerful and well-trained force known as the Windhund (Greyhound) Division, because of its speed and success in Russia. An officer from one of its panzergrenadier regiments described its status as almost equivalent to that of the élite SS Panzer Divisions of 1st and 2nd SS Panzer Corps, and with comparable strength.

The 116th comprised one panzer regiment of two battalions of Mark Vs (Panthers) and Mark IV tanks with a total of 160 to 180 armoured vehicles; two panzergrenadier infantry regiments of two battalions each; an artillery regiment; a reconnaissance detachment; and an engineer battalion.

"Morale and spirits in the division are very high," the division war diary noted. "Cooperation among the units of the division is excellent; they are clever, quick, and reliable."[3]

Its commander, Lieutenant-General Gerhard Graf von Schwerin, was a skilled veteran of the eastern front and a proud and aloof Wehrmacht career officer who had little use for Hitler or his SS divisions. Count von Schwerin was, in fact, also a major player in the assassination conspiracy. So far, he had managed to elude the Gestapo's list of suspects.

The 116th, then posted near Rouen, received its orders to proceed to Normandy on 14 July. As they were always in combat and weapons readiness to move, they broke camp that same night. But moving a force of 12,000 men and 180 tanks under determined Allied air raids was a daunting challenge.

There was any number of reports of the hazards of daytime travel. SS-General Sepp Dietrich, travelling by day in France, claimed he had to leave his car eighty to ninety times and seek cover from air attacks. Only half the ammunition trains that left Paris ever reached their destinations, and a normal three-hour trip now took an average of three days.[4]

Originally it was decided to send the tanks of 116th Panzer Division by rail to spare extra stress on engines, treads, and petrol supplies. The troops would march to the Seine and be ferried across.

The plan proved unworkable. The Allied air forces had damaged all train lines that ran east–west into Normandy. The tanks would have to travel on their own by road and then queue up to cross the Seine by ferry. This took two extra days.

Moving the 12,000 troops presented more hazards. The division war diary reported that,"for reasons of camouflage, and because of the heavy enemy air activity in the lower Seine area, marches were only made at night. The days were used for resting and for servicing vehicles. The engineer battalion was detached to the ferry crossings in advance in order to regulate traffic and help with the ferrying."[5]

The distance was a mere 120 miles. It took 116th Division six days to reach its destination. During that time the troops hid by day in the woods or in hastily dug slit trenches, with sporadic food supplies and no protection from dive-bombing Typhoon aircraft. They marched through the long night hours, often in driving rain.

When the division finally arrived, it was first put in reserve at the Caen front. Soon afterwards it came under command of 47th Panzer Corps, the force of four panzer divisions newly created for Hitler's counter-attack at Mortain. The corps' commander was fifty-three-year-old SS General Hans Freiherr von Funck, a general officer who had risen from military attaché to Spain during the Civil War to succeed Rommel as commander of 7th Panzer Division. To the Wehrmacht, this SS officer was "brutal, captious and unbeloved."[6]

The Windhund Division was first moved into combat in the British sector at Vire, a key point southeast of St-Lô. Here the troops met "stubborn fighting," clashing with the full might of General Horrocks's British 30 Corps. For another three days the division was locked in "defensive battles and reconnaissance skirmishes, under heavy air activity."[7]

It was while the 116th was in the middle of a brutal battle that Funck ordered Schwerin to "disengage." Disengaging was easily ordered, but not so easily achieved, as Count von Schwerin undoubtedly told his superior officer, whom he considered "narrow-minded and obstinate."

The personal animosity between these two men exploded into a bitter fight. Funck accused the division of "passive resistance, cowardice and inability" and ordered the newly arrived 84th Infantry Division to relieve 116th Panzer from the British front at Vire.[8]

This didn't sit well with the aristocratic 116th commander, who held a poor opinion of the combat abilities of the newcomers. "This new division was not up to the difficult conditions of war against superior heavily armoured forces; its armament and equipment were completely inadequate," Schwerin argued. "After the first appearance of these troops, all commanders of 116th Panzer Division were fully aware of the danger of such relief."[9]

Funck also arbitrarily transferred an entire panzer battalion from the 116th as well as half of its anti-tank battalion to fill the shortfall of 2nd Panzer Division. Its reconnaissance battalion had already been seconded.

Schwerin fumed. Through Funck's meddling, 116th Panzer Division had lost one-third of its armoured strength—a bad beginning to a major counter-attack. Inwardly he resolved to oppose the counter-attack by the "passive resistance" for which he was being accused. As long as he was commander, his division would not fight in *Operation Lüttich*. [10]

Kluge's strategy for the Mortain counter-attack depended on surprise. To achieve this there would be no preliminary artillery barrage. He had also been assured that the predicted weather conditions would ensure dense ground fog in the morning of 7 August— an essential element to avoid air interference.

Two panzer divisions would advance in stealth at midnight: Lüttwitz's 2nd SS Panzer, reinforced by a combat group of 17th SS Panzer Grenadier Division, would recapture the small town of Mortain, now enjoying its third day of liberation. At the same time, 2nd Panzer Division would attack the village of St-Barthélmy, ten kilometres to the north. The division was to be reinforced by Schwerin's 116th and by a tank battalion of 1st Leibstandarte-SS Adolf Hitler.

An essential element was the Luftwaffe guarantee of substantial air support—three hundred fighters to form a protective ring around the operation.

Sunday, 6 August: Kluge was in a panic. H-Hour was set for 2200 hours. As it neared, more crises arose. Patton's Third Army had reached Le Mans, almost encircling the Seventh German Army. Hitler still hadn't given his final approval for *Operation Lüttich,* and was still holding out for a postponement until the remaining panzer divisions arrived. He was even suggesting that Eberbach replace Funck. Kluge declined; it was too late to change commanders. Finally, at 1905 hours, the telephone rang: the Führer's permission to attack was granted.

A fresh problem presented itself. Initially, 1st SS Panzer informed Kluge that they were delayed leaving the Caen front. Their second call informed the already agitated commander that the 1st SS Tank Battalion—an essential element in reinforcing 2nd Panzer's spearhead attack on Mortain—could not arrive until morning. Ironically, a British Typhoon shot down by German anti-aircraft fire had crash-landed into the leading Panther on the road, blocking it. The entire column would have to reverse out and find a new way around the narrow defile.

The final blow was a call from Funck. He insisted on a two-hour postponement of the attack because of the delays in getting his formations prepared. H-hour was changed to midnight—2400 hours.

Kluge feared that the bottom was falling out of his operation. His battle plan was compromised; his general officers were feuding. There was pressure on him to fire one of the most capable commanders, Schwerin.

The bottom was about to fall out of his life, too. He could not help wondering if in trying to placate Hitler by launching this flawed operation he had raised a question mark of his own loyalty. *Der kluge Hans*—"Clever Hans"—so careful to keep his political balance, may have gotten a bit too clever for his own safety.

He suspected, as well, that the Americans might well be on to his surprise attack. He turned flatly to his son, Lieutenant-Colonel Klaus von Kluge, chief of staff of 47th Panzer Corps: "Our Intelligence has intercepted enemy signals. The Allies may have recognized our intentions and discerned our army regroupings. The pressure of superior forces compels us to launch the attack.

"It is now or never."[11]

What he couldn't realize was that the Allies had the use of Ultra's top-secret radio intercepts and knew *exactly* what the enemy was doing. In this case, the first radio communications the Germans made pertaining to the raid were on 6 August, that very morning. By the time Ultra decoded the transmissions at Bletchley Park in

England, then translated and relayed them through to General Bradley's headquarters at U.S. First Army, it was thirty-eight minutes past midnight.[12]

General Bradley had just moments of warning. But it was sufficient to divert three American divisions and redirect them towards the sector of the enemy offensive. He also asked for full Allied air support for the next morning.

But the 30th Division combat troops at the sharp end had barely any warning at all. Had the attack been launched at 2200 hours as originally planned, they could have been completely overrun and surely annihilated.

That crashed British Typhoon pilot who so stalled the advance of the powerful 1st SS tanks did his Allied friends a very large service: he gave them a two-hour reprieve.[13]

Shortly after midnight on 7 August, two panzer divisions—two of the eight Hitler had originally demanded—milled about in the confusion of the start-line. Jumping off with whatever units they could assemble at short notice, 2nd Panzer and 2nd SS Panzer divisions launched *Operation Lüttich*.

The *Suisse Normande* terrain made the going perilous. Dense thickets of trees masked sharp drops and gullies. Narrow, winding lanes made navigation treacherous, despite the clear light of a full moon.

One hundred and twenty tanks, each carrying German infantry and engineers, advanced cautiously in single file to avoid alerting the enemy with the noise of crashing trees. The tank commander, on foot, led his tank at a steady walking pace, using only pinpoint light. His skill determined their safety.

The 2nd Panzer troops advanced on the northern flanks in two columns. At 0100 hours, its reconnaissance battalion crossed a small river, the Sée. Ahead they could see the shrouded outline of Hill 314, a sheer outcropping of tree-covered high ground standing like a sentinel blocking the approaches to the small town. A thick fog rolled off the river.

Maintaining silence, the reconnaissance battalions stealthily skirted the hill on the north side, bypassing an American roadblock.

They were so close they heard English voices in their foxholes. They pushed on another eight miles until daybreak, almost reaching their objective of Le Mesnil–Adelée before enemy resistance stopped them. Avranches was within reach, a mere twelve miles farther on.

In their wake the remaining 2nd Panzer column, proceeding without resistance, confidently approached St-Barthélmy, three miles north of Mortain.

One more such push and Patton's army would be cut off.

"Bad weather is what we need, Herr General," von Lüttwitz's chief of operations said. Indeed, the thick fog was a sure guarantee that dawn would not bring the rocket-firing aircraft.[14]

Meanwhile, the lead 2nd SS Division, reinforced by 17th SS Panzergrenadiers, started out just three kilometres east of Mortain. In less than an hour the panzergrenadier infantry troops—500 men, faces blackened, rifles poised—poured furtively down the main street of the town.

Operation Lüttich—Hitler's gamble—was on.

8

THE BATTLE
OF MORTAIN

After the grim forty-nine-day battle through the *bocage* and the bloody capture of St-Lô, 30th U.S. Infantry Division, "Old Hickory," was relishing some hard-won rest and relaxation.

On 1 August, a Tuesday, the troops had their first baths since D-Day. Fresh laundry and replacements of tattered shirts and worn boots boosted morale—as did grub that didn't come out of a tin, and jokes that didn't emerge from the black humour of the foxholes. Attractive American girls serving coffee and donuts from the Red Cross clubmobiles gave snatches of stateside memories.

On Friday, a USO show featuring Edward G. Robinson wowed the troops, though possibly the film with Lucille Ball and June Allyson wowed them even more. Thirtieth U.S. Division commander, Major General Leland Hobbs, for once mellowing his loud, gruff-talking manner, commended the men for their fine efforts in fighting their way through the *bocage*. First U.S. Army had finally escaped the confining Cotentin Peninsula. Hobbs liked to win.

Among the soldiers were 1,200 replacements that had been moved up to join the division because of the heavy casualties from the *bocage* battles. It is never easy to assimilate so many new men, especially during heavy fighting.

"We had a crack outfit when we came over the Channel," 1st Sergeant Thomas "Tops" Kirkman of 119th Infantry noted. "We'd been together for two years. We'd worked together in England, trained together; we were good. But since we came to France, it'd been a steady drain. We'd been shot up pretty bad. We'd lost a lot of swell men.

"Now we get replacements who show no signs of that training. We get clerks and mechanics and cooks who have suddenly become

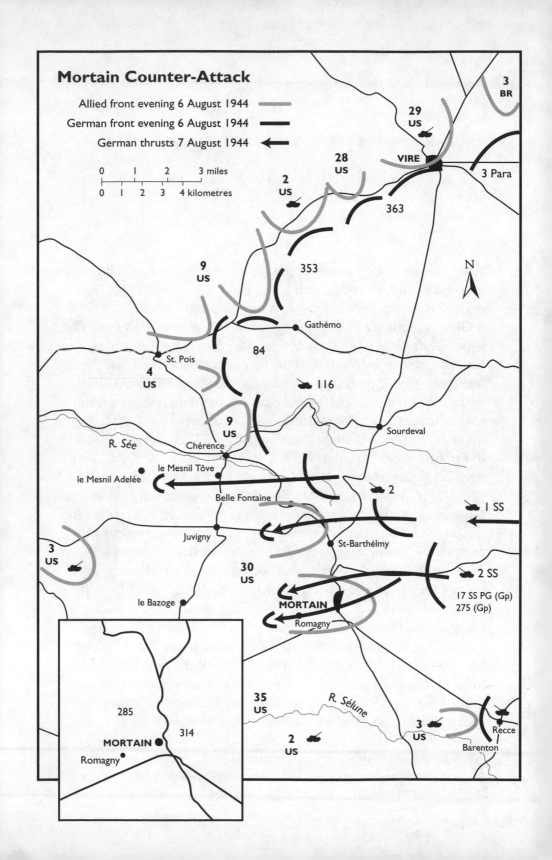

Mortain Counter-Attack

Allied front evening 6 August 1944 ——
German front evening 6 August 1944 ——
German thrusts 7 August 1944 ◀——

0   1   2   3 miles
0   1   2   3   4 kilometres

3 BR

29 US

VIRE

3 Para

363

28 US

2 US

353

9 US

N

Gathémo

84

St. Pois

4 US

116

9 US

Sourdeval

R. Sée

Chérence

le Mesnil Tôve

le Mesnil Adelée

Belle Fontaine

2

1 SS

Juvigny

St-Barthélmy

3 US

30 US

2 SS

le Bazoge

MORTAIN

17 SS PG (Gp)
275 (Gp)

Romagny

35 US

R. Sélune

3 US

Recce

2 US

Barenton

285

MORTAIN

314

Romagny

riflemen. Why, I remember in a group that recently arrived—I asked for somebody to handle a machine gun and not one of them spoke out. None of them had ever handled one. Finally one of them said, 'Hell, Lieutenant, I'll fire the damn thing.'

"Look at the list of NCOs. Most of them are privates with stripes. We have to have somebody in those jobs. That's why they were upped.

"And now we go in with a bunch of replacements who haven't had a chance to learn north from south, or whose arches have fallen after the first five-mile hike. The new non-coms rattle around in the old ones' shoes.

"But the old man says to jump." He grinned. "So, we jump."[1]

The old man—the division commander—did say "jump." But first the division, the old sweats and the new, young replacements, had the heady experience of marching as liberators along the main road of the small town of Mortain, a hamlet that few of the GIs had even heard of—but they all enjoyed to the hilt. First U.S. Infantry Division had actually freed the town three days earlier; the townsfolk could hardly believe their good fortune in having two liberation parades!

> *Diary of René Langlois, a Mortain schoolboy:*
> *Mortain, Tuesday, 3 August.*
>   *About 0700 hours we saw the first Americans. All of us, every-one in the whole district, ran out toward them, not thinking of the danger. At the same time, to announce our liberation, the bells of the Collégiale began to peal, making us believe that the nightmare was over. Or so we thought . . .*[2]

In pre-war days, Mortain was a tourist's playground. Built halfway up a hillside in an attractive wooded gorge, the foaming waterfall, La Cascade, was the town's centrepiece attraction. An imposing rocky spur on the town's eastern edge rose 314 metres above sea level. Hikers (ironically, French, British, and German in particular) found the clamber to the top of Hill 314 a popular Sunday excursion. A narrow lane curved up through a landscape of rocky outcroppings towards the summit. It passed, on the way, the twelfth-century L'Abbaye Blanche (so named because its nuns wore white homespun robes). The adventuresome ignored the road and, instead, scaled the sheer rocky crag on the southwestern summit of Hill 314, known as Montjoie.

A dazzling view rewarded anyone who would stand perilously on the out-jutting rocks behind the tiny church, La Petite Chapelle. Thirty kilometres to the west, one could see as far as Avranches, the gateway to Brittany, and beyond it, the glistening Atlantic waters of the Bay of Mont-St-Michel. Due south were the flat plains of the Sélune River, bordering the province of Maine. A full turn north revealed the Norman countryside, the *bocage* terrain that tourists loved for its beauty. And soldiers despised for its treachery.

> *Diary of René Langlois: Saturday, 5 August.*
> *Americans came to see us . . . They were warmly welcomed by everyone in the district, and given cider, coffee, and, obviously, Calva [Calvados]. Which they seemed to appreciate!*

On this balmy summer Sunday, 6 August, elated townsfolk of Mortain finally believed they were free. They crowded the avenue, throwing flowers, laughing, and cheering in the joy of being rid of the Nazis. Not a few ran up to the troops with hugs and *mercis* and always-welcome bottles of wine or the local apple liqueur, Calvados. The townspeople—some 1,600 souls—were grateful that their ancient buildings had emerged from four years of occupation and three days of liberation with only a single shell hole, harmlessly landing in the park.

> *Diary of René Langlois: Sunday, 6 August.*
> *On Sunday we were sitting beside the road and passing Americans gave us whatever they had: cigarettes (in packets of three or four), chewing gum, little packets of coffee and tea, little pots of jam.* [3]

Arriving in Mortain on that sunny Sunday afternoon, the three regiments of U.S. 30th Division headed for their assigned defensive posts: 117th Regiment took over the defences of the tiny village of St-Barthélmy, just north of Mortain. The 119th was in reserve nearby, and 120th was assigned the task of defending the town of Mortain and its surrounding hills.

Colonel Hammond Birks, the commanding officer of 120th Infantry Regiment, was amazed at the carnival atmosphere of Mortain. "This town is *wide open*," he told his aide-de-camp. "The hotels are full. It should be an excellent place for a little rest and relaxation."

But his counterpart from the departing U.S. 1st Infantry Division unit uttered a prophetic warning: "Hill 314 is the key to the whole area. In case of emergency this hill has to be held at all costs."[4]

For General Bradley and his Allied commanders, and for Hitler and his generals, that modest peak in the *Suisse Normande* would become the focus of tactical scrutiny. Whoever commanded its summit commanded all movement of the troops below. In short, Hitler's troops could not reach Avranches without taking and holding Hill 314. Bradley's troops could not avoid being overrun unless *they* held it.

Birks assigned the defence of the town of Mortain and Hill 314 to his 2nd Battalion, warning that the enemy was located in strength northeast of Mortain. "If any trouble develops it will come from that direction," Birks told 2nd Battalion's commanding officer (CO), Lieutenant Colonel Eads Hardaway. "Put roadblocks on all approaches to the 2nd Battalion position."

It was the intersection at L'Abbaye Blanche that concerned him the most. Four roads converged on it. The main north–south road to Mortain ran right through it. As well, three others angled into it.

"If that roadblock does not hold, the resulting gap will permit the enemy to smash through our line," Colonel Birks declared. Lieutenant Tom Andrew was put in command of a seventy-man force to hold the barricades at L'Abbaye Blanche. He had two 57mm guns from the battalion's anti-tank platoon, a machine gun and mortar section, and a rifle squad. To give added firepower Birks sent over Lieutenant Tom Springfield's platoon of four guns from 823rd Tank-Destroyer (TD) Battalion.[5] The 15-pound shells from the Springfield's 3-inch anti-tank guns were capable of penetrating three inches of armour at 2,000 feet.

Lieutenant Andrew did a quick survey of his post. "There is no time to start building new defensive positions before dark," he said grimly. "We'll have to use these ones the Germans just left. They are in good natural positions."

He sited his 3-inch guns on either side of the main road with two, 30-calibre machine guns on each side. Then he placed a bazooka and BAR (Browning automatic rifle) team and half a squad of riflemen in former enemy dugout positions along a small hedgerow north of the railway bridge. A 57mm anti-tank gun covered the end of the road.

Immediately south of the railroad bridge, Andrew placed riflemen and bazooka teams. He had two belts of mines laid near the bend in the road and these were covered by the bazooka and BAR teams. Every one of his seventy men had a vital role to play.

They were ready.

From his battalion headquarters at the old Grande Hotel on the main square, Lieutenant Colonel Hardaway swiftly dispatched some 600 men from 2nd Battalion to establish defensive positions on Hill 314.

"We had to carry everything up that damn hill—guns, tripods, ammo, everything!" recalls Private John Weekly of "H" Company. "We didn't have a jeep or an ammo carrier. I was carrying the tripod for our 50-calibre machine gun. We set up in an orchard. It was a machine gunner's paradise. You could see for miles and miles. The problem was we only had minimal ammunition. We brought all we could carry, but that wasn't much."[6]

The men found that inheriting 1st Division's hastily installed temporary defences created a lot of problems. "They had only dug down about eighteen inches," Private George Neidhardt of "F" Company said scornfully of his predecessor's foxhole. "I went down four feet, deep enough to stand in up to my armpits."[7]

There were other snags: the phone net was unusable and had to be completely rewired. There were few large-scale maps. There had been no chance to install fortifications or minefields.[8]

Still, they reckoned there was plenty of time to correct these deficiencies: "Perhaps the battalion was suffering from a false sense of security," Lieutenant Ralph Kerley admitted.[9] Kerley, a seasoned veteran, had been wounded as a platoon commander before the St-Lô battle. He had just returned to the line to take command of "E" Company. The men worked hard at their tasks of consolidating the position, grateful for the lateness of midsummer light that let them toil away until midnight.

*

The Germans launched their attack with a bombing raid and haphazard shelling on the town's centre. A number of fires broke out, forcing the civilians into shelters.

> *Diary of René Langlois: Sunday, 6 August.*
> *At midnight, there was a German bombing raid. In our parents' house there were also several families. In the cellars, we were all curled up, listening to the explosions. Where would the next bomb fall?*
>
> *After the bombing, which had set fire to the whole town, the people of Mortain left for the surrounding countryside. Some families went to a mine, where there were 800 people in the end. They had some problems feeding them.*[10]

Amid the screech of flying mortars and the crash of exploding shells, no one heard the more ominous drumming noise of tank treads rumbling towards them. At 0125 hours, enemy small-arms fire was heard to the east of the 2nd Battalion command post (CP). It was while he was stringing telephone wire across the town streets, working by the illumination of the fires, that Sergeant Robert Bondurant happened to look up and gasp: "There they were at the other end of the street—German soldiers. Maybe thirty or more. All with burp guns. The town was full of them."

Bondurant immediately reported the crisis to Colonel Birks. "Hold the town at all costs," Birks ordered him. "Stay at your post."

He stayed.[11]

Five minutes later the full force of an enemy attack fell on the Allies. Second SS Das Reich Panzer Division had managed to bypass a roadblock on the southeast approaches to Mortain, enabling them to encircle the town.

> *Diary of René Langlois: Monday, 7 August.*
> *On the Monday, we wanted to go out quickly and beg some more from the convoys we could hear passing. But when we got to the first hedge, we realized they were German tanks going up the road.*
>
> *The local policeman's wife [had been] killed. He stayed behind*

to watch over his wife's body during the counterattack and was reported missing. No trace was ever found of him or of her. [12]

The Americans were forced to withdraw to the high ground of Hill 314. Lieutenant Ronal Woody had just come off the hill when he spotted the enemy troops: "When the firing started I knew I had to get up to where my men were, up on top of the hill, so I went up the cliff," he said. "They were shooting all around me as I climbed. Somehow I made it up there. When I looked back and saw the way I'd come, I couldn't believe I had climbed it."[13]

At 0345, Hardaway signalled Birks urgently: "The Germans have taken part of Hill 314."

"Send Company 'G' to drive them off," Birks commanded him.

Minutes later, Hardaway called back with an ominous message: "Enemy tanks and armoured vehicles with accompanying infantry are entering Mortain in strength."

By 0700 hours he was desperate. "I've got to get out of Mortain," he pleaded.

"You get up there with your troops on Hill 314!" Birks ordered sternly.

The next call from Hardaway's HQ Company came a few hours later. With him were his executive officer, his communications officer, and a dozen men of Battalion Headquarters Company—some twenty-seven men in all.

"We tried to sneak out of town between the buildings but ran into Germans blocking any access to the hill. Then we had to duck into another building. I am cut off from Hill 314 and unable to join my troops," he signalled.

"My staff and I are in hiding; my radio batteries are low."

Then—silence. Nothing more was heard. It was assumed that the commanding officer and his entire headquarters staff had been taken prisoner. (This was later confirmed by one of his staff who escaped.) Command of 2nd Battalion was given to Captain Reynold Erichson.

Meanwhile, a number of other 2nd Battalion men still roamed the outskirts of the town. Overrun and out of communication, the small isolated bands were striving to find their way through enemy lines to join their comrades on Hill 314. Some were killed; some managed to sneak through or to hide out in the hedgerows or barns for several days, dodging Germans.

Some, like Sergeant Robert Bondurant, were captured. The young signaller had stayed at his switchboard to the end, as ordered. The SS troops rounded up all their prisoners and forced them to sit in the middle of the road. The frightened sergeant could only think of the reported 2nd SS massacre of hundreds of French civilians in Oradour-sur-Glane.[14]

"I thought they were going to shoot us," he said. "Instead they walked us back to an aid station. Wounded were lying around everywhere, both German and American."[15]

> *Diary of René Langlois: Monday, 7 August.*
> *The German counter-attack was becoming fiercer, and getting nearer, and this forced us to draw further back into the country. Were we aware of what was at stake not far away? We youngsters, full of the carelessness of inexperience, slept the night without hearing too much of the noise of the battle . . .[16]*

One of the last outsiders to reach the summit of Hill 314 was Captain Delmont Byrn, who was commanding "H" Company (Heavy Weapons). He found Ralph Kerley's company and was stunned by the sight of wounded men lying around the command post: "It was my first week of combat," he said. "I was kind of shocked to see injured men lying there in the open, being hit again by shrapnel."

Erichson, now in command of 2nd Battalion, had rounded up what stragglers he could, about forty, and managed to find an unguarded trail that led steeply up the hill. He quickly pulled all the companies into a communication link, established an all-round defensive position on the summit and alerted the watches and the men positioned on the roadblocks leading to the hilltop. Dense fog rolled in, adding to the darkness of the night; visibility was nil.

Erichson took stock.

The battalion, or what was left of it, was now isolated on the summit of Hill 314. The six hundred men were surrounded on all sides by one of Germany's most élite panzer divisions that even at reduced strength numbered some nine thousand men.

Its acting CO, Erichson, was a twenty-four-year-old captain, in peacetime an Iowa farmer. Three of its company commanders had never before commanded a company (Captain Delmont Byrn, Lieutenant Joe Reaser, and the irrepressible Lieutenant Ronal Woody). One, Ralph Kerley, was a hell-for-leather soldier, but noted for being unorthodox.

However, they had, as powerful tools, two forward artillery observation officers (FOOs). These FOOs were the eyes of the divisional artillery that was securely positioned several thousand yards behind them. From their hilltop observation posts, FOO lieutenants Robert Weiss and Charles Bartz could see all of the surrounding countryside, and thus direct and correct effective fire from the American guns against the enemy. Although telephone communication no longer existed, they still had battery-run radio communication with which to call down targets to the gunners from 230 Field Artillery Battalion on the flats below. Thanks to these two men, counter-attack after counter-attack by determined panzer troops were thwarted.

The battalion could hold out—as long as the batteries lasted.

Meanwhile, some three kilometres northwest of Mortain, two battalions from 117th Regiment arrived to take over the defences of the tiny crossroads village of St-Barthélmy. French resistance had tipped off the CO of 1st Battalion, Lieutenant-Colonel Robert Frankland, that German troops were massing in the northeast. He directed two of his companies to cover roads coming in from that direction.

"A" Company seemed hardly a match for the might of 2nd Panzer Division. Its commander, a lieutenant, had been with "A" Company for just a week; 3rd Platoon had no officers; a sergeant commanded it. Of its strength of 135 men, fifty-five were replacements who had come in two days before. The company had no bazookas and no artillery support.[17]

Frankland would have been horrified to learn that 1st SS Panzer Division—the powerful Leibstandarte Adolf Hitler that had been stalled the previous night by the crashed British typhoon near Caen—had now caught up with Funck's counter-attack force towards dawn. Its task was to follow and overtake 2nd Panzer, picking up the lead for the final drive to Avranches.

Frankland's tiny force was all there was to block its advance through St-Barthélmy.

*

The attack came on Monday, 7 August, at 0600 hours. Panther tanks from three directions poured into St-Barthélmy, overwhelming the crossroads defenders. The tanks converged on the U.S. 823rd Tank Destroyer Battalion's anti-tank and tank-destroyer guns. George Greene, a twenty-two-year-old lieutenant commanding a platoon of four guns, had joined the 823rd TDs just a few days before, and barely knew even the names of the men under him. Greene and his men hung on, knocking out tank after tank, until the Panthers had, one by one, destroyed their guns. Then he grabbed a machine gun and fired an entire belt of ammunition at the enemy, giving his men the chance to escape.

By 0700 hours, at least eight enemy tanks had fought their way into the town. Because of the thick fog that "rose and fell like a stage curtain," fighting was chaotic. Attacker and defender groped for each other, fighting blindly, viciously, often trading blows and even bayonet thrusts—a rare occurrence in WWII. Two German tanks came to within 250 yards of Colonel Birks's command post.

"The Germans rushed the positions, throwing potato mashers over the hedgerows, and some of them even jumping the hedges right into company positions," Sergeant Grady reported.[18]

Colonel Frankland still had clear radio communication with his companies. "Stay in place," Frankland told them urgently. "Let the tanks break through and then get the infantry that follows." It was a tactic the Germans so often and so effectively used against the Allies in Normandy.

The outnumbered GIs of 117th Infantry fought back with incredible tenacity and resourcefulness, and their guns and bazookas took a heavy toll on the German infantry. The men of the hapless "A" Company were dead in the path of a column of Mark IV tanks from 2nd Panzer Division. One tank crashed through a gap in the hedgerow directly in front of a foxhole shared by Staff Sergeant Abbie Riviere and Sergeant Grover Wright.

"Should we shoot him, Abbie, should we shoot him?" Wright asked excitedly.

But neither man had a bazooka with which to shoot the tank.

Wisely, Riviere ordered his squad to withdraw, using the thick fog as cover.

Short on trained manpower or effective weapons, but long on sheer courage, the company was virtually wiped out in those first few minutes. Only one officer and twenty-seven men, out of one hundred, escaped being killed or captured.

The panzers then penetrated the town and, unknowingly, surrounded Colonel Frankland's advance command post. "The colonel heard noises at the rear of the house and went to investigate," one of his staff recalled. "He got there just as two of his radiomen were being forced out the back door with their hands up. The colonel followed them out and shot the two Germans. The command group immediately escaped out the window."

A second unconfirmed report claims that the colonel also shot the commander of the tank that was attacking his headquarters. He is then said to have jumped up on the tank and started blasting away down the hatch with his .45 automatic, killing the whole crew.

Frankland's 1st Battalion and its supporting 823rd Tank Destroyer Platoon suffered heavy casualties: more than 334 men killed, wounded, or missing. One of those casualties was Lieutenant George Greene, the newcomer to battle, who made his mark on 7 August. Greene was wounded and taken prisoner. In the early afternoon (he couldn't be sure of the time as a German soldier had stolen his watch), he and the other American prisoners from St-Barthélmy were loaded into trucks packed with German soldiers for a nightmare trip into German lines. Every time the convoy was strafed by Allied Typhoons, the German troops "were able to jump out of the truck and hide in the ditches. We had to stay in the trucks."[19]

But still the battered companies fought on. Survivors dropped back to a new defensive line on a low hill just west of St-Barthélmy. The 117th regimental commander, Lieutenant Colonel Walter Johnson, grabbed every man that could hold a gun—including his kitchen staff and drivers—and set up a defensive line just in front of the stone farmhouse that served as regimental HQ. A battalion from 823rd Tank Destroyer provided fire support. The men soon changed the name of the house that served as the regimental command post to "Château Nebelwerfer" as German artillery registered all their guns and mortars on it.

The Germans were fewer than four hundred yards away. They fired everything they had. Every square yard around the house seemed to be hit but, amazingly, the house was untouched. Once the attack was under way, Colonel Johnson refused to back down. He thought it would affect the men's morale if he changed the command post location.

That morning, before the fog could lift, the Germans attacked again, this time just with infantry. Right over the hedgerows they came. They wore stolen American uniforms and field jackets, and carried trench knives. Close hand-to-hand fighting, even fistfights, followed for about thirty minutes.

But the obstinate defenders of St-Barthélmy, though driven out of the village, achieved their goal. They had delayed what was supposed to be the main thrust of the German attack for six vital hours until air support could arrive.

By early afternoon, 1st SS Panzer Division, still sixteen miles from Avranches, had been forced to a standstill, unable to bypass the tenacious Americans. The 2nd Panzer Division's reconnaissance battalion had managed to spearhead the northern column's drive, advancing six miles towards Avranches at daybreak and forcing one infantry company to abandon its vehicles and guns. A roadblock established by the reserve 119th Infantry Regiment stopped the rout. The panzers were being threatened, too, by the first elements of the armoured reinforcements that VII Corps commander Lieutenant-General Joe Collins had rushed up to prevent the Germans from breaking into the vital Avranches Corridor.

While they had initially seemed to have the whip hand, 2nd German Panzer Division at nearby Mesnil–Adelée also came to a halt. With just twelve miles still to go, they had now to wait for the remainder of 2nd Panzer and 1st SS to catch up.

Those six hours bought for them by the Americans in St-Barthélmy had proven to be of vital importance.[20]

In that exact time span, the fog had dissipated from the River Sée. General von Lüttwitz had been praying for continuing fog to provide a protective mantle from air observation over his attacking troops. Sunlight breaking through would bring the dreaded American and British air forces into the Battle of Mortain. If he could just be free from the harassing fighter-bombers for a few more hours!

He knew from past experience that when the Jabos attacked he had no choice but to order his foot soldiers to take cover and his armoured columns to get off the roads and cover their tanks with camouflage netting.

But brilliant noonday sun began filtering through the lifting fog, casting unwelcome shafts of light on the Mortain aggressors. Lüttwitz quickly ordered his tanks off the roads. It was too late. The Allied gunners and airmen could now target their prey.

The Day of the Typhoons was at hand.

9

MORTAIN'S
LOST BATTALION

As the fog burned off Hill 314 in the late morning, FOOs Lieutenants Weiss and Bartz grinned broadly at each other. The view
below them was an artilleryman's dream: "Columns of enemy
armour and foot troops streaming [towards us] from the east and
northeast."[1] The battalion's hold on the hill had become a festering
sore to the enemy, as an extract from the diary of 2nd Panzer Division shows:

> *1000 hours, 7 August 44: A battle group consisting of elements
> of the 17th SS Panzergrenadier Division has not been able to
> budge the stubborn American defenders on the Hill. Hill 314
> provides American artillery observers with an excellent view of
> the entire countryside for miles around."*[2]

A very effective collaboration was developing between the American infantry at the L'Abbaye Blanche roadblock and the artillery
FOOs atop Hill 314. Weiss and Bartz would spot the enemy armour
and infantry concentrations approaching from the east and radio
their positions to the American artillery emplacements several miles
away to the west. They then would observe the fall of shot and,
when necessary, correct the range and alignment. This broke up the
German concentrations before they could attain full momentum.

Any vehicles or infantry getting through this hurdle then came
under fire of the seventy-man L'Abbaye Blanche roadblock team of
Lieutenants Tom Springfield and Tom Andrew's 823rd Tank
Destroyers.[3]

But Andrew soon realized that in using the old German dug-in
defence positions he was letting himself in for a lot more fire. The

enemy now demonstrated that they had full knowledge of these positions and had targeted them for their artillery. "Whenever they opened up, our troops would have to abandon them and take shelter in the nearest house or barn," Andrew said. When the artillery fire ceased, the troops returned to their positions and found that "everything we left there such as gas masks and clothing had been completely riddled."

The Germans pounded the roadblock with every weapon they could lay their hands on—flame throwers, grenades, 88mms, and non-stop artillery bombardments. Combat patrol attacks were directed at the roadblock from every direction.

The 30th Division's artillery, criticized as being slow at first to respond seriously to the German counter-attack, now threw its vast weight of twelve-and-a-half field artillery battalions—some three hundred guns—at the enemy. "Air Ops [operations], working out of little low-flying Austers, were invaluable in identifying targets, especially because of the position of the sun in the late afternoon," artillery commander Brigadier-General James Lewis noted. "We established a record, firing thirty artillery concentrations [stonks] on enemy gun positions in one hour at dusk. There was a tremendous drop in the enemy's artillery fire the next day."[4]

The Allied air forces had been tipped off by General Bradley (through Ultra) to pour on an "all-out effort." They had been watching the skies just as anxiously as Lüttwitz had.

They decided to split the job. As soon as the fog lifted, Major-General Elwood "Pete" Quesada's 9th Tactical Air Force P-51 Mustangs and P-47 Thunderbolts engaged the Luftwaffe over their base near Paris. The RAF 2nd Tactical Air Force's rocket-firing Typhoons had the task of tackling the German armour and infantry at Mortain. This cooperative effort of both tactical air forces produced the greatest concentration of fighter-bombers yet deployed in the west.

After an inauspicious beginning, the Typhoon had found its forte, ultimately becoming the most deadly air-to-ground attack aircraft of the war. Able to outrun the German ME-109 and the FW-190, the single-seater Typhoon fighter was highly manoeuvrable at low level.

The Luftwaffe's promise to Kluge of producing three hundred fighter planes in support of *Operation Lüttich* dissolved under the impact of two hundred sorties by the American P-51 Mustangs. As visibility improved, they swarmed the German fighter planes as they took off from their base, rendering the Luftwaffe completely impotent.

Kluge, expecting dog fights, got no protection at all. Luftwaffe colonel Schultz admitted apologetically, "Our fighters were hard pressed by enemy fighters from the moment they took to the air. They could not reach the target area."[5]

At 1215 hours, Wing Commander Charles Green, a burly South African who was something of a legend with the RAF, spearheaded the first flight of Typhoons. These would total 294 sorties by the end of the day. When he and his wing man took off from Le Fresne Camilly fighter strip, the fog still lingered, putting doubts to their chances of being able to spot enemy targets, or even being able to put back down on the airstrip after their reconnaissance. But the two men got lucky. Although the cloud base was so low they had only a split-second's glimpse before they pulled out of their dive, they had spotted their quarry.[6]

The German armour has already stopped on all fronts, they reported back gleefully. They're sitting ducks.

Flying from primitive, hastily constructed air bases in France, not far from the D-Day landing beaches, the Allied pilots operated in teams. Planes would take off together in pairs, or sometimes fours or eights, to make the fifteen-minute flight to target. Then they would attack, and return to base to rearm. Thus they maintained a continuous cycle over the target from 1230 hours until dusk.

This was, as Flight Lieutenant Charles Demoulin describes it, desperately dangerous: "The average survival rate for a rocket-firing Typhoon pilot since mass sorties at low level were introduced was around seventeen operations. After that, he lived on borrowed time. Veterans stood a better chance of living than the younger ones, whose average number of operations before 'buying it' was no more than five.

"They learn by trial and error, on the spot. Most casualties occur on the first few operations, through lack of experience. I am sorry for these sprogs [newcomers], who will probably not get past their first ten sorties before 'going for a Burton.'"[7]

Flight Lieutenant Bill Baggs was one very lucky sprog. Enlisting straight out of high school in 1942, Bill was the only Canadian in 164 Squadron, RAF. The squadron was a regular "united nations of pilots" from eleven countries.[8] He started flying close army support on 14 July, and from that date he flew in combat for many months, with as many as three sorties a day against enemy strongpoints.

Early in July he was hit by heavy flak, an 88mm shell, resulting in nineteen holes in his aircraft. Incredibly, he got home. His early brush with death "sort of woke me up," he said. From then on Baggs flew daily in close support sorties. "Initially, when you started flying on your tour, you didn't really see very much. You were too involved in keeping in formation with your leader. As you got more experienced you could see what was going on, on the ground.

"In an attack, we would climb to about 9,500 feet. That was supposedly above the light and medium flak and below the heavy flak. Then we rolled over on our backs and started a sixty-degree dive to the target, releasing our rockets at about 2,000 feet."

The dives were steep—so steep that sometimes the pilot would black out for a few seconds as he pulled out of them. "It was always nice to wake up at about 10,000 feet, not having been hit," Baggs added, grinning.

As soon as the Germans realized they'd been spotted, Baggs said, "they let go at us with everything they had and tracers zipped past on all sides. But nothing except a lucky shot can stop a Typhoon diving at five hundred miles per hour.

"We could look over our left shoulder as we climbed back up and see if a tank had been hit. Then, if there wasn't too much light flak, we would take additional passes with our four 20mm cannons. We [in the RAF] had eight rockets with 60-pound warheads.

"We could fire two at a time or all of them at once in a salvo. That would be equivalent to a salvo from a light cruiser. The Canadian Typhoon squadrons had bombs instead of rockets: one 500-pounder or 1,000-pounder under each wing."[9]

Flak was the main reason for the very high casualty rate of Typhoon pilots: 151 pilots were killed between D-Day and the end of August. "The flak could be so bad that in shows of just twenty minutes or half an hour, we would lose two or three men out of the original eight," Bill Baggs recalled.[10]

New Zealander Desmond Scott, who at twenty-five was one of the youngest group captains, gave a vivid description of one attack: "As I sped to the head of this mile-long column, hundreds of German troops began spilling out into the road to sprint for the open fields and hedgerows. There was no escape. Typhoons were already attacking in deadly swoops at the other end of the column and within seconds the whole stretch of the road was bursting and blazing under streams of rocket and cannon fire. Ammunition wagons exploded like multi-coloured volcanoes. A large long-barrelled tank [probably a Tiger] standing in a field just off the road was hit by rockets and overturned into a ditch. It was an awesome sight: planes smoke, burning rockets and showers of coloured tracer."[11]

On the receiving end of this carnage, Warner Josupeit, a German machine-gunner with 1st SS Panzer, remembers the terror. "The fighter-bombers circled our tanks several times. Then one broke out of the circle, sought a target and fired. As the first pulled back into the circle of about twenty planes, a second pulled out and fired. So they continued until they had all fired. Then they left the terrible scene.

"A new swarm appeared in their place and fired all their rockets. Black clouds of smoke from burning oil climbed into the sky everywhere we looked. They marked the dead panzers. Finally the Typhoons couldn't find any more panzers so they bore down on us and chased us mercilessly. Their rockets fell with a terrible howl, and burst into big pieces of shrapnel."[12]

Josupeit was describing the Typhoon tactic known as "cabrank," in which a group of orbiting aircraft was directed by a ground controller onto a specific target.[13]

"We'd be circling overhead—just like a bunch of taxicabs circling the Regent Palace Hotel in London," Flight Lieutenant Baggs recalls, "and that's how it got its name. Cabrank was a highly successful technique that we used about 50 percent of the time in Normandy. We would take off, not knowing what our target would be. An officer of the Canadian army would give a target to an air force officer who was with him on the ground. The latter would adapt the coordinates on his map and radio the encircling Typhoons and we would be briefed in the air."[14] The contact would also pass on information about the target and provide a detailed description of landmarks, such as roads, villages, and woods. After carrying out the attack, with their rockets used up, the pilots either returned to base just a few minutes away to refuel or reload aircraft, or looked for another target of opportunity.

If the Typhoon pilots had been successful in knocking out the target, the army would radio them a "strawberry"—a message of appreciation and thanks.

The job of identifying the targets from the ground was not an enviable one. Baggs related his experiences at this job later in the war. His boss at 123rd Wing, Group Captain Desmond Scott, sensed he was becoming a little "twitchy," and needed a rest. "So he sent me out to the Fourth Canadian Armoured Brigade as an air force control officer. His idea of a rest and mine were entirely different. I got the hell scared out of me riding around in a tank much more than I ever did in an aircraft!"[15]

The shattering Typhoon attacks of 7 August brought overwhelming horror, destruction, and defeat to every German soldier in the eye of the attack—from the ordinary panzergrenadier to his army commanders.

The staff report to General Hausser attested to the success of the Typhoon attack: "Continuation of the ground attack during the midday hours was made impossible because of enemy air superiority."

General von Gersdorff, Chief of Staff, Seventh German Army, echoed this. "The attack has bogged down since 1300 hours because of heavy enemy fighter-bomber operations and the failure of our own air force." He added, "OKW never attached enough importance to the air situation that made the movements and the supply for the operations doubtful."[16]

Hausser himself told Kluge at 2150 hours, "Terrific fighter-bomber attacks. Considerable tank losses. The corps have orders to continue their attacks as soon as air activity decreases."

Unofficial RAF communiqués initially claimed that the Typhoons had put 162 tanks out of action with 81 destroyed and 54 seriously damaged. Three Typhoons were lost.[17]

U.S. historian Martin Blumenson downgrades these figures somewhat, and concludes: "Of seventy enemy tanks estimated to make the original penetration, only thirty were judged to be in operation at the close of the day. On the morning of August 8, the estimate was reduced to twenty-five still remaining behind American lines."[18]

However, further investigation also credited the U.S. artillery with many of the "kills."

Meanwhile, General von Funck was increasingly concerned about the faltering efforts of the northern flank of his counter-attacking force. He had been forced to immobilize it at midday. Now he badly needed Schwerin's 116th Panzer Division's seventy-five tanks in action. Funck charged Schwerin with refusal to engage in the battle. "He was ordered to support 2nd Panzer *and he did not. Therefore he is the reason we failed!*"[19]

Schwerin was having none of this buck-passing: "How and with what should I have conducted this strong attack you wanted?" he asked sarcastically. "You've taken two-thirds of my tank strength. Then you insisted I hurriedly throw my troops, who were not ready for offensive combat, into an attack. The enemy was occupying my forward assembly area. Half of my infantry had to be employed in the rear to prevent the collapse of my lines of communication. Moreover, a strong enemy with tanks and very heavy artillery cut short every attempt to attack by my advanced infantry."[20]

Funck stormed furiously to Kluge's command post. "That man must be immediately relieved of his command!" he demanded.

At 1600 hours on 7 August—still Day One of the Mortain counter-attack—Generals Hausser and Funck fired Schwerin from his command and replaced him with Funck's chief of staff, Colonel Walter Reinhard. Thirty minutes later Reinhard obediently ordered the division into action. The troops almost immediately came to a standstill.[21]

Major Heinz Günther Guderian, an officer with Windhund 116th Division at Mortain, had witnessed many successful panzer attacks staged over the years by his father, the famed tank commander.

"To begin an attack with the idea that it is without hope is not a good idea," Guderian said. "We did not have this hope."[22] The Mortain counter-attack had no such chance of success and Schwerin was too professional a commander to send his troops into battle with such a flawed plan.

*

If Kluge had doubts about the unlikelihood of success of *Operation Lüttich* before it was launched, he surely was convinced of its folly twenty-four hours later, when he was informed that Allied troops were closing in on him from three sides. General Horrocks's 30 Corps, just thirty-five miles northeast of his position, had seized Mount Pinçon, the coveted jewel of the *Suisse Normande*. Further east, he just learned that First Canadian Army had launched a massive night armoured attack on 7 August from Caen toward Falaise. *Operation Totalize* kicked off at 2300 hours with more than 600 tanks. A RAF force of 1,000 planes, including heavy bombers, dropped more than 5,000 tons of bombs in front of the ground troops, and 720 artillery pieces shelled the enemy.

Patton's Third Army encircled him from the south. Major General Haislip's XV Corps was just now rolling into the town center of Le Mans, just sixty miles south. The Canadian thrust south of Caen was imperiling General Meyer's 12th SS Hitlerjugend. Each of these outside threats pinned down panzer divisions that Kluge urgently needed at Mortain.

But Hitler insisted that he persevere with the Mortain attack—and one does not refuse the Führer, especially when one is under deep suspicion of having been a conspirator in the assassination attempt.

In truth, as General Eberbach later observed, "this would have been the right time for Field Marshal von Kluge to act against Hitler's orders to save the two armies [Seventh and Fifth]. But after 20 July, he was watched in such a sharp way that it would have been especially difficult for him. The result would have simply been his substitution for a more manageable tool."[23]

The operation was to plod on for four more days, with heavy losses on both sides and few gains. By 9 August, Lüttwitz's 2nd Panzer was forced to give up the ground it had won and was back to the start-line, having lost 30 tanks and 800 men.[24] On 10 August, Kluge begged Hitler to let him transfer some of the force southeast to stem the American push on Alençon. He was ignored and, instead, was commanded to remount the Mortain operation on 11 August, with General Eberbach replacing Funck as commander of Panzer Group.[25]

*

Meanwhile, conditions on Hill 314 were grim for the beleaguered battalion. The Germans realized that this little band of American GIs was blocking the advance of four panzer divisions; they were desperate to dislodge them. German infantry, armoured cars, and tankers viciously threw everything they had at the beleaguered force: flame-throwers, mortars, rocket guns, hand grenades and sniper fire.

On the first day of their isolated stand, 7 August, the Americans were bombed and strafed ten times by both friendly and enemy aircraft (a few having evidently slipped through the net) and heavily shelled. At 1507 hours, two enemy tanks advanced to within 250 yards of their command post. Private Joe Shipley, a switchboard operator, grabbed a bazooka—a gun he had never held, much less fired—and successfully knocked out one tank, scaring off the second. "He didn't even leave his seat!" marvelled one commander.[26]

The shelling of the regimental command post continued so heavily into the next day that they were finally forced to move it to another location.

At 1100 hours on 8 August, Acting CO Captain Reynold Erichson radioed a report to regimental HQ: "Need radio batteries, medical supplies, food and ammunition. Men holding their positions. Forward observers, Lieutenants Bartz and Weiss, doing splendid work. Enemy has been prevented from organizing armour and infantry to affect an attack of overwhelming strength."[27]

At 1828 hours, 9 August, an SS officer, accompanied by an enlisted man carrying a flag of truce, issued an ultimatum to surrender to 2nd Battalion. The officer approached Lieutenant Ralph Kerley's "E" Company headquarters on Hill 314.

"You are entirely cut off and surrounded," the German said, his English stilted but impeccable. "We have captured your commanding officer [Colonel Hardaway] and many other prisoners. The position of the Americans on the hill [is] hopeless. If you do not surrender before 2000 hours, we will blow you to bits."

He soon learned that you don't give Ralph Kerley ultimatums.

"Kerley was kind of a loose cannon," Captain Delmont Byrne said of the sandy-haired Texan. "He was rough, tough, unkempt, unshaven, profane, a heavy drinker and disdainful of red tape and protocol . . . a great combat leader, utterly fearless."

Wounded men lying nearby heard the German demand. They called out to Kerley, "No, no! Don't surrender!"

"I will surrender when every one of our bullets has been fired and every one of our bayonets is sticking in a German belly," Kerley replied, stalking off angrily.

That night, the enemy struck again. They swarmed up the hill with tanks, machine gunning the entire American front. German voices could be heard yelling, "Surrender! Surrender!" After a stiff fight they were driven off.

The exhausted defenders were forced to hold their positions in relays to beat off constant combat patrols. "One tank came within fifty yards of our observation post, fired a few rounds, called for us to surrender or die, and left," Kerley reported.

At one point, warning his men to dig in, Kerley called down artillery on his own position. The men huddled in foxholes or rock crevices. For five minutes hundreds of shells pounded directly on top of the American headquarters, driving the enemy off.

Although they were desperately in need of food, ammunition and medical supplies, their most urgent shortage was for fresh batteries—their lifeline. Without batteries, their FOOs would be unable to radio German positions to the artillery units below the hill, and they would be quickly overrun.

When the battery scarcity became acute, Robert Weiss would give rapid (and increasingly faint) directions to the artillery, then yank out his batteries and lay them in the sun, trying to coax one last iota of power from them.

> 2nd Bn Report, 10 August:
> American C- 47s accompanied by fighters flew over Hill 314 and dropped food. Unfortunately, at least one-half of these rations were dropped in enemy held territory. The hungry men of Hill 314 organized patrols and went out during darkness to retrieve what rations they could, always under sniper fire.

There were nine local French farmers isolated with them on the hill. They contributed a little milk and shared what they could. To fill out the slender diet some of the men foraged in the farmers' fields to wolf down raw carrots, potatoes and radishes. Sergeants

Kozere and Murphy of "C" Company even managed to secure some rabbits they had found in cages.

Any milk was given to the wounded. Deep slit trenches were dug for these men who endured the greatest of privation and pain without complaint. There were no doctors on Hill 314 and scarcely any medical supplies. Although the aide men worked steadily, constantly performing miracles, soldiers died.

The 230th Field Artillery attempted vainly to fire plasma, morphine, and medical supplies in 105mm shells, normally used to fire smoke or propaganda material. The priceless fluids smashed on contact; only bandages were recovered.

Morale was slipping. Exhaustion, hunger, and helplessness were taking its toll. The stench of the dead in the August heat was an ugly reminder of a fate that seemed more and more inevitable to them all.

Then there was a transformation. Anger and resolve replaced despair. The turning point was Ralph Kerley's pointed rebuff of the arrogant SS officer.

In the pre-dawn hours of 12 August, the Germans withdrew from Mortain as silently as they had come six days earlier. The Americans awoke to . . . nothing. No shells. No mortar. No enemy.

The 35th Division Quartermaster Company loaded a truck with food, water, and medical supplies. Every driver volunteered to make the run up Hill 314.

Of the seven hundred men who had reached the hill on 7 August, 357 were able to walk off on 12 August. Three hundred were killed or wounded.

Colonel Hammond Birks, 120th Division's regimental commander, hurried forward to L'Abbaye Blanche roadblock force after the battle. The Abbaye defenders, grown to 150 men and the company mascot—a dog appropriately named Mobile Reserve—had maintained the roadblock for six days under intensive enemy armour and infantry attacks from four roads. The Americans had inflicted heavy casualties and a great deal of damage to the counter-attacking Germans. Incredibly, their losses were minimal. They suffered only three killed and twenty wounded.

Tom Andrew said modestly, "I think we knocked out twenty-four vehicles, sir." But Birks, investigating the road, believed the number was closer to forty.

"The road was littered with knocked-out enemy armour. You won't find better testimony to the accuracy of the roadblock's fire," Colonel Birks said. "It was the best sight I had seen in the war."[28]

> Diary of René Langlois: 16 August.
> We went up to the Petite Chapelle [on Hill 314] by the path below the cemetery, and there, by the last bend before the chapel, we saw the bodies of seven Germans in a heap, almost completely burned. There was no sign of the bodies of any Americans.[29]

Birks was also there to warmly welcome the men of Hill 314 for their heroic stand as they came off the Hill. He clapped Ralph Kerley on the back. "Did you *really* give that quote to that Associated Press correspondent William Smith White, where you said you would surrender only when every one of our bayonets was sticking in a *Bosche* belly?"

Kerley cleared his throat and said, in mock apology, "No sir. I was not quite so dramatic. What I really said was short, to the point, and very unprintable."

"That's telling the son of a bitch," Birks grinned.[30]

10
EVERYBODY BREAKS...
SOMETIME ...

Fear, exhaustion, and misery—these are the three main ingredients that cause combat stress. Yet they are also the common ingredients of every battle. It's the intensity and mix of these three factors that determine whether at a given moment a man will be simply scared, bone tired, and depressed—because that is the state of all men in battle—or over the edge and out of control.

This type of casualty was becoming more and more prevalent among troops who had been in action for weeks on end, constantly under fire, constantly facing death and seeing their buddies blown to bloody bits. As the war intensified, one in every four non-fatal casualties was attributed to this condition.[1]

"Everybody breaks; nobody can say that they were never scared," Padre Jock Anderson of the Highland Light Infantry (HLI) maintains. It was manifested in many different ways: "Some go completely wacky. I remember them bringing in one lad and he couldn't move a muscle. He just lay there; you couldn't get through to him. I asked, 'What'll happen to him?' And they said, 'Oh, when he gets back to where he is safe he is likely to just snap out of it.'"

"And then there was another officer, he just took to his heels and ran and ran and ran until he got all the way down to the beach and then collapsed.

"I broke once, once," Padre Anderson admitted. "The greatest thing is that it lets you see that everybody else has a breaking point too." The padre's collapse came in Normandy after the battle of Buron, when 262 of his HLI infantry were wounded and 62 killed. The sheer ordeal of helping take 262 wounded men off the battlefield created a genuine exhaustion. The stress of losing so many of his boys overcame him. "I couldn't control myself; I started to cry."

The time-honoured remedy—an injection that knocked a man out for twenty-four hours—was all it took to bring the personable chaplain back on his feet. But later, when he saw men in a similar agony, he found he could deal with them with deeper concern.[2]

Australian journalist Alan Wood wrote movingly of young Canadian soldiers who confronted fear—and won. "Theirs is not always the courage of men who know no fear, but sometimes the courage of men who overcome it. A few short weeks ago, most of these Canadians had never seen action. Many of them are young, many of them inexperienced. I think of a dispatch rider, only nineteen; he joined up when he was sixteen.

"The strain and terror of the battle told more and more on the faces of some of these men as they came back. One or two seemed at times almost to have reached the breaking point. Sometimes they would come in sobbing. But they would rest a little, nerve themselves afresh, and then always go back into battle again."[3]

As the Normandy campaign settled into grinding battles of attrition, the incidence of combat exhaustion escalated in direct ratio to the incidence of battle failure. It reached crisis proportions in July, during the stalemate, when the lack of progress and the high casualties induced a feeling of futility in the men.

British historian David French summed up this all-important aspect of combat efficiency when he wrote,

Morale . . . was more fragile in veteran divisions brought back from Italy than it was in those divisions which came to Normandy fresh. Unsurprisingly, it was most fragile in infantry battalions, because infantrymen were exposed to the most discomfort and maximum danger on the battlefield. It was probably strongest in those battalions which, through luck, were able to retain a cadre of officers and NCOs who were known to their men and who took a personal interest in their welfare.

Finally, the typical deserter—exhaustion-case or victim of a self-inflicted wound—was another rank of infantryman who had recently joined an infantry battalion as a reinforcement, or a veteran soldier who was asked to take part in one battle too many.

"Morale," French concluded, was "the willingness of soldiers to fight rather than absent themselves from the battlefield."[4]

A historian describes a sad incident when a fine, once-proud battalion in 3rd British Division whose morale, just briefly, had crumbled. Their leaders, the "old sweats," had fought one too many battles, seen one too many friends killed or maimed, had been themselves wounded once too often. A Spandau opened up and they went to ground. The young reinforcements, new to the grim realities of fighting, simply followed their leaders' example. A similar episode was documented in another battalion when, at the height of battle, the reinforcements saw officers they respected and depended on gravely wounded. They panicked.[5]

The greatest number of NP [neuropsychiatric] casualties occurred when the troops were very tired, very static, dug-in and under heavy counter-attack. The high number of Canadian casualties in the August slog to Falaise also saw an increase in cases of battle fatigue. By contrast, the large numbers of battle exhaustion in American troops reported during the miserable fighting in the *bocage* dropped sharply with Patton's dramatic breakout at the end of July.

"The fear is there." Private Adolf Rogosch learned this fundamental philosophy of killing as a seventeen-year-old German infantry private fighting for his life in Normandy. "Everyone was afraid when they got close. No one can say that they were unafraid. [It's] either me or you. The fastest one was the winner."[6]

Fatigue was "the biggest single threat" to troop morale; sound leadership was its most vital stimulus. As long as there is hope, even just a glimmer, a man will usually accept the risks, if he is well led. Soldiers eyed their commanders warily. Will he get us killed? they wondered.

Denis Whitaker was commanding officer (CO) of the Royal Hamilton Light Infantry (RHLI). "I believed that the men were concerned with two things: survival and success. If a CO demonstrated understanding of the task and consideration of the men who would achieve it, and if he had then developed a sound plan, he would win the confidence of the officers and, through them, of the troops.

"The morale in the RHLI was high; I think success brought a good deal of that about. We had seen others fail where we had succeeded. And our officers were strong; that made quite a difference. Through their own qualities of leadership, they could instill confidence in the other ranks.

"One of my corporals described leadership more simply: 'When you climb out of that slit trench . . . if you were to look around and find that you didn't have an officer, boy, that would have a tremendous effect on you psychologically.'"[7]

Captain Charlie Mackay, RHLI carrier platoon commander, recalls the battalion's successful fight to seize Verrières Ridge: "At that point we didn't know what battle fatigue was all about. We were told to capture that ridge and we did it; we were the only regiment in the Second Division that got to our objective and held it.

"The next few days we were under mortar and shell fire the whole time. I got a call to bring up three medics. When I got these three guys—one major and two captains—they said they were psychiatrists and they wanted to know what caused battle fatigue. They were going to spend two days in the front lines with us. I took these officers one at a time under heavy fire up to battalion headquarters. The next morning the phone rang and I was told these fellows had changed their minds. They didn't think they needed to spend two days here. They want to leave right away. These guys found out about battle fatigue; they found out in the first half-hour what caused it."[8]

Or maybe they realized they were looking in the wrong place? The battalion was pumped up with the justifiable pride of having pulled off a victory when no one else had been able to do it. Battle fatigue? Those men were too elated to be NP candidates.

The Royal Winnipeg Rifles (RWR) of 3rd Canadian Infantry Division had been in action fifty-four days—"hardly a one of them with respite from shelling, bombing, attacks, and the ordinary daily discomforts of living in slit trenches and eating when the exigencies of the service permitted."

RWR Captain Cliff Chadderton confided in his diary what it felt like to be under heavy shelling. "The ground shakes and shakes. There is dust, creaking of tank tracks and noise everywhere. Somehow the fear comes and goes. With me it is bile in the gut. Figure I am lucky because I hold a rank. Hopefully, I could not show any fear. But what about the ordinary guys—particularly those who have just come up as reinforcements. Somehow they stand it.

"Normandy will always be a blur to me. Dust, heat and worst of all the dead guys. I only look at their boots. I do not want to see the RWR shoulder flash or the face. Having been with the battalion since the start, I might know the guy too well. What else? Oh yes, goddamn dysentery. That with lack of sleep and tiredness. How the jeez could we function; but apparently we did."[9]

That "goddamn dysentery" was a violent form of diarrhoea known as "Normandy Stomach." With its gut-wrenching cramps and cold sweats it was becoming a major factor compromising optimal combat effectiveness in the hot August weather.

Hives was another. Lice drove the men nuts. The troops blamed the recurrence of hives and dysentery on the food. The medics disagreed. They attributed these minor symptoms to mosquitoes—attacking the men sleeping in the open in slit trenches—and to the soldiers gorging on those sweets in the Compo rations!

"About half the boys in the section have got hives. They are a damned nuisance; they make you itch like hell. The medic tells us that we are eating too many sweets when we are not used to them," one soldier wrote to his mother.[10]

"I am well bitten by mosquitoes," a signaller in 3rd Medium Regiment, Royal Canadian Artillery (RCA), reported home. "They make attacks on me during the night. I got up last night and my left eye was swollen, both the backs of my hands and my right cheek were swollen and [I had] a nice egg over my right eye."[11]

The lice were German hand-me-downs, picked up when men used slit trenches and dugouts abandoned by the enemy. "Everybody is having to scratch continuously," another rifleman complained.[12]

But it was utter tiredness that most debilitated the soldiers of Normandy. The Royal Regiment recalled the agony of sleep deprivation—virtually a non-stop, weeks-long jet lag in today's vernacular. "Night after night passed without sleep and day after day was spent with no more rest than was afforded by the odd cat-nap. Men fell asleep as they drove carriers along a road, as they plodded in single file with their sections, or as they huddled in slit-trenches under bombardment. Weariness built up until it laid its hand upon the very spirit. Men went for days on end in a sort of dazed mental stupor, in which they could not remember the events of an hour before, and in which they were utterly incapable of speculating upon the future."[13]

"I'm smoking far too many cigarettes to keep awake," a British trooper scrawled in his diary. "Between sixty and eighty a twenty-four hour day; my mouth and throat are like a kipper. God how tired we were! I took my boots and socks off for the first time . . . in twelve days."[14]

Royal Winnipeg Rifles' Captain Cliff Chadderton described the "hard lines of fatigue" that were moulded on the faces of the young soldiers of the Rifles after fifty-six days of bitter fighting. "They had tasted the cruel slaughter of an invasion landing; they had withstood the fury of the German counter-attack; they had felt the consequences of an assault . . . they had become accustomed to the incessant danger from shells, bombs and snipers' bullets that the infantryman takes along with his daily rations. . ."[15]

At some point—to keep his sanity—every man had to develop a philosophy towards killing and being killed. Perhaps hardest to bear was seeing your closest friends brutally shattered. Do you learn to hate the enemy, and relish his death? Or do you pity him?

"Most people seem able to accept casualties," Trooper Ken Tout wrote, "but for my part I can never overlook the tragedy that each one means to some far away, stricken home. The sadness of it all is always with me."[16]

A more resigned Englishman eyed the fact of war: "We no longer think or talk of our comrades who have been killed—killing is our life and our past life is unreal."[17]

It is said that some airmen expressed their antipathy to their enemy by peeing in a bottle and dropping same when they flew over Germany. Chadderton remembers an incident when an RAF bomber flew over an enemy position down the line. "The roar of the mighty warplanes continued and the watchers could see the bombs leave the planes' bellies and arc toward the earth. Seconds later the burst would scatter earth and other objects high into the air.

"Joe Sakolinski, who came from behind a store counter in Brandon to join the Rifles in 1940, was . . . a lance-corporal and had done much good work in the preceding month, so that his companions looked upon him with pride and respect.

Joe watched with relish. "It sure does my heart good to see those bastards getting a 'treatment like that.'" The exhilaration of seeing their enemy disintegrate under the weight of these bombs spread through them like an intoxicant. They gave vent to suppressed feelings, running to and fro to get a better "seat" and gesticulating wildly. "Jeez, my morale has gone up a hundred percent," one corporal said gleefully.[18]

But other men felt no joy in destroying their enemy, as British Trooper Hewison wrote sadly in his diary, "There's ordinary blokes on each side with no desire to kill each other, yet here we are."[19]

Or as Flight Lieutenant Duke Warren mused, "We didn't feel an overpowering hate of the Germans, but rather an intense dislike and revulsion at what Germany was doing. One killed Germans to win the war."[20]

In all the Allied armies, the emphasis was on returning battle-fatigue cases back to the front quickly. The U.S. army pioneered the importance of forward psychiatry. They'd come a long way from the crude face-slapping techniques in Sicily in 1943 by General George Patton, who, still unrepentant in August 1944, made a snide reference in his diary to "war-wearies—a new name for cowardice."[21] His biographer, Carlo D'Este, explains that "Patton was simply unable to understand that soldiers have different breaking points. He thought all soldiers had to live up to a high standard. And in Patton's mind, bravery was the highest virtue that a soldier could have, and cowardice was the deadliest sin."[22]

Cases of exhaustion were kept at their aid stations for up to seventy-two hours. The first twenty-four hours focused on rest, usually under light sedation. In the second twenty-four-hour period, the men got hot food, showers, and clean clothes. On the morning of the third day, they had a personal interview with the psychiatrist.

The U.S. 29th Infantry Division outlines the three directions to which each man must be sent: immediate return to duty; enrolment in the training program (where confidence is built up by short refreshers in such essentials as battle drill and weapon training); or reclassification as unfit for further combat duty.

The newest conscripts had the biggest problems. According to the infantry division, "The biggest fault we find upon arrival here is the disregard of orders. They have not had obedience to orders sufficiently emphasized. Such disregard may easily result, on the battle line, in useless casualties."[23]

As American historian Stephen Ambrose notes, three-quarters of them returned to their foxholes.[24]

German soldiers became similarly disturbed by feelings of futility as the Normandy campaign advanced. The penalty for desertion was the death sentence, yet many German soldiers did lay down their arms. In their landmark study on battle exhaustion, military historians Terry Copp and Bill McAndrew wrote that, in Normandy in late July and August, many Germans surrendered "in a condition suggesting complete physical exhaustion and serious nervous fatigue."[25]

Later, when the frenzy of battle abated, the padres with their driver-batmen would go back to the battlefield to bury the dead. They took shovels and dug burial places; then they conducted private, very meaningful services for each. The dog tags and personal items were brought back, some to send to their families, and the perishables to distribute to their mates.

If the bodies had lain there overlong, there was the added danger to the padres that the corpses had been booby-trapped by the Germans. Padre Jock Anderson, HLI, recalls: "I used to carry in my jeep a long anchor and a long rope. I would hitch it on to the casualty's belt and then my driver Mitch and I would go back to my jeep and pull. If nothing happened, then we knew it wasn't boobytrapped. But any body that was left out for any length of time posed a risk."[26]

Few Germans made attempts to rescue their dead comrades. The corpses lay sprawled grotesquely around their trenches, the agony of death lining their faces and locking their bones in a horrible rigidity.

On an ambulance ship, typing on his old Hermes typewriter that he always carried with him, Winnipeg Rifles' Captain Cliff Chadderton set down these personal recollections of the aftermath of battle:

Khaki-covered shapes, huddled in the grimness of life's end, told of unfortunate Canadians. They lay where they had fallen and were usually covered with a gas cape or ground sheet. Their rifles were stuck into the ground beside the body, with the butt-end protruding skywards. These rifles, the sentinels of the dead, were left thus as a guide for burial parties. Often the soldier's helmet would be suspended in the air on the butt of the rifle.

Dark-stained, discarded clothing, accompanied by outer casings from shell dressings and a pile of equipment, marked the spots where wounded men had been bandaged by stretcher-bearers and hauled away to medical aid posts.

The smell of battle—acrid smoke, burned-out vehicles, death itself—hung about. Stillness was everywhere.

The sun was just rising . . . as a padre made his way to Charlie company. He was greeted by Captain Fred Allen, second-in-command.

"Mornin', Padre."

"Hello, Fred. How are things with you?"

"Oh, fair enough."

"This is an awful business," the padre said, as he swept his arm around to take in the whole battlefield. He was like that. He was sincere and the boys adored him. He would go anywhere and was never afraid. But he hated killing, and whenever he was face-to-face with death, it showed on him. One of his main tasks was conducting burial parties and although this padre was always left shaken for hours after an ordeal of this sort, he never let his feelings interfere while doing his job. His services were simple and beautiful.[27]

There were times when it was not possible to recover the fallen. A Scottish trooper summed up this anguish: "This last forty hours we have been asked to accomplish three tasks not normally asked of human beings. First, to face appalling wounds, burning and possible fearful death at fifty yards' range; second, to destroy other human beings; and third, to leave our own dead unburied."[28]

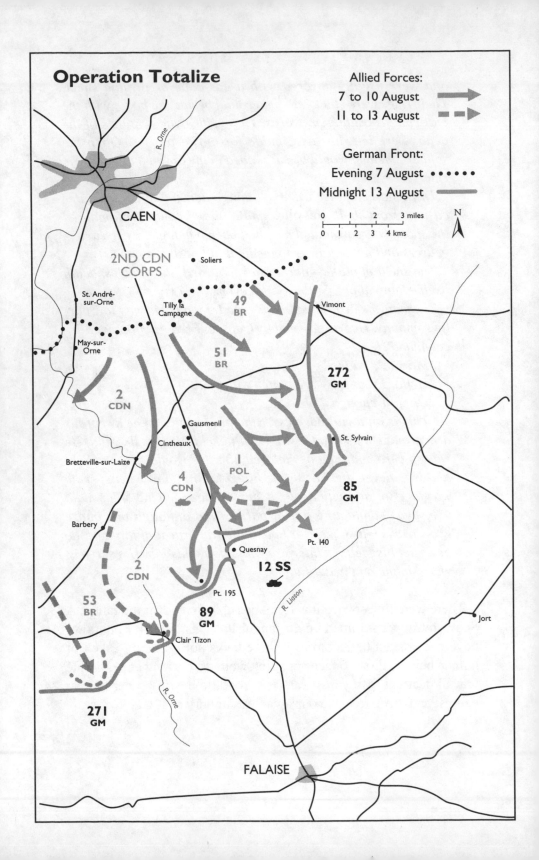

Operation Totalize

Allied Forces:

7 to 10 August →

11 to 13 August ⇢

German Front:

Evening 7 August ••••••

Midnight 13 August ▬▬▬

0   1   2   3 miles
0 1 2 3 4 kms

N

CAEN

R. Orne

2ND CDN CORPS

Soliers

St. André-sur-Orne

Tilly la Campagne

49 BR

Vimont

May-sur-Orne

51 BR

272 GM

2 CDN

Gausmenil

Cintheaux

St. Sylvain

Bretteville-sur-Laize

4 CDN

1 POL

85 GM

Barbery

Quesnay

Pt. 140

2 CDN

12 SS

R. Liason

53 BR

Pt. 195

89 GM

Jort

Clair Tizon

271 GM

R. Orne

FALAISE

I I

OPERATION TOTALIZE

Monday, 7 August 1944

While the beleaguered men of U.S. 2nd Battalion were hanging on grimly to Mortain's Hill 314, and the Wiltshires, with Captain Denny's 13th/18th Hussars, were relishing their conquest of Mount Pinçon, 2nd Canadian Corps was gearing up for the bloodiest fight yet in the Normandy campaign.

Tank crews confined to the ruggedness of the *Suisse Normande*, or the hidden terrors of *bocage* fighting, thought often and wistfully of the kinds of terrain over which they had trained: the wide open, gently rolling plains of the English Downs. Now, gazing south down the dead-straight Caen–to–Falaise road, the tankers realized that these next twenty miles were not going to be the cross-country romp they had imagined. It would prove to be "the worst possible country for Allied armour. . . . There were few bumps or depressions where a tank could take a hull down position and provide covering fire."[1]

The pastoral panorama revealed a series of softly rising ridges, blanketed with fields of corn, grown to August height, and wheat, still unharvested in the stress of the Normandy conflict. But this undulating, open land offered the Germans endless defensive opportunities.

Each of those panoramic ridges would become a battlefield, strongly held by a fierce enemy force guarding its approaches. The Germans could clearly see even the twitch of a corn stalk from as much as a mile away. The numerous Norman farming villages, modest stone cottages clustered around the inevitable church, had become a network of fortresses, heavily fortified with mines, mortar installations, and camouflaged anti-tank guns. The spires offered excellent observation posts for the enemy. Thick hedges of bramble or poplar concealed panzerfaust parties waiting in ambush.

Following their usual tactics, the Germans had transformed the wheatfields into death traps. They rigged haystacks to explode, spraying steel fragments. They erected scores of wooden tanks with dummy guns, hulled down near the crest of a ridge to intimidate and confuse the enemy. They booby-trapped dead bodies.

In early August, Lieutenant-General Guy Simonds, at the age of forty-one Canada's youngest corps commander, was ordered to mount *Operation Totalize*, a major assault opening the way to Falaise. At this point in the campaign, the British were still struggling through the *bocage* to reach Vire and Mount Pinçon. The Americans had just burst through the Cotentin Peninsula and reached the Atlantic port of Avranches; Patton's breakout was still a gleam in his eye. The Germans were engaged in the bitter struggle for Hill 314.

"Trap the Germans on the British front," Montgomery further directed Simonds. Guy Simonds was just the man—perhaps the *only* man—for the job. He was tough, young, smart, ruthless, and intolerant of inefficiency. In a single day early in the Normandy campaign, he fired one brigadier and two lieutenant-colonels, all close friends. It was said he came in two temperatures: hot of temperament and cold of manner.[2] In short, "the count," as he was known, was widely admired and universally considered to be a bit of a bastard.

To mount the operation, Simonds was given command of three infantry and two armoured divisions, plus two armoured brigades. On paper this was a powerful force of more than 100,000 men, but the two armoured divisions, which had just arrived in Normandy, had never been in combat. The infantry divisions Simonds planned to use, 2nd Canadian and 51st Highland, had lost so many men that their rifles companies were at half-strength. At the sharp end Simonds could employ about 5,000 infantry and 300 tanks in the first phase of *Operation Totalize* and then call upon his two full-strength armoured divisions, each with 200 tanks and 1,600 infantry, to carry out phase two.

Simonds was squaring off against the youngest divisional commander in the German army. At thirty-three, Standartenführer (Colonel) Kurt Meyer was every bit as clever, as handsome—with blue eyes as piercing as Simonds'—and every bit as tough. Every bit the bastard.

Both protagonists knew that the final confrontation was coming.

Caen had finally fallen. The next step was obvious: an Allied break-out south to Falaise to link up with the Americans and drive the Germans out of Normandy.

A fresh German division from Fifteenth Army's reserve had replaced 1st Panzer Division on Verrières Ridge. The 89th Infantry had been formed in Norway early in 1944 with veteran cadres from the eastern front. Transferred to France in June, it trained in the Dieppe area before crossing the Seine in late July. The division was "well equipped with personnel and material" and, in common with other German pocket divisions, contained a high proportion of infantry with automatic weapons, mortars, and gun batteries. Out of a total strength of 12,000 men, 7,000 had served in direct combat roles.[3]

Meyer positioned the 12th SS battlegroups behind the 89th as a counter-attack force, ready to pounce on Simonds' divisions when they made their move, ready to block them from their final objective, Falaise.

In addition to 12th SS, Meyer had 100 of the long-range 88mm of 3rd Luftwaffe Flak Corps, and a regiment of carefully camou-flaged Nebelwerfers (Moaning Minnies). His proven strength lay in his Tiger and Panther tanks, which far outgunned the British Shermans.

The Hitlerjugend commander predicted that the Allies would lay on their usual set-piece attack, with a heavy preliminary artillery barrage to get the infantry troops forward, followed by an armoured assault. It will be soon, he told his battlegroup commanders.

Back in Caen, Simonds was trying to outthink his adversary. It won't work, the set-piece, he thought. A preliminary barrage will warn the enemy of the coming attack. Infantry advancing across those open slopes will be massacred, tanks shot up like ducks in a row. But how can we get two divisions of men across open country under the eyes of a watchful enemy?

Surprise and concealment were the only answers. If he could lay on the attack at night, without alerting the Germans by a preliminary artillery barrage, and then overrun the enemy defences in darkness before they could retaliate, he might have a chance. But how?

Moving several thousand fighting men with their tanks and equip-ment through unfamiliar territory at night invited chaos. With no illumination and with compass readings made unreliable because of the tank's metal plating, they would be totally lost. During the next two weeks, working up to twenty hours a day, Simonds' fertile mind conjured up a hat full of tricks, many of them untried.

By bouncing the rays of huge searchlights off low clouds, sufficient light could be produced to guide his men to their objectives. On previous attempts, although successful, the troops had dubbed it (not always with enthusiasm) "Monty's moonlight." The attacking divisions won't be able to identify their boundaries? Bofors guns streaking green phosphorescent tracers along the flanks of the columns—another Simonds innovation—will help to lead the force to its destination.

Compasses won't work inside metal tanks? Use radio beams, signalling a series of dots and dashes on the tank commanders' earphones if they veer too far right or left.

Replacing the pre-attack artillery barrage designed to keep the enemy's heads down, Simonds had an idea that had never, ever been tried. "I'll get the air force to bomb the hell out of the German lines along our flanks just before we go forward," he told his skeptical staff officers. "We'll save the artillery barrage until the actual assault."

There followed an intense period of negotiation to sell the crazy, complex Canadian plan for air support to a testy Royal Air Force. Air Chief Marshall Harris was "horrified." His bombers had never been trained to the task of close troop support, never mind at night. How could they accurately identify bomb lines in the dark without endangering the men on the ground?

Simonds had an answer for that one, too. Artillery would fire coloured concentrations of smoke to indicate the targets. Pathfinder planes could then come in low, dropping markers that would be confirmed by a "bombs away" signal from the "Master Bomber."[4] (So meticulous was his planning that a special planeload of cotton wool was flown from England—enough to make 100,000 earplugs to avoid the dangers of blast deafness.)[5]

Another important element in this surprise attack was to figure out a way to bring the infantry forward along with the armour, and to protect the troops from enemy small-arms fire and shell fragments. Historically, infantry's role had been to move up on foot ahead of or closely behind the tanks to protect the vulnerable armour from hazards such as enemy bazookas and anti-tank guns. Infantry was mowed down every time they crossed the open ground.

Everyone knew the infantry would be more effective if they had armoured personnel carriers to keep them up to the pace of the tanks. Simonds did something about it. The artillery had traded in their self-propelled guns, known to all as "Priests," for the more familiar towed 25-pounder guns. The D-Day beach areas were cluttered with these abandoned Priests. Why not convert them into armoured troop-carrying vehicles?

He called in his engineers. In an apple orchard near Bayeux on 2 August 1944, 250 engineers from fourteen British and Canadian units of mechanical and electrical engineers (REME/RCEME) converged on a field full of Priests and began the "defrocking" process to convert them into armoured troop carriers.

This ad hoc Advanced Workshop Detachment (AWD) was code-named "Kangaroo" and the troop carriers were named for them. (The troops irreverently dubbed their carriers "unfrocked priests" or "holy rollers.") The conversion entailed stripping them of their guns, welding armour plating around the gun aperture, and completely overhauling the engines.

Finding enough armour plate became the major challenge. The "Kangaroo Men" went on a spree. They cannibalized some from "W" crocks (tanks beyond repair). They raided a steel mill near Caen. The navy complained crossly that hunks of steel plating were being cut from stranded landing craft.

Each Kangaroo Man was assigned a task, to be monotonously repeated over and over on successive vehicles. Cfn (Craftsman) A.M. Campbell of 2nd Tank Troops Workshop concentrated solely on track tightening. As he later recalled, he worked steadily for four days from 0400 to 2300 hours, "so busy he didn't even know what the next fellow was doing."[6]

Working these eighteen-hour stints the engineers had managed to reconstruct seventy-two troop-carrying Kangaroos, each capable of transporting a dozen men. At 2000 hours on 5 August, they were declared ready for troops to practise embussing and debussing.

For the first time in the history of warfare, at least some of the 10,000 attacking infantry—in this case, 10 per cent—could follow close behind the tanks and disembark right on to their objectives.

Remaining riflemen would be carried in bulletproof vehicles or by hanging onto the backs of the armour. The rest were assigned a "walking infantry" role as mop-up troops.[7]

"A pity we did not have something like that," Private Bill Hinde, Queen's Regiment (British 7th Armoured Division) noted enviously. "It would have saved a lot of lives."[8]

Finally, it was time to brief the commanders.

The 9th Brigade commander, Brigadier John Rockingham, described the "O" (Orders) Group when Simonds unveiled his startling plan: "We were ordered to advance our tanks and troop-carrying vehicles at night. But navigation was nearly impossible in the dark. Guy said we had to use direction finders to keep the armour on direction. 'You know perfectly well you can't put compasses in tanks,' we told him. 'There's just too much metal around them.'

"But Simonds just said he'd figure a way, and he did."[9]

One 51st Highland Scottish officer, less impressed, noted, "I well recall his 'O' Group before *Totalize* when the several division commanders sat in a circle under the pine trees (all being much older than GGS [Guy Simonds] and some with desert sand in their shoes) to whom he opened, 'Gentlemen, we will do this attack at night with armour.' Their jaws dropped."[10]

The attack, he told them, would be centred on an unusually narrow front. Two infantry divisions and two armoured brigades, packed "closer than Piccadilly Circus at rush hour" into twenty-eight tight columns, would form one enormous battering ram of men and armour to smash a hole through the German line. (It was, some remembered, a tactic that had served Napoleon well, using cavalry.) Furthermore, Simonds went on, for the first time, instead of foot soldiers leading armour, the 350 tanks would head up the assault, followed by the mounted infantry. More jaws dropped.

The main north–south Caen–Falaise road would be the dividing line between the Canadians and the Scots. Fifty-first Highlanders with 33rd Armoured Brigade would advance down the left, or east side; 2nd Canadian Infantry Division and 2nd Canadian Armoured Brigade, with 8th Recce Regiment, would be on the right of the road.

For the second phase of *Totalize*, at 1400 hours the same afternoon, Tuesday, 8 August, there would be another massed armoured push, this time by the newly arrived 4th Canadian Armoured and 1st

Polish Armoured Divisions. These would pass through the leading troops and attack the second belt of defences, pushing through to Falaise. Flying Fortresses from the U.S. Eighth Air Force would lay on a massive bombing raid to clear their way.

There had been some initial misgivings in using the Highlanders. As was true of the Desert Rats—and for much the same reason—the keenly honed fighting spirit of the Highlanders had dulled following their elated victories of Alamein, the Western Desert, and Sicily. Their commander inspired little confidence. Montgomery solved this.

> *Top Secret. Personal and Eyes Only for CIGS from Field-Marshal Montgomery:*
> *Regret to report . . . that 51 Div is at present not. repeat not. battleworthy. It does not fight with determination and has failed in every operation it has been given to do. It cannot fight the Germans successfully. I consider the divisional commander to blame and I am removing him from command. I consider that the best man to put to 51 Div in its present state is Rennie and I have confidence he would bring it up to its former fine state.*[11]

Late in July, his arm still in a sling from wounds incurred in an earlier Normandy battle, Major-General Thomas Rennie was brought in to replace the hastily deposed division commander. An officer of 7th Battalion Black Watch describes the electric effect Tom Rennie had on the troops: "The morning we knew he was coming back—he was arriving at 11 a.m.—you could just *feel* the morale go up. We were back on top again. Rennie understood the Scots; he was an old friend coming back."[12]

From that moment, 51st Division gradually regained its spark: "He was the most accessible and least pretentious of generals, whom every officer and man could boast as a friend," the chronicler of the Black Watch related. "He had an impish sense of humour, and a cheerfulness which was proof against every crisis or disaster. He had a great flair for doing things the right way, and complete confidence in his own judgement, which was shared by all around him. His courage was far beyond the ordinary, but there was nothing flamboyant about him. . . .

There was no Jock in the Division who did not know his duffel-coated figure."[13]

Rennie made it his business to ensure that non-Scots—the English and Irish reinforcements, and the Canadian Canloan officers who came to join the Highland Division—were quickly assimilated as "instant Jocks." These honorary Scotsmen soon picked up the flavour of their adopted fighting mates: the wry humour, the verve, the clannish loyalties, and, above all, the flat-out, hell-for-leather Lochinvarian courage.

Shortly before midnight on Monday, 7 August, 1,020 RAF bombers thundered overhead and the largest armoured/motorized attack in the Battle for Normandy was launched. A startled enemy force looking skyward that night saw a terrifying sight: a *son et lumière* of huge proportions. The pyrotechnics: an enormous green glow on their right, a red one on their left; a sky splintered with brilliant streaks of green tracer fire. The ear-shattering noise: a thunderous roar of more than a thousand heavy bombers, the crash of some 3,462 tons of bombs cratering the ground on the flanks.

At the start-line, the two-mile-long column of one thousand tanks and armoured vehicles of the mounted infantry simultaneously revved their engines with a collective roar that shook the earth. This huge battering ram of steel was packed so tightly together that a squadron leader of the Sherbrooke Fusiliers, Major Sidney Radley-Walters, walked the length of the column, jumping from tank to tank, with his feet never touching the ground.[14] As the tanks crossed the start-line, a massive barrage of neutralizing artillery fire was then unleashed, adding new agonies for the German defenders.

To keep his direction, each tank commander clung desperately to the tracer fire and to the faint pinpoint of light from the tank ahead, eyes smarting from the acrid smell of exhaust fumes and cordite. The impact of the powerful bombs on rain-starved August plains raised a cloud of dust that almost obliterated vision for the drivers. The smoke and exhaust from hundreds of heavy vehicles added to this dense fog. Often their only recourse if trouble developed was to jump down from the tank and lead it on foot.

In the ensuing confusion and chaos, the tanks forged ahead blindly over uncharted rough country. They rammed their way through hedges, lurched into ditches, flushed out enemy snipers lurking in cornfields and behind hedgerows. Incredibly, the armour led the infantry to their designated points of disembarking. The tanks reached their objectives and quickly consolidated to beat off the anticipated counter-attacks.

The Germans were stunned by the devastation caused by the bombs and heavy artillery falling around them. Cornfields had new crops now: dead bodies of animals, and the torn and burned corpses of young men dressed in field grey. Cottages and churches were hulled ruins; blackened haystacks silhouetted the skyline.

The "walking infantry"—Canadian 6th Brigade and Scottish 152nd—followed in the wake of their mounted comrades. They had the so-called mopping-up tasks, clearing out villages that the armour had been ordered to bypass. These proved to be the toughest-fought battles of all, and the most successful for the Allies.

It was historian John Keegan who observed "the dangers inherent of cornering first-class German formations, however worn and whatever the odds stacked against them." This was never more true than during the early morning battles on 8 August.[15]

The German defenders had fortified these garrisons and vowed they would never surrender them. Over the previous two weeks, the Canadians had been thwarted every time they had tried to seize them.

In May-sur-Orne, enemy troops in this small hamlet held out against Les Fusiliers Mont-Royal so desperately and for so long that, finally, Crocodile flame-throwing tanks were brought up. The terrifying jets of flaming fuel finally flushed out the defenders. Snipers in Rocquancourt held the village for six hours against the South Saskatchewans. The Queen's Own Cameron Highlanders of Winnipeg had a stiff fight at Fontenay, which they finally captured—but at what cost: the commanding officer was badly wounded; the brigade major who took his place was killed, and four senior officers wounded. Companies led by lieutenants and a sergeant major eventually wore down the German resistance.

Another of these villages was Tilly-la-Campagne, a picturesque farming hamlet of grey Norman fieldstone originally defended by the fanatic 1st SS (Leibstandarte Adolf Hitler). After two weeks, during which the SS fought off countless attacks, the grey stone had become smashed rubble, stained crimson with German and Canadian blood. By this time, the SS had been shifted to Mortain, turning over their carefully constructed defences to the newly arrived German 89th Infantry.

The job of capturing Tilly was finally given to the seasoned Highland 152nd Brigade, who ordered 2nd Seaforth to lay on the initial attack. No dent was made. Then a company of 5th Seaforth was sent in as reinforcements. The fierce fighting and tragic consequence to the company was described in the Scottish history: "Their commander, Grant Murray, was killed along with ten of his men. Captain Murray was found lying in front of the German defensive line with the dead of No. 17 Platoon round about him. They had obviously had a fierce hand-to-hand struggle with the enemy, for one or two bodies were found actually in the German line with dead *Bosche* beside them."[16]

Finally a squadron of tanks from 154th Brigade attacked Tilly from the rear, and after two attempts they liberated the village and captured the only survivors: one German officer and some thirty infantry men.

By midday on Tuesday, 8 August, the *Totalize* force had penetrated enemy lines by some six or seven miles. They were on their objectives, digging in and looking forward to breakfast. The German reaction was swift. General von Kluge radioed Hitler: "A breakthrough has occurred near Caen the like of which we have never seen."[17] This was a double blow to the German High Command. News was filtering in that morning that the Mortain counter-attack was not going well. They learned, too, that the British had captured Mount Pinçon the previous day.

General Eberbach was concerned enough to rush forward to meet Standartenführer Kurt Meyer at 12th SS Panzer headquarters, just a mile or two from the approaching Allied forces—an almost unheard-of act by an army commander. Meyer, aptly known as *der schnelle Meyer*—"Rapid Meyer"—informed his senior officer of the events in the early hours of the morning. When he had seen the artificially illuminated sky and realized that the long-expected attack had been launched, Meyer jumped into his scout car and drove north along the Caen–Falaise road toward the attacking force. Through his

A German soldier with an MG-42 machine gun.

The North Shore New Brunswick Regiment on patrol.

German magazine features 12th SS Hitlerjugend,
defenders of Normandy.

A menacing Tiger Tank at close range.

TOP: A German tank crew camouflages an 88mm self-propelled gun.
MIDDLE: A dead German gunner slumped behind a Nebelwerfer.
BOTTOM: A German tank crew atop a Tiger.

4th Canadian Armoured Brigade at an "O" Group, August 7, 1944.

Nursing sisters.

Capt. Reynold Erichson

Michael Wittman

Lt. Sydney Jary

Maj. Ned Amy

Lt. Cliff Chadderton

Kersten T. 05

Cpl. Sidney Bates, VC

Maj. Leonard Dull

Capt. Bill Whiteside

Lt. Wladyslaw Klaptocz

Maj. S.V. Radley-Walters

Sgt. Curtis Culin

L E F T : Twin brothers and F/Ls Douglas and Bruce Warren of 165 Squadron, R A F.
R I G H T : F/L Bill Baggs pictured with a Typhoon.

An R C A F Spitfire nestled in a French wheatfield.

A Typhoon of No. 121 Squadron.

Wrecked German vehicles near St. Lambert-sur-Dives.

Canadian troops—respite from battle.

British troops and tank crews in action in Normandy.

Preparation for Operation *Tractable*, August 14, 1944.

NAC/111565

NAC/111586

T O P : "As close as we shall ever get to seeing a man win a Victoria Cross":
Major David Currie (third from left, holding pistol) at St. Lambert.
B O T T O M : German prisoners at St. Lambert.

MOOREHEAD SENDS THE GREATEST NEWS OF THE WAR:

'No doubt now—the German armies have been decisively defeated in the west'

COMPLETE VICTORY—AND GERMAN ARMY IN ROUT

'Further power to resist in France has gone'

AMERICANS REACH THE SEINE

A high staff officer at General Montgomery's headquarters said last night: "The battle of Normandy is certainly won. German power effectively to resist again in France is now gone. The enemy sent a reserve army over the Seine to try to stop the gaps, but owing to lack of mobility they arrived not in bulk but in series. They arrived too late."

He also revealed that American patrols have reached the Seine.

General Eisenhower yesterday visited the advanced Normandy lines.

A broadcast last night from his headquarters reported that he predicted "final catastrophe" for the Germans.

From ALAN MOOREHEAD: General Montgomery's Headquarters, Friday

THE German armies have been decisively defeated in the west. Savage fighting will still go on, but you can now accept it as a fact that the crisis of the battle is passed and we have won. The bulk of von Kluge's Seventh Army between Argentan and the Seine is rather surrendering than dying or attempting to make a full-scale fighting retreat to the east.

Books-to-the-wall call to Germany

'Trying to finish us

Paris itself becomes a military side-issue as a result of this victory, and must fall as a prize. Even if the Germans try to defend it, the main issue—the breaking of the major German Army in France—will not be affected.

With the situation changing from day to day one has hesitated until today to come out with a flat statement that a victory, the biggest Anglo-American victory of the war, has been won. But after the events of last night and this morning it is impossible to delay any longer.

— COMMENTARY —
by Morley Richards

ROUTED ARMY SPLIT

IN the ranks of the routed German Seventh Army Waffen S.S. troops and the regular Wehrmacht men are fighting among themselves. The retreat to the Seine has become a rout. Chaos is everywhere. S.S. General Paul Hausser commanding the army has lost control of his forces.

Groups of troops are wandering about roads that lead only into the Allied blocks. Large pockets of the enemy are cut off and walk only to be rounded up.

The S.S. men are trying to get away and are stealing, at the point of the gun, transport from the Wehrmacht, which is being sacrificed in their frantic efforts to escape the steel jaws of the Allied armies closing round them.

Prisoners have confirmed that the disorganisation in the Seventh Army are deep and widespread. Unless and widespread some sort of coherence very quickly the remnant of his army will be lost in the cul-de-sac while separate fighting force is already ended.

Ninepins

After noon yesterday—up to then cloud had hampered air operations—the Allies swept the straggling German columns fearful traffic jams started up again in daytime, knocked over, like ninepins, and those trying to reach the Seine and unable to find cover in time

NEARLY IN PARIS

Another secret 35 mile advance by Patton : Planes blitz 2,000 vehicles

FAST-MOVING American tank spearheads are only 12 miles from Paris, according to a German report last night. The point was not specified. Fighting was reported outside Rambouillet, 17 miles from Versailles, 25 miles from Paris.

Other German messages spoke of U.S. advances along several more roads to the capital.

Another dramatic move in the great drives to cut to shreds the German remnants was reported by the German Overseas News Agency.

The Germans said that strong Allied forces covering Patton's Third U.S. Army have swung north to Gacé and Laigle, both north of the Argentan-Falaise area.

It appears that these formations have made 35 miles from the Alencon area.

Other German messages report the Canadians sweeping through Thun, south-east of Falaise, have smashed into the Germans within six miles of Lisieux.

Allied planes yesterday destroyed or damaged 2,000 vehicles.

East of Caen, General Dempsey's troops are pushing eastward at a rapid pace.

TRANSPORT GOES UP IN SMOKE

Every pilot joins in air hunt

From NORMAN SMART: Normandy, Friday night

HUNDREDS of thick, black smoke pyres from burning German transport were rising in the sky east of the Falaise Gap tonight when Allied aircraft completed Day of Reckoning Number 2 against the fleeing Germans.

It was a greater day than, yesterday. Plots counted about the roads in thousands instead of hundreds. They were nose to nose, going eastwards as fast as the Germans could force them.

The horses bolted when they could escape from the harness of gun and wagon while hundreds of the drivers fled into the fields.

The Germans tried to camouflage their vehicles with lately bought brushwood, tree branches, even feeble attempts to sling corn over the silhouettes of our aircraft, as they went over the columns at less than 100 feet.

Car in Flames

One wing-commander saw what looked like a battery racing along a side road in the heart

At midnight the German News agency gave the staggering news of the ''advance'' 30 miles south of ''Tours '' is an enemy hands.''

I think it is right in the heart of France. But the report did not say.

After four years...

2 a.m. LATEST

binoculars he was stunned to view what he later described as a menacing landscape of 150 Allied tanks lined up for an attack. Strangely, the force was motionless.

On his way, he encountered soldiers from the German 89th Infantry Division, retreating in disorder after a night of terror from the Allied bombing and artillery. The SS commander paused to light a cigar and strolled out in their path. Ever the showman, he challenged the deserters. So! Am I to fight the British by myself? Are you such cowards that you run away?[18]

As the sun rose on the waiting battlefield, the day was clear, hot, and windless. The smoke and dust still hung shroud-like, the ground mist thickened by enemy smoke shells, mortars, and artillery shellfire.[19]

There was a strange hush of expectancy. With the original attacking *Totalize* force firmly on their objectives, the next wave of 10,000 men—two fresh armoured divisions, 4th Canadian and 1st Polish—were assembling on the start-line to initiate their part in the overall plan. These units had landed in Normandy only a few days earlier, and had not had an opportunity to rehearse the plan, as had the veterans spearheading the assault.

Because of the inexperience of the units, Simonds had gone to some lengths to organize protective bombing with the American air force. This, by the plan, was to herald the second phase of *Totalize*. Simonds had ordered all units to wait while his second daylight-bombing raid was launched. The timing was precise: the launching of the armoured attack would coincide with the conclusion of the bombing raid: 1355 hours.

Just a few miles south, however, Meyer was ordering his units into position to mount a counter-attack. The 12th SS H-hour was coordinated for 1230 hours.

The Allies looked up expectantly as the Pathfinder for the 678 silver American B-17 Flying Fortresses circled enemy lines, preparing to drop a directional marker to guide the American bombers to German positions. Meyer, too, spotted the Pathfinder as it flew overhead several times, dropping visual markers. He quickly grasped the implications and raced to his radio: "Get closer! Get closer!" he yelled to his commanders. He reckoned that if his panzers remained on high ground they would be destroyed.[20] His men obediently sped for cover nearer to the Canadian lines, safe from the bombs that now crashed uselessly onto their former positions.

The bombers came on with what one observer described as an aura of "ghastly relentlessness. The first huge flight passed directly over our farmyard and others followed. . . . And then the bombs came. They began up ahead as the crackle of popcorn and almost instantly swelled into a monstrous fury of noise that seemed surely to destroy all the world ahead of us."[21]

The Allied soldiers were horrified to see two groups from the U.S. air force, each consisting of twelve planes, become directionally confused by the ground fog that lingered in the smoke-filled windless air and mistakenly begin dropping the bombs on their own, densely packed units. Worst hit were the Poles and infantry from the 3rd Canadian Division, who suffered 315 casualties in all, 65 killed. The 3rd Division commander, General Rod Keller, was badly wounded. The North Shore Regiment lost 100 officers and men.

"It was a grim thing to witness just before going into battle," the Algonquin Regiment history relates, "To see your own people bombed by your own people. The thing that finally stopped this horrible mistake was a little Moth artillery observation plane that flew up between the bombers and the bombed."[22]

A normally hard-nosed and tough Scottish regimental sergeant major, seeing the blast kill his lads behind the lines, summed up the grief and horror in a simple sentence: "No trace of 'em. Not even a hand to shake goodbye to."[23]

In the first moments of the first battle for these wholly inexperienced Canadian and Polish divisions, they were smashed by their own aircraft. Now they were to be confronted by Meyer's quickly assembled panzer counter-attack, which stormed into their midst even while the air force bombs were thundering around them.

Regrouped and reenergized, the German 89th Division was reinforced with SS-Sturmbannführer (Major) Hans Waldmüller's armoured Kampfgruppe (battle group) with thirty-nine Mark IV tanks in addition to Hauptsturmführer (Captain) Michel Wittmann's troop of Tigers, and Kampfgruppe Krause.

At 1335 hours, the Polish 24th Lancers, with fifty-two Sherman tanks, advanced confidently onto the battlefield to launch the second phase of *Totalize*. They could not know that the Luftwaffe had

moved a strong battalion of 88mm guns into range, or that a venge-
ful panzer troop was waiting, hunkered down out of sight in a gully.
Guns capable of shattering a Sherman turret at 2,000 yards were
now within 200 yards. The German gunners, flabbergasted at their
good fortune, fired shot after shot at the hapless Poles. The Lancers
bravely fired back at the enemy they could not see.

In five minutes, forty tanks were in flames. "The sight of men on
fire, scrambling out of the blazing vehicles was viewed in horror by
their British allies, who described it as "like watching a field full of
haystacks set on fire by an arsonist."[24]

The panzers then turned their guns on a troop of Northhamptonshire Yeomanry. Their diary told the sad story:

> Our 2 Troop, after inflicting losses on the enemy, disappeared
> into oblivion from the wireless network like a Roman legion
> marching into the forests of an earlier-day Germany or like an
> aircraft disappearing over the Antarctic. Except that [Number
> 2] was only about three minutes' walk from where we sat on the
> open hillside. . . . Somewhere in those woods beyond the gully,
> 2 Troop perished.
>
> We counted their survivors as they trudged back from the
> gully, but there were not enough survivors. Count them how
> many times we would, the mathematics of our sadness and
> desperation still failed to tally with our hopes.[25]

Meyer sent out his powerful kampfgruppe of Tigers, stressing the
urgency of the situation. The legendary panzer ace, thirty-year-old
Michel Wittmann, shook hands with his commander. "Our good
Michel laughed his boyish laughter and climbed into his Tiger,"
Meyer recounted. "Until that moment, 138 tanks had become his
victims. He adjusted his throat microphone and ordered, 'Panzer
Marsch!' "[26]

As was his style, Wittmann led his troop of four Tigers in a wild
charge across open country. It had worked for him at Villers Bocage
in June, where, in five minutes, he single-handedly destroyed
twenty-five tanks and twenty-eight other tracked vehicles and self-
propelled guns (SPs) of 3rd County of London Yeomanry (British
22nd Armoured Brigade).

This time, it would backfire. This time he was in the gunsights of "Rad" and Tom—Major Sidney Radley-Walters, commanding a Canadian squadron of the Sherbrooke Fusiliers, and Captain Tom Boardman, commanding "A" Squadron, 1st Northamptonshire Yeomanry.

Radley-Walters and his squadron had hulled down in a protected wooded area, waiting for the second phase of *Totalize* to start. He spotted Wittmann's troop of four Tigers and their supporting force of Mark IVs and self-propelled guns storming up the east side of the Caen–Falaise highway. Rad was not aware that the guns of "A" Squadron, 1st Northhamptonshire Yeomanry, on the opposite side of the road, were also beading in on Wittmann and his squadron. It was, in fact, an ambush the like of which tankers only dream—a Tiger kill.

The Tiger was the most feared weapon in Normandy. Neither Sidney Radley-Walters nor Tom Boardman had any idea that their quarry was Michel Wittmann—they were not even aware of the identity of the "Black Knight."

Radley-Walters describes the event: "I had moved into the little village of Gaumesnil. We got behind some bush that had a rock wall around it and we cut the rock down so we could get our tank guns over the front to be well protected. I only had two 17-pounder Fireflies; the rest were all 75mms—twelve altogether.

"When we saw the German attack coming in I just kept yelling, 'Hold off! Hold off!' until they got reasonably close. We opened fire at about 500 yards. The lead tank, the one closest to the road, was knocked out. Behind it were a couple of SPs. I personally got one of the SPs right on the Caen–Falaise road."[27]

At about the same time, Tom Boardman fired as well, but from 1,700 yards. A shot struck the turret of the lead tank. The Tiger started to burn. More shots hit the next tank in line, and the next one after that. Suddenly there was an explosion. Wittmann's tank blew up in a sheet of flames. The Black Knight—the ace who knocked out 119 enemy tanks on the Russian front and several score more British ones at Villers Bocage, this German super-hero with the Knight's Cross with Oak Leaves—was dead.

There can be no conclusive proof as to which squadron, Canadian or British—or which commander, Rad or Tom—actually brewed

Wittmann's tank, but the results were spectacular, and to troopers who had taken a lot of beating from Tigers, no small victory.[28]

The first stage of *Operation Totalize* had been by all counts a brilliant success, meeting all its objectives: the Allies had loosened the enemy's hold on the long-elusive Caen–Falaise highway.

One Highland division officer, remembering the troops' low morale earlier in the month, spoke for all the men who fought there, who had endured the fears of fighting blindly through the night, the heat, the thirst, the pain, the terror of being constantly shelled, the sadness of losing their friends: "*Totalize* put us back on our feet again! The battalion felt it was getting back to its old form."[29]

12

HILL 195

General Simonds was gambling for high stakes in *Operation Totalize*. So far, his gamble was paying off. His night attack had taken the enemy by surprise and had propelled 60,000 combat troops eight miles deep into enemy territory in the early hours of 8 August. But the ill-fated bombing raid later on the same afternoon that was to initiate the next phase of the attack backfired. It failed to subdue the Germans and, in fact, caused heavy casualties and confusion among the unfortunate Allied soldiers caught by "friendly bombs."

The 1st Polish and 4th Canadian Armoured Divisions—fresh to Normandy and totally unrehearsed in the battle plan—were plunged into exactly the situation Simonds had tried so hard to prevent. They clashed head-on in broad daylight, with no support, against a well-entrenched and heavily armed enemy. That they managed to advance at all was a great achievement. For one infantry battalion, the Canadian Argylls, it was a superb effort, ranking in tactical brilliance and raw courage with the best in any war. For another armoured unit, the British Columbia Regiment (BCR), it was a gallant effort, but one of the most disastrous of the war.

Hill 195, a gentle knoll midway between Caen and Falaise, was a green and pleasant picnic spot in peacetime. It was now a formidable obstacle in war. Guns dug into its rise could command movement from every quarter. It was the key to the capture of Falaise.

During the rest of the afternoon of 8 August, the units in *Totalize*'s second phase had run into a seemingly impregnable wall of fire from the Luftwaffe's one hundred 88mm guns. Meyer's counter-attack force, coupled with the disastrous casualties from friendly bombing, had shattered many of the units. Late in the evening, an impatient Simonds fired out an order, very succinctly, to the British Columbia Regiment: "Take Hill 195! Now!"

Lieutenant-Colonel Don Worthington, the commanding officer, ordered the assault. It would be his first battle, personally, and the first for his armoured regiment. He was determined to succeed.

The BCR's fifty-five tanks moved off into the darkness at 0200 hours on 9 August, with their supporting infantry, the Algonquin Regiment. They were driving blindly into countryside unrelieved by any landmarks, on a complex route, with enemy on all sides of them. Encountering sporadic pockets of resistance, Colonel Worthington dropped off one squadron of tanks and one company of infantry to deal with any further enemy attacks.

At 0650 hours they climbed the rise to what they believed was their objective and frantically dug into the gravelly hilltop before the inevitable counter-attack. They radioed brigade headquarters of their successful arrival on the position. Brigade was puzzled; the fix given of the BCR position did not correlate with any map reference.

In one of war's strange, grotesque convolutions, Worthington had taken a wrong turn in the night and ended up four miles east of Hill 195. He was deep in enemy territory and totally surrounded by an agitated German force.

Worthington was now waiting for reinforcements to consolidate his hold—reinforcements that would never come because he was, in effect, lost.

Kurt Meyer was puzzled, too. How had the Allied tanks penetrated so far into the German lines? He sent one of his lieutenants in a scout car to reconnoitre; the officer did not return. Clearly, he had been captured.

Meyer became concerned; the situation was dangerous. This penetration by the Allies gave their gunners a clear view of the Laison Valley—Meyer's last possible defensive position north of Falaise. Furthermore, a fresh German infantry division, Lieutenant-General Fiebig's 85th, was moving in momentarily and had been assigned Worthington's Hill 140 as its headquarters.

Meanwhile, Worthington innocently hung on to what he still believed was his proper objective. He saw Sherman tanks approaching—relief at last. It was a Polish squadron, but the enemy quickly drove it off. He saw Typhoons attacking and signalled them with yellow smoke to indicate an Allied presence.

They obediently dived on the attacking enemy, but later sorties blasted defenders and attackers alike. The Typhoon pilots had no means of communicating with ground troops. It never occurred to them that the tanks were part of Worthington's force.

The BCR dilemma was partially a result of the obstinacy of the Royal Air Force, which refused to establish a system where ground troops could communicate directly with aircraft. The U.S. 9th Tactical commander, Major-General Pete Quesada, had introduced the technique to the American armoured brigades the previous month with great success, but the British weren't to be budged.

Canadian historian Terry Copp recently noted that, "if such a method had been available to 4th Canadian Armoured Division on 9 August, the Typhoons and Spitfires, which repeatedly bombed, rocketed and strafed friend and foe alike [around Worthington's position], would have received targeting information from Worthington and would have informed . . . headquarters of their exact location."[1]

At daybreak, Meyer's panzers, recovering from the surprise of this major breakthrough, now poured every kind of retaliation on the helpless Canadian tanks and infantry. Tigers and Panthers attacked from every direction, inflicting huge casualties. But the Canadians refused to give in.

One Algonquin officer recorded the grim scene: "The crash of exploding shells, the quick, lethal scream of the 88s going over, the cries and groans of the wounded, and the indescribable odour of burning flesh now began to have an effect on the defenders. Firing became wilder; men would rise out of their slits, stand up and curse the foe that was invisible, yet so close, and so inexorable. It was difficult to hold the wounded down, many of whom were now delirious with pain and thirst. The morphine supply had long since been used up, water was exhausted, and there was little that could be done with the stricken except to hold them down out of the direct fire line."[2]

With dwindling forces and a diminishing supply of ammunition, Worthington ordered his last eight tanks to make a run for it, taking to safety as many of the wounded as they could. He covered the initial dash himself with machine gun fire. They got out safely to Polish lines, but still the position of the isolated Canadians was not relayed to brigade.

Although suffering mortar wounds himself, Worthington now

reorganized the defences so well that they were, at least for a brief time, secure. A British officer who was in the position wrote later: "At 1830 hours a strong enemy counter-attack came in. The infantry and tank crews met it with small arms and grenades. Serious losses were inflicted on the enemy who then withdrew. At this stage of the battle I saw one soldier, shot through the thigh and with a broken leg, still throwing grenades. Every man who was still conscious was firing some type of weapon."[3]

"At about this time," the official Canadian history relates, "Lieutenant-Colonel Worthington, who had directed the fight with cool courage throughout the day, was killed by a mortar bomb. At dusk, as a final German attack was coming in, the surviving Canadians who could, slipped out of the position. Most of them succeeded in making their way into the Polish lines."[4]

The British Columbia Regiment was savaged. Forty men were killed, thirty-four were taken prisoner, and another thirty-eight were wounded. The regiment lost forty-seven tanks—almost its entire tank strength—in its first day of fighting. The Algonquin Regiment's casualties over two days came to 128. Forty-four Algonquin officers and men were killed or died of wounds; forty-five were taken prisoner. The rest were wounded but evacuated.

The prisoners managed to carry one badly wounded soldier with them, who was finally taken to a first-aid post. The rest of the wounded were left behind by the Germans and brought in sometime later by the Allies.

As darkness fell the whole area was lit up by the dozens of tanks on fire. In a letter to a fellow officer, Major Keith Stirling of the Algonquin Regiment described the ordeal of being captured by the Germans: "A Jerry approached holding his rifle in the air. All of us were gathered up and taken out on the road and searched . . . but not very well. We were marched down the road and then during the march I remembered the notes in my book about all the supporting arms, etc. So, as I walked, I tore page after page out and tore it to bits. I took the book out and turned it over and did the same with the other side. I did this not being able to see which side had the writing on it. I had about five maps but as they were bulky I decided to wait to get rid of them."

Stirling described being marched to a little village (about four kilometres) and taken to a headquarters in a barn. "I managed to hide the maps under a pile of hay. We were searched and all the stuff put on a table and an Intelligence Officer went over it."

A German confiscated his watch, wallet, and other contents of his pocket. "I was so tired I don't remember getting my stuff back from him, but the next day I had the pen and pencil set, my wallet (without any money) and a few pictures.

"By this time our group consisted of about twenty-five or thirty men, mostly all Algonquins but a few strangers. The Jerries gave us all a card, which if we filled [it] out would inform our relatives where we were. On this card was a Red Cross. The information they wanted on the card was correct (except for the name of the company). I advised [our group] not to fill them out, but many did.

"We marched all the next day to a place that used to be a racing stable. There we had our first food, a bowl of soup, since we were captured. There were a lot of prisoners in the place, including Americans and British. We stayed in this place for a few days, and then started our march across France to Germany, to POW life."[5]

Hill 195, that still-elusive knoll so essential as the gateway to Falaise, remained in enemy hands. Again brigade orders come through: "Take it!"

This time it was the Canadian Argyll and Sutherland Highlanders who were given the job. Commandeer any tanks or guns you need, the brigadier told commanding officer, Lieutenant-Colonel Dave Stewart. Just take it.

Argyll Captain Bill Whiteside related the outcome: "Our boss, Dave Stewart—while he didn't refuse to follow orders, he changed them if he had a different idea."[6]

"Different" was what Dave Stewart was all about. "He didn't like brigade telling him what to do," Captain Bob Patterson of the Argylls agreed. "He was quite a guy; a good soldier. But he didn't like authority.

"Dave never wore a steel helmet. He just would wear his little Balmoral tam, at a cocky angle. He thought about the men, not the job, and the men loved him."[7]

On the night of 9/10 August, Stewart put his plan into action: no tanks, no artillery, no tracer, no bombing. Just his men. Silently.

Patterson relates: "We had an excellent scout platoon leader, [Lieutenant Lloyd Johnston, who was subsequently killed] and he had an excellent scout platoon. He posted his platoon at the various junctures of the path to guide us up to the top.

"Dave went himself and surveyed a sort of a back-door route into Hill 195," Whiteside added. "The scouts were placed at points to keep people in line, let them get through fences and that sort of thing, and company after company moved up the hill into position."

Bob Patterson: "The battalion followed the scouts perfectly up to the top in total silence. Then we surprised the Germans, got up without any casualties. The enemy counter-attacked later on but they didn't make it; so we had a dominant position at the top of Hill 195 and it was successful. It was one of the best things the Argylls ever did."

Bill Whiteside: "My part was the anti-tank guns and I didn't have very much to do because at no time did tanks attack us. We knew where they were, because our forward company could see them. They put in an infantry attack, but we were able to mow that down. About six abortive efforts were made.

"Then at about six o'clock in the morning, a funny thing happened. We'd been taking this sporadic mortar fire, not heavy but it just kept coming. Somebody said to me, 'There are Germans in those trees about a quarter of a mile or little bit further from here. From the trees they can see the whole of our area.'

"So we spun our anti-tank guns around and we knocked those buggers out of the trees. You could see them falling out!"[8]

The Argylls, led by one maverick CO, had outwitted the determined force of Meyer's 12th SS and Fiebig's 85th Infantry in grasping and holding this important enemy defensive position. They had penetrated two additional miles behind enemy lines.

They achieved this with the cool wit, the ingenuity, and the verve that was becoming a trademark of these citizen soldiers of Canada.

13
PATTON:
FARTHER AND FASTER

Like a cork out of a bottle—one that had contained a wildly impatient Lieutenant-General George Patton long enough—Third U.S. Army burst from the Avranches corridor.

Patton flung all three corps of his newly activated Third Army, some 150,000 men, in three directions across France—west, south, and east. Incredibly, with over a hundred miles separating each flank, the circus master had all three rings going hell-bent towards their objectives. He was everywhere. In his low-flying L-5 Liaison plane, he criss-crossed his battlefields, devising new routes and tactics to get farther, faster. Then, in his jeep, he screeched up to the lead troops, even leaping onto the vehicle's hood to urge the men on. He would be seen marching in the ranks, standing at a crossroads or on a bridge, waving the units through.

Patton's energy and enthusiasm were contagious. He harnessed the two skills that are inherently American: mechanization and improvisation. The media loved him. At last they had something to write about. And the tank crews loved him. Finally he had those much-maligned American Sherman tanks doing what they did best—fighting a mobile action.

His aide, who scarcely ever left his side at this time, described him as "pushing, pulling, exhorting, cajoling, raising merry hell, and having the time of his life." He was completely unconcerned for his own personal safety. On at least one occasion he drove right through a German division. "He had an uncanny gift for sweeping men into doing things which they did not believe they were capable of doing, which they really did not want to do."[1]

The Americans had broken out against only light opposition. Their infantry were being treated as heroes, riding jubilantly atop

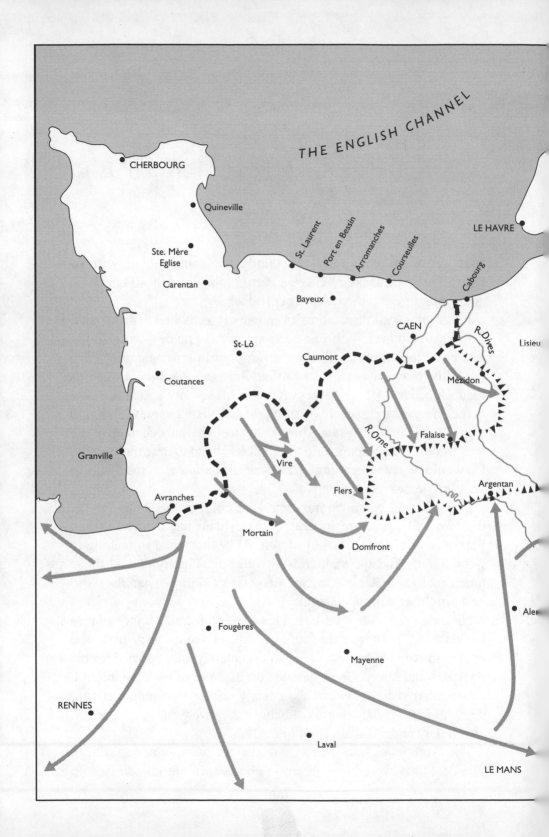

THE ENGLISH CHANNEL

CHERBOURG

Quineville

St. Laurent
Port en Bessin
Arromanches
Courseulles
Cabourg

LE HAVRE

Ste. Mère
Eglise

Carentan

Bayeux

CAEN

R. Dives

Lisieu

St-Lô

Caumont

Coutances

Mézidon

R. Orne

Falaise

Granville

Vire

Argentan

Avranches

Flers

Mortain

Domfront

Ale

Fougères

Mayenne

RENNES

Laval

LE MANS

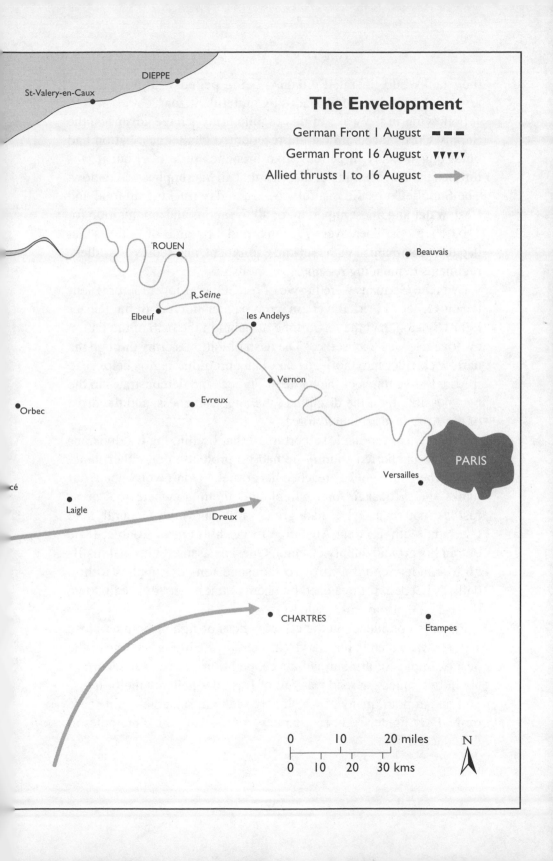

The Envelopment

German Front 1 August ▬ ▬ ▬
German Front 16 August ▼▼▼▼▼
Allied thrusts 1 to 16 August ➤

St-Valery-en-Caux

DIEPPE

ROUEN

Beauvais

R. Seine

Elbeuf

les Andelys

Vernon

Orbec

Evreux

PARIS

Versailles

cé

Laigle

Dreux

CHARTRES

Etampes

0   10   20 miles
0   10   20   30 kms

N

their tanks into liberated villages, being pelted with flowers and rewarded with shots of Calvados by grateful citizens.

Following in the wake of this mobile army's huge advances, the Supply Corps faced almost unprecedented challenges. Patton had burst out in many directions, like branches on a tree, but it was through the narrow trunk of that tree that all his supplies had to flow. The Supply Corps did manful work each day trucking up food and fresh water and, most important of all, weapons and ammunition for 150,000 troops. There were 700 tanks and thousands of vehicles that had to be maintained with fuel and equipment, and scores of artillery regiments demanding re-supply of shells.

Even the Germans were in awe of him. Obergruppenführer (Lieutenant-General) Fritz Bayerlein, commander-in-chief of the Panzer Lehr Division, had the misfortune of being in the path of the Patton cyclone. He was to observe: "The dash of Patton's army through the narrow corridor into the deep rear of an unfamiliar region belongs to the boldest ventures of the battle in France, and demonstrates in the best possible light the discipline, the aggressiveness, and the drive of the American armoured force."[2]

Patton wasn't in the least perturbed that by flinging his divisions deep into uncharted country he had no protection on either flank. Everywhere he went he preached his gospel: "Don't worry about our flanks; our tactical air force will clobber them; go where you can as fast as you can."[3] He had great faith in Major-General Pete Quesada's 9th Tactical Air Force to get him out of trouble. If he outran his ground-supply channel, Quesada assured him that his B-26 Marauders could airlift two thousand tons of supplies to him daily as needed. If threatened by enemy attack, he would call down the P-47s, those much-dreaded Jabos.

Patton's confidence in the effectiveness of fighter-bomber close support was noted in his diary: "Just east of Le Mans was one of the best examples of armour and air cooperation I have ever seen. For about two miles the road was full of [disabled] enemy motor transport and armour, many of which bore the unmistakable calling card of the P-47 fighter bomber—namely, a group of 50-calibre holes in the concrete."[4]

*

On 8 August 1944, two events influenced a dramatic switch in Allied planning. Up until that moment, the Allies had assumed that Hitler's next move would be to withdraw his forces to a new defensive line along the Seine, towards Paris. No one expected him to attack further west, as he had at Mortain, thus putting his divisions even more firmly in the Allied net. Certainly no one expected him to persist on keeping his troops there when the Mortain counter-attack failed.

In fact, Montgomery, for one, was delighted. He was praying that Hitler would hang on at Mortain.

> 7th August 44.
> Personal for CIGS [Chief of the Imperial General Staff] from General Montgomery (Cipher one time Pad):
> If only the Germans will go on attacking at Mortain for a few more days it seems that they might not, repeat not, be able to get away.[5]

Ultra gave reassurance that the German supreme command still planned to persist in the *Operation Lüttich* plan and in fact drag even more forces into the pocket instead of evacuating them. A huge window of fresh opportunity opened up to the Allies: the possibility of encircling the German armies. The Canadians and British in the north were on the road to Falaise; the Americans were completing the encirclement from the south.

On the evening of 8 August, General Dwight Eisenhower had dinner with General Omar Bradley, commander of First U.S. Army. The supreme commander had moved the previous day from England to set up his advanced headquarters in France. He was now on direct telephone communication and an easy drive to Montgomery's and Bradley's command posts. Also, he finally had close, continual, first-hand observation of the battlefields. This was an essential first step for Ike: he had just announced that he would take overall command of all land forces from Montgomery when he fully established a headquarters in France.

On the heels of this move, Eisenhower promoted Bradley to command a newly created 12th U.S. Army Group, comprising Patton's Third and Hodges's First Armies. Monty was left with the

British and Canadians of 21 Army Group. While Ike was vague as
to who was actually in charge for the next few interim weeks, until
he was fully established, the assumption taken by many historians is
that, when he was on the battlefield, the supreme commander bore
responsibility for major strategic decisions.[6]

In the 12th U.S. Army map room, Eisenhower and Bradley were
impressed at the incredible numbers of German troops from the most
élite panzer divisions, which were well behind Allied lines at
Mortain. They've stuck their heads in a trap, they both agreed. Let's
slam the trap shut on them.

A quick call to Monty's HQ brought the three men into total
accord. Why not continue advancing Monty's British and Canadians
from 21 Army Group south to Falaise? They were making good
headway in that direction. At the same time, send Patton's and
Hodges's armies north to take Argentan. The two army groups can
seal the trap on a line between Argentan and Falaise.

Minutes later, a delighted Patton received a telephone call from
his boss. We've shortened the goal line, Bradley told him. Forget the
Seine; you're going to link up with Monty's forces and cut off the
Germans on a line between Argentan to Falaise. Bradley then gave
him the go-ahead to concentrate the bulk of his armoured power
eastward towards Argentan.

Patton wasted no time in issuing his orders. Major-General Wade
Haislip's XV Corps was selected to make the end run to Argentan,
by way of Le Mans, Sées, and Alençon. Haislip, a stocky, balding
Virginian, would carry the ball with two armoured divisions (5th
and 2nd French) leading, and two infantry divisions following in a
mopping-up role.

While so far these divisions had achieved their objectives on the
breakout, they had not met any real opposition. So Haislip was a
curious choice for such an important mission. An infantry commander of World War I vintage with little armoured experience, he
hadn't impressed Patton, who grumbled that Haislip had been
"sitting around the War Department in swivel chairs so long, he's
muscle-bound in the ass."[7]

The corps commander's spearhead divisions were also untried in
the Normandy battlefields. Bradley himself had said he wished the
5th Armoured Division, leading on the right, was more "battle-

wise." The 2nd French Armoured Division (also known as 2ème Division Blindée), in taking the lead on the left, was an even riskier gamble. This was the vulnerable side of the spearhead, wide open and exposed to enemy forces within striking distance. The 2nd French Armoured had more experience, having fought in Africa, but its commander had a reputation for being temperamental. In Bradley's eyes Major-General Jacques Leclerc had three strikes against him: he was "notoriously undisciplined and did not speak English; and his sole ambition seemed to be to liberate Paris."[8]

Leclerc was a pseudonym for aristocrat Vicomte Jacques-Philippe de Hautecloque, changed of necessity to protect his wife and six children from Gestapo reprisals. His passion to return to—and liberate—Paris after four years of exile, to the exclusion of all other demands, was to have a strong influence in the coming weeks.

XV Corps swept across the lightly defended interior of France. The French populace went wild with joy when Sherman tanks with the tricolour markings of the Free French pounded through their villages.

"General Leclerc always adapted the corps plan to suit his own type of fighting of 'liberating and celebrating.' He set a pattern of action for his division," remembers Tony Triumpho, a lieutenant in an American artillery battery with the Free French: "He would have a meeting of his officers to set out his own battle plan. Invariably he would say, 'Our objective is there but we will go on to here because I will contact my friend the mayor, or a friend in the underground, who will order a feast to be prepared for us.'

"After taking an objective, there would be a splendid meal with wine and champagne."[9]

A captain with 3rd Armoured Division described the bacchanal sight of 2ème Division Blindée at war: "I saw French soldiers spread over the fields, and spilling in and out of houses, and bivouacked *with campfires going*, and singing and feasting and wine flowing. The whole scene . . ."[10]

Field Marshal von Kluge had always found pleasure and a certain serenity contemplating the view of the Seine River from his headquarters at Château La Roche Guyon. The château was built into chalk cliffs rising steeply above river, winding its way from Paris to the sea.[11]

On 9 August 1944, there was no tranquillity on his horizon. Pressure from the Allies was growing steadily more intense as they closed in on his two German armies.

From the west and north there was a triple pressure. The American First Army had pushed the Germans back out of Vire after a week of violent fighting and was advancing south to Mortain; Second British Army on their left had just won the battle for the high ground at Mount Pinçon. Moreover, the Canadian breakout the previous day had brought them just eight miles north of Falaise. The German panzer divisions at Mortain had been put on the defensive, told to hold on, and this they were barely doing.

But it was over his left shoulder, southward, that Kluge was anxiously looking.

Patton's XV Corps, sweeping southeast at lightning speed, had advanced an incredible one hundred miles in less than a week. Kluge had just been informed that U.S. Third Army had captured Le Mans that morning. The Americans were now fifty miles closer to Paris and the Seine than were the nearest German panzers—and Kluge's divisions at Mortain were a dangerous eighty miles into Allied territory, surrounded on three sides.

Now he had the "unpleasant and unexpected surprise" of learning that Patton was veering north towards Alençon. Clearly his aim was to cut off the German supply base centred there. His next step would be to encircle and annihilate the German Fifth and Seventh Armies.[12]

"We have no forces on hand to repel this envelopment," Major-General Fritz Bayerlein told him grimly.[13]

The commander-in-chief of Seventh Army, Major-General Gersdorff, told Kluge flat out that "judging the enemy's advance on Alençon, it was quite clear that this was to be the 'knock-out-blow' and the end of the army as well as the whole Western Front.

"The decision is not up to me; it is in the hands of Hitler—the supreme commander," he was told.[14]

Field Marshal von Kluge was a traditionalist, a Prussian career officer with an exemplary record through two world wars. He commanded a battalion on the western front in 1914–18. He was chosen to replace von Rundstedt as C-in-C West because he was more "energetic and aggressive."

Bayerlein noted that "Von Kluge played a more active and personal role and spent more time at the front checking on troop conditions. Personally, I thought he was a good leader of troops. But he was no armoured general."[15]

Kluge in fact frequently spent many hours on the road traversing the routes from his headquarters to the forward lines of two armies. He had viewed the Mortain attack, *Operation Lüttich*, merely as a means of getting the enemy off balance long enough to move the German armies back, preferably to the Seine River, where they could establish a new defensive line. Despite Hitler's optimistic belief that they would sweep the Allies back into the sea, Kluge was too shrewd a soldier to think this was possible.

"We are underestimating the striking power of the American Army," he observed to an associate, theorizing that such a highly industrialized state had the resources to rapidly improvise a good army.[16]

The Führer had cast all the blame for the failure of the Mortain counter-attack on Kluge. "Von Kluge did that deliberately," Hitler said spitefully to General Warlimont. "He did it to show me that my orders were incapable of being performed!"[17]

Having found a scapegoat, Hitler could now justify ordering a remount of the attack that afternoon, this time under command of General Heinrich Eberbach. Kluge met Eberbach at his command post at Château La Roche Guyon.

"By the Führer's orders you will put together an emergency staff as Panzergruppe Eberbach, and with a number of panzer divisions mount a repetition of the counter-thrust on Avranches," he instructed.

Eberbach tried to beg off. "Sir, I consider this offensive impossible and hopeless. I therefore request that someone else be put in charge."[18]

Hitler was not to be dissuaded. He had chosen Eberbach as a last-minute replacement for the ill-tempered Funck on the eve of the first Mortain counter-attack, believing the former to be more aggressive. Kluge had refused to make the switch then; this time he could not refuse.

But both men received a temporary reprieve. The Canadian attack the previous day, *Operation Totalize*, sabotaged the remount. Kluge could not afford to pull additional panzer divisions from the British/Canadian front at such a critical time; even Hitler agreed.

Now the Führer was demanding a *re*-remount of the Mortain counter-attack two days hence—on 11 August.

"*Madness!*" thought Kluge. Did he not understand that the main German supply base at Alençon was about to be overrun?

I have 500,000 troops in danger of encirclement, Kluge thought desperately. They need fuel for their tanks, ammunition for their weapons and food for their bellies. We must forget about Mortain and confront this new danger first. People there live in another world, he mused.

Still looking over his shoulder, he saw twin threats to this latest idea of the Führer. By defying Hitler he would be fired; then the Gestapo would question him about his role in the assassination conspiracy. By conforming, the German armies could be wiped out.

Kluge felt as though he, too, was in a vise. It was squeezing the breath and heart out of a great soldier.

Wheeling north from Le Mans on 10 August, U.S. XV Corps reached Alençon the next day, capturing (as Kluge had feared) the Seventh German Army's supply base. On Friday, 11 August, Haislip ordered both armoured divisions to advance north to Argentan. To this point, the German resistance had been negligible. At Sées, all that the battered 9th Panzer Division could muster up in the way of opposition was a company of bakers.

Patton's mood was mellow, and justifiably so. "Third Army has advanced farther and faster than any army in history," he bragged happily of his 170-mile advance.[19] So far, the 2nd French Armoured Division had earned all manner of praise for their fine achievements on the drive north: "Be sure to bring along a bag of Bronze Stars for Leclerc's sons of bitches," Patton joked with his aide.

On Saturday, 12 August, Patton's mood was quite different. Haislip's orders had been clear enough to each of his divisions. Ahead of them, five miles south of Argentan, was a large forest, the Forêt d'Écouves. The Germans were notoriously skilled at using forests as a defensive position. Haislip called for an air strike to clear it. Fifth Armoured was therefore ordered to skirt the woods on the right, using the main N158 road to Argentan. Leclerc was similarly told to bypass the forest, taking the road around it on the left, or west, side.

Leclerc had other ideas. Eager to advance, he sent his units up *all three* roads. Fortunately for his troops in 2nd Armoured, the bombing was cancelled in time to avoid a tragedy. But the ensuing traffic chaos caused its own kind of fireworks.

There is possibly no traffic jam comparable to that created when one armoured division (French) collides with a second one (American) at a village crossroads. Thousands of troops, not understanding a word of each other's language, milled about in the village square at Sées. Scores of wildly excited just-liberated townsfolk frolicked while several hundred tanks and armoured vehicles meshed hopelessly at the congested corner.

"You have no right to be here," shouted the 5th Armoured Division's chief of staff.

"We're only passing through," replied the French commander haughtily.

"Argentan is our business. Our tanks need the N158," insisted the American.

"And Écouves is ours," replied Leclerc, his cold blue eyes flashing steel.[20]

Leclerc was not to be budged. Haislip roared his frustration at the Frenchman to Patton.

"Hell, Wade, don't get so upset. He's only a baby," his boss retorted.[21]

The "baby" had in fact stopped the war—or one element of it. The 5th Armoured's tanks ground to a halt, its gasoline supply vehicles hopelessly entangled as the French pre-empted their road.

Six valuable hours were lost in this débâcle—six hours that marked the difference between an enemy in total disarray and a German force once more given time to mount a defence of sorts against the American onslaught.

Late that same Saturday evening, 12 August, General Wade Haislip, commanding XV Corps, reported to Patton that he expected to capture his last objective—Argentan—the next morning. What were his further orders?

Here was a chance to cut off the German army—an opportunity too great to pass up. Without hesitating, Patton replied, "Push on slowly in the direction of Falaise" and "continue to push on slowly until [you establish contact with] our Allies."[22]

Patton then phoned his superior, General Omar Bradley, to report the sensational news. To his surprise and anger Bradley told Patton "nothing doing. Stop where you are and build up on the shoulder. The German is beginning to pull out. You'd better button up and get ready for him."[23]

Both Bradley and Patton were acting in character and carrying out their roles. As an army group commander, Bradley was always cautious; as an army commander, Patton always preferred action. But it was Bradley's job to consider the overall picture, and Patton's to pursue the immediate goals of his army. Bradley interpreted intelligence on the build-up of Panzergruppe Eberbach as a threat to the extended American flank. He preferred "a solid shoulder at Argentan to the possibility of a broken neck at Falaise." Patton thought this cautious approach was typical of Bradley and a monumental error.

Patton was also a proponent of the "rock soup" approach to orders. If he could persuade Bradley to give a little—a piece of "rock" to boil for soup—vegetables and even some meat might follow. His orders forbade an advance beyond Argentan, but who knew what might happen during a battle for the city.[24]

At 1130 hours Sunday morning, Patton was again given the order by his boss Bradley: *Stop!* The red light infuriated him. He had within reach the closure of the gap between Argentan and Falaise—the entrapment of two German armies. And he was told to stop?

"You're kidding!" Patton exclaimed with some bitterness.

Patton urgently called Bradley. He found him at Eisenhower's headquarters. But his pleas brought him no comfort. They knew through Ultra that the four German divisions that had done so much damage at Mortain were trying to mount a fresh attack on the American flank.

You are overextended, Bradley told his upset commander. You are wide open to attack. There's a gap of some twenty-five to fifty miles between your Third Army at Argentan and the nearest American force, First Army, still back at Mayenne on your left flank.[25]

Eisenhower, who apparently was in the room, was to say (at the time and later in his memoirs): "I completely support Bradley."[26] Clearly, as British historian Major-General Essame noted, "By his very physical presence in Normandy, Eisenhower assumed direct responsibility for the decision—a responsibility the American people expected him to exercise."[27] Martin Blumenson, an American authority, agreed. "Eisenhower could have done [it]."[28]

In the early hours of Sunday, 13 August, 5th Armoured Division approached the outskirts of Argentan. They were too late. The 116th Panzer Division (under new command after Schwerin had been sacked) had taken advantage of the confusion of Saturday's traffic jam at Sées, and the ensuing six-hour delay, to infiltrate Argentan and reinforce its slender defences. Elements of two more panzer divisions arrived a few hours later. The Americans were driven back with "surprisingly heavy" losses.[29]

Despite the momentary success, Kluge was deeply worried. His defences at Argentan were too weak to hold out for long. His line was so thin that enemy reconnaissance units had managed to bypass the town and probe eight miles beyond Argentan, reaching a point just six miles south of Falaise. Less than fourteen miles now separated the Anglo/Canadian and American spearheads. The German encirclement was imminent.

Unaccountably, while staring at defeat, Kluge was astonished to hear that the American attack had come to an "abrupt and surprising halt."[30] He would have been even more amazed if he knew that General Bradley, furious at having his standing order disobeyed and worried about the consequences, had been the commander who stopped Patton's advance.

General Patton's indignation at being halted on the threshold of victory evaporated with extraordinary alacrity. The next day the mercurial commander dreamt up a new plan. Now he would drive east towards the Seine and Paris and shift three of his corps away from the Argentan/Falaise front. Bradley approved the idea, without consulting Montgomery, and by nightfall it was executed.

Patton's Diary, 14 August.
I flew back to see Bradley and sell him the plan. He consented.
It is really a great plan, wholly my own, and I made Bradley think he thought of it. I am very happy and elated. I got all the

corps moving by 2030 so that if Monty tries to be careful, it will
be too late.[31]

Moving over a dozen divisions, some 180,000 men and all their equipment and vehicles, on a whim, in less than twenty-four hours was an amazing feat. Clearly, the fact that he didn't get his way in closing the Argentan/Falaise Gap motivated this action has never been determined. His gloat in his diary that he had shifted this force away without Monty's knowledge and moved them out of range is some indication of his pique.

Patton's Diary, 15 August.
Bradley came to me suffering from nerves. There is a rumor,
which I doubt, that there are five Panzer divisions at Argentan,
so Bradley wants me to halt my move east. I am complying with
the order and by tomorrow I can probably persuade him to let
me advance [farther].[32]

Patton had persuaded Bradley to change his focus of encircling the Germans at Falaise to the broader encirclement at the Seine— and, incidentally, give Patton's ego a boost by becoming the liberator of Paris.

The only question now was, could the three unproven divisions left behind—Leclerc's 2ème Division Blindée, and U.S. 80th and 90th— manage to achieve what Patton had been blocked from doing: attempting to close the southern jaw of the trap on two German armies?

THE SCAPEGOAT

War Diary: General Eberbach: 12 August 1944.
The whole day MG fire was heard from a short distance. Every
moment the enemy might appear at the headquarters. Fighter-
bombers, however, made the transfer of the headquarters
impossible. The enemy was forcing its way toward Argentan.[1]

From "Wolfschanze" in East Prussia, Hitler issued a fresh order to
General Eberbach. He was to attack southwardly past Alençon
immediately "as a preparation for the attack on Avranches."

Eberbach was stunned and incredulous. Hitler still has not given
up on *Operation Lüttich*, the Mortain/Avranches counter-attack? He
still thinks we have divisions enough to mount *two* counter-attacks
when we do not have sufficient for even one? It was as if Hitler was
no longer aware of realities; his confidence in a successful assault on
Avranches still persisted.

General Heinrich Eberbach was unhappy with his orders but
obedient to them. When the forward units from 116th Panzer arrived
on 12 August, he sent them to engage the Allies at Sées. He
dispatched 9th Panzer Division to the forest to confront the French
Armoured Division.

In the evening, a report of crisis proportion reached his headquarters near Argentan. The American XV Corps had destroyed one
hundred of his tanks that day and had taken 1,500 prisoners. Units
of 116th Panzer Division had been destroyed by heavy fire from
massed enemy tanks. Ninth Panzer Division was virtually annihilated and had but the strength of a company.

War Diary: General Eberbach: 12 August.
In the night, both of the headquarters made a shift to the region
of Chenedouil, 20 kilometres west of Argentan. This shift took

six hours. The whole supply service for one and a half armies
was congested on the few roads between Falaise and Argentan.
The columns were able to move only in the night hours. A big
number of burnt-out motor vehicles created many bottlenecks.
In consequence all streets were congested and the traffic was
moving merely at a walk. The loss of Alençon deprived 7th
Army of its supply base. It is now entirely dependent on the 5th
Army [for] gasoline and ammunition.[2]

Still, in that six hours provided him by the French traffic snarl,
Eberbach had been given breathing room, a chance to stiffen his
defences.

By Sunday, 13 August, Panzergruppe Eberbach—a sorry lot of
unkempt troops, their tanks chugging sluggishly on their last dregs
of fuel—had straggled in piecemeal after having made the last of
their seventy-mile route march from Mortain in darkness to avoid
Allied air attacks. Their numbers were so depleted that the counter-
attack Hitler had ordered against U.S. Third Army, and that Eberbach was attempting to mount, had to be cancelled. Eberbach could
use his troops only for defensive tasks, to hold the paper-thin line
at Argentan.

> *War Diary: General Eberbach: 14 August.*
> *I sent my last special-mission staff officer to the Army Group*
> *High Command with the following report:*
> *"Enemy attack with a presumable strength of two Panzer divi-*
> *sions and one Infantry division. He has surprised 2 Panzer Divi-*
> *sion and 1st SS Panzer Division Liebstandarte causing heavy*
> *losses to them. Parts of 116 Panzer Division annihilated. Rest*
> *holds against heavy enemy attacks both sides Argentan. 9*
> *Panzer Division has company strength.*
>
> *"Owing to fighting bombers at daytime and traffic congestion*
> *at night, fuel and ammunition situation very serious. Lack of*
> *fuel caused 1st SS Panzer Division to blow up a number of*
> *tanks. Under flank protection a quick withdrawal from encir-*
> *clement of the 7th Army imperative in order to avoid catastro-*
> *phe. Success improbable."*[3]

While Eberbach was imploring Hitler to authorize the withdrawal of the Seventh Army beyond Argentan, Field Marshal von Kluge was urging the Führer to withdraw all German divisions even further, all the way back to the Seine.

Eberbach told his boss, Kluge, far more frankly than he dared tell Hitler, that the German troops had lost the will to fight.

"The fighting morale of German troops has cracked," he said. "The German troops in the west have now to wage a war of the poor man against an enemy who has everything in abundance; who is fresh while the German soldier had already been engaged in hard fighting for five years and, moreover, during the last two years suffered only defeats.

"He feels himself betrayed. He no longer fights with the belief in victory and a reliance on his command but only from a soldier's pride and for fear of defeat."

Eberbach cited sorry examples of the depths to which the soldiers' spirits had sunk: "For the first time not only Poles and Alsacians but even single Germans deserted to the enemy. Tanks are left standing without being blown up, MGs thrown away, guns left lying, stragglers without arms are numerous. Catch lines [to intercept deserters] in the rear of the front had to be inaugurated. Even the SS were no exception. First SS Panzer Division Liebstandarte had never before fought so miserably as at that time."

Perhaps, Eberbach hinted to Kluge, this would be the right time for him to act against Hitler's order to save the two armies (the Seventh and Fifth). But he could do no more than hint. He was well aware that the Gestapo was watching Kluge with growing suspicion.[4]

At his command post at La Roche Guyon, Kluge, "Clever Hans," was feeling increasingly not so clever. Always the conciliator, he had hoped that by appeasing Hitler, even when his military training told him the Führer's demands were ridiculous, he could dissuade his leader from believing that he supported the assassination attempt. It hadn't worked.

He had, in Hitler's eyes, failed at Mortain and now he would be blamed for the disaster at Argentan. He was the scapegoat. He had his family to worry about too: his wife, and his son, Klaus, a lieutenant-colonel and chief-of-staff with Panzergruppe Eberbach.

In anticipation of a withdrawal order from Hitler, Kluge had set the wheels in motion prematurely. All non-combat units were to be dispatched back to the Seine: "Rear elements, repair tanks, half-tracks, artillery, anti-aircraft artillery, crews without tanks and armored infantry cadres."

Now he realized it was imperative that he meet with his army commanders to inform them of his actions. On 14 August, he saw General Dietrich at 5th Panzer HQ in Bernay. Dietrich had only bad news. The Canadians had laid on a massive attack that day; Falaise would soon be in their hands.

At dawn the next day, Kluge set out with his usual entourage, a motorcycle escort and a communications truck, to see Eberbach and Haussar. His 1000 hours rendezvous was at Nécy, some forty miles south and halfway between Argentan and Falaise. The convoy advanced perilously, with maddening slowness, over the cratered roads.

Suddenly they were dive-bombed by a Typhoon. Kluge leapt to safety in a ditch; his communications vehicle was smashed, its crew killed. He sent his aide ahead to inform Eberbach of his delay. Alone, Kluge tried to get back on the road. Again and again fighter-bombers attacked the unmistakable Porsche command car.

At Nécy, after waiting two hours, Eberbach and Hausser returned impatiently to their headquarters. Further bad news awaited them: the Americans had successfully invaded the south of France that morning.

They reported Kluge's disappearance. We cannot reach him, they told Army Group B headquarters at La Roche Guyon. He is not on the radio net.

15 August: Adolf Hitler to General Eberbach: "Establish where-abouts of Field Marshal Kluge. Report results hourly."[5]

"The inquiries by the Supreme Command were not prompted by an anxiety for the personal fate of Kluge," Eberbach noted wryly, "but by the suspicion he might have had a meeting with American officers in order to capitulate or surrender personally."[6] Indeed, Eberbach had heard through German intelligence that the Allies were rumoured to have been in contact with a German general that day. That was all Hitler needed. His suspicions were confirmed that Kluge was impli-cated in the assassination conspiracy of 20 July.[7]

The nightmare trip ended for the field-marshal at midnight.

Exhausted by the heat and the effort of crawling in and out of ditches, frustrated at being out of communication with his armies, he limped into Seventh Army headquarters. A new nightmare was just beginning.

By now, Kluge's twelve-hour disappearance had fuelled Hitler's paranoia about the man. He was a traitor.

Within forty-eight hours, Field Marshal von Kluge was removed from his command in disgrace and ordered to Berlin for interrogation by the Gestapo. On his way to Berlin, he swallowed a cyanide capsule provided him by his physician son-in-law.

The pounding of heavy guns from the American sector near Argentan—and a new thundering from the north, nearby and menacing—disturbed his final moments on earth.

The Canadians were closing on Falaise.

It was all over, anyway.

15

BARBERY CROSS

On Monday, 12 August 1944, Hitler authorized the German retreat from the Mortain counter-attack. The German forces began a slow withdrawal towards the Falaise Gap. The gap was being closed from five directions by five nations: Patton's XV Corps with the 2nd French Armoured was nearing Argentan, fifteen miles south of Falaise; the British were squeezing the retreating enemy units from behind, forcing them more and more tightly into the narrow escape hatch. On the ridge overlooking the Laison River, the Canadians and Poles were exerting pressure from the north and north-east. They were eight miles from Falaise.

A mere twenty-five miles separated the two jaws of the trap.

At 0500 hours on 19 August 1942, two brigades—5,000 men—from 2nd Canadian Infantry Division had been ordered to mount a "reconnaissance in force" on German defenders in France. The objective was a small fishing village named Dieppe. The cost was 3,367 casualties.

Two years later, at 0500 hours on 12 August 1944, two brigades from the same infantry division were again ordered to mount a reconnaissance in force on German defenders in France. The objective this time was a small farming village named Clair Tizon, just west of the Caen–Falaise road on the Laize River and some four miles to the south in the direction of Falaise. On the way they were ordered to take out the tiny hamlets of Barbery and Moulines.

As the August sun beat down on the advancing foot-soldiers of the Royal Hamilton Light Infantry (RHLI), who had fought on the main Dieppe beach, the coincidence was hard to shrug off.

The same sweltering weather, the same scratchy wool battle-dress and wretchedly uncomfortable steel helmet; even the flies dive-bombing sweaty faces seemed the same. And the pre-battle dread—heightened for some of the lads by recollections of that bloody day almost two years before—that was the same.

The Rileys (RHLI) led off the assault on Barbery. This dubious distinction was probably a spin-off from an earlier meeting with Montgomery following the RHLI's hard-punching attack at Verrières, when it was the only battalion in 2nd Canadian Corps to seize and hold its objective in *Operation Spring*. The battalion adjutant, Captain Bill Parker, was present when Montgomery congratulated the men: "He told us that we did what good infantry regiments should do: we took the ground and we held it against counter-attack. Then he said that he would 'honour' us by letting us lead the next big attack."[1]

Some "honour" it turned out to be!

The Barbery attack had been designated as 2nd Corps' main effort that day, meaning that the Rileys would have all the resources of Second Division in support: the armoured vehicles of 8th Reconnaissance Battalion, tanks from the Sherbrooke Fusiliers, and the entire divisional artillery plus two Army Groups Royal Artillery (AGRAS).

Following behind them, the Royal Regiment of Canada and Essex Scottish would advance in single line, each to leapfrog over the unit ahead as it achieved its set objective and consolidated. Then the 5th Brigade battalions, all with armoured and artillery support, would follow, emulating this tactic until the final objective, Clair Tizon, was reached.

These single line "advance to contact" tactics were standard infantry operations, well rehearsed in battle drills prior to D-Day. The infantry learned to plan not only the attack, but also—and just as importantly—what to do when the attack succeeded. The Germans were certain to counter-attack. To prepare for this, tasks had to be assigned to the rifle companies and all its supporting arms: artillery, machine guns, armour, and engineers. The infantry also had to formulate a counter-counter-attack plan.

It had seemed fairly straightforward, practising it in England. But it had never before been put into effect in Normandy. No amount of practice could prepare you fully for an exercise under heavy enemy fire. The rules often changed.

If the attack succeeded, the assault would catapult the Canadians well behind enemy lines, taking the pressure off the British on their right and off Simonds' pending Anglo-Canadian attack towards Falaise on their left.

Royal Regiment patrols confirmed that the German 271st Division was withdrawing in stages.[2] They were digging their artillery into new defensive positions on the high ground along the Laison Valley. Scout patrols described a slope with orchards and woodlands—the kind of landscape that offered the enemy every opportunity for stiff resistance.

The ground had been carpeted with land mines. The Germans were trained to booby-trap ordinary roadside articles with hand grenades and trip wires: a pump handle on a well, a doorknob on a cottage, a bottle of wine on a window ledge—even corpses on the side of the road. All were rigged to maim and kill.

Reconnaissance patrols were a battalion's eyes and ears. The scouts' pre-battle sorties into and behind enemy lines detected the German dispositions—their location, strength, and weaponry—and where possible even the placements of the lethal obstacles.

It took a special sort of man to volunteer for the scout platoon: someone with a natural instinct for the use of the ground; someone with skill, agility, and all sorts of courage. It was the élite unit of every regiment, with tasks of such priority that its commander, a lieutenant, worked directly under the battalion commanding officer.

Company Sergeant-Major Charlie Martin of the Queen's Own Regiment describes his vast experiences operating in some seventy-five patrols in Normandy alone. "Speed, timing, teamwork, and sometimes physical strength were important. The ability to work together in silence was vital. For example, I'd never take along a man who had any sign of a head cold—that's what we meant by total silence. We didn't want to hear a man breathing. We had to be very closely tuned to one another, communicating in the subtlest way—quick and quiet.

"Some could move like a ghost. One moment he'd be there, the next moment, gone.

"Then there was the danger of panic. It was necessary to train our men to 'freeze.' Only movement could be seen. A man frozen motionless, particularly if next to a tree, was virtually invisible. Don't fire—unless the enemy opened up.

"Frozen silent in the ghostly flare, black face, muffled weapon, no helmet—a helmet looks just like a helmet and can cause a rattle—there's every chance a man will not be spotted or will even look to the enemy like a stump or part of the terrain."[3]

There were three seven-man sections in a scout platoon. "Our training was very concentrated and of a special nature," Corporal Doug Shaughnessy of the RHLI recalls. "We worked in pairs mostly."

Shaughnessy—known as "Sandy" for the colour of his hair—and Harold Green—"Harry" to all the guys—had been training together in the scout platoon for five months prior to D-Day, always a team.

"We were given the best possible training in camouflage and concealment, marksmanship, map and compass reading, unarmed combat, all aspects about enemy rank structure, vehicles, weapons and aircraft recognition, demolition and about anything else required to survive by our own wits."

Sandy turned twenty shortly after the division landed in Normandy—"Not a boy any longer, but not quite a man either." On the eve of his last day as a teenager he found himself alone, hunkered into a hastily dug slit trench, experiencing his first heavy enemy bombardment.

"I didn't sleep that night . . . one is more apt to be frightened of things he cannot see or a situation he cannot fully understand . . . but I was not alone. Somewhere out there in the dark were some six hundred other members of the RHLI who I am sure were preoccupied with their own special feelings."

Since second Division's landing in Normandy in July, the RHLI's leader, Lieutenant Hugh Hinton, had led them on any number of patrols, usually at night, to glean information of the enemy. "Military maps do not necessarily show all the detail that may be found on the ground and this was particularly true that summer in Normandy."[4] Hughie Hinton himself had spent so much time in the enemy lines the scouts kidded him that he should be drawing German rations.[5]

"Harry and I moved out quietly," Sandy Shaughnessy recalls, "sometimes crawling on our stomachs, sometimes moving in a crouched position, but always hopeful that we would not end up in an enemy minefield or pull one of those hateful trip wires that would set off a flare or explosive charge.

"Listening patrols were a nasty business because you had to get as far forward of your own position as possible and remain there until early morning, then get back just before daylight. Quite often, listening patrols gave the first warning of enemy attack and more often than not they were the first to be taken prisoner of war—or worse. Then, too, there was the problem of getting back through your own line in the early morning hours when everyone was on 'Stand-To.'"

Crawling back through no-man's-land, often ducking fire from both sides, was daunting enough—worse if you couldn't get past the battalion sentry because you didn't remember the nightly password. "It was a very serious business," Shaughnessy recalls. "Many a man had been seriously injured or even killed because he forgot the password.

"It was always a double-barrelled word, such as apple-pie, or orange-juice. As you approached our lines the sentry would say, 'Halt!—Apple!' You had to reply, 'Pie!'"

One night the password was 'Holy-night.' Shaughnessy, on guard duty, challenged an incoming scout: "Halt! Holy . . . ?"

The scout, Ace Bailly, "a Nova Scotian and a real character," shouted: "Holy. . . holy . . . holy shit! I forget!"[6]

Once back to the relative safety of his unit, the scout immediately starts digging his slit trench. It was often tough work, digging four or five feet down in Normandy's hard-packed clay. But it wasn't an option. No matter how exhausted he might be, he knows that a rifleman's survival often depends on how deeply he has dug his slit, and how quickly he can get into it before the mortars come crashing around him. He has learned—often by seeing his buddies killed—that his trenching shovel is almost as important for survival as his rifle, and without it a man would feel "as naked as a man in Piccadilly without his trousers," as historian John Ellis described it.[7]

The French farmers had not harvested their wheat in this hot, dry summer from hell. The Rileys marched chest-deep through dense, dusty wheat fields, avoiding the mined road. They were soaked in sweat, hating the chafing wool uniforms.

Major Joe Pigott's "C" Company led the advance. Joe was twenty-two years of age, "tall, magnificently handsome and put together like a strip of hard steel." The men called him "King," with a lot of respect.[8]

"He was very cool, almost lackadaisical," Corporal (now Colonel) John Williamson recalls. "Nothing ever seemed to bother him. He just went calmly on, doing his job to the best of ability. He was the only person of the battalion to wear body armor—the rest of us got rid of it, but it saved his life."[9]

On Pigott's left was another of the "old sweats," Major Huck Welch, commanding "B" Company. Welch, thirty-one, moved ahead lithely as the all-star Hamilton Tiger football player he had been.

They reached the crossroads village of Barbery, with nothing but the reassuring clank of the Sherbrooke tanks breaking an almost eerie silence. The village seemed deserted; nothing stirred. At the end of the road stood a life-size crucifix. "Quite a sight in the middle of a war," Sergeant Arthur Kelly observed to his buddy. "I hope the peace that Jesus thought He died for prevails today" was the fervent reply.[10]

They advanced a few hundred yards further, warily eyeing the copse of woods on a small rise ahead. Abruptly the quiet was broken with the staccato drumming of machine guns and the shrieks of mortars as the woods on the left came alive with sheets of enemy fire, directly on Pigott's company.

Pigott, now under continuous fire, urged his men to attack. Lieutenant Hughie Hinton, the Rileys' scout leader, led his section in a rush across the Barbery crossroads against the German defences, throwing grenades and firing his Sten. He was the first to fall.

German Tiger and Panther tanks roared out of the copse, knocking out the vulnerable Sherbrooke Shermans and spraying intense machine gun fire on the Rileys. The Germans closed on the attackers. Bayonets and knives swung wildly. "They were fanatical devils," Pigott later recalled. "We started to have casualties right away. There was hand-to-hand fighting as these fellows came running out of their slits, firing rifles and throwing grenades."

Meanwhile, on the right flank of the attack, Welch's company had got on its assigned objective without serious opposition. "We were spread out wide on a lateral front," recalls Lieutenant Colin Gibson, commander of 12 Platoon in Welch's company. "Our orders were to start digging in when we had got on the ground we were to take and then hold our position. I found some old German slit trenches and got my men in these."

Gibson made a dash for Welch's HQ to report his position: "That's when the stuff started flying. I ducked part way under a carrier when an 88mm shell from a German tank exploded near me. The blast broke my right leg; I was in pretty bad shape. Gordy Holder got out of his trench even while we were under fire. He came over, stuck the shell dressing on me and gave me a jab of morphine. It was one of the bravest acts I can remember. While he was doing that he got hit in the shoulder and I got hit again, this time in my other leg and arm. Right after that I turned my platoon over to the senior NCO."[11]

By then the entire battalion was under "the most intensive mortaring and shelling the unit ever witnessed," as its intelligence officer, Lyle Doering, later noted.[12] At 1800 hours a mortar shell smashed into battalion HQ and five men, including the Riley CO, Graham McLaughlin, were wounded.

The RHLI history recounts the final moments of the battle. "Towards twilight the enemy armour moved in for what appeared the *coup de grâce*. 'The [German] tank commanders had no nerves at all,' Major Huck Welch reported later. 'They stood exposed in their turrets looking for targets through their binoculars, their guns traversing all the time.'[13] Suddenly they stopped, made a last desultory sweep with their machine guns, and left the field of smoking hulks, the dead and wounded."[14]

The Germans pulled out to replenish their ammunition and dig in a new defensive line further back, against what inevitably would be a renewed Canadian attack.

The Rileys had responded valiantly to General Montgomery's challenge; they took the ground and held it. The cost: twenty dead and one hundred wounded in one bloody afternoon. Some honour, Monty.

A survivor, Sandy Shaughnessy, recalls the next hours. "We were detailed with the padre and a couple of other guys on a burial party to the Barbery crossroads. We saw Hughie Hinton first. He had a burst of machine gun fire in the chest. So did Billy Lister; he was just a short distance from him. It could have been from tanks with self-propelled guns in the bush beyond the crossroads or from a MG-42.

"We found the others, about eighteen or twenty, all killed there. We picked up Hinton, Billy Lister, Sunday Soldo, and Eric Hughson—he had a brother with us in the battalion who was devastated."

Then Sandy picked up the next body lying sprawled across the Barbery crossroad: Harry Green, best pal and scout buddy of a lad who had just turned twenty.

It was one hell of a way to grow up fast.

Meanwhile, the remaining 4th Brigade battalions—the Royal Regiment of Canada and Essex Scottish—advanced through the Riley lines, still in chaos. Tanks were still blazing; the ground was strewn with bodies, dead and dying. The Royals met bitter opposition at the village of Moulines, but managed to capture it after close-quarter fighting.

At the height of the firefight, a sixteen-year-old boy got the scare of his life. Gunner Bill Knox was a schoolboy in Canada when he pounded the doors of Canadian enlistment centres until he found one that bought his fib about his age. He was fourteen when he enlisted and now, two years later, he was on his first tour of duty as carrier crew for a forward observation officer from the 4th Field Regiment. Without warning, an 88mm shell ripped through his carrier, barely missing the young gunner—a literal baptism of fire for a spunky kid.[15]

Billy was lucky. Twenty Royals were killed that day; seventy-four more were wounded.

Shortly after midnight on 13 August, the Calgary Highlanders of the 5th Brigade continued this dangerous game of leapfrog, setting off into a "vicious dark night" on a nerve-wracking march through rough, heavily wooded and uncharted terrain.

"The battalion had only maps and compasses to guide them over narrow trails and along sunken roads," the Highlanders' war diary records. "They came across dirt tracks not marked on the map, never knowing for certain which way to turn. The night was still and the air thick with mist. The men moved in an eerie world of deserted woods, empty villages, and quiet orchards, all the time uncertain as to where the enemy was, and waiting for the sound of German mortar, machine gun, or 88mm fire which would signal their discovery."[16]

The men were physically and emotionally spent. They had not eaten for twenty-four hours and had had only one night's sleep—under heavy shelling—in the past week. As one history describes it,

> The long marches, weighed down with personal equipment, shovels, weapons, and extra ammunition for the Brens and PIATs; the frantic digging in at each stop to get below ground as fast as possible to gain shelter from shelling and resist the inevitable counter-attack; and the never-ending tension that comes from living minute to minute, alert and ready to react to every rustle of air, knowing that the worst could happen at any moment—all combine to guarantee that those who do survive attack after attack after attack exist at the outer limits of their endurance, in a state of fatigue that defies description.[17]

Still they forged ahead. At first they encountered pockets of Germans who were ready to surrender, some carrying safe conduct pamphlets promising them good treatment if taken prisoner. The Allies had printed these translated invitations to quit, crammed them into shells and fired them over enemy lines.[18] (Both sides also found the pamphlets to have a secondary use as toilet paper.)

Then resistance stiffened. The enemy was becoming alarmed at this threat to their main position on the Falaise road. They heavily reinforced their defences on the high ground overlooking the west bank. The Highlanders nevertheless seized their bridgehead at Clair Tizon, the battalion's objective on the east bank of the Laize River.

The final attack to conclude the operation was the daunting task of crossing the narrow bridge spanning the Laize and attacking up the road, in full daylight and dead in the face of the German guns. The job required the strength of a brigade but it was given to one seriously understrength company of the Régiment de Maisonneuves, badly hurting for a lack of reinforcements.

A screen of hostile fire repelled every attempt. Finally the company commander, Major Alexander Dugas, ran out ahead and made a dash for it. Safely across, he brought his men over in twos and threes. Lieutenant Charles Forbes of "D" Company was close behind him. "There was a terrific concentration of enemy mortars and artillery coming down on the bridge. Dugas and Lieutenant

Daoust were killed, and many others. "D" Company was sent forward to push through. . . . We took a position some three hundred yards past the bridge, in a field near a woods. During the night we heard German voices coming from the woods."[19]

In darkness, fresh troops from the 6th Brigade waded across the river and secured the high ground. Falaise was now barely six miles south-west of them. The end was in sight. Second Canadian Division was well south of any other Canadian or British unit. The official history recorded the price: "These gains were only made at the cost of stubborn fighting against an enemy who resisted every attempt to advance with ferocity and who counter-attacked with vigour before yielding any ground."[20]

Fourth Canadian Infantry Brigade's "butcher's bill" on this sunny summer August weekend, fighting a diversionary action that barely made it into the history books, totalled 214. Forty of these young men were now lying in hastily dug graves, each marked by a rifle with the despised steel helmet atop.

It was a grisly garden.

16

OPERATION
TRACTABLE

Hunkering down for a precious few hours' sleep at the front line presents interesting choices.

You can dig a deep, narrow trench, about the size of a coffin— that's if you can find a spot where the soil hasn't been turned into cement by the hot, dry August weather. Then you might have to employ an axe. Alternatively, you can use a slit trench abandoned by a retreating German soldier. The risks here, assuming one isn't overly fastidious about using a dank, lice-ridden hole in the ground that served as bedroom and latrine for some considerable period, are twofold. The trench may be booby-trapped; its exact position may also be registered with the enemy's artillery.

If you are a tanker, no problem. You simply burrow down under the security of your tank and hope it isn't laagered on a swampy area, causing it to sink—with you underneath.

Finally, you can kick aside the rubble and bed down in a bomb-shattered farmhouse, hoping it won't be shelled again . . . if you are lucky enough to find one still standing.

Major Alec Balachi, second-in-command of 8th Recce Regiment, 2nd Canadian Infantry Division, had just got lucky. He found a mattress (intact) on the kitchen floor of a farmhouse (semi-intact). An urgent message woke him at midnight.

"Sir! General Foulkes is holding an 'O' Group at 0200 hours. Second Division forward headquarters is at Jacob Mesnil, an hour's drive from here. The colonel [Lieutenant-Colonel Mowbray Alway] is LOB [Left Out of Battle] at rear echelon and you are replacing him."

Balachi and his driver barely made it to the meeting on time. The division intelligence officer was distributing sheafs of paper for

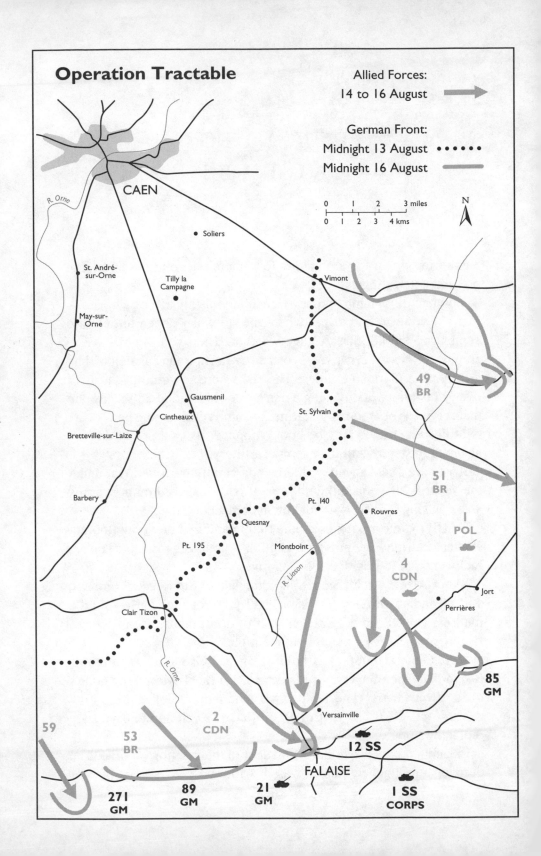

Operation Tractable

Allied Forces:
14 to 16 August

German Front:
Midnight 13 August ••••••
Midnight 16 August ▬▬▬

0   1   2   3 miles
0 1 2 3 4 kms

N

CAEN

R. Orne

Soliers

St. André-sur-Orne

Tilly la Campagne

May-sur-Orne

Vimont

49 BR

Gausmenil

Cintheaux

St. Sylvain

Bretteville-sur-Laize

51 BR

Barbery

Pt. 140

Rouvres

I POL

Quesnay

Montboint

Pt. 195

R. Liason

4 CDN

Clair Tizon

Jort

Perrières

R. Orne

85 GM

59

53 BR

2 CDN

Versainville

12 SS

FALAISE

271 GM

89 GM

21 GM

I SS CORPS

Operation Tractable. It would seem that the next big push was on for noon that day, 14 August. General Simonds was re-creating *Operation Totalize*, using the same immense numbers of armour and motorized infantry as a phalanx to smash through the German anti-tank defence ring. But this time, instead of using darkness to blind the enemy guns, he was attacking at high noon, substituting dense, man-made smoke to mask the attack.

The immediate objective, described by the divisional intelligence officer, was the Laison River Valley. The river, really just a narrow meandering creek that curled through a valley north-east of Falaise, could pose problems for the tanks because of its high banks. The long-term objective was the capture of Falaise, Trun, and Chambois, and closing the circle around the Germans.

Predictably, the Germans had their anti-tank weapons well dug in on the high ground overlooking the valley.

The major task, Balachi noted with some relief, excluded 2nd Canadian Division. It was still dusting itself off from the intense Barbery/Clair Tizon battles and starting a renewed advance towards Falaise from the north-west.

Operation Tractable was assigned to four seasoned brigades of infantry and two armoured brigades (2nd and 4th Armoured; 7th, 8th, 9th, and 10th Infantry). As well, 2nd Canadian Corps would have under its command British 51st Highland and 1st Polish Armoured Divisions, supporting the eastern flank of the operation.

Alec Balachi was an experienced soldier, "blooded" in the battles of North Africa, and a "damned good 21C," his CO was to say.[1] Urgent, middle-of-the-night "O" Groups were nothing new to him.

He packed the new ops order in his map case, climbed wearily into his Humber scout car, and told his driver to get him back to regimental headquarters on the double. "We can take a shortcut through here," he instructed the corporal, indicating the route on his map.

Typical Normandy landscape, then and still today, is a maze of narrow farm tracks criss-crossing each other like spider webs on the rolling countryside. Many are uncharted. Place names, like the scores of "Le Mesnils," are frequently duplicated several times throughout the region, further confusing accurate navigation.

Groping in the darkness, they had only pinpoint lights on the vehicle and no signs to direct them. "He and his driver somehow took a wrong turn and got lost," Lieutenent Colonel Mowbray Alway recounted. "They went into enemy lines. Then they tried to turn around and get out but they couldn't do it and drove straight into a German patrol."

A shot rang out. Balachi slumped over, mortally wounded. The enemy swarmed the frightened corporal, pulling him roughly out of the jeep. German soldiers searched the body of the young major and discovered the sheaf of papers that were so recently handed him.

The complete operational plan for *Tractable* was in German hands.[2]

The intelligence officer at General Fiebig's 85th Infantry Divisional headquarters at Jort quickly scanned the document and contacted Major-General Kurt Meyer at 12th SS HQ. "The Canadians are mounting a massed attack with some two hundred and fifty tanks and eight thousand infantry. H-Hour is 1200 hours today," he reported urgently. "Their start-line is from Estrées-la-Campagne, just east of the Caen–Falaise highway, on a north-east axis to Soignolles, opposing our 1st SS Panzer Corps and the left wing of 86 Corps."

The Canadian objective, he explained, was to cross the Laison River and cut south towards Falaise and Trun.

"Are they planning their usual preliminary artillery barrage?" Meyer demanded to know.

"No, sir. They don't want to alert us to the operation. The Allies won't open up their guns until just before H-hour. Then they intend to lay down an immense smoke screen to mask their actions, as well as to pound our anti-tank positions. The RAF are planning two bombing attacks. The first will be at H-hour when they will bomb our gun positions. The next will be two hours after the attack goes in."

The SS commander responded with typical speed. "It's almost daybreak now. We have no time to relocate our defences, nor do we need to. We have been expecting a Canadian attack. After all, there is only one open approach to Falaise left.

"So, we are ready for them. We now have twelve thousand men from 85th Division positioned on the ridge opposite the attack line. They are fresh troops; the Canadians and British are tired.

"We also have asked that Lieutenant-General Wolfgang Pickert's 3rd Flak Corps' 88mm guns are prepared for H-hour. (A strategic irony was that the army wanted the 88mm guns forward to stop

Allied armour; the air force, who controlled the guns, wanted them used in an anti-aircraft role.) The 102nd SS Tiger Battalion, and 89th and 271st Infantry Divisions will hold the line to the west of the Caen–Falaise highway. Alert these forces to the H-hour. It is extremely useful to know their start time."[3]

Meyer had inserted battle groups of 12th SS troops into each battalion as "battle police." Their job was to stiffen the fighting morale of each unit. Fiebig was instructed to alert them, too.

"They must not allow the inexperienced men of 85th and 89th divisions to cave in," he said harshly.[4]

Ironically, the focal point of the German defences was a ridge overlooking the Laison River—the same ridge that Lieutenant-Colonel Worthington and his brave band of British Columbia Regiment and Algonquins had stumbled on four days earlier. The bodies of forty Canadians were still unclaimed as 12th SS began to dig in their fortifications around them.

A crimson glow tinted the eastern horizon. Soon the sun's first rays gave promise of another hot, cloudless August day. Canadian tanks and troops milled about the forming up place (FUP).

First among them were 79th Armoured Division's "Funnies." This strange menagerie of tracked vehicles was specially designed by Major-General Sir Percy Hobart shortly after the Dieppe Raid to overcome a variety of obstacles, primarily minefields and ditches.

The initial creation was the "Flail." This was a Churchill or Sherman tank modified to carry up front a rotating drum with chains attached. The chains beat the ground to explode mines as the tank moved forward, thus clearing a passage through a known or suspected minefield for vehicles and foot soldiers.

Then in rapid succession came a number of other inventive ideas. The "Crocodile" was a flame-throwing tank that spread panic and fear in its wake. The versatile AVRE performed as a cannon, firing a highly penetrating and destructive charge capable of demolishing concrete emplacements. The AVRE could otherwise carry a small bridge to span narrow gaps or drop bundles of fascine into smaller anti-tank ditches, making them passable for armour.[5]

Shortly before noon on 14 August, the guns roared into action and bombers thundered overhead. Above the din, commanders leading the tightly melded force shouted as one: "Move now!" The assault was launched.

"Speed is essential," the tankmen were told. Accelerators were jammed to the floor and engines roared as 160 tanks all abreast plunged headlong through the fields of unmown wheat in what the First Hussars termed a "mad charge." Ninety more tanks followed in tight formation.[6]

"Follow the sun" was the next command. This was deemed the only way to keep direction in the smoke and dust churned up by armour and artillery. But the glaring sun was soon reduced to a faint pinpoint. Even that light became obscure as the gunners blasted their 25-pounder smoke shells into the valley. Before long an impenetrable grey-white mist obliterated all visibility, blinding both ally and foe.

Kurt Meyer's hastily rescheduled pounding of the start-line was immediately felt by the Canadian Scottish Regiment, as their war diary notes:

> *The Bn [battalion] immediately came under intense enemy fire from various heavy weapons and MGs [machine guns] raked the area. This was undoubtedly the most intense and persistent barrage yet laid down upon us by the enemy . . . almost completely eliminating close support transport for the Bn.*[7]

The Lake Superior Regiment moved off immediately behind the tanks "so as to gain some concealment in their dust."

Grenadier Guards squadron commander Major John Munro recalled the regiment as having "all sorts of battle courage. . . . The Lake Sups were an efficient, fast-striking force of skilled infantrymen. They were heavily tracked—their carriers looked like battleships—and they had every weapon they could get on them. They were over-sized, over-strength and very tough guys—just great to work with."[8]

Heavy shellfire slammed against the unit at the start-line. Undeterred, the intelligence officer defiantly lifted his trumpet to sound a stirring chorus of the regimental march "Light of Foot."

Nearing the woods, the vehicles were held up. The commanding officer, Lieutenant-Colonel R.A. Keane, dismounted, strode to the front of the column, pulled out his pistol, and coolly shot two Germans in a slit trench.

Meyer's beefed-up anti-tank defences exacted a hefty toll on the armour. Soon the valley was chequered with flaming hulks of steel. In the mêlée, many tanks went off course. One of the early casualties was Brigadier Leslie Booth, commander of 4th Canadian Armoured Brigade.

Though a diminutive five-footer in height, Booth was a tough veteran of the Italian campaign, earmarked for higher command. His entire armoured headquarters was obliterated by a nest of German tanks, whose guns killed his intelligence and liaison officers and several of his crew.

One of his officers cradled his body, one leg nearly torn off, and ferried it on top of his tank towards the regimental aid post. But Booth was beyond help. He died shortly afterward, and the ambulance driver quite properly placed his body on the side of the road to take on two freshly wounded men. Booth was dressed for battle: black coveralls with no identifying rank tabs. It wasn't until well into the next day that he was found, brought in, and identified.

The loss of their commander added to the confusion in trying to keep direction in a dense fog. The *Tractable* armoured force nevertheless plunged determinedly forward.

By 1300 hours the first infantrymen, the Glens (Stormont, Dundas and Glengarry Highlanders) were nimbly wading across the river. Soon all units of foot soldiers began mopping-up operations in the valley.

The troopers had a tougher time finding crossings over the Laison River for their tanks. For more than an hour, the defile of the riverbank "seethed and boiled with a disorderly confluence of armour," as their war diary records.[9] While the river was not deep, its steep-sided banks caused a few tanks to flounder in the mud. Some troops reconnoitred sites where the banks were less steep. The lumbering Churchills with their huge bundles of brushwood deftly improvised bridges. Other tanks unfolded "scissors bridges"—ingenious contraptions from the "Funnies" menagerie that opened like scissors to provide bridges capable of spanning a thirty-foot gap and carrying thirty tons.[10]

On the corps' left flank, the armoured cars of the Manitoba

Dragoons probed deeply into enemy territory, netting several hundred prisoners.

By nightfall the Laison valley was fully breached. Despite isolated episodes of bitter fighting by determined 12th SS troops, all units were consolidated on their primary objectives on the heights of the southern bank of the river. Over one thousand prisoners were taken from the shattered 85th Division.

Blinded by smoke and dust, deafened and bewildered by artillery shells and bombs, the enemy's gunners had frantically searched for their assigned defensive fire zones. Many of the German 85th Infantry Division troops understood the utter uselessness of trying to resist the weight of steel bearing down on them from every direction; others who attempted it were crushed as their positions were overrun. As the attack gained momentum, prisoners became so numerous that they were merely sent back unescorted.[11]

The division that had arrived in Normandy only a week before now was decimated, with 1,010 Germans taken prisoner. "In a six-hour major battle, the division lost the bulk of its infantry and artillery and therewith its actual fighting potential," Lieutenant-Colonel Kurt Schuster reported. "It was only with the most severe casualties that . . . we were able to succeed in preventing an enemy breakthrough to Falaise. This success was however out of all proportion to the losses."[12]

In the wake of the forward troops, two supporting arms poured in, each with essential tasks. The engineers opened up supply routes. The Royal Canadian Army Service Corps (RCASC), following closely behind the troops, kept them supplied with the essentials of war. A mobile army could not get far without ammunition, petrol, food and water.

By nightfall on 14 August, the fascine and scissor-bridge crossings were replaced by Bailey bridges, sturdy enough to withstand the poundings of Polish Division vehicles crossing at the rate of six hundred per hour.

Sappers clearing roads still under enemy sniper and mortar fire found themselves in unaccustomed infantry roles, scooping up prisoners. The German retreat had been too swift to allow them time for much deliberate mine laying on a large scale until the sappers reached the outskirts of Falaise.[13]

With the roads established, however primitively at first, the RCASC (Service Corps) lads swung into action to re-supply the forward troops. Eighty thousand tonnes of essential goods were hauled to front echelon dumps in thirty-six hours in the *Totalize* operation. Much of this activity was conducted while the enemy artillery was still sited on the newly liberated Laison Valley battlefield. Tanks pulling back into shelter to refuel were often under fire, as the Governor General Foot Guards reported.[14]

Corporal Adam Kreuter was a mechanical electrician with 1st Polish Armoured Division. His job was to keep forty-three lorries and motorcycles on the road. There were two units: one for food and one for gasoline. They quickly discovered they weren't interchangeable—troops grumbled that the margarine was starting to taste like petrol!

"We carried petrol to the front. We'd go back to get more gas and sometimes we had to go all the way back to the coast. The need for supplies never stopped. We were on the road twenty-four hours a day. Sometimes we would get three hours' sleep but we always had to keep going. Once I drove way back but there was no gas—I kept on going farther back until I found some and then drove all morning to get it to the tanks. The commanding officer said, 'My God! I'm glad to see you!' Without our service an armoured division would have become an infantry division in no time."

Kreuter recalled that snipers were "all over the place. They shot one of my friends right off his bike."[15]

It had been a day of great achievement for the weary Canadians. They attacked twelve thousand fresh troops at a place and time known to the enemy and still pulled off a significant victory.

17

"MY GOD! WE'RE BOMBING SHORT!"

At the very hour when Major Alec Balachi was sleepily groping his way in the dark to the last-minute "O" Group about *Operation Tractable*, another hurriedly convened meeting was taking place many miles away.

At Bomber Command at High Wycombe, Buckinghamshire, an extraordinary request was being made. Bomber Command was accustomed to having sudden bombing operational orders hit their desks a short period before an operation. In practice, a few penetrating questions were asked and answered and the operation was approved before dawn for launching that day or night. On this occasion, their time was cut to a very brief few hours.

H-hour for *Operation Tractable* was 1200 hours, 14 August. It wasn't until late in the evening of 13 August, as Air Chief Marshal Arthur Harris himself noted, that "details of the operation were brought over to the Headquarters."[1] Brigadier Churchill Mann, chief of staff of First Canadian Army, instigated the request for RAF bomber support (via the RAF air liaison representative).[2]

Bomber Command and its C-in-C, "Bomber" Harris, had provided close bomber/infantry support in the Normandy campaign. However, this request provided no time for proper briefings. It provoked serious reservations from the senior air staff officers, which they underlined to Brigadier Mann and his staff.

Their first concern was with Bomber Command's inexperience in daylight raids. "The risk of bombing our own troops exists to a serious degree. Our heavy bomber force has had very few daylight missions," they insisted. The only way to avoid this would be to route the aircraft entirely over enemy lines—and directly in the path of enemy anti-aircraft fire.

Harris demurred. He knew well that the casualty figures for bomber crews were staggering. Of every hundred RAF aircrew, fifty-one were killed on operations. Twenty-six more were either killed or seriously injured in crashes in England, or were taken prisoner when shot down. That left only twenty-four men who theoretically got home alive. Ten thousand aircraft had already been lost.[3]

He realized, and Canadian pilot and author Murray Peden confirmed, that

> ... the crews faced formidable odds, odds seldom appreciated outside the Command. At times in the great offensives of 1943 and 1944, the short-term statistics foretold that less than twenty-five out of each two hundred crews would survive their first tour of thirty operations. On a single night Bomber Command lost more aircrew than Fighter Command lost during the Battle of Britain. Yet the crews buckled on their 'chutes and set out with unshakeable resolution night after night. They fell prey to the hazards of icing, lightning, storm and structural failure, and they perished amidst the bursting of shells of the flak batteries. But by far the greatest number died in desperately unequal combat under the overwhelming firepower of the tenacious German night fighter defenders.[4]

Harris' response was unwavering. "I [am] not prepared to subject my crews to this additional risk in order solely to lessen the risk of bombing our own troops. Their casualty rate is far in advance of anything suffered anywhere by our ground troops," the air chief observed grimly.

Then Harris expressed serious concerns about the visibility of the targets. "There would be a tendency for smoke from the initial target to obscure the remainder," he pointed out.

Following this gloomy prediction, he asked two final, urgent questions: "Is there any possibility that ground troops would use pyrotechnics [coloured smoke signals] that could confuse the bombers?"

Incredibly, the Canadians make no reference to standing orders issued pre-D-Day by SHAEF (Supreme Headquarters Allied Expeditionary Force) that yellow flares or yellow smoke would be the standard signal for forward infantry to identify themselves as friendly troops.

"Absolutely not," the Canadian liaison officer appointed by Mann replied.

"Then do you enter this venture, as does Bomber Command, in full knowledge of the possible risk to our own troops?"

"Absolutely."[5]

With this, a quick telephone call confirmed the raid to the waiting RAF squadron bases in northern England.

At 0700 hours on 14 August, some six thousand air force personnel in Yorkshire and Durham dug into a breakfast of bacon and eggs (real eggs for the air crew, powdered for the ground crew).

A total of 811 aircraft were designated for the operation—Halifaxes, Lancasters, and Mosquitoes. While they were being fuelled and armed, the aircrews crowded the briefing areas.

For the first time, the men learned their mission: a daylight bombing raid on five German strong points in support of *Operation Tractable*, a massive Allied infantry/armoured/air attack near Falaise.

The flight path over Allied positions added extra hazards to the mission. The pilots had a very limited view of the ground. Therefore, a precise bomb-line was delineated to navigators. North of it was Allied; south was enemy. This addressed the very real danger of pilots' "short bombing"—that is, dropping the bombs prematurely on their own troops.

Another safeguard was the use of Pathfinders. These aircraft would fly in ahead of the bombers, lighting "proceed with bombing" flares to guide them in over the bomb-line to their targets— yellow target indicators, the briefing officers emphasized. There was no other way the aircrew could identify ground targets at eight thousand feet.

Flight time was three hours. They would fly a timed run in from the coast to a crossroads at Caen, and then a timed run from that crossroad to the target. This would be the final safeguard against short bombing.

To be sure of timing, the navigators were given stopwatches. The sweep of the second hand of a watch would govern the blind release of thousands of tons of bombs.

It was a daunting assignment. The airmen had been trained only for night raids—not for daylight raids, visual recognition of targets, or flying in formation.

As Air Chief Marshal Harris had pointed out, the turnover rate among bomber crews was very high. Few crews gained experience before they were killed. Those that did were veterans of harrowing tours—flying many nights a week for five solid weeks—on night raids on France and Germany. They lived with danger and with death, often witnessing their close friends become statistics.

Flak sparked universal fear. "Everybody gets hit by flak, no question," Flight Sergeant Roy Clarke, a wireless operator on the Falaise attack, noted.

"When you run into flak it sounds like handfuls of gravel being thrown against a tin garage roof. Going into a target you can see black puffs straight ahead of you. Sometimes they were so heavy you'd think you could get out and walk on top of them. Those German flak batteries were bloody good. If the flak gunners got you with a direct hit, there was no way you were going to come out of it—just boom! and that was it.

"If it was predicted flak—when the flak guns down below got a range on you—the skipper 'jinked' the aircraft by moving it slightly to starboard or port, to get away from the flak.

"The scary part was when even at nighttime you could see the shape of an airplane to the right or left or above you and all the sudden you saw the thing blow up. That's what kind of shook you. Sometimes you knew whose airplane it was. It could be your own squadron, your best friend."

Another worry was collision. "With the sky filled with a thousand or so aircraft, you had to be careful. We all watched for other aircraft, even fighters."[6]

The constant stress of losing close friends, of wondering when you yourself would be killed, often created a physical twitching or stuttering known as being "flak-happy"—a condition that almost all the men endured but few gave in to. And while the air men got used to fear, they just didn't show it. Far worse would be a transfer from action with LMF (Lack of Moral Fibre) stamped on your papers.

Flight Lieutenant Jim Llewellyn, a Welshman with No. 4 Group RAF, recalls an incident typical of the "stiff-upper-lip" air force tradition. "I was hit by flak coming back from a raid and crash landed in a field. My rear gunner, a good friend, was killed; we were all badly shaken. When we finally made it back to base, all my CO said was, 'Where the bloody hell have you been?' "7

It was a tough lesson for a twenty-one-year-old.

At high noon on a sultry 14 August, crews of over eight hundred aircraft pulled on warm boots and heavy, fleece-lined jackets or flying suits. Temperatures could dive well below zero in unheated craft at high altitudes. They butted out a last cigarette, buckled parachute straps, and prepared for take-off. Some three hours later, the giant armada, stretching over ten miles, as far as the eye could see, crossed the French coast.

On the approach, navigators watched for that key crossroad at Caen. At this point they carefully marked the speed and time by seconds to the target.

"We bombed by time instead of looking for a target," confirms Flying Officer Ken Fulton, who flew as navigator in the first wave of the *Tractable* raid with No. 426 Squadron. Fulton's log reflects in minutes and seconds the precision of the flight: *Cross coast: 14:46:10 hours. Timed run from coast to road west out of Caen: 3 minutes, 18 seconds. Speed 180 mph. Altitude: 8,000 ft. Timed run from Caen crossroad to target: 4 minutes, 57 seconds.*

As he neared the target, Fulton's aircraft ran into predicted flak from German *ack-ack* guns. As an experienced airman, he knew too well how deadly this could be. Radar-directed predicted flak was so accurate the Germans had been known to shoot down a single plane at 20,000 feet with one or two rounds of an 88mm (at six to eight shells per round).

He glanced at his stopwatch. Still over a minute to go to target. The pilot, experienced to this danger, kept a straight and level course, trying hard to ignore the lethal fire exploding around him. Fulton looked out his window. At last: the Pathfinder below was dropping yellow target indicators. Fulton deactivated his safety switch, a precaution that prevented the bomb-aimer from releasing his bombs prematurely. Anxiously, he watched the bombs descend and explode. The smell of cordite was strong; *200 yards from target*, he noted in his log.[8]

Coming that close to a target from 8,000 feet was considered to be very accurate. He was sure the plane's photographs would confirm a good result.

But there was no time for cheering. Within a few seconds the flak became dense. Now, free of their bombs, they were able to manoeuvre to avoid it. The pilot corkscrewed, diving to port and climbing to starboard in a zigzag pattern to avoid being hit.

Corkscrew to 4000 feet, Fulton logged. *Small arms fire commences. Plane receives bullet holes.*[9]

Fulton's squadron headed for home. They were lucky. As the first wave in, they had clear vision—no smoke or dust. The damage they inflicted on a number of enemy strong points would be a huge contributor to the success of *Tractable*.

Moments later, the second wave made its approach.

Below, in the deep Hautmesnil quarry, men from the Royal Regiment of Canada were enjoying a few free hours after 4th Brigade's gruelling battles to liberate Barbery and Clair Tizon. The portable baths had been brought up and they were revelling in the warm, sunny day and the chance to catch up on laundry and letter writing. Nearby, Lieutenant Ken Turnbull and his platoon of machine gunners of the Toronto Scottish had hunkered down into a large German dugout. They had ordered up their first hot meal in days, and were idly cleaning their guns, enjoying the respite. They spotted Polish troops moving into a nearby field.[10]

Elated at the sight of the heavy RAF bombers flying low overhead, many of the men waved and yelled at their protectors. No one had any qualms about the accuracy of Bomber Command, which had made six similar army support raids without causing a single Allied casualty.[11]

Following after the first wave, Flight Lieutenant Russell Curtis (an American flying with No. 428 Squadron, No. 6 Group, RCAF), and Flight Sergeant Roy Clarke's craft (in No. 419 Squadron) were in the next run-ins to the target area. By then "bomb creep"—the smoke and dust that filtered back from the earlier bombing—was obliterating the target, just as Air Chief Marshal Harris had feared.

Peering through the smog, the pilots saw yellow flares and believed they were the agreed signal described in their briefing. They heard the master bomber, or "master of ceremonies," as he was called, break radio silence to instruct "bomb the yellow target indicators."

What they didn't realize was that the master bomber had his attention focused only on the first-wave bombers, who were successfully on target.[12]

They could not know that some Canadian troops, watching the huge bomb bay doors open, panicked. They rushed to light their Verey pistol flares, as they had been trained, to alert aircraft of friendly troops below—yellow flares.

"It would only take one crew to bomb short," Flight Sergeant Clarke believes. "Then the troops would start sending up the yellow Vereys and, once that started, some of the crews behind them would say, 'Oh, they've changed the target!'"

This, in fact, happened to Clarke's crew. But after the bomb-aimer had dropped the bombs, the navigator went up behind the pilot and Clarke wriggled into the dome behind him. "The navigator was yelling, 'My God! We're bombing short!'

"We could see the bomb bursts going down to the yellow Verey flares, a paler colour than the intense yellow of the target indicators. You could definitely see the difference. I saw it myself.

"The master bomber could see it, too," Clarke remembers. "He started screaming and shouting 'You're bombing short, for God's sake! Don't bomb those yellows coming from the ground!'"

Wing Commander Chester Hull faults the Canadian Army for the arbitrary assignment. "There were five targets all in a row along the front and the Army insisted they be bombed in a certain order, one after the other. So the smoke from the first target drifted over the others. That was a cause of the confusion."[13]

Each of the five targets had a master bomber, each on a different radio frequency. Most of the remaining pilots of the operation flying in the next waves were unaware of any problems. As ordered, they used their stopwatches to put them on target for accurate bombing. But 10 per cent of them forgot to use their watches and, hence, neglected to time the run. They depended instead on visual identification. Tragically, they dropped their lethal loads on their troops below.

On the ground, elation turned to horror as tons of deadly bombs poured down on them relentlessly. Hundreds of troops at Hautmesnil and St. Aignan dove for slit trenches as the attack continued. Direct hits were made on the troops and on the vehicles that were massed in the quarry prior to moving out that evening. The 12th Field Regiment incurred serious casualties.

Seeking cover in the slits was probably the worst thing they could have done. When Lieutenant Turnbull saw the bombs, he thought, "Holy Jeesuz, here it comes! We're goners if we stay in this dugout."

Turnbull's quick thinking saved many lives that day. "Get the hell out of here!" he yelled at his men. "Get to the open fields!"

"We threw everything into the carriers—our guns were dismantled and we just tossed in all the parts in a jumble—and took off for the next open field. We felt awfully vulnerable, standing there in the open, but we were lucky. I lost one sergeant, wounded in the arm, that was all."[14]

In the Polish sector, terrible carnage was experienced. In all, 397 men were casualties. One hundred and fifty were killed.

"The absurd thing was that there was no direct ground-to-air communications, which could have stopped it at once," observed the Gordon Highlanders' diarist, who experienced the same futile helplessness as bombs thundered about him.[15]

The war diary of the Royal Regiment described the terror of the men on the ground:

> *For more than half an hour the stunned survivors hid in what shelter they could find while this dreadful hammering beat upon the battalion. At last it stopped. Here and there men emerged from the wreckage to find the area unrecognizable.*
>
> *No one expected to see many survivors, but gradually men returned to find vehicles destroyed and their personal equipment buried. The resulting casualties were six killed and thirty-four wounded. The loss in vehicles amounted to twenty-six, and great numbers of wireless sets and weapons had been smashed to fragments. Such was our painful revelation of what had been imposed on the enemy.*[16]

A thick pall of smoke hung over the area as the men gradually crawled out of their trenches. In anger and dismay they viewed the terrible scene. "It was the only time our morale really sank. We couldn't go anywhere to escape the bombs," Corporal John Angus McDonald remembers. McDonald was one of three brothers in the Stormont, Dundas and Glengarry Highlanders. His younger brother, Francis, was wounded on 19 July in Caen and died the next day. (His other brother, Jim, a corporal, would be shot in the knee at Boulogne in September.)

McDonald said, "They kept coming closer and closer. Joe Liscomb said to me, 'Which way do we go? We've got to get out of here!' I said, as far as I can see east, and as far as I can see west, they're bombing, so we might as well stay right here in our trenches and take our chances. We could see them opening the bomb bay doors. There was not a thing we could do. There's our own people trying to knock us off."[17]

The Chaplain of 2 Derbyshire Yeomanry (51st Highland Division), Major N.F. Jones, comforted the "horribly shattered" Scots.[18]

A British gunner, Sergeant J.G. Perry of the 15th Medium Regiment, Royal Artillery, stumbled into his base camp. His clothes were torn, his body bruised and filthy. Shakily, he recounted to startled friends the story of his escape from being buried alive. Two 1,000-pound bombs had exploded a hair's breadth away from him, one ten yards to his right and the other six yards on the left. By some sweet miracle he eluded death. His diary records:

I was in a fairly shallow slit trench face downward (about 2 ft deep). The bombing continued after that as wave after wave came over & released those loads. All HELL was let loose & the earth jumped up & down as each stick of bombs crept near to where I was.

Thoughts kept flashing in my mind as I lay there, my loved ones, home, everything that was dear to me & finally as I was gradually getting buried alive, a prayer. Two noises like thunder which deafened me literally lifted me out of the trench, dropped me back in & plastered earth & debris on top of me. . . . I thought it was all over. I MUSTN'T PANIC. I realized that if I didn't make a tremendous effort in a second or so I would just suffocate . . . .

My knees moved & I got a bit of leverage & heaved for all I was worth (mentally thanking God that I had strong leg, back, & stomach muscles). Finally when I was beginning to feel that all was over I saw a small shaft of daylight. I took a deep breath then I rested for a second. Another deep breath & then a heave for all I was worth.

The patch of daylight widened. I began to dig upwards with my fingers towards the light & eventually got my head out— another short rest & then one shoulder & then the other. After that it was comparatively easy. I lay panting on God's good earth.

Then I realized that another squadron was coming over. I nearly panicked then, but almost immediately came the thought—I MUSTN'T PANIC. I dragged myself to my feet & forced myself to walk to my own slit trench. I got there before the next lot came. My own trench was comparatively heaven & inhabited by a Canadian. I dived in & we huddled together sideways with our helmets over our heads until the bombing stopped.

None of the chaps around me were killed. One is still missing having panicked & just run God knows where, & one man was evacuated in a state of complete nervous collapse. Other units were not so lucky & ambulances were streaming backwards & forwards along the road for an hour or two afterwards.[19]

Of the 811 aircraft, seventy-seven bombed "short." The majority—90 per cent—performed their tasks with great skill and accuracy, and were a major factor in the success of the operation. As one historian later noted, "in the wide open rolling country north of Falaise the neutralization of a dozen key anti-tank positions spelled the difference between success and failure."[20]

Clearly, the blame for the tragedy was shared two ways. Canadian Army headquarters was at fault: for not alerting Bomber Command to SHAEF's policy of using yellow flares as an infantry signal, and for arbitrarily insisting on the sequence of targets that produced "bomb creep." Also to blame were the 10 per cent of air crew who did not follow clear orders to time their runs. On both sides, remorse and guilt were acknowledged.

"We (and myself in particular) might be considered as having some responsibility," Brigadier Churchill Mann noted in a gross understatement in a memo to General Harry Crerar shortly after the event.

Ironically, two other planners of the disaster very nearly became victims themselves. From a vantage point at Hautmesnil, General Simonds and the senior air officer at 2nd Tactical Headquarters, Vice Air Marshal Coningham, arrived to "watch the 'heavy' show."

"Bombs are mistakenly unloaded some 300 yards from their jeep," recorded 2nd Corps' war diary. "Very lucky escape."[21]

The air personnel of the seventy-seven bombers who bombed short were also victims in a very real sense. Most of them first learned of the disaster when they returned to base for the debriefing. Sadly, forty-four of these craft were, like Flight Lieutenant Curtis's, flown by members of the Canadian air force. Bombing their own countrymen bore an extra sting.

Flight Lieutenant John Turnbull of 424 Squadron, No. 6 Group, RCAF, would normally have been flying on this mission. Luckily for him, he was grounded that day. "My flight commander took the station's group captain with him; they flew in the second wave. So I only sat in on the briefing."

Turnbull was back at the base, waiting to attend the debriefing of the men on their return. "They didn't know that they had bombed short until we debriefed them. They were chagrined . . . very unhappy people."[22]

The risks that had been initially pointed out to the Canadian Army—sending aircrew on a mission for which they had little or no training—had been tragically realized. Turnbull offers an explanation: "It was not an unusual thing to have a creep back [bombing short] of the bombing on our night flights. It took a lot of guts to fly right into the target with flak coming at you. That's why we used to tell our bomb-aimers [to] keep your finger off the bomb-aim button until you are really on the target. Otherwise they tended to bomb a little bit short."

More importantly, unused as they were to "timed runs," a number of navigators neglected to set their watches on the Caen crossroad. Because they were on a day flight, they were using a visual observation of the flares more than a stopwatch. Then, seeing the army's yellow signal, they thought they were on target.

"The smoke and dust were very strong factors in the erroneous bombing. It was blowing into the approach," Turnbull believes. "Even my flight commander and his group captain [flying as a passenger] got sucked into the same mistake."

Bomber Command's reaction was swift and uncompromising. "The whole squadron was put under a form of house arrest for about twenty-four hours until they got the thing straightened out," Turnbull recalls. "They had to turn in their log books and no one could leave the base or even use the telephone."[23]

Flying Officer Ken Fulton also attended the debriefing that broke the news to the squadron. "Every aircraft was sealed and they took every camera out of the aircraft. I believe there were a few people in other squadrons disciplined for bombing short. We got pictures of the target and all of our squadron was fine. There was a lot of consternation. I never did hear who did it and of course we never talked about it. It was all hushed up."[24]

Judging by the London *Daily Mail* account the next day, the hush-up even included a British correspondent, Colin Bednall, who actually flew on the raid: it was a glowing account of total success, with no mention of the disaster: "Aerial policemen were on duty over the target areas right through the bombing to ensure that the bombs did not creep across the narrow line marking the positions of our own ground forces. They gave frequent directions over the radio to the bombers. . . . They were part of an intricate organization to ensure that the attack went right home to the mark."[25]

After the investigation, disciplinary measures taken against those crews found responsible included demotions of one or two ranks, reprimands, and "starring" them from participating in similar raids without further training.

No discipline could ever redress the terror and anger the victims of the errant bombing endured. One gunner reported seeing men six months later, just returned to the line after long treatment for battle exhaustion induced by the bombing in the quarry, "break down again after heavy shelling."[26] Even forty-five years later there were scars. "I met a captain from my home town who was in charge of the artillery unit that we bombed," Ken Fulton remembers. "He lost quite a few men and he was still very bitter that he had been bombed by our side, still bitter, after all those years."[27]

But no punishment could match the hell the aircrews put themselves through after that day of bombing their own countrymen. Their lack of training was not their fault, but their carelessness was.

The sting of his reprimand continued to be keenly felt by Flight Lieutenant Russell Curtis, 428 Squadron, until a night raid over Dortmund on 3 November 1944, nearly three months later. Flying through heavy anti-aircraft fire, he was severely wounded, incurring a compound fracture of the head.

Lieutenant-General Chester Hull, CO of 428 Squadron, tells a story of an incredible vindication: "Having been chastised by me for bombing short at Falaise, Curtis was determined to prove that this time he had bombed where he was supposed to have. He hung on long enough to enable the bomb-aimer to drop the bombs, and then for another couple of minutes to take the picture of where the bombs hit."

Curtis then collapsed. The air bomber, Flying Officer Douglas McGillivray, took over the controls although he had never previously landed an aircraft, much less a four-engine Lancaster. With the help of the remaining crew members he brought the craft home, managing an emergency landing despite having a tire, that had been hit by flak, burst on landing.

The entire crew was decorated for the feat of fulfilling their objective and returning the plane home with their pilot unconscious. Curtis received the DSO. "I don't know of any other crew when all the living members were given a decoration for one incident," Hull added.[28]

It was a brave apology to the men in Hautmesnil Quarry.

18

JUST ONE GUTSY LEADER

The battle from Caen to Falaise had been a bitter two-week drive, ridge by bloody ridge, mile by grudging mile, across the rolling cornfields of the Caen plain.

Simonds' *Operation Tractable*—propelling some fifteen thousand men and their armour across the Laison River under a mask of smoke—had been an innovative success. In this battle of attrition, the Laison Valley victory, one of the most remarkable assault operations in the war, leapfrogged the Allies a vital five miles. They were at last within striking distance of Falaise and Trun, their objectives for so many weeks.

Just one more ridge to conquer. Just one more river to cross.

But from here on, the drive to close the gap became a deadly struggle.

Despite the near annihilation of German 85th Division on 14 August, the 88mm guns of Luftwaffe General Pickert's 3rd Flak Corps continued to create a curtain of formidable fire. It was virtually impossible for the Allies to advance in broad daylight across open country against an enemy with well-sited and dug-in anti-tank guns overlooking the battlefield. Minefields covered by the anti-tank weapons also slowed progress.

The enemy panzers still roamed the heights as predators. At Soulangy, the Fort Garry Horse lost six tanks to the gun of a single Tiger in the space of a few minutes.[1]

With no thought now of winning, the Wehrmacht tactics were designed to create major delays in the Allied advance. Buying time was what it was all about: time to permit the orderly retreat to the Seine of all non-combative units; time to keep the narrowing neck of the Falaise Gap open long enough to allow the panzer units still escaping from Mortain to elude the Allied encirclement.

"The German habit of leaving snipers and machine-gunners as

ambushers could be both tough and expensive," the Queen's Own Cameron Highlanders war diary noted. "Two or three men could hold a battalion up for hours."[2]

A German panzer officer, Helmut Ritgen, described their tactics: "We always tried to delay them and we succeeded. We erected road-blocks just from leaves, twigs of trees, flower boxes and so forth, which we took off the houses. We put them on the road. Then we painted a sign ACHTUNG MIENEN! [Beware of Mines]."[3] That bought the German army more time, too.

As they fell back from the Laison, the Germans firmly entrenched a new defensive line some three miles north and north-east of Falaise. The accepted battle-school wisdom dictated that the attacker must have three to five times the strength of the defender to over-come a well-dug-in defensive force.

The Allies had nothing like those numbers.

First Canadian Army's battalions were at half strength. Exhausted troops were fighting with determination and little hope of immedi-ate rest. Casualties among officers created strange command situa-tions: majors became acting commanding officers; lieutenants took over companies; and sergeants or corporals led platoons.

There were no easy answers. Hulks of smouldering Shermans dotting the landscape gave mute evidence of that. Allied recovery units cannibalized parts from wrecks to keep the armour going. Crews frantically welded on extra tracks to give added protection to tanks inadequate in this static warfare.

Although squadrons and battalions faltered at times in the face of dogged resistance, individuals shone. The skill to lead and the passion to win were never more evident.

In battle, it is the leaders who inspire the men to fight. The Normandy fighting saw more than a dozen Canadian commanding officers killed, wounded, or replaced. In just one twenty-four-hour period, three commanders of the Governor General's Foot Guards were killed or wounded. Fourth Armoured Brigade lost three commanders to wounds; one, Brigadier Leslie Booth, was killed. The commander of 3rd Canadian Infantry Division, Major-General Rod Keller, was severely wounded. This turn-over of command upset the continuity of leadership style and rocked the solid confi-dence within the battalions.

The Glens (Stormont, Dundas and Glengarry Highlanders) watched sullenly as the commanding officer who had led them onto the D-Day beaches, Lieutenant-Colonel G. H. Christiansen, was summarily dismissed from his command. Lieutenant-Colonel Roger Rowley was parachuted into the job. Just turned thirty, with a major operation to launch (*Totalize*) in just three days, Rowley had some eight hundred somewhat resentful front-line soldiers with whom to forge a new relationship that could mean life or death to them all.

"They loved their CO, Christiansen, and they were mad because he was fired," Rowley explains. "So they didn't like me. The only two people I knew when I arrived at battalion headquarters were my driver and my batman, and I brought them both with me. I had a pretty rough time there for a while, but we got along well at the end."[4]

The eighteenth-century Château d'Assy, pleasantly situated in an orchard bordering the Laison River, was the assigned objective for the Glens. It was also a fortified defensive strongpoint of 1053rd Regiment, a horse-drawn unit in Fiebig's 85th Division.

The Canadians warily crossed a shell-cratered moonscape of littered human remains and pieces of horseflesh. Shattered apple trees, now stripped of their young fruit and blackened, stood among the craters. Rowley's men swiftly cleared the château and rounded up the prisoners.

A young Glen reinforcement, new to the line, spotted a German Tiger tank that had suddenly appeared two hundred yards away. Turning to his company commander in the passenger seat of a Bren carrier, he asked, "Sir, is that one of ours?"

"If it isn't, we've had it!" the major snapped. A moment later an 88mm shell crashed into the carrier. The officer was instantly killed; the private leapt safely into a ditch amid machine gun fire.

Rowley, up forward as usual with his lead companies, called for fire from a nearby 6-pound anti-tank gun, and the tank was dispatched. But the well-dug-in enemy machine gun nests stubbornly kept the Canadians at bay. Rowley ordered the "Wasps" to attack. These flame-throwing Bren carriers could wreak fearful damage, hosing liquid fire on positions more than forty yards away.

The sight and sound of seared and screaming dead and dying

victims of this deadly weapon would live long in the minds of the young soldiers.

As darkness drew in, Colonel Rowley was in a dangerous position. His left flank was wide open, and he was out of communication with Rockingham's brigade headquarters. He established his command post in the château's pitch-dark wine cellar. It was a sinister place, made more eerie by the head of a dead horse plastered like some grotesque carving over its entrance. The floor was awash in wine from burst vats.

Finally, communication was restored with brigade and M10 tank destroyers were sent up to knock out some five Tigers that had been stalking the regiment.

"We were the only guys who got there and stayed there," Rowley would say of the battalion's efforts in capturing and holding its objective. "That was one tricky battle."[5]

The achievement of bonding eight hundred fatigued and dissatisfied men into a smooth-running effective machine capable of holding off German panzers—all in less than two weeks—had been one tricky feat for the thirty-year-old commander.

In this sense, the battle for Falaise became a series of outstanding acts of initiative by small groups of riflemen—or by *just one gutsy leader*.

Lying in ambush on the high ground above Falaise—Hill 159—Kurt Meyer was ready to pounce on the leaderless 4th Canadian Armoured Division. He observed the Canadian Grenadier Guards and the reconstituted British Columbia Regiment moving up Hill 159. He was aware, too, that the Americans had just captured Alençon and were closing in from the south. It was imperative that he hold the line as long as possible if the German Seventh Army was to have any hope of escaping the trap.[6] The terrain made his task easier: rolling wooded country studded with stone farmhouses that offered good defensive positions, and fortified ridges.

"Hill 159 is a boiling mountain," Meyer reported. "Shell after shell explodes around us." The Hitlerjugend commander, wounded in the head by a shell splinter, continued to tough it out "with a half-shaved head and a couple of stitches."[7] Meyer ordered 3rd SS

Artillery Battalion to open fire. The multi-purpose 88mm guns pinned down the Canadians. The Grenadier Guards were reduced from fifty-six to thirty-nine tanks.

Meanwhile, the Canadian Scottish Regiment was also moving towards the coveted hills above Falaise. Heavy mortar fire poured down on the Canscots, and their supporting tanks came under intense anti-tank fire, driving them back.[8]

Their war diary describes the grim encounter with a 12th SS battlegroup: "All ranks of the Scottish now stepped into a molten fire bath of battle. They were tired, hungry, and thirsty. These conditions made them doubly mad.

"The SS defenders fought back bitterly but could not stop the momentum of the [Canscot] advance. Few prisoners were taken; the enemy preferred to die rather than give in. [German] snipers were posted along hedgerows covering each tiny field with rifles and MG-42s.

"B Coy [Company] slugged its way through all opposition to be the first company to consolidate on its objective, where they were counter-attacked by Tiger tanks and armoured cars."[9]

A bitter action now took place. So close was the fighting that the Canadian Scottish ducked for cover underneath the hostile tanks that were milling around them through the rocks and hedges of the heights. From the midst of the chaotic violence, "B" Company yelled over the radio net for tank support. The only reply that came through to them was a BBC announcer benignly introducing the program "Music While You Work."[10]

But if the Germans were determined, so also were the Canadian Scottish, who pushed stubbornly on despite their losses. Company Sergeant-Major J.S. Grimmond won the Distinguished Conduct Medal by leading his company headquarters against two German tanks and supporting infantry.[11] *Just one gutsy leader.*

But the price was high. By 1645 hours, one company was halved to forty-six. The thirty-seven men killed and ninety-three wounded marked the most costly day of the Normandy campaign for the Canscots.[12]

*

A mile or so east of that attack, the Winnipeg Rifles had similar success with an assault on the ridge. The company commander, Captain Cliff Chadderton, noted in his diary, "I gave the okay and we went up the hill after I had ordered some smoke and covering fire from the Garrys [Fort Garry Horse]. We got onto the objective (four or five farm buildings) and took eighteen to thirty prisoners. Great big mystery—there were two SS *feldwebels* [sergeants] but the rest were from ordinary [Wehrmacht] divisions."[13] This, in fact, was more evidence of Meyer's tactic of inserting small combat groups of his 12th SS into ordinary infantry companies to "stiffen" them.

Still further east, 51st Highland Division provided left flank support for the Canadians. The Highlanders approached St. Pierre-sur-Dives, a picturesque riverside village. (A lustful Scot, not under-standing the French pronunciation "Deeves," chortled, "Dives! Real French dives at last!")[14] Meanwhile, 1st Polish Armoured Division seized a crossing of the same river at Jort following a bitter fight.

The eastern arm of the Allied encirclement was inexorably clos-ing in towards Trun and Chambois, the Germans' escape route.

On the night of 15 August, the Highland Division padre N.F. Jones wrote in his diary:

> *Tuesday we eventually moved to South of St. Sylvain. We found some lovely Jerry gun sites with slit trenches. We spent quite some time digging in the half-track & then getting our own slit trenches ready. It was just as well. When night came we had a concentrated Jerry bombing all round. This was coincident with the first heavy downpour for some time. It was the most uncom-fortable night I've spent for years as the rain poured into my trench. In the morning the sun came out quickly & we managed to dry out.*[15]

The Luftwaffe maintained a rare patrol over the Falaise area that night, dropping clusters of parachute flares, a prelude to anti-personnel bombing raids. The skies would suddenly fill with a virtual blizzard: thousands of whirling white phosphorous frag-ments, each no larger than a bar of soap, tumbled down. Lieutenant Robert Weiss of the U.S. army recalled the horror of it: "Where the particles landed on shirts and trousers they sizzled and burned. We brushed our clothing frantically . . . If any of the stuff touched the skin; it could inflict a horrible burn, increasing in intensity as it burrowed into a man's flesh . . . Another shell. Another missile from hell. Fiery snow!"[16]

A young Canadian lieutenant, Edward Glass, a Canloan officer newly arrived in Normandy, had moved into position minutes before. He had just sent off a letter to the commanding officer of his regiment in Toronto, 48th Highlanders, telling them of the warm welcome he had received by the affiliated British regiment, the Gordons, when he arrived ten days ago.

"The CO has insisted that I wear our regimental flash alongside their own," he reported proudly.[17]

Gazing skyward in astonishment Glass saw the white slivers cascading down, almost like a Canadian snowfall. Then he heard an eerie swishing noise as the shower came through the air . . . and his final sound on earth: the steady drumming as they exploded.

The Highlanders dived for their slits. Major Martin Lindsay, acting CO of 1st Gordons, recorded the next moments. "Unfortunately "D" Company, the last to arrive, had only dug down about eighteen inches by this time and they had twenty-three casualties. Most were only lightly wounded, but two were killed and one of them was Glass, the young Canadian officer who came to us ten days ago."[18]

It was a deadly blizzard.

On 15 August, General Simonds ordered 6th Canadian Infantry Brigade to capture Falaise. Immediately!

The proud home of William the Conqueror was in ruins. The twelfth-century castle where he was born was perched on a high rock (or *falaise*, giving the town its name). Allied bombing and shelling had made the roads through the historic town almost impassable.

Fanatical young SS Hitlerjugend snipers were sheltered behind broken walls or in ruins of buildings. They knew that in savage street fighting, a single machine gun could hold up an entire battalion. This was their mission: to delay the attackers as long as possible so that other panzer units could escape the Allies' net.

A German anti-tank gun at the gates to the town had pinned down and stopped the South Saskatchewan Regiment, moving in from the west. The squadron commander of the supporting Sherbrooke Fusiliers, Major Radley-Walters, was astonished to see a lone man running forward from the rear of the battalion. After a sprint of several hundred yards, this unknown soldier reached the forward company, dropped to the ground, and opened fire at the anti-tank gun, silencing it.

After that astonishing feat, without a word of command from anybody, the infantry and tanks came to life. They leapt to a renewed attack and, within minutes, were pouring into the town square.

"It was a fine example of one man moving the whole bloody battalion without a word, just through his own example," Radley-Walters notes. "That man was Lieutenant-Colonel Freddie Clift, the CO of the South Saskatchewans."[19] *Just one gutsy leader*.

It was now 2300 hours and the battalion had penetrated the town. They reached the château square, still under heavy fire and surrounded by snipers firing on all sides from the upper windows of the buildings.

Clift saw one of his company commanders shot between the eyes, the bullet exiting from behind his left ear. That decided him. "We can't stay here all night, being shot at," he told his staff. "Line the battalion up, put the forward platoons in carriers and we'll charge straight through to the far side of the town."

The plan worked. Clift himself climbed aboard the forward carrier to direct the attack. He noted a large house on his map, laid on a hasty flank assault, and captured what turned out to be the enemy headquarters.

A brigade staff officer advised him that it would be safer to press on out of town. "That's bullshit," the doughty commander bellowed. "My boys haven't slept for thirty hours. We'll set up defences right here."[20]

The man who had single-handedly inspired his troops to fight was clearly able to demonstrate his compassion for them.

Next morning the Cameron Highlanders of Canada broke into the town, their supporting Sherbrooke tanks having been held up by huge craters. Then it was up to Les Fusiliers Mont-Royal to mop up the last resistance.

12th SS commander Bernhard Krause ordered his Hitlerjugend troops to withdraw. The order failed to reach a group of SS Grenadiers holed up behind the thick stone walls of the École Superieure.

The band of some fifty or sixty young Nazis hung on until dawn. Their NCO held a ballot to decide which two would be sent out to report to Sturmbannführer (Major) Krause. A ballot was necessary because not one of the SS wanted to leave his comrades in this last fight.

When the Fusiliers stormed the fortification at 0200 hours, setting fire to the buildings and plastering the school with machine gun fire, they found only the corpses of the defenders.

The battle for Falaise was won. But a twelve-mile gap was still open. Chambois and Trun had become the keys to sealing the trap on the escaping enemy.

19

THE TYPHIES
AND THEIR
LOVABLE ERKS

When the early morning mist lifted on 17 August, pilots on a routine reconnaissance sweep rubbed their eyes in disbelief. Below them, across the entire twelve-mile width of the Dives Valley between Falaise and Argentan, the German Seventh Army was executing a mass exodus.

No. 35 Wing, RAF, the tactical reconnaissance wing providing intelligence to ground forces, heralded what was to be "three days of the largest scale movement, presenting such targets to Allied air power as has hitherto only been dreamed of."[1] It was a stunning sight. Thousands of trucks, armoured vehicles, half-tracks, ambulances, horse-drawn carts, and even soldiers on bicycles and on foot, were nose-to-tail three abreast, on every road and country lane that led to the east.

The final order Kluge had given before he swallowed the cyanide capsule—the evacuation of all non-essential units—was being executed to the fullest measure. Some 65,000 non-combatant soldiers had been steadily evacuating their administrative and rear-echelon units, making their way out in horse-drawn carts or on foot. Only combat troops and their key headquarters staff were left in the trap.

For the first time, the Germans did not limit their troop movement to nighttime. They wanted *out*—and were prepared to sacrifice untold lives to achieve this. The retreat was on; the rout was yet to come.

The reconnaissance fighter planes were the eyes and ears of the army; their camera shutters clicked furiously as they catalogued the catch. As historian Christopher Evans noted, "They kept a general watch on road and rail movement and on shipping. They flew over rivers to observe barge movement, bridging and ferrying sites; they made detailed searches of specific areas at the request of 21 Army Group to detect possible concentrations for counter-attacks. They also carried out intelligence missions in search of gun sites, dumps, supply centres, etc., and for purposes of bomb damage assessment.

"A measure of just how active reconnaissance aircraft were during the campaign is the sheer volume of photographs taken in such a short span of time: 1,481,000 prints were produced during the Normandy campaign.

"These photographs were distributed widely, often down to the platoon level, providing the ground forces with up-to-date information on enemy dispositions, thereby allowing for a more informed plan of attack. Information was to come from other sources too. With fighter aircraft operating almost constantly over forward enemy positions on other missions they constantly reported back on what they saw, supplementing the dedicated reconnaissance squadrons many times over."[2]

Thus alerted, Allied fighter squadrons based across France raced for the kill. Hundreds of fighter-bombers swarmed the skies: American Thunderbolts, Mustangs and Lightnings, and British and Canadian Spitfires and Typhoons.

For almost three months of the Normandy campaign, these pilots had stalked their prey. They had done incalculable damage to the enemy and his morale, knocking out hundreds of tanks, armoured vehicles, and self-propelled guns. Equally important, they had intimidated the Germans to such a degree that, as the weeks of the Normandy campaign wore on, the enemy increasingly dared not risk daylight movement.

The costs to the Allied air forces had been massive. The Luftwaffe's anti-aircraft guns had shot down or damaged a large percentage of the total available fighter aircraft since D-Day. Whole squadrons had been replaced. But Typhoon casualties were by far the highest: 151 men had been killed. That represented losses of 128 per cent in three months. All of the wings had experienced soaring losses.[3]

*

In the face of statistics like that, what kinds of men would voluntarily hurtle through the skies, bearing tons of explosives in highly vulnerable craft, with hundreds of potent guns waiting to blow them up?

Airmen had always been a little different from the other arms of military service. They wore rather spiffily tailored dress uniforms; the foot soldier rarely got to change his socks in mid-battle. In a single day their experiences could swing wildly, from the terror of being hit by flak to flying a damaged airplane home, to seeing their friends die in an exploding aircraft, to enjoying a cold beer and a good dinner that same night. The doughboys spent the day in sodden slits. Their dinner was C-rations.

The airmen even had their own vernacular, graphically described by air historian Hugh Halliday.

> A "gong" was a decoration, "gen" was information, "ropey" and "dicey" were adjectives for dangerous . . . If there was a "flap" on, the situation was confused or unpleasant. On a patrol one might report a "bogey" (unidentified aircraft) which could turn out to be a "bandit" (hostile aircraft). If a man had been jilted by his girl, the men would nod their heads wisely and say, "Poor old so-and-so. He was shot down in flames by his popsy." A flyer who had been killed or was reported missing had "gone west," "bought it" or "gone for a Burton." Supply officers were "grocers," scientists were "boffins," the intelligence officer was referred to as "the spy" or "the Gestapo," soldiers became "pongos" or "brown jobs," and sailors were "blue jobs."[4]

There was one other essential difference between air and ground troops. While the latter had to cope with just one enemy—the Germans—the airman had two: the Germans and the elements—wind, rain, hail, fog, and dust.

As air bases were hastily established on the Normandy beachhead, the dry, hot August weather was causing another serious problem: dust. When the planes' wheels touched the landing strips, a fine dust, inches thick, rose like a cloud, infiltrating and damaging the motors and firing mechanisms of cannons and guns.

Allied engineers who constructed the landing strips even tried spraying the field with water or oil to keep the dust down.[5] Ingestion of these particles of sand and dust also had disastrous results on the cannons, causing misfiring and structural failure. "Stoppages were always a problem," Bill Baggs of 164 Typhoon Squadron, RAF, said.

The mechanics who toiled all night to get the plane serviceable for the next-day's combat were "loveable erks." Their bosses became "chiefies."[5]

It was those magnificent Typhoon mechanics who made significant contributions in solving the problems. One such erk became known among his peers as "The Hero of the Falaise Gap."

David Raymond Davies was a leading aircraftsman (LAC) with 123 Rocket projectile (RP) Wing, which operated Typhoons. His expertise was as an armourer for the 20mm cannon. When cannon stoppage became a serious problem, someone figured out that Davies' squadron, number 183, was experiencing fewer cannon stoppages than the others operating in the same sandy conditions of the beachhead airstrips.

Davies' grandson, Dr. Jonathan E.C. Tan of Muncaster, England, gives this account:

> They sent a senior armament officer from the U.K. to investigate. He discovered that in setting up the rounds of 20mm cannon on his workbench, Davies had positioned the ammunition slightly in advance of the specified settings. The consequence was that the cannons had been firing slightly faster and had thus let less sand/dust into the firing mechanisms.

When these new settings were communicated throughout the group, Davies earned his justifiable reputation.[7]

Davies' resourcefulness was also exercised—somewhat cunningly—in speeding up the work crews charged with breaking open and unpacking urgently needed ammunition. Dr. Tan recalls:

> My grandfather and his closest comrade came up with a plan. They slipped a spurious "letter from home" that they penned into one ammunition box. The letter supposedly was from a young lady, working in a munitions factory, thinking about the boys out there. The next day, the letter was "found" with much shouting and prompting from the two partners in mischief.

Never had they seen men work so fast, tearing open all the other ammunition boxes in the hope of finding further letters.[8]

Each type of aircraft had a specific role. Typhoons were used mainly against tanks and strong points. The Spitfire's was to ensure air superiority, safeguarding the devastating, low-diving Typhoons from Luftwaffe harassment. Spits also did armed reconnaissance and performed fighter-bomber attacks against troops and trucks, or "targets of opportunity." The Spit carried two 20mm cannons and two Browning machine guns, and could also carry one 500-pound bomb or two 250-pound bombs. The Typhoon or "Tiffy" had eight rockets with 60-pound warheads or two 500- or 1,000-pound bombs, as well as four 20mm cannons.

A third British fighter plane, the fast and deadly Mosquito, had an all-plywood structure. Its specialty was as a night intruder, hunting down German night fighters that preyed on RAF bombers. For one month, from just after D-Day until the RAF destroyed the launching pads, the "Mossies" intercepted Hitler's terror weapon, the lethal V-1 "Doodlebugs" that rained so much havoc on the English in 1944, killing 5,500 civilians and injuring 16,000 more.

A Canadian ace, Wing Commander Russ Bannock, was one of the fifty thousand Canadians in the Commonwealth Air Training Plan. He set something of a record for kills. His Mosquito, "Hairless Joe," carried a long string of swastikas and V-1 symbols to indicate his tally: nineteen flying bombs destroyed (plus eleven enemy aircraft shot down). That actually made him a double ace. His technique was uniquely Canadian: "I used my duck-shooting experience," he admitted. "You had to shoot the V-1s from the side. If you shot them from the back, the resulting explosion could knock your aircraft out, too."[9]

Their fellow Spitfire airmen were confused when the Warren twins, Bruce and Douglas, checked in at B-16, one of Normandy's first operational airstrips.

"What is your name?" an airman would ask one of the twins.

"Duke," was the reply.

"Well what's *your* name?" the other brother would be asked.

"Duke," again, was the reply.

The twins were used to the confusion about their names. It had begun in the first grade; "Our teacher, trying to explain that we were identical twins, said we were duplicates of one another," Warren said. In the playground, the word was transposed and the brothers were called, none too kindly, "Dupes." After "a bit of persuasion," the nickname was softened to "Duke." It stuck for both of them.

So, here at B-16, at the height of the Normandy battle, were two "Dukes." Solution? "My twin was called Duke Mark I (he arrived there first). I was Duke Mark II."

But they never called each other by name; they didn't need to. Their communication was so intuitive they could finish each other's sentences.

Both men, now twenty-two, were skilled and experienced fighter pilots and flight commanders. Initially they flew the single-pilot Spitfires as a section of two. "It was excellent as we had complete confidence in the other's ability," Duke Mark II explained. Even when flying in different sections, they still managed to watch out for each other. But they made a pact: if one of them was shot down or killed, the other would not go "foolish" in a rage.

They both knew the risks. "Low-level attacks by their nature were dangerous," Duke Mark II recalled. "The flak was plentiful and accurate." Losses had been heavy. When hit at low altitude, there was very little time to bail out.[10]

Flight Lieutenant Roy A. Crane, a pilot in 124 Typhoon Wing, was lucky. He managed to get his parachute open:

> On the 2nd of August 1944 I was shot down after twice being hit by flak near Falaise, parachuting from low level into a German SS camp and was quickly surrounded by about twenty hostile SS. I was rescued by the German air force gun crew, one an *Oberfeldwebel*, who had shot me down. Later I was taken in an open staff car with an armed motorcycle escort. We had only travelled a short distance when, passing some German tanks in a wooded valley, we were signalled to stop by German soldiers standing as lookouts under some trees. Much panic ensued and I was pushed by the *Oberfeldwebel* into a ditch. It was quickly evident we were being attacked by Typhoons which came round again, and again firing their rockets and cannons. I have since established there were six Typhoons being led by my best man,

Phil Strong, an Australian from 182 Squadron, who went out to seek revenge after hearing I had been reported killed.[11]

For the aircrews, the chase was on. The German exodus meant that the flak was lessening and the escaping Seventh Army provided endless targets of opportunity. At first the Allied tactical air forces were restricted from harassing the fleeing troops and their vehicles by the constraints of the bomb-line in the valley. But a special arrangement with the Allied armies opened up these targets to an "August bank holiday" of Spitfires, Thunderbolts, and Typhoons, careening and wildly diving over the valley. For three days, operating in almost perfect flying conditions, hundreds of fighter-bombers converged on the narrow country lanes where a hapless enemy was attempting to escape in increasingly chaotic conditions.

Action reached its most intensive pitch on 18 August. All day long, the Allied tactical air force attacked the German columns that jammed the roads, flying more than three thousand sorties that day. The possibilities of mid-air collision were enormous.

Maintaining the aircraft under such intensive use was a Herculean effort. Again, the "lovable erks" came to the rescue. One Typhoon squadron's history describes the challenges: "Amidst the dust and noise, the erks performed minor miracles of servicing and repair. Aircraft could be refueled and repaired in eight to nine minutes; propeller changes were made in forty-five minutes; radios were changed in less than ten."[12]

The air became filled with the screech of airplanes and the thunder of the artillery as the Allies pounded the escaping enemy. Although the Germans clung to the shelter of wooded paths, narrow twisting lanes and sunken hedgerows, terrible damage was inflicted on them and on the once-beautiful Dives Valley.

Duke and his twin especially felt the anguish of the animals. "When we attacked horse-drawn transport along with staff cars and trucks, the German soldiers would hold the horses' bridles as the horses reared in fright and pain. Duke and I, having grown up on a farm with an intimate knowledge of horses, felt specially sorry for the animals because they could not understand what was happening to them."[13]

A Canadian officer who was captured but escaped two days later described what he saw in the Falaise Gap on 18 August: "All roads, and particularly the byways, were crowded with transport two abreast, grinding forward.

"Everywhere there were tanks and vehicles towing what they could. And everywhere there was menace in the air. . . . On many vehicles an air sentry rode on the mudguard. At the sound of a plane every vehicle went into the side of the road and all personnel ran for their lives. The damage was immense and flaming transport and dead horses were left in the road while the occupants pressed on, afoot."

The officer also noted a phenomenon that had been blatantly obvious to many Allied troops throughout the Normandy campaign: the enemy's misuse of the Red Cross. "There were Red Cross signs everywhere—on staff cars, and even on ammunition vehicles."[14] The airmen were furious to confirm that some able-bodied German troops were being brought out in ambulances.

Flight Lieutenant Cecil Brown, a renowned Spitfire pilot, related the quickly improvised solution: "We would send one pilot down, not firing, just to make a simulated attack on an ambulance. When the back doors opened and troops started to bail out, the rest of us would come down behind and let them have it.

They didn't do that very long. We massacred those [fake] ambulances."[15]

20

CHEERS!

As the weeks of anguished fighting went on, keeping up the soldiers' morale became increasingly important. The comforting reminders of home—warm meals, clean clothes, family letters, and, above all else, peaceful rest—took top priorities as morale boosters to the troops.

Food, though plain, was ample. Front-line men were issued "Compo Rations," boxes each containing enough food for seven men for two days (or fourteen men for one day). They usually contained an assortment of M and V (tinned meat and vegetables), dried fruit, biscuits, and pudding (different each time). "Finding you've been given the one with the can of peaches is like winning a lottery," Canadian gunner Captain George Blackburn recalls.[1]

As well, coffee, powdered milk, sweets, cigarettes, and toilet paper were included. The British added "compo tea"—cubes containing a dried pre-mix of tea, milk, and sugar. But the Americans had the best, as one Canadian soldier noted in disgust: "Them buggers know how to do things. You seen their fuckin' K-Rations? They get Spam and beef stew and coffee. We get jeezly bully beef and tea! Shee-it!"[2]

Finding fresh food was an ongoing challenge. Highland Light Infantry padre and honorary captain Jock Anderson believed in loot—of an edible and legal sort. He still remembers a sack of fresh baby potatoes which he found dug up by tank treads on a French farmer's field: "They were wonderful; you will never have any idea what they tasted like until you haven't had anything fresh for a long time."[3] Major Ray Hodgins recalls that "Jock also managed to get hold of a crock of real farm butter that he'd share out with any of us."[4]

Bartering for food went on everywhere, sometimes in a very lopsided way that reflected the extraordinary needs of both parties. One soldier managed the bargain of a lifetime: a chicken in exchange for two boxes of matches. Many others swapped compo ration edibles for eggs and milk. A Middlesex officer saw an elderly French woman standing in the doorway of her cottage munching an army hardtack biscuit. "Les gateaux anglais sont magnifiques," she said to him.[5]

The padre was probably the only man ever to swap a jeep for one dozen eggs. It happened this way: a German major who was taken prisoner had somewhat reluctantly handed over an amphibious German vehicle in good condition. After driving it for some time, Anderson learned that anyone caught operating a German vehicle would be put on charge. He went to a Frenchman's farm. "I'll give you this car for one dozen eggs," he offered. "The farmer said that was a deal if we would help him hide it up in his loft. So we hauled the thing up, covered it with hay and we got our dozen eggs."[6]

The importance of fresh food for the troops was appreciated even at the highest levels. Company commanders learned to look the other way when the squawking of a chicken was soon replaced by the heady aroma of *ragoût de poulet* wafting from behind a barn. When Lieutenant-General Sir Brian Horrocks took command of British 30 Corps in Normandy, he was startled to find himself also commanding a barnyard of chickens and cows. There were so many stray cows and so much poultry wandering loose in bomb-shattered Normandy, that 30 Corps troops who had been farmers before going to war were put in charge of collecting them for a kind of mobile farm. "We were thus able to supply our casualty clearing station with fresh eggs, milk, and meat," Horrocks noted with satisfaction.[7]

Letters home revealed how the men rated their daily fare. Of 5,219 examined by the censors, only one complained of poor food:

> *"Food is getting better every day. Fresh meat every day is more than we ever expected when we left England."*
>
> *"All our food is canned and it is monotonous. It's good and wholesome and well cooked and served, but one would appreciate a change to fresh meat and vegetables."*
>
> *"The only hardships are lack of fresh vegetables and meat, also bread. We've been living on compo rations for quite a while now. They're quite good and miles ahead of the last war."*[8]

However, food brings out strange attitudes in men. A British signaller reported a near mutiny when officers in his unit invited a troupe of entertainers for dinner, "serving specially cooked pies and other delicacies," while the other ranks resentfully chewed their compo rations.[9] Another man, a Royal Air Force pilot, dropped his Mars Bars ration from the plane every time he flew over Germany. He knew it was a vain hope that one might somehow get to his brother, who was a prisoner of war there—but it made him feel better to make the gesture.

It also brought out a strange bravado in front line troops. The U.S. 743rd Tank Battalion history describes an incident where one man, Sergeant Perry "Cock" Kelly, seemingly thought that a cup of good old American coffee was worth risking his life for: "When mail call included a sister's present of real coffee, Cock treated it as the treasure it was, but discovered nothing was stowed in his new tank in which to prepare it. He spied a nearby bombed-out farmhouse and set off, trudging across the open field between tank and farmstead."

On his way back, Cock came under mortar fire. Tucking the pot against his chest "he broke into a run propelled by fear, zigzagging, ducking, and turning as exploding mortar shells stalked their elusive target. Corrected for distance, each shell measured Cock's progress across the field. With each explosion that rained stones, the pot was hugged even tighter until they reached the safety of the trees protecting the tank."

As he blissfully sipped his hard-won brew the next morning, the intrepid sergeant realized how close a call it had been: the backs of his legs were tattooed with shell splinters.[10]

Fiery Calvados—it being after all a Norman product—was easier to come by than coffee. French hard cider, too, could be "liberated" from almost any farm cellar. A tot of rum, and even occasional bottles of beer, were issued on occasion, especially before a battle. Many of the younger soldiers, being of the recession era or just out of school, were unused to the potent drinks and sometimes it showed. As one seasoned front-line commander noted, "a steady diet of cider with the occasional shot of Calvados kept me awake on long night watches."[11]

Curiously, soldiers were given a tot of rum *before* they went into battle; air crew were given theirs *after* a raid.

Increasingly, though, as the humid weather set in, water became the most important thing of all. "Men can fight without food, but not without water," wrote the *Wyvern News*—a chatty front-line newsletter for the men of British 43rd Division: "British infantry who have tramped and fought in the choking dust that has often lain over the roads and battle areas will tell you that the next best thing to the old pub at home is the 'Water Point' on the Normandy road-side—the mobile water pumping and purifying unit which provides the only safe water supply for the troops in the forward areas.

"There have been days in Normandy when the unending convoys, and the rumbling tank squadrons on the move, have covered the roadside hedges and the fields alongside with a thick layer of dust. Through it all have come the marching troops—appearing like workers in a flour mill."

A team of four men established one water point for the 43rd Wessex infantrymen within three-quarters of a mile of the German positions, providing 58,000 gallons of water a day while under constant fire from "Oscar"—their flippant term for the enemy mortar.

"There's 'Old Faithful,'" a corporal of London-Irish extraction boasted of their purifying plant. "Oscar knocked her about a bit—she's like a sponge. We plugged the shrapnel holes with bits of rag and wood. She's taken more bashings than I'd like to take—and she's still grinning."[12]

Understandably, to men whose skin has been imbedded with dust and grime for days or weeks at a time, mobile baths and laundries set up at "A" echelon, not far behind the front, meant a lot to the men. The Ordinance Corps, a seldom-recognized service arm that brought up all such services and supplies, played a huge role in maintaining troop morale. A private soldier in the Royal Regiment of Canada wrote home happily: "We went for a complete change of clothes and a shower. We went in one end of the tent dirty as a coal bin and came out the other end looking like a new recruit in his first uniform. We felt 100 per cent better afterward."[13]

Even on the front lines, the men were encouraged to wash and shave. "The platoon seldom went unshaven," a British officer in the 43rd Wessex observed. "Never once did I have to reprimand a man for uncleanliness." However, proximity to enemy lines did make for primitive toilet arrangements. "Newspapers and food cans were our resort."[14]

The outgoing mail from the front was censored for security reasons. But the censors also noted factors in the letters—gripes or elation—that could influence a soldier's morale. They read time and again how widely the men appreciated the Postal Corps. These men braved enemy fire to deliver news from home to the front. Allied troops got letters from mothers, wives and friends in incredible speed. Mail arrived from the U.K. in two to three days. ("What a lovely letter is yours of the 26th. And here it is the 28th!")

From Canada and the United States, it took six to nine days. ("Our mail from home is coming first rate, which sure is a blessing. Out here a letter is a million times more precious than gold.")[15]

Royal Hamilton Light Infantry private Bill Grant wondered at some of the strange things people from home would send. "The other day I received from my old Scout leader a book called *Rovering to Success*. The book cautioned me to eschew tobacco, strong drink, loose women and bad language—suggestions not too relevant to my present situation."[16]

No matter how tough the campaign, how imminent the battle, there came a time when it was imperative to give the men a respite, however brief, from the anguish of war. An effort was made to take every unit out of combat periodically to specially set up rest centres. "Out of the line at rest at last! Really out, after fifty-four days and I've worn pyjamas for two nights running and have been in bed ALL night long! It's marvellous. The men are like kids out of school and the officers much the same."[17]

The troops were also given a few hours of fun by stars of the entertainment world. No prima donnas here; they sacrificed comfort for comforting. The YMCA and the Salvation Army produced glitzy Hollywood and London show personalities like Lana Turner and Edward G. Robinson. George Formby held a concert for five thousand men ("a bit vulgar," one officer confided to his diary) and films shown on the mobile cinema were a popular feature—even reruns.

"You should see our theatre here," a private soldier from the Calgary Highlanders raved to his mom. "The only place in one piece that was large enough was the stable and in no time we had it all set up with about fifty chairs and the show was on."[18]

American troops got a kick out of the Red Cross "donut wagons" driven to the front by U.S. volunteers. The 305th Engineer Combat Unit noted that "at Argentan the Red Cross Clubmobile visited the battalion with hot coffee and donuts and music. Four real American girls attended it. These were the first American girls any of us has had seen since our arrival in France. It was a real treat to see a petite *mademoiselle* who spoke English! Here we saw a movie for the first time, ten years old, but enjoyed by all."[19]

But for others, just sitting quietly under an apple tree without the incessant thunder of artillery was restorative. Northamptonshire Yeomanry lance-corporal Ken Tout described an evening when troopers—their tanks laagered for the night in a lull of battle—found solace tuning in to a BBC wavelength to listen to the Promenade Concert from London. "Into a five-man tank a dozen of us push and squeeze as though playing at sardines. Outside, another batch of Moaning Minnies screams and thunders down. Somebody closes the turret hatches. There are not enough headsets to go round. We could, of course, spread ourselves around several tanks with ample supplies of headsets. But that would not be such fun. It would not be in the spirit of the Proms."[20]

Front-line journalism came of age in World War II. The Allied countries had columnists and radio commentators whose professionalism and skill, often under fire, has seldom been matched. The United States had Ernest Hemingway (writing for *Colliers*), Ernie Pyle, and Bill Maudlin, creator of "Willie and Joe." Canadian war correspondents like Ralph Allen, Greg Clark, Charles Lynch, Wally Rayburn, Ross Munro, and Fred Griffin, and radio commentators like Matthew Halton, had equal expertise, as did British writers and news commentators such as Alan Moorehead, Chester Wilmot, and Richard Dimbleby.

Troops received home-town newspapers with amazing efficiency. But their front-page stories weren't always good for morale. The men followed the course of the war with a discerning eye, and sometimes disagreed with the wartime journalists' interpretation—especially if it had been focused on their particular battlefield. British soldiers receiving next day newspapers, or hearing the hourly BBC news broadcasts, became not a little disgruntled at the attention focused on Patton's Third Army's sensational breakout. The British units that had been slogging away, mile by agonizing mile, to distract German opposition from the American front to their own, got little attention. Canadians, curiously, felt ignored because of British achievements. ("Over here it is always what the Limeys do; you never hear about the Americans and Canadians at all . . . .")[21]

These resentments were alleviated to a large extent by the publications of Canadian and American army newspapers. Brigadier Richard Malone, founder of the *Maple Leaf*, bet (and won) a case of whisky from his American counterpart that his *Maple Leaf* Canadian newspaper, published in Normandy, would roll off the presses in Caen before the Yanks could produce the *Stars and Stripes* in Cherbourg: "Each time I saw the RAF bombs dropping on Caen, I prayed that they would miss my little newspaper plant," Malone grinned.[22]

The Canadian Army Film and Photographic Unit (CAFU) had fifty trained cameramen posted to operational filming on the continent. Of these, three were killed and several were seriously wounded. They received numerous awards for bravery, among them the Medal of the British Empire (MBE), the Military Medal (MM), and Mention in Dispatches (MID). On D-Day, several "firsts" were credited to the Canadian Army Film Unit. They were the first Allied cameramen to land on French soil, having been dropped in Normandy with the paratroops. They were also the first Allied cameramen to step ashore with the sea-borne assault troops; and the first to provide film of the landings, which was sent to London (in several hours) and to New York (in just over than a day).

The CAFU war dairy proudly claims that more than 2,100 individual stories had been shot. Many of them appeared in British, American, and Canadian newsreels and were also shown to our troops in action. Unhappily, a claim that "a permanent film record of the Canadian Army overseas is thus readily available for reference or reproduction in the future" turned out to be mere wishful thinking.[23]

The wire services of the three countries cooperated fully with one another. But reporters, under pressure from home-town editors to produce dynamic articles, occasionally got carried away. The unfolding saga of a young Canadian lad in Normandy who stumbled into international—if momentary—fame in the press illustrates the zealousness of stateside editors to develop a story.

It began with a small item filed by war correspondent Bill Wilson that was picked up by international media. A follow-up query to the Defence Department in Ottawa triggered this immediate cable to the Canadian Press Camp in Normandy: "Aug 22/44: US newsreel editors all much interested story today of Pte Earl McAllister, Canadian who according to Wilson BUP War Correspondent single handed captured 150 enemy near Trun thus outstripping Sergeant York. Stop. Suggest something special by Army Film Unit if rushed will make feature spot all newsreels. Stop. Advise soonest if anything done or can be so may be prepared for film getting special play."

Back came the reply next day: "Trying to obtain material. Will advise if successful."

And then another query from an anxious editor: "Is story now confirmed?"

While the search was on for the young man, McAllister—unit still unknown—was going about his war, innocently unaware of the furore. But the newsmen wouldn't let go. They wanted that story, even if they had to exaggerate or even stage it: "Reels scream for story even re-enactment of Private Earl McAllister of Hamilton capturing 160 [sic] armed Germans near Trun. This exceeds Sgt York's record."

On 25 August, the reply finally came: "McAllister prisoner story exaggerated but we are tracing him and will obtain some coverage." The outcome was this article published in New York by *Time* magazine:

"Hamilton's York. Canada At War," September 5, 1944
Last week Canada had its own Sergeant York—Pvt. Earl ("Scotty") McAllister, 21 and 5 ft. 3.

Scotty left his furniture factory job in Hamilton, Ont. two years ago, joined the R.C.A.F. Sidetracked from pilot training, first because of his small size, then because of an ear defect, he finally joined the army as a private.

In Normandy, reported United Pressman William Wilson, Scotty was driving down a road when six Germans crossed in front of him. He fired. The Germans surrendered. Then some

French resistance fighters told him there were more Germans in a nearby woods, asked him to send a tank. Said McAllister, "Tank, hell!" He walked to the woods alone, fired a few bursts from his Sten gun. Eighty-five fully-armed Germans emerged, threw down their arms. Then some Frenchmen told him that there was a Nazi tank farther down the road. It turned out to be an armored car escorted by 60 to 70 German soldiers. Scotty jumped into the armored car, ordered the Germans to surrender. They did.

Total catch, some 160 Germans, as compared with Sergeant York's bag of 132 Germans captured, a score killed, in one memorable day of World War I.

Said Scotty's mother (who has two other sons in the service): "It was just like we figured. We thought he had too much courage for his size. When he went away we said, 'Either he comes back a hero or he doesn't come back at all.' "[24]

No one was more thrilled than the parents of the twenty-one-year-old Canadian from Hamilton, Ontario, to see a hero's write-up, photo and all, in *Time* magazine. Scotty McAllister, a "hitherto anonymous Argyll," in actual fact became, briefly, the hero of his battalion by "bagging" one hundred (though not 160) POWs at St. Lambert-sur-Dives.

His buddies' pride and the spirit of comradeship that were engendered at the front were perhaps the greatest morale boosters of all.

Sadly, his mother's prophecy was not fulfilled. Scotty *did* become a hero; but he never came back. Promoted to the rank of sergeant, he fought "gallantly" until he was killed in action in Germany.

The Trun-Chambois Gap: 18 August

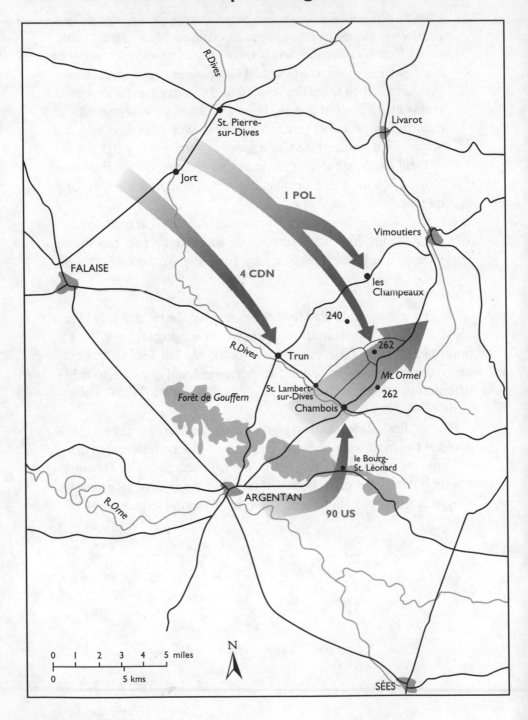

R.Dives

St. Pierre-
sur-Dives

Livarot

Jort

I POL

Vimoutiers

FALAISE

4 CDN

les
Champeaux

240

R.Dives

Trun

262

Mt. Ormel

St. Lambert-
sur-Dives

262

Forêt de Gouffern

Chambois

le Bourg-
St. Léonard

R.Orne

ARGENTAN

90 US

0 1 2 3 4 5 miles

N

0   5 kms

SÉES

"BLOODY WARSAW"

By the morning of 17 August 1944, the Allied senior commanders were beginning to realize just how many Germans were still trapped in the Falaise pocket. With the U.S. 90th Division blocked at Le Bourg-St. Léonard, it was up to the 4th Canadian and 1st Polish Armoured Divisions to close the gap. General Simonds issued firm orders: 1st Polish Division, he insisted, must thrust on past Trun to Chambois to meet the U.S. 90th Division "at all costs and as quickly as possible."[1]

Fifteen thousand men from 1st Polish Armoured Division had planted their feet on French soil on 1 August—the first step, they hoped, in the long road home. It had been almost five years since their ignominious retreat from their homeland in the face of advancing Nazi troops. Now they felt that at long last victory was in sight.

When the Germans attacked Poland in September 1939, the Poles mustered a military force of some million and a half men, determined, but ill equipped, to defend their country. Such a man was Michael Gutowski, a cavalry captain with 17th Lancers and an outstanding Olympic horseman. In those early days of the war, Captain Gutowski twice led successful cavalry charges against the invaders, "pushing the Germans quite energetically with very bloody fighting, 99 killed."

Although wounded, he dared not seek medical help. "Being in hospital meant becoming a prisoner of war," he explained. During the next weeks the Poles stubbornly fought on. Gutowski and his unit covered close to one thousand miles on horseback, caught up in numerous skirmishes and battles as they tried vainly to stem the onrush of Germans. Twice again wounded, he still managed to avoid capture.

The crisis came on 19 October 1939. "There was no place to go, no fighting left. I found civilian clothes and with a pair of horses I went back to western Poland to find my wife and children."

Gutowski was horrified to discover that many of the prominent people of the country had been rounded up by the SS and put in concentration camps. His wife and young children, a three-year-old and a six-month-old baby, were among them. When he tried to free them, he was himself arrested.

"I have orders from the SS to shoot you tomorrow morning," the commandant told him. At dawn the next day they came for him. To his surprise, instead of marching him out to a firing squad, they released him. "For the moment I am able to save your life," the commander, an Olympic equestrian admirer, said. "At least you won't be shot. As soon as you leave the barracks, disappear. Change your name. If the SS get their hands on you, you won't live twenty-four hours." His reputation as an international equestrian had saved him.

Gutowski joined an underground resistance group. When he later learned that his wife and children had been released and were safe with friends he decided to leave the country, skiing over the mountains to Slovakia and Hungary. Finally, in May 1940, he reached France and joined other escapees trickling in to reform the 10th Cavalry Brigade. A month later France fell and the Polish military were evacuated to hastily erected camps in Scotland.

Through the next four years this nucleus grew and flourished. Poles like Gutowski came from around the world, including Canada, the United States and South America as volunteers for the Polish army, navy and air force. By 1944, 1st Polish Armoured Division, under the seasoned command of General Stanislaw Maczek, was ready to fight in Normandy.[2]

Their determination to fight was sharpened by a crisis that by coincidence broke out in Poland on the same day as their landing in Normandy: 1 August 1944. The 30,000 Polish Home Army in Warsaw had staged a bloody uprising against the Nazi oppressors. Their objective was to liberate Warsaw from German rule and establish independent Polish control before the approaching Russians, now just twelve miles away, could impose their own Communist regime on Poland.

It was a valiant but futile effort. The Germans rushed in

reinforcements, including the Hermann Goering Panzer Division. The Resistance captured the whole city but had ammunition for only seven days. Armed with only 1,000 rifles and 25,000 homemade grenades, they were trapped in the inner-city cellars, where they fought on for some weeks with little more than their bare hands and courage.[3] The Warsaw Uprising created a symbiotic and very emotional bond with the Poles liberating Normandy. Both were fighting the Nazis to free their homeland: the one army from within the country and the other from without.

"What news of Warsaw?" was the first question Polish airmen would ask when they returned to Britain from bombing raids. Air crew and artillerymen symbolically scrawled "For Warsaw" across bombs and shells before releasing them. In France, bomb-shattered roads south of Caen bore signposts that read "Caen-Warsaw." The Normandy Poles in their slit trenches hung on to hourly BBC reports of the progress of the Warsaw uprising.[4]

One Polish tanker remembers that "near the command vehicle, a crowd gathered. The news was on: 'This is the home service of the BBC. Here is the news.' Faces looked serious—Warsaw was rising. The names of familiar districts, streets and buildings were mentioned.

"Warsaw was fighting.

"We knew what fighting meant. We knew from bitter experience what Tigers were like. And Warsaw had no 17-pounders with which to fight Tigers, had no flame-throwers to burn the Germans out of the city, had no tanks, no guns, the weapons, no ammunition . . .

"Faces grew grim.

"The broadcast was very short. It ended with the chorale *'Z dymen pozarów'* [with the smoke of the conflagrations . . .]."[5]

The Home Army in Warsaw faltered, weakened by lack of ammunition. They were finally starved out of their cellars under the city and defeated. Thus sprung the tragic Polish adage, "If you take a handful of Warsaw soil and squeeze it, the blood will run from it."

Every Polish soldier in Normandy felt the anguish of Warsaw. Their hatred of the SS deepened. Their determination to defeat the Nazis grew.

Unhappily, ill fortune marred the initial efforts of 1st Polish Armoured Division. They were now fighting under command of

Simonds' 2nd Canadian Corps. Twice they had been victims of friendly bombing: the first on 8 August, by the U.S. Air Force, and next on 14 August, when *Operation Tractable*'s ill-fated RAF bombing mission saw ninety-three Polish soldiers killed or missing. Then, during the advance to Chambois, when the 1st Polish inadvertently crossed the bomb-line into enemy territory, they came under fire from strafing Spitfires. In three days, from 16 to 18 August, 72 Polish troops were killed and 191 more were wounded by Allied planes.[6]

It was a tragedy that Allied commanders tried hard to avoid. The established "bomb-line"—an imaginary line drawn on the map connecting a number of locations—was well forward of troop positions. The bomb-lines were updated on a frequent, sometimes daily, basis. The sole purpose was to avert Allied air attacks on Allied forces. Liaison between air and ground forces tried to ensure that both were well aware of the current bomb-line location. It worked often, but not often enough for troops on the receiving end of mistaken bombings.

Despite these losses, the Poles seized an important crossing over the Dives River at Jort and at Simonds' urging pushed on during the night of 17/18 August in a remarkable twenty-mile night march through enemy lines towards Chambois.

General Maczek had noted on his map an imposing summit overlooking Chambois. The contours, with twin hills each 262 metres high, somewhat resembled a mace or two-headed axe. On the northern "head" of the mace was a fifteenth-century stone manor house, Château Boisjois. It had witnessed a decisive conflict in the Hundred Years War. It would soon witness a battle even more bloody.

The twin hills were divided by a narrow, sunken road running from Chambois to Vimoutiers—a road that would prove critical in the coming battle. Again, the road's contours reminded Maczek of a long handle of a mace. To preserve security he codenamed the entire battlesite "Maczuga," the Polish word for mace.[7]

It has become a name, and a battle, that the Polish even today revere. The road would come to be called the "Corridor of Death."

The soldiers' gruelling cross-country route led them through the Pays d'Auge. This lush corner of Normandy had long been an attraction for tourists. Its steep hills, meandering creeks, and winding lanes bordered by dense overgrown hedges invited hikers. At the end of a day on the trails they could enjoy the local specialties of Camembert cheese, Calvados, and cider.

It was a country for tourists, not tanks. Some of the most difficult fighting terrain in France was found in this untamed land. "Surely we must be on the borders of Switzerland!" one Polish trooper exclaimed in wonder.[8]

Traversing it at night with no maps and no light was a daunting task for the Poles. One of the two armoured units—the 2nd Armoured Regiment with riflemen of the 8th Light Infantry—took a wrong turn. This surprised no one as its commander, Colonel Koszutski, was known to be so anxious to forge ahead that he was "inclined to lead with his heart, not his head."[9]

Koszutski took that order from General Simonds very literally: ". . . *at all costs and as quickly as possible.*"[10]

It was midnight; his troops were asleep on their feet after a forty-eight-hour advance; his supply lorries had not caught up with him. So keen was he to obey that he set forth immediately "without refueling and without replacing spent ammunition."[11]

His men called him the "Happy Wanderer."[12]

Wander they did, that strange dark night of 18 August—straight into German lines. At the precise moment when the Polish tanks cut across the Auge hills towards Maczuga and Chambois, a motorized enemy column was struggling through the same terrain but on a different tack, from south to north.

Captain Ted Walewicz of the 2nd Polish Armoured Regiment recalls: "It was a terrible night, I remember it well . . . dark, not a pleasant night, especially after a whole day of fighting. We were driving at night through the German lines and the enemy began coming up in front of us."[13]

The two columns, Polish and German, encountered each other at a crossroads. The German policeman with white gauntlets stopped the north–south convoy and waved the Polish tanks through, not knowing, or not wanting to know, their identity.

Captain Gutowski confirms the strange encounter. "The German traffic police ordered the Polish tanks to go first and the Germans to move aside; in the middle of the night they didn't recognize our tanks."[14]

Certainly, neither protagonist welcomed a close battle in darkness.

Did they tacitly ignore each other's insignia? They were later to discover that these were units of 2nd SS Panzer Division, escaping from the Allied encirclement, regrouping for their counter-attack to save their trapped comrades.

To make the night trek even more bizarre, the French guide had misunderstood the Polish pronunciation of their objective, Chambois. "We were given the order to secure Chambois," Captain Walewicz explained. "But we were led instead to les Champeaux. It was unbelievable.

"It was the headquarters of a German division. I know because we found in one of the houses in les Champeaux a German staff officer's uniform."[15]

The Poles had penetrated well behind enemy lines and had in fact stumbled on the headquarters of 2nd SS Panzer Division. A firefight ensued. The Poles captured an enemy command post and found two generals' uniforms and a number of suitcases filled with loot. These "various trinkets" from the fashion houses of Paris included "beautiful furs from Rochas . . . dresses made by Maggy Rouff . . . ladies' underwear, silver cutlery—everything carefully folded and beautifully packed," the division history records.[16]

General Maczek had directed half of his division to head down the valley towards Chambois to drive the Germans from the village and its surrounding area, as General Simonds had ordered.[17]

But his experienced eye saw a flaw in the plan. That won't keep the Germans from infiltrating the line and escaping east to the Auge hills on one of the many country paths and lanes, he thought.

To counter this he ordered his remaining units—1st and 2nd Armoured Regiments and three infantry battalions—to seize the high ground of Maczuga some two miles beyond the Dives River.

The men were exhausted. They had been fighting for three days. Their all-night, twenty-mile trek had been a test of endurance. The infantry had marched or clung white-knuckled to the sides of the tanks, fearing that if they dozed off they would tumble to the ground and perhaps be crushed. The heat inside the tanks was stifling; drivers' grips on the steering levers were weakening. They were hungry. Water was scarce.

But they hadn't come down this long road home to quit now. The next morning, 19 August, Polish soldiers and their tanks attacked

Hill 262 at the northern end of "the mace" and drove out the German infantry company defending this critical vantage point.

At 1240 hours the first Polish troops—2nd Armoured Regiment with 8th Infantry Battalion—rolled into Boisjois, the stone manor house on Hill 262. Pierre Grandvalet, a Norman farmer who lived in the manor with his wife and two young children, recalls the excitement of the liberation:

A German came to my house and asked me to give him some potatoes. He said he hadn't eaten for three days. I pointed him toward a neighbour's field. He busied himself putting the potatoes on the cooker in the kitchen and after a while he ran outside and warned me, 'The English are coming!' He left the house in a great hurry. My wife and I ran into the cellar and waited. A short while later we heard voices in the courtyard. The Polish had arrived. Next a convoy of tanks came. They were very thirsty and hot. We brought out carafes and bottles of cider. They were welcomed with great joy.[18]

By late afternoon, the 1st Armoured Regiment and Lieutenant-Colonel Szdlowski's 9th Infantry Battalion were digging in, using trenches recently abandoned by the Germans. Two thousand Poles with eighty-seven tanks and well-sited artillery had taken firm possession of Maczuga.

One of the officers assigned to the Polish Armoured at Maczuga was a French Canadian artillery captain with the 4th Canadian Medium Regiment, Pierre Sévigny. His role at Maczuga was to serve as forward observation officer (FOO).

"I trained with the Poles in Scotland," he recounted. "Since their second language was French, particularly so with the soldiers, they requested a French-speaking officer who could communicate with English-speaking senior artillery officers at Canadian Army HQ when massive fire was needed."[19]

From the high ground of Hill 262, Sévigny would be able to identify enemy positions and radio these to Canadian Medium artillery. He had the authority to call down, in an instant, all the available corps' firepower—hundreds of guns—in whatever strength he deemed necessary to knock out the menace.

As General Maczek had shrewdly surmised, the Polish position at Maczuga commanded far-reaching views in every direction. As if in the best balcony seats, they could see across the broad valley of the Dives River below them. Here and there were glimpses of the Dives. It seemed incredible that the blue line on their map—a river wide and steep enough to stop tanks—could be that narrow, tree-lined creek they glimpsed meandering through the old Norman farming villages of Chambois, St. Lambert-sur-Dives and Trun.

The local Norman populace rated the hilltop views in their luxuriant country by the number of steeples that dotted the landscape. "On a clear day, from Mont Ormel, one could see 30 steeples in all directions," local inhabitant Robert Chombart noted recently.[20]

So it was that the Poles could use these landmarks to identify friend and foe. Four miles southwest they could make out the distinctive hundred-foot towers marking the corners of the 12th-century fortress in Chambois. Here their comrades—Major Zgorzelski's 10th Polish Dragoons, with the 10th Mounted Rifles (the regiment in which Captain Gutowski served) under command, were preparing to attack.

Beyond Chambois, the Forêt de Gouffern obscured the steeples of Argentan and Le Bourg-St. Léonard. But through their binoculars, they could see artillery flashes that identified the positions of the 2nd French Armoured and Bradley's 90th and 80th infantry divisions as they attempted to seal the gap from the south.

Veering their gaze slightly to the west they could see the church steeples of St. Lambert and Trun, where, on this August 19th, the Canadians were attacking to close the gap from the north. "From our hill there was a panoramic view of the combat zone," Sévigny recalled: "At our feet the battle raged for the possession of the villages of St. Lambert and Chambois. We could see the Shermans advancing, blazing away with their guns and machine guns. The attacking tanks and infantry exploited the folds in the ground for cover."[21]

And just two or three miles beyond St. Lambert, more steeples marked the several small farming villages clustered amid the woods and high hedges of the Dives Valley. Tournai-sur-Dives, Villedieu les Bailleul, le Bas-Aubry, Meri, and Nécy: they had not yet been badly touched by war. The tawny stone of their modest barns and cottages still took on a warm amber glow in the July sunshine, in dramatic contrast with the awful destruction of larger centres north and south of them. The apples in their bountiful orchards, nearing maturity, were unmolested by bomb splinters or tanks. Their cattle grazed contentedly, plodding at will down trails that led to the nearby Dives River.

It was here that remnants of twenty divisions of the German 7th and 5th armies were now harbouring. They had only one escape route left: to cross the Dives River and head north-east over one of the two main roads that led to Vimoutiers and the safety of the Auge hills.

Both escape routes cut through the high ground near Mont Ormel; both led directly into the positions at Maczuga that the Poles had so triumphantly seized.

The villagers who now so unwillingly shared their safe harbour had no such escape.

22

DAVID CURRIE'S
DESTINY

When war broke out, Canadians—unlike the Poles—were very remote from the issues that provoked World War II. Yet Canada had its own special motivations for supporting the war effort. As a young nation, it was loyal to its mother country. In its own right, Canada abhorred the tyranny of Nazism.

As well, the Depression had caused many of Canada's young men to be unemployed and restless. They welcomed the opportunity to join the armed forces.

When Great Britain declared war on Germany following the Nazi aggression in Poland, Canada swiftly followed suit, making its own declaration of war on 10 September 1939. By 1944, 1 million men and women—a full 10 per cent of the Canadian population—were directly involved in the war effort, all as volunteers. Some soldiers fought in the Dieppe Raid in 1942, or in Sicily and Italy in 1943, but many saw their first action in Normandy on or shortly after D-Day in 1944.

However, 4th Canadian Armoured Division, like 1st Polish Armoured Division, was kept waiting impatiently in England for close to two months after D-Day before being committed to battle. These neophyte units, with little or no previous battle experience, saw their first day of action on 7 August, spearheading the second phase of *Operation Totalize*. There never was a single day of more difficult fighting than on that steaming August afternoon when two inexperienced divisions were ordered to attack in broad daylight across open country against a pre-warned and strongly armed enemy.

Those who survived the cruel toll of that day became "blooded" troops, determined and tough in the demands of war. One such man was Michael Gutowski; another was a Canadian major, David Currie.

*

The mean, lean years of the 1930s in Canada had created a national crisis of unemployment and economic despair: the Great Depression. The nation was brought to its knees: productivity was almost halved, and one-fifth of the population became destitute.

Half a million farmers—5 per cent of the Canadian workforce—were on relief. Two hundred thousand of these came from the province of Saskatchewan. It was a cruel time.

Drought and blight contributed to a market downslide of wheat that devastated the province. With few buyers, the railways began to lay off workers. Surviving this woesome decade took special skills of patience, tolerance, endurance . . . and stubbornness.

These were qualities that David Currie nourished in himself as he grew up on Canada's prairies. He was a seventeen-year-old Saskatchewan lad when the Depression began, a boy of modest background who had to settle for a technical-school education when he had his sights set on university.

Stubbornness was what kept him going despite the miseries of prairie life: the long dark winters of bitter cold and biting wind, the summers of intense heat and bugs so voracious you huddled indoors. Endurance helped him stick to a meanly paid job as an automobile mechanic and welder.

He steadfastly plodded through the "dirty thirties," shrugging off the degradation of the Depression while embracing his personal achievements: a steady job, a supportive wife, and a young son, his namesake, whom he cherished.

When war came, years of dogged training in the militia and subsequent wartime training boosted him up to the rank of major. Currie, at thirty-two, was given command of a tank squadron with the South Alberta (29th Armoured Reconnaissance) Regiment. His division, 4th Canadian Armoured, landed on the Normandy beaches in late July.

Lieutenant-Colonel Gordon Wotherspoon ("Swatty" to his friends; "Sir" to the officers and men in his regiment) had studied and identified the man's strengths, as he did all his officers. "[Currie] wasn't a brilliant tactician, but he was very stubborn, and if you gave him an order to do something that was within his capabilities, he would do it—period."[1]

Not a man among them had fired a gun in anger. They were

hopeful that under Wotherspoon's skilled and tough training they had learned the basics of tank warfare.

By 18 August 1944, the regiment had been in action only two weeks. Currie's unflappable leadership had bonded his squadron into a cohesive fighting force. What each soldier didn't know—and was in some ways afraid to find out—was how he would react under fire. It's one thing to carry out a manoeuvre on the English Downs; it is quite another when mortars are exploding around you and a German 88mm gun has you in its sights.

Happily, the South Albertas made one of the farthest advances of any unit in the second phase of *Totalize*. "Our outfit is doing better than the rest of them," Trooper Bob Clipperton wrote to his wife with understandable pride. "We are called the Fighting 29th."

As the SAR (South Alberta Regiment) history explains it, "the first two weeks of action are crucial for new soldiers because, until they experience combat, men do not know how they will react and there is always the danger that fear will destroy their self-control.

"If a soldier can survive this period without any unduly traumatic experience and can acquire the basic knowledge necessary for survival in his new and terrifying environment, he gains self-confidence because he has seen the worst (or thinks he has) and is still alive."

One corporal from the South Albertas summed it up like this: "[We] had our answers now to the questions that had been in the backs of our minds as we approached the front line." They had "seen our tanks hit, men wounded, killed, burned to death, and we found that we were able to handle it. You were always afraid, but you accepted what was happening and you did what you had to do."[2]

By mid-August, having survived its first two weeks without suffering any of the disasters that had befallen some other units, the South Alberta Regiment was beginning to "shake down." It had lost men but its casualties were the lowest of the four armoured regiments in 4th Canadian Division.

"As the men gained confidence, so did the unit."[3]

On 18 August, the regiment thundered through the bomb-shattered streets of Trun, many of its houses in flames. Defeated German soldiers were still wandering down the road, trying to give themselves up. Currie's "C" Squadron pulled up at an orchard overlooking the Dives River, marvelling at the dramatic sight of the German exodus eastward across the rolling valley. Only this single six-mile ribbon of land along the Dives, running from Trun through St. Lambert to Chambois, barred the way out for the retreating enemy.

"In the distance, we could see rising clouds of dust," Major Currie noted. "We were witnessing . . . the remnants of the German forces in France trying to escape the pocket. The columns were about three to four miles from our location and seemed to consist of every type and kind of vehicle, gun, tank, and horse-drawn equipment that the German army possessed. The column stretched as far as we could see. It was an awe-inspiring sight, and from the distance, it appeared to be a crushing force."[4]

At 1500 hours, Wotherspoon radioed Currie to report to regimental headquarters. Orders were waiting, orders filtered down from Montgomery through Crerar and Simonds to the commanders on the ground: it was "essential" to plug that gap. St. Lambert was the key.[5]

Wotherspoon handed the job to Currie. "I've got a tough assignment for you," he said grimly. "The German withdrawal has to be stopped—now! The Allied success in Normandy depends on it. There is no time to bring the artillery into range before you launch the assault. You'll have to 'go in naked' until we can move the guns forward."[6]

Both men knew that laying on an attack without close artillery support was a very daunting operation. Only the urgency of the mission could allow this risk.

Currie's squadron was understrength for the assignment. He was down to fifteen tanks from the normal nineteen, with a force of just seventy-five officers and troopers from the normal one hundred. And the infantry backup he would have under command, just one company of the Argyll and Sutherland Highlanders, was also understrength.

Normally an infantry company's fighting strength is about ninety combat troops. After the ravages of the past ten days of battle, the Argyll infantry company was down to a depleted strength of about fifty-five all ranks. Added to Currie's fifteen-tank squadron of officers and troopers, this force that was to close the St. Lambert escape route initially numbered a mere 130 men.

Still, Wotherspoon knew his man. Currie might not be the most brilliant tactician of his squadron commanders, but he had the determination to get the job done. Take St. Lambert. "That's all I had to say. And I knew, having said that, that he'd stay there."[7]

There's a strong tie between armoured squadrons and infantry battalions that in war can be, literally, life-supporting. Tankmen are highly vulnerable to attack by enemy infiltrators armed with the lethal hand-held panzerfausts. Their infantry pals, therefore, had a protective role to rout out opposition. On the other hand, foot soldiers badly need the fire support of powerful tank weaponry.

Swatty Wotherspoon was very understanding of that relationship between tankmen and infantrymen and tried to fit each squadron to each regiment. He considered that Dave Currie fitted best with the Argylls. Wotherspoon was certainly recalling the Argylls' stunning exploit nine days earlier when their commander Lieutenant-Colonel Dave Stewart ignored standard procedure and devised a silent night attack up the back trails of Hill 195. The Argylls captured it without a shot being fired.

Currie and Stewart were similar characters. Together they would make a tough team, with the abilities and determination to get the job done—one way or another.

Returning to his squadron, Currie held a quick "O" Group with his four troop commanders. "The assignment given us by the colonel is to take the village of St. Lambert-sur-Dives," he told them as they grouped around a map of the area. "I reckon this will place us squarely in front of the vast array of the German forces that we had been watching most of the day."[8]

He set up a communications plan with Captain John Redden, his second-in-command. Redden was his rear link, charged with relaying all signals between Wotherspoon and Currie.

The maps and recce photos showed clusters of small houses and farms hugging a dusty chalk road (actually the highway between Trun and Chambois). The road dipped sharply down to the village and wound through its modest centre for less than half a mile.

It could be any small farming hamlet of clapboard houses in the Canadian prairies, they thought, except for the distinctively Norman stone construction of the buildings. The key elements were two small bridges over the steeply-banked Dives River—the only two escape hatches that were allowing the columns of retreating enemy tanks and vehicles to cross it.

H-hour for the attack on St. Lambert was 1800 hours on 18 August.

Pre-battle anxiety was lessened by the practical joke of one of the troopers. As Currie recounted, "The boys brewed tea, and made the last-minute preparations for the coming battle. Just about one minute before we pushed off, an infantry sergeant came along holding his mess tin.

"I was sitting on top of my tank. He asked me if I wanted a drink. I said, 'Sure, what is it?' He said he didn't know and passed it along to me. I took a good healthy swallow and almost choked to death. His remarks at my antics, 'Sure is hot, ain't it?' was the understatement of the year. I found out later that I had had my introduction to that fiery Normandy speciality known as Calvados."[9]

This gambit produced a rare smile from the reserved major: "A small grin from Dave meant the same as hilarious laughter from another person," one of his troop leaders recalled. "Dave was always a very private individual but he was also easy-going and very matter of fact. He gave his orders clearly and distinctly and had confidence in his abilities. Everybody in the regiment held him in high regard."[10]

At exactly 1800 hours the tanks pushed off down the long hill that led to St. Lambert. No.1 Troop (four tanks) led off with Currie's Squadron Headquarters (three tanks and a first-aid vehicle) close behind. The remaining two troops followed, with Major Ivan Martin's Argyll infantry company clinging to the backs of the final eight tanks.

"Embus on Carriers etc in another mad drive," Argyll CSM (Company Sergeant-Major) George Mitchell recorded, dreading a replay of the experience infantry had, hanging on for dear life to the outside of the hot and thrashing metal as the tanks bumped down the dirt road.[11]

Within minutes the squadron came under fire from the extreme left flank. A false alarm. "One of the tank commanders from the Polish Armoured Division had become a little excited at the appearance of our tanks and had fired first and looked later. They apologized and assured me that it would not happen again," Currie explained to his men.[12]

Then a German 88mm suddenly opened up. Trooper Wayne Spence can still see it: "when all the shooting started and flares went up, it was just like daylight."[13] The lead tank was hit and although its commander, John Slater, and a crew member were wounded, they all managed to bail out.

Moments later, more fire: this time it was two Royal Air Force Spitfires confusing them for an enemy. They dove down, making one pass over Currie's headquarters squadron.

"The back end of my tank is on fire!" Currie shouted, grabbing a fire extinguisher. The Spits attacked again. This time, Currie dove for safety into the ditch beside the road. Four of his men lay wounded. His first-aid ambulance vehicle was out of commission.

"The hatch on our turret was not closed," Lieutenant Gerry Adams recalls. "Bullets ricocheted inside the turret. My Gunner, Coates, had a face injury and my right arm and leg were wounded."[14]

The normally mild-mannered Currie was furious. Captain John Redden, "mad as hell," tried to nail one of the aircraft with his turret gun but they were too fast. "Our CO wanted our own ack-ack troop to open fire but the padre talked him out of the idea," Redden remembers.[15]

Currie's tank crews frantically threw out yellow smoke canisters to no avail. It was "like poking a hornet's nest, they got so agitated and came back twice as bad," Lieutenant Don Stewart complained.[16]

The frustrating aspect for the troops was the inability to communicate ground to air. Yellow smoke was the recognized signal identifying the bomb-line. In fact, one battalion even posted a warning to its companies that there was a likelihood of us being RAF'ed unless forward troops displayed yellow smoke. However, dust and distance sometimes obliterated the efforts on the ground.

The pilots made every effort to respect the new bomb-lines that delineated friend and foe. But the battle was so fluid that no line on a map could keep up with the ebb and flow of the troops of five Allied nations on the ground. There were a number of unfortunate "friendly" strafing incidents.

General Crerar finally issued a directive to all Canadian units. He suggested that being strafed and wounded by your own aircraft was a necessary evil: "There have been a number of attacks by our own aircraft on our own tps [troops] during the last two days and particularly today. It is necessary to stress the peculiar difficulties to the Allied air forces caused by the convergence of U.S., British and Canadian armies on a common objective, with air action against the enemy force within that Allied circle desirable up to the point of their surrender."

The directive went on to itemize the damage done to scores of enemy tanks and trucks by 2nd Tactical Air Force: "Tanks flamers 77, smokers 42, damaged 55. Mechanical transport flamers 900, smokers 478, damaged 712." He stressed that if the Canadian units would "compare their vehicle casualties proportionately to the above they will obtain some idea of the tremendous military balance in their favour."[17]

For the Albertans it was a tough beginning to a tough battle. Two of their fifteen tanks had already been disabled, and six men wounded in the initial minutes of the attack. Now they discovered a Tiger tank positioned squarely in their path, prohibiting any advance into the village. They had to get around it before they were spotted.

It was then that Currie made the decision that first marked him as a man of great—of greatest—courage and determination. Ordinarily, when a commander required urgent information about the enemy, he would send out a reconnaissance patrol of men especially trained for the job.

Not Currie. He made up his mind to go alone on foot into the village centre that night to find a way to somehow outflank the German tank that controlled the main road into town.

As dusk settled into darkness, and rain clouds hovered threateningly over St. Lambert-sur-Dives, Major David Currie strode purposefully down the road that led into the silent village. His findings were not encouraging. The Dives River, curving through the town, would prevent them from manoeuvring around the Tiger's lethal 88mm gun.

In the darkened streets of St. Lambert, there was an eerie hush. Not a single villager was present; not even the barking of a dog. But there were German troops entrenched in the silent cottages and hedges along the road. Currie was convinced of that.

"I could hear voices of Germans in some of the buildings, but did not run into anyone during my reconnaissance on foot," he reported back to Wotherspoon.

Let me lead the men on foot tonight to wipe out that Tiger, he urged his commander.[18]

Sit tight until morning, was the reply. Attack at first light.

There was little sleep that night at South Alberta Regiment head-quarters on nearby Hill 117. Tanks and infantry were harboured in an orchard one thousand yards north of St. Lambert, waiting for the attack to go in. A soft rain, the first in weeks, brought the threat of cloud cover and the fear of no air support for their morning attack. Less than a mile away, an entire German army could be down there, determined to keep the escape gap open.

"Everybody stood to waiting for some movement which would start things flying," the South Alberta Regiment war diary reported.[19]

The terrifying thought came to each of the 130 men peering out into the eerie silence: how can a handful of men and fifteen vastly inferior Sherman tanks stand a chance against thousands of escaping enemy equipped with the awesome Tigers and Panthers?

Inevitably their eyes rested on the tall profile of David Currie, leaning casually on the side of a tank, gaze fixed determinedly upon the dark ridge beyond the Dives Valley.

Yet there was something in his stance. "He was so cool, it was impossible for us to get excited,"[20] one of his NCOs later recalled.

They would have been surprised to know the turmoil of his thoughts at that moment. His greatest fear, he was to say, "was the possibility that I might not measure up."

He confronted that fear. "Well, Dave," he thought, "up to now this has been a pretty good war, but this is it!"[21]

23

BRAVERY
AT ST. LAMBERT

Daybreak: Saturday, 19 August
The South Alberta attack went in at dawn.

The lead tank moved ahead. David Currie and the Argyll Company advanced on foot to support it. They knew their Sherman tank was no match for the German Tiger. Their only hope of destroying it lay with nimble-footed and courageous infantrymen. They had to stalk the tank, get in behind it within close enough range—say, ninety yards—with just one chance to get off a shot with their PIATs before the Tiger spotted them. The PIAT was a hand-held anti-tank weapon, fired from a prone position, and had a terrific recoil. Its firer needed strong nerves. "Even in short-range tests, it scored only 57 per cent of its hits. Failure meant probable extinction."[1]

The South Alberta tank got a third of the way through the village. So far, so good. Suddenly, a German armour-piercing (AP) shell slammed into the Sherman. The three crew nearest the turret of the disabled tank scrambled to get out. (The crews had trained for years for such an emergency. "We [always] knew something like that would happen!" Trooper Wayne Spence said.)[2] But before the driver and co-driver could escape, a second AP shot smashed into the Sherman, setting it on fire. Both men were badly burned as the tank brewed.

Currie spotted the two enemy tanks creating this havoc—a Tiger and a Mark IV—a quarter of a mile down the road at the southern end of the town. Sonofabitch! He had no radio to alert the squadron. It was his rear link, Captain John Redden, who saved the day. Realizing that he'd lost communication with his commanding officer, Redden abandoned his tank and sprinted up to Currie's. He was able to pinpoint one of the German tanks, the Mark IV, in the gun sight and fire on it. He destroyed it. It was a first confirmed "kill" for the Albertas. (Currie's crew got the colonel's prize—a bottle of rum.)

Meanwhile, Major Ivan Martin's Argyll infantry company of fifty-five men was working in support of the armour. They had the dangerous job of clearing pockets of Germans from each house along the road. The Tiger had pulled back out of sight, but a 45-ton Panther had drawn up beside a cottage. It towered ominously over the foot-soldiers as they now had to tackle the horrific job of destroying it.

Lieutenant Gil Armour asked for volunteers. The lads in Armour's No. 10 platoon were used to following Gil on crazy missions: "A suicide squad," Private W.F. Cooper muttered, but he volunteered with the rest of them. They had Armour pegged as "a little wild, but the guys wouldn't hesitate to follow him. . . . He knew his stuff as well as anybody."[3]

Lieutenant Armour climbed on top of the tank with a 36–grenade in his hand. As he was about to drop the grenade in the open turret, a German officer armed with an automatic pistol thrust his head out. The two men wrestled furiously and Armour forced his adversary out of the turret. Face to sweating face, they grappled on top of the tank until the Canadian finally gave a mighty lunge and shoved the German to the ground, tumbling down as well with the effort.

Private Jimmy LaForrest, one of his platoon volunteers, grabbed his rifle and shot the German, seriously wounding him. Moments later, Armour scrambled on top and dropped his grenade in the turret, immobilizing the Panther. A PIAT was brought up to finish the kill.

By mid-morning, Currie could signal Wotherspoon that the village had been cleared. Now, with just twelve tanks and some sixty infantrymen left, he faced the job of holding it against almost inevitable enemy counter-attacks. He ordered Lieutenant Armour to consolidate his platoon on the vital southern crossroad, with three tanks in support. That left just nine tanks and some three dozen men to hold the rest of the village. They dug in facing the western edge of town, where most of the German fire seemed to be coming from.

During the afternoon, fighting became spasmodic but the country-side around the town fairly seethed with small groups of Germans, some wandering aimlessly, giving themselves up without a fight. As

Currie was walking back up the street, two German officers rapped hard on the window to get his attention. Currie gestured them out of the building and accepted their surrender, but not the gift they offered with it—a small puppy.

One group surrendered with about a dozen American GI prisoners who had been captured somewhere to the south. A South Alberta trooper grinned to see the Yanks "going around [to] different tanks bumming smokes."[4]

Other Germans, more militant, took their toll as snipers. Captain John Redden, already a hero for coordinating the attack earlier that day on the enemy Mark IV tank, pushed his luck—and was taken in by an old German ploy: "Suddenly about a dozen two-ton trucks loaded with enemy troops blundered into our area," Redden described. "We used a high-explosive round to stop the lead truck, and two rounds of AP on the rear of the convoy."

Redden decided he would "be a hero by conning these bastards into giving up." A German approached, waving a white flag. "I popped out waist high to talk," the Albertan said. His driver spotted trouble: "Another German came around the corner with a Schmeisser. . . . The guy with the [white] flag went down and ducked out of the line of fire." Redden went down, seriously wounded.[5]

German prisoners began to pour in. Currie organized them into groups, establishing a first-aid post for those that were wounded, under the direction of an English-speaking German doctor. He was too thin on the ground to spare any infantry to escort them back, so he sent them off in batches of three or four dozen, with a "watch dog" tank trained on their every move. Of 2,500 POWs, only one tried to escape. "He took off through the fields but did not get very far."[6]

It was during this midday lull that the media turned up on the battle scene. Canadian Army photographer Lieutenant Donald Grant, with his unit from the Canadian Army Film and Photographic Unit, cameras slung over their shoulders, had been up the road in Trun when they heard rumours that the long-awaited link-up between Canadians and Americans was about to take place.

Grant, a seasoned newspaperman with veteran front-line experience, had been awarded the Military Cross for heroism on the

Normandy beachhead. He commanded (and in a few days would be the only survivor of) a seven-man media unit. Another of the photographers, Sergeant Jack Stollery, had been awarded the Military Medal in Italy.

At St. Lambert the photographers got their scoop the hard way. Donald Grant will never forget that afternoon: "About 1 o'clock we heard vehicles coming so we ducked off the roadway. Along came a motorcycle and sidecar and an armoured half-track full of [German] soldiers."[7] An arrogant-looking officer, complete with peaked cap, goggles and high leather boots, sat in the sidecar, furious that he had stumbled into a South Alberta ambush. Major Currie personally took the officer captive. "He was a cocky little bugger. He didn't want to surrender to a lowly major."[8] Grant's photograph of the event became a front-page picture for the September issue of *Canada Weekly*—and in newspapers and books around the world. The official historian captioned it "as close as we are ever likely to come to a photograph of a man winning the Victoria Cross."[9]

But Grant's adventure wasn't over yet: "Before we got the prisoners in the vehicles totally out of the way, the rest of the convoy or the same convoy came in sight, saw us and tried to retreat."

The war diary recounts their next anxious moments: "The group of Jerries were called upon to surrender by these photographers, but they took a belligerent attitude and fired on our men." The Canadians prevailed and caught "possibly [the] first picture of Germans before capture."[10]

Grant remembers that his two drivers (one spoke German) helped out as "traffic cops controlling prisoner traffic." At one point he and Stollery also "acted as extra guns" for Currie, backing him up when he went into a building and captured six Germans.

Before they returned to Trun, Stollery and Grant capped their scoop with another picture series that was "fantastic."

"We actually saw Germans running through a young orchard. We could see their feet and glimpses of their heads as they ran away. I wrote in my diary, 'It was now about 3:30, the burning tanks were exploding, and at the end of the day we even followed a patrol, who had an argument with a couple of soldiers behind a haystack at the left fork of the road. They lost the argument and were killed.'"

To Grant's great regret his standard lens camera couldn't capture the scene, "but Stollery's movie camera had a turret and a long lens."

It was late afternoon when the photographers decided to return to Trun. "Our movements were limited . . . space under control was small." They had in their rolls of film a photograph that would make history; at the time, they just "knew it was good." (Returning to St. Lambert the next day, the unit was shot up by a German machine gun; four of the five men were wounded.)[11]

Their departure seemed to signal a rekindling of action.

"Up to this time I had lost two officers," David Currie recounts. "During the rest of Saturday, the fighting was bitter." So far, the Albertas and Argylls had been fighting "naked," with no artillery support. Finally, the guns had been moved into range. Now they were supported by the field artillery (three regiments) as well as the medium guns.[12]

Captain Fred Clerkson, the FOO for 15th Field Regiment, RCA, set up an observation post on Hill 117, the South Alberta's forward HQ. From the high point he had an incredible view of the Dives Valley.

Lieutenant-Colonel Swatty Wotherspoon and the FOO began calling down fire on the fleeing Germans: "It was an OP officer's dream," an amazed Clerkson said. "Below in the valley targets appeared one after another. Roads and fields were full of Germans moving eastward seeking a way out of the trap. The resulting carnage was terrible."[13]

American artillery at the Forêt de Gouffern on the southern ridge of the Dives Valley also pounded the hapless escaping German troops.

From his vantage point on Hill 117, Swatty Wotherspoon could see "small parties of Germans" in the surrounding woods. To guard Regimental Headquarters (RHQ) from infiltration, he made the highly unusual move of bringing up the whole rear echelon and arming them with PIATs for permanent defence around regimental headquarters. "He was then in a formidable position with a view of the whole gap," Lieutenant Danny McLeod noted. "He was very instrumental in formulating the artillery plan."[14]

During the three days of the German withdrawal, the skies had been brilliantly clear. The artillery and tactical air forces were having a field day shooting up the packed columns of retreating Germans.

In the village, the situation was getting desperate. An apparently never-ending stream of enemy was wading across the Dives into the town and attacking the small band of defenders. Emboldened by their superiority of numbers they swarmed the Canadian tanks, even leaping on board to attack the troopers. Currie described those tense moments. "The tanks were running around in circles firing at one another to keep the enemy from climbing on top of them."

Drastic measures were required. Currie requested a massive artillery concentration directly on his own position. He shouted a warning to all his men, "Get under cover!"

It came down with lethal force, far greater than he had expected. Instead of the 25-pounders he had ordered, 100-pound shells from 4.5-inch medium guns crashed within fifteen metres of his position. It was a powerful-enough explosion to wipe out his whole squadron.

This was a seldom-used tactic, only employed in desperate situations. The Germans were out in the open; the Canadians were dug in. "We were lucky," Currie said. "We suffered no casualties from our own guns, but it had a very devastating effect on the Germans."[15]

Now the Albertas faced a new problem: their tanks were running low on ammunition. Refuelling mid-battle poses special kinds of nightmares for the rear-echelon boys. With enemy shells pounding the roads, it was far too risky for the three-ton trucks, each hauling more than one thousand gallons of petrol and quantities of ammunition, to approach the battleline. At St. Lambert they devised a shuttle system.

The trucks deposited their volatile cargo on a hill several hundred yards behind the front line. This was picked up in smaller loads by South Alberta Regiment Crusader tanks and brought in by back roads to Currie's HQ. One by one each tank would then pull back to the headquarters to refuel and rearm.

By late afternoon Currie's small band was fighting off ever-increasing German pressure from the west. Sniper and shellfire were heavy both in the town and up on Hill 117 at regimental headquarters. Wotherspoon requested reinforcements. He warned brigade HQ that "unless relief comes Germans will move back in."[16] Yet forty infantrymen were all the reinforcements that Brigade could muster to help the desperate Canadians.

At this point, 4th Canadian Armoured Brigade was rudderless. The commanding brigadier, Leslie Booth, had been killed in the opening hours of *Tractable*. His replacement, Lieutenant-Colonel Murray Scott, broke his ankle when his tank ran over a mine. In both cases, the casualties weren't immediately reported and confusion ensued. The final replacement brigade commander, Lieutenant-Colonel Bob Moncel, had consequently been delayed five days before taking command, leaving the brigade without consistent leadership during that critical time. Perhaps for this reason, while the South Albertas fought for their very survival, the other three armoured regiments of 4th Brigade spent the day out of combat waiting for orders.

At 1800 hours a token reinforcement—two half companies of infantry—arrived: a second Argyll company and another from the Lincoln and Welland Regiment, both gravely depleted in strength. Currie personally led the reinforcements into key positions, while still under heavy enemy fire.

Wotherspoon had also been assured that Brigadier John Rockingham's 9th Infantry Brigade, then in Trun, would be moved up that night. The three battle-proven battalions of this brigade would clearly provide essential support—if they made it in time. But the enemy was still attempting to break out through Trun. The Lincoln and Welland Regiment, supported by the machine guns of the New Brunswick Rangers, reported that they were holding off repeated attacks by "madly shouting gray-clad men."[17]

There was only one crossing over the Dives that could sustain the weight of the German tanks and heavy vehicles: the stone bridge at St. Lambert. There were also two crossings for foot soldiers. One was a footbridge at Moissy, just south-east of the village. A second was a small bridge built to carry farm equipment at the Château de Quantité farm and mill half a mile west of the town.

With darkness falling, Currie's forces were too extended to be able to maintain strong control of all the vital crossings over the Dives. He tried. He consolidated his force in a tight defensive core in the centre of the village, guns sited on every escape route.

Nearby, at the mill at Quantité, Currie had directed Number 15

Platoon Lincoln and Welland under command of Lieutenant Arkle "Junior" Dunlop to dig in near a group of farm buildings at the edge of the river. The Argylls were on their left. To add to the mêlée, dozens of terrified villagers huddled in the barns and outbuildings.

Two South Alberta Sherman tanks supported the outpost. Dunlop was grateful for the backup for several reasons. "The tanks supplied the radio communication between our little force and the main force in St. Lambert." Besides, he was hungry. He figured out that "the tank men had more and better rations than we had, and the commander of the tank in my particular area [Lieutenant Don Stewart] was a nice fellow who was willing to share his."

Disorganized bands of Germans continued their sporadic entries into St. Lambert. As night fell, Dunlop saw "literally hordes of Germans cross the river . . . I would think that between 1,500 and 2,000 prisoners of war went through our combined positions.

"They were a sad-looking lot. Their uniforms were ragged and dirty," Dunlop recalled. The Canadians removed all their weapons —mostly grenades and revolvers—putting them into a farmer's wheelbarrow. It soon overflowed.

"To get them back to the main force, we gathered them in lots of perhaps 100 to 150, and marched them directly across the field with one of our chaps escorting. I remember we were careful to tell the escort that he must take them only to the town and then return for more since we were extremely short of help. Through the tank radio they were able to notify HQ when another flock of prisoners was coming.

"One of our chaps, who was armed only with a rifle, asked if he might perhaps have a Sten gun, in case some of the prisoners decided to turn on him or escape. To this I recall Sergeant Schuler replying, 'If they do that, it won't matter a damn whether you have a Sten gun or a rifle, you'll be dead anyway.'"[18]

The prisoners were herded into a large flat field near Currie's headquarters. "That night, up on Hill 117 just above Dave," Lieutenant Danny McLeod relates, "we had a couple of tanks with headlights. The Germans were lying prostrate and we were saying, 'Don't bloody well move or we'll fire!'"[19]

Argyll private Art Bridge never forgot the wistful tune that drifted out in the deepening twilight when one of the prisoners picked up his squeeze box and started playing *La Paloma*.[20] There would be no sleep that Saturday night for the captives—or for the weary troops who guarded them.

To some of the Canadians, it was a disconcerting experience to see these Germans whom they had regarded as enemies become just ordinary men: "A couple of days ago you were fighting with them. And you start to wonder . . . if these guys have got families . . . because you start to think about your own family . . . and if you're ever going to get back. There's no hostility."[21]

Wotherspoon positioned the Albertas' "B" Squadron (commanded by Major Darby Nash) on a hill east of the town, where their guns could fire direct on any escaping enemy. It was a gamble. Orchards and woods—and Germans—surrounded the tankmen and gunners. But guns cannot see in the dark and tanks are helpless against enemy infiltrators.

In the blackness of night, it was the infantry, barely more than one hundred men in total, who had to guard each woodland, each slope, each narrow farm track of the entire area surrounding the town.

Currie had sent a platoon of the newly arrived Argyll "C" Company under Major Winfield south down the D13 in the direction of Moissy and Chambois, to "possibly make contact with the Poles who were supposedly in Moissy, and if not there, in Chambois."[22]

There was no hint, on that Saturday evening just two miles away in Chambois, that officers from the U.S. 90th Infantry and the 10th Polish Dragoons were at that moment shaking hands and toasting each other with drinks of Polish vodka in a historic encounter. Only one mile away was the Moissy ford, just a cluster of trees, and a handful of outbuildings on the Argyll maps. It had traditionally been a meeting-place where washer-women laid a plank from one bank to the other to carry their heavy baskets of wet laundry across the Dives. Now, German orders groups were being held that night in wooded hideouts a short distance away. Moissy had taken on more sinister importance as an important escape route for the German Seventh Army.

CSM George Mitchell remembered that night patrol through St. Lambert to Moissy as "terrifying." The men got about two miles down the road when they ran into enemy small-arms fire and grenades. "We couldn't tell where the fire was coming from so we hit the ditch," Art Bridge remembered. "I ended up on top of an ant hill . . . the nasty little buggers bit me everywhere!"

Several of their group were wounded, including the major in command who, though his wounds were slight, evacuated himself out. As there were indications that they were dangerously behind enemy lines, and they had lost their leader, the men cut back cross-country, creeping through back lanes, sometimes crawling on their bellies. They made it back to St. Lambert in three hours. Had Winfield managed to carry out the order, the gap could have been closed.

Art Bridge only found out later that the company was on top of something hotter than an anthill: "Little did we know that we were right in the line of march of an entire [German] army trying to get out of the gap. We didn't encounter any opposition until we actually reached Moissy, although . . . the fields and lanes were full of them. When we were fired on, our situation was not much changed. We could have kept right on going along the same road to Chambois, and no doubt we'd have reached that town relatively intact. I have often pondered the decision to find our way back to St. Lambert.

"But one understrength infantry company didn't stand much chance of stopping the swarms of Germans who started moving through Moissy the next morning."[23]

24

POLISH VODKA
AT CHAMBOIS

Saturday, 19 August 1944

While Canadian troops battled at St. Lambert to seal the gap from the north, a series of bizarre events continued to thwart the American efforts to close the gap just four miles south, at Chambois. When Patton, in a fit of pique, impetuously pulled out the bulk of his units from the Argentan/Falaise front on 15 August, he left behind three divisions—three of his shakiest—under the command of his chief of staff, Major-General Hugh Gaffey.

One of these divisions was General Leclerc's 2ème Division Blindée. Leclerc had already amply demonstrated a cavalier attitude to obeying orders. For example, he ignored clear directions and sent his division wheeling up a road reserved for the U.S. 5th Armoured. He created a traffic snarl in the Forêt d'Ecouves that took six hours to unravel, thereby granting the German 116th Panzer Division a bonus of six hours to retrench and mount a vigorous defence that stalled the capture of Argentan for two days.

Leclerc badly resented his division's being left behind when Patton took off for the Seine and Paris. That was *his* job, *his* moment of glory. He refused to risk incurring heavy casualties fighting or being stranded in this Norman backwater, and even tried to sneak part of his division towards Paris. (General Gerow told him to "get the hell back where he belonged.")

The second division Patton left in Normandy was the inexperienced U.S. 80th Infantry. The third, U.S. 90th Division, had somewhat redeemed itself from its sorry reputation established in earlier Normandy fighting as the "single worst division in the European theatre."[1] The 90th had been so far from being combat effective in the battles to capture Cherbourg and St-Lô that Bradley twice sacked the commanding generals. There had even been talk of breaking it up to provide replacements for other units. However, under a new commander, Brigadier-General Raymond McLain, the 90th was given another chance.[2]

Although all three divisions had shot ahead successfully as part of Patton's dazzling breakout force, they had met virtually no opposition. Now, as a result of considerable fighting in the struggle to seize Argentan, the French Armoured was being somewhat "chewed out" by the German 9th and 1st SS and 2nd Panzer Division. The 90th was heavily engaged with the German 116th at Le Bourg–St. Léonard, a small hamlet three miles south of Chambois.[3]

Patton appointed General Gaffey to take command of his abandoned divisions for the U.S. Third Army. Gaffey established his headquarters in Sées and issued instructions for all three divisions to attack and clear Argentan and seize Chambois. However, he was unaware that General Bradley had also ordered Major-General Leonard Gerow to command the divisions under the First Army's V Corps. Not only had they been orphaned when Patton took off for the Seine, but now they had two commanders from two different armies—and neither one could find them. The divisions had seemingly disappeared.

Gerow spent a frustrating night driving around in a belting rain looking for the missing units. The commander noted in frustration that "V Corps that night was composed of ten rain-soaked officers in three jeeps out searching the countryside for three divisions."[4]

Gerow finally located 90th Infantry Division and set up temporary headquarters a few hours later in the bar of the Hôtel de France in Alençon. His first act was to cancel Gaffey's battleplan.

"It resulted in a strange situation," the unit history reports. "Here were two major-generals, both charged with the command of the same divisions. Both wanted to attack immediately, but one [Gaffey] had to wait for orders from above, while the other had been given authority to act on his own."[5]

The outcome of this bungling was that while all three units had been ready to do battle on 17 August, by the next day, none was cleared to launch the attack. The situation remained "obscured," as the war diary described it, while urgent radio messages flashed back and forth between the higher commands.

It was this fiasco that gave the Germans an unexpected bonus: extra time to bring many more units out of the gap and at the same time, keep it open for those still attempting to escape.

Finally, on the morning of 19 August, 90th Division was given the green light to approach Chambois from the south, meeting enemy opposition on the way. Chambois had been a tranquil little village bordering the Dives. Many of its citizens had fled the town during the week of intensive shelling. But not all. The baker of Chambois, who made all the bread for the three hundred people of the village, stayed on. He devised an unusual pocket of serenity for his wife, their four children, and the other youngsters left in town. "There was a big trench where the children were put," he recalled. "We made them sing songs to the violin while the artillery raged."[6] As shrapnel burst over their heads, the familiar notes of *"Un petit moulin sur la rivière"* brought some comfort to the fearful children.

U.S. Major Leonard Dull, commanding 2nd Battalion, 359th Infantry Regiment, had orders to block the roads and cover the village by fire only. An hour later there was a shift in orders. Dull was instructed that Chambois was to be occupied. Now the village was to become a battlefield. This "snafu," as Dull later called it, caused a major delay while he reorganized his battalion and disengaged his men from the firefight with the enemy outside the town. In mid-afternoon he sent patrols into Chambois and at about 1730 hours elements from two companies waded across the shallow waters of the Dives south of Chambois and managed to penetrate the village.[7]

At about the same time, Major Zgorzelski's 10th Polish Dragoons were advancing on Chambois from the north, preceded by the 10th Mounted Rifles reconnaissance regiment.

"We advanced to the top of a hill just south of Chambois," Captain Michael Gutowski of the 10th Mounted Rifles reported. "There was a ravine in front of me and buildings of the village around it. Suddenly we came under fire from panzerfausts."

Gutowski sent a foot patrol to investigate, which radioed back anxiously: "The valley is black with Germans!" Gutowski ordered his squadron to dismount and attack on foot—an unusual and highly dangerous tactic for an armoured reconnaissance unit.

"My squadron had sixteen tanks left, each with three men. We attacked with machine guns and hand grenades; there was nobody else to support us." The small band engaged in a fierce firefight for some thirty minutes, capturing and killing many Germans.[8]

At 1630 hours, the forward observation officer, Captain Sévigny, noted the action from the heights of Boisjois. He reported that the lead Polish troops had passed from his sight as they reached the orchards and hedged enclosures on the outskirts of Chambois itself. Major Zgorzelski's 10th Dragoons, and its Recce Regiment, the 10th Mounted Rifle, were herding along the great number of German prisoners as they entered the village.

Second-Lieutenant Karcz, a troop leader in the 10th Dragoons, described the scene as they entered the town: "The place was on fire. The roads leading to it and the side streets were jammed with German armour already alight or smouldering, enemy corpses and a host of wounded soldiers. No civilians were to be seen." From every orchard, ditch and house they collected prisoners until their numbers grew enormously. As they approached the Dives River they came under a hail of bullets from the houses; a Polish grenade silenced this.[9]

Elements from Major Dull's 2nd Battalion, by chance approaching the town at about the same time (but from the south), were equally overawed by the scene of destruction.

Captain Gaskins, commanding officer of "F" Company, reported it was the first time he ever had living proof of the old phrase "rivers of blood—blood was actually running in sizable streams in the gutters." Houses were burning, the stench of dead and burnt flesh was almost unbearable; there was an unbelievable clutter of dead Germans, horses, and vehicles. Ammunition exploding all around the place made him think incongruously, "It was just like a Fourth of July!"

Suddenly, Lieutenant Karcz's second-in-command shouted news of the approach of a battalion of enemy infantry attacking across the fields. Before they could open fire, they were able to identify from their helmets that these were American infantry.

"An American captain ran toward me and, still running, caught hold of me and lifted me in the air as if I had been a child," Lieutenant Karcz remembered.[10]

This encounter between a 10th Dragoon Squadron and a patrol

Capt. Michael Gutowski, Polish Armoured Division, rests on his tank.

The Polish Armoured Division on the move.

Captured German officers.

Sniper hunt, Falaise, Les Fusiliers Mont-Royal.

David Currie, VC.

A knocked-out German tank, August 16, 1944.

"B" Company of Le Régiment de Maisonneuve, August 16, 1944.

Canadian troops enter Falaise, August 16, 1944.

GI with German paratrooper.

Tanks of U.S. 5th Armoured Division.

GIs hunting snipers.

Prisoners from the 25th Infantry Division, Operation *Tractable*.

The rubble of Argentan, August 21, 1944.

A Canadian soldier watches for snipers, Falaise.

The Corridor of Death.

from Major Dull's 2nd Battalion, 359th Infantry Regiment, was a historic moment: the first time American and Polish troops had ever met on a battlefield.

The 90th Infantry Division historian reported another such encounter in an after battle report: "Major Booth, the Regimental S3, met the Polish commanding officer who, although he spoke English, said when asked his name, 'Here, give me a book and pencil. You'll never be able to pronounce it anyway so I'll write it down.' He was Major Zgorzelski of the 10th Polish Dragoons."[11]

Zgorzelski scrawled his name and unit on a scrap of paper torn from a notebook: Captain Laughlin Waters, commanding "G" Company, 359th Infantry, reciprocated.[12] These two allies appropriately commemorated the occasion with a toast in Polish vodka (from a bottle fortuitously liberated from a German officer's jeep). Elbows bent in quick succession to a lusty round of drinks and many "*Vive les Americains* and *Vive les Polognes.*"

"This meeting on the Chambois/Mont Ormel road, although one of several 'first' contacts reported, seems to be the one nearest to the 'first,'" the 90th Infantry Division historian noted. Several others took place almost simultaneously, however, so the point is debatable. As it turned out, the Polish unit which was contacted was a flying column which had shot ahead of its main body and was almost completely out of supplies when it met the Americans."[13]

After this first contact by the advance units of two divisions, both brought up their forces quickly: the Dragoons handed over some two thousand German prisoners to the Americans, explaining that their resources were too limited to keep POWs. The new allies then worked out a mutual plan for defence of the town.

The Poles had seriously outstripped their supply lines. They had not been resupplied since their amazing twenty-mile night march three days earlier. Just prior to their exodus they had lost half of their petrol stores and much ammunition to RAF bombing during *Operation Tractable*. Now the division was cut off both from its own units at Maczuga and from all of their other allies, excepting this one tenuous and, so far, unproductive link with U.S. troops.

"Our position is very flimsy," Captain Gutowski emphasized to the Americans. "We are out of food. We have no water, no gasoline and no ammunition. Some tanks have no more than five or ten shells left. For machine guns there is maybe ten minutes' firing left." They asked the Americans for help.[14]

"Major Dull contacted his higher echelon and informed them of the situation," the battalion history records. "I had one hell of a time convincing the higher authorities of the actual conditions," Dull confirmed. "The Poles did not have enough gas left in their vehicles to allow them to go the few miles south to Le Bourg–St. Léonard. Finally, after urgent negotiation up and down the chain of command, the American 1st Army, through V Corps, supplied the Poles with 4,000 gallons of gasoline, 140,000 rounds of machine gun ammunition and 189 rounds of 75mm ammunition for the guns of the tanks."[15]

The 1st Polish Armoured Division history applauded the generosity of the Americans. "[They] shared with us their rations, ammunition, gasoline and were very generous with their cigarettes. It will be difficult to forget the supply officer, Major Miller, who, being short of working hands, helped personally to load ammunition boxes on our trucks."[16]

But all of this negotiation took time—too much time. In the waiting period, both units were too thin on the ground to develop a solid barrier against a determined enemy. They had no resources to extend their line the mile north to Moissy, as per General Simonds' orders, where a small ford offered the enemy a shallow crossing over the Dives.

In fact, it was on that same evening that "C" Company of the Canadian Argylls probed south from St. Lambert as far as the small village of Moissy. Had the Canadians or the Poles been able to reach out that extra mile or two, the pocket enclosing the German army would have been at least technically sealed.

Although they were, like the South Albertas and Argylls down the road at St. Lambert, celebrating the formal closing of the Falaise Gap, in truth the Allied defenders on the Dives were finding it hopeless in the rough and wooded terrain to block small groups of enemies from filtering through their lines.

They had no knowledge that this misgiving would be put to a test within a few hours. A massed enemy breakout, heralding twenty-four hours of violent conflict, was planned for dawn the next day.

*

On 13 August, celebrants of Sunday mass at Tournai-sur-Dives were distracted by an unusual clatter outside. They emerged into the sun-filled square to witness a terrifying sight: the narrow lanes of their small hamlet were jammed with German vehicles and military equipment. The German army was escaping before their very eyes.

"We are caught in the middle of the battle!" Abbé Marcel Launay exclaimed to his parishioners. There were 314 townsfolk in Tournai, but their numbers had swollen as refugees from stricken towns sought refuge in the formerly peaceful village.

Launay could offer little consolation to his parishioners. The Germans must cross the Dives to break out of the Allied trap, he told them. All roads leading to the river go through Tournai-sur-Dives. So our small village is a rallying point for an army in full retreat.

"They are escaping with three vehicles abreast everywhere they can," the padre noted tersely in his diary that day. "Some towards Vimoutiers, some towards Chambois. Allied planes are constantly strafing them. This afternoon, between St. Lambert and Trun (3.5 km) 12 German vehicles are in flames. Two of these are ammunition transports and explode for hours."

An eyewitness described the exodus: "German vehicles of all kinds, tanks, small and large trucks, motor bicycles and carts fleeing en route for Chambois. Some of the cars had lost their windows, others had no doors left . . . one had no front tires and another had only three wheels."

Who were they, these fleeing Germans? A comrade described the hodgepodge of non-combat personnel: "Infantrymen without weapons, civilians employed by the Wehrmacht, workers from the Atlantic Wall, newsreel operators, buyers from ministries . . ."

The villagers didn't care who the stragglers were. They were leaving, that was the important thing. "Get going! It's your turn to run now!" one shouted gleefully at the retreating foe.

In the next few days, panicky civilians in neighbouring villages reported increasing misery. By day, enemy trucks and tanks were camouflaged in increasing numbers in sheds and under apple trees. "As usual," Launay wrote, "as the sun sets we hear Germans on the move." French villagers were forced to hand over food and drink. Some were ordered to drive their cattle towards the German border.

In one afternoon every chicken in Villedieu was slaughtered to feed German troops.

Launay noted that: "People are sleeping where they feel the safest, some in the dry drainage ditches of the fields. In Villedieu the local prison and the quarry passages are filled with people trying to find shelter. The Germans take advantage of this situation to pillage their homes of all items of value."

Not only did the Germans cause suffering and death to the villagers, but the Allies also created havoc. As the Americans closed in from Argentan and the Canadians and British from Falaise, the townspeople were caught in the crossfire of their guns. On the 14th, the padre wrote, "the Allied artillery has concentrated on Trun and Chambois which both suffer terrible damage."

At 0530 hours on 15 August, the day of the Feast of the Assumption, Abbé Launay arose early and went out of the presbytery into the street. His entry in his diary that day was horrified: "A troop of German tanks were setting up at a nearby school. Worse, one of their soldiers had been shot. The commander declared the town of Tournai under siege. Three Frenchmen had been arrested and detained in the school basement. The SS lieutenant decreed that for every German harassed or threatened, 10 French civilians would be imprisoned."

Launay and the mayor negotiated the release of the civilians, but the lieutenant, fearing more resistance, forbade any man of the village to attend the important religious celebrations that day.

The next day, the mayor asked the SS lieutenant if he intended to fight it out in the town. He received a grim response: "We are here to fight, and we expect to fight the 'Tommies' soon."

"The villagers start preparing themselves for this outcome," the padre noted. "The civilians move their belongings into cellars and build shelters as best they can. The shelling continues unabated all day. The Germans, who are in the midst of a fighting retreat, occupy the abandoned houses and refuse to let the French civilians back into them to get some of their belongings."

Civilian casualties increased, but many doctors refused to come out because they were afraid to be on the road during the invasion. The allies thought that if you were on the road you must be a German. And so they were strafed and killed.

Some French risked their lives to loot the escaping Germans. Tires were removed from smashed vehicles. Their contents, often perfumes and elegant ladies' wear that the enemy himself had looted, were snatched back. Bodies were searched for watches or money. Boots were stripped from corpses.

The villagers were furious to hear the monstrous story of a farmer in a neighbouring hamlet. The SS had occupied his home. His wife and four children cowered in a shed. The Germans ordered the children to fetch them water from the well. As the youngsters crossed the farmyard, an Allied mortar made a direct hit, killing all four children. With his wife in hysterics and his neighbours scattered into ditches, the wretched man was left with the solitary and grisly task of burying his own four children.

On 18 August the Abbé wrote: "The American artillery is stronger than ever as they smash Argentan and the Trun-Chambois road. The fleeing Germans are forced to go by Tournai: their last possible exit. But in fact, once in Tournai they are stuck in a terrible traffic jam with their comrades [escaping] from Mortain. Everybody wants to get to Chambois quickly, and with our narrow streets everybody must wait their turn, but everyone wants priority! Once in a while an officer is forced to dismount his vehicle and pull out his pistol to ensure his unit's passage."

By now, Allied bombing and shelling had increased to a frenzied level. Every 13 minutes, from 2230 to 0500 hours a shell falls in the centre of town. "We are stuck in the middle of an artillery duel between the Allies and the Germans," the padre said helplessly.

"We are now at war. The battle has begun."[17]

25

TRAPPED!

Saturday night, 19 August 1944
Oberstgruppenführer Paul Hausser sat at the edge of a ditch, studying a map.

Even in this rude setting, the sixty-three-year-old SS general maintained his demeanour: back ramrod-straight, uniform impeccable, black patch neatly adjusted on the eye lost on the Russian front, expression as aloof as ever.[1]

He ignored his staff, hurriedly setting up a new command post—an old stone quarry near the village of Villedieu les Bailleul. He seemed unconcerned that his new CP was a mere two miles west of the Allied positions on the Dives and could be overrun at any time.

He took no notice of the August sun, just now setting on this eighteenth day of the month. He had seen seventy-three suns go down over Normandy since the D-Day invasion.

The task that absorbed his attention now was how to extricate his men from almost certain capture or death as the Allied trap closed around them.

General Hausser had just returned after personally visiting on foot the headquarters of each of his four corps threatened with encirclement. With them, he explored a means of organized escape.

It was true that for the past two or three days endless columns of German troops and even some equipment had been pouring east across the Dives Valley, finding sanctuary in the ruggedness of the Auge hills. They were part of the exodus initiated on 14 August by General von Kluge. In all, five panzer divisions and two infantry divisions had managed to get most of their rear-echelon troops safely out of the entrapment. Supply troops and a large mass of *matériel* were also saved, although few of their vehicles, being mainly horse drawn, had survived the passage. They had followed the secondary roads and trails that led from villages west of the

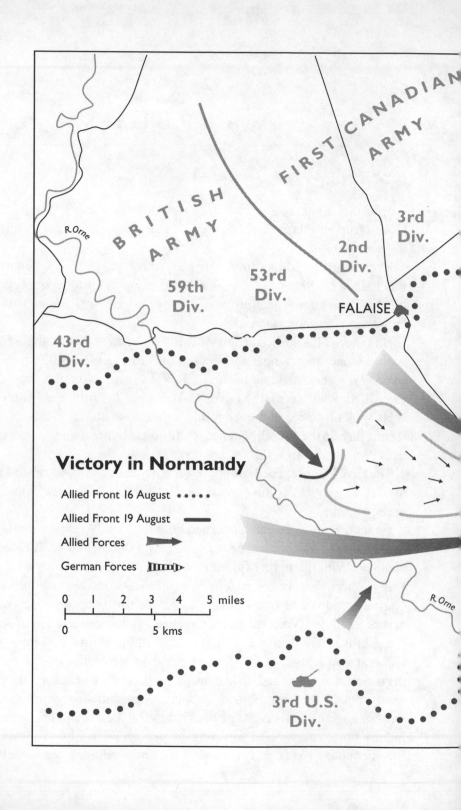

Victory in Normandy

Allied Front 16 August	•••••
Allied Front 19 August	▬
Allied Forces	➤
German Forces	⫞⫞⫞▷

0   1   2   3   4   5 miles

0   5 kms

R.Orne

BRITISH ARMY

FIRST CANADIAN ARMY

59th Div.

53rd Div.

2nd Div.

3rd Div.

FALAISE

43rd Div.

3rd U.S. Div.

R.Orne

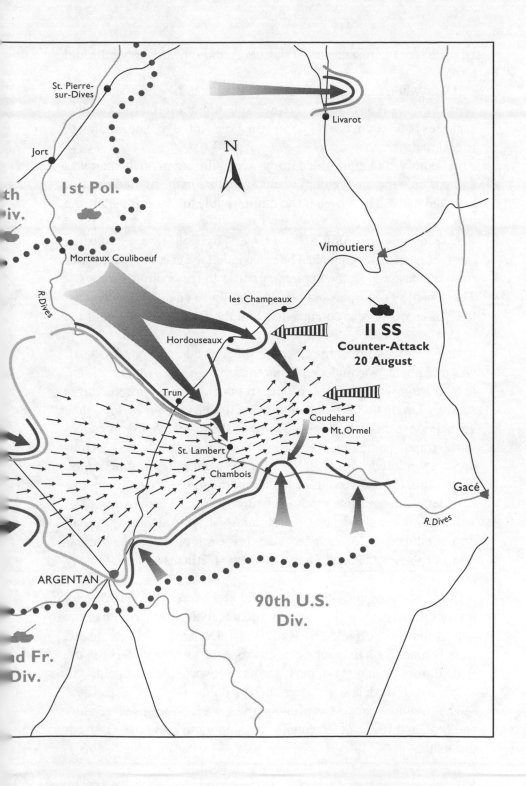

St. Pierre-
sur-Dives

Jort

th
Div.

1st Pol.

Morteaux Couliboeuf

R.Dives

les Champeaux

Hordouseaux

Trun

St. Lambert

Chambois

ARGENTAN

d Fr.
Div.

Livarot

N

Vimoutiers

II SS
Counter-Attack
20 August

Coudehard
Mt. Ormel

Gacé

R. Dives

90th U.S.
Div.

Dives River to crossings at St. Lambert and onwards toward Mont Ormel.[2]

It was while following this escape route that they had been intercepted by the Poles during the previous night's trek. The German escapees had "courteously" waved the Poles through, not wanting to reveal their intentions.

Incredibly, although Allied troops were closing in on them, it was still possible for small groups to elude capture in the myriad wooded hills and paths. The terrain made it impossible to seal completely the gap.

A reconnaissance unit of 21 Panzer Division, now established north of Les Champeaux, had been assigned the task "to reconnoiter from the east unoccupied points of sortie to the encircled troops."[3] These battle groups, probing the Allied lines, enabled the clandestine passage of senior commanders and their staffs in and out of the pocket.

Hausser's chief of staff, Oberst Freiherr Rudolph von Gersdorff, was making his way independently through the gap to attend a high-level meeting with General Model (replacing the disgraced Kluge) at Army Group "B" Headquarters at La Roche Guyon. He brought a grim description of the plight of some of the miserable troops caught in the trap: "Things look black inside the pocket," he said. "Hundreds upon hundreds of vehicles [have] been put out of action by enemy fire. Untended wounded (and) innumerable dead characterize a battlefield in a manner rarely seen throughout the entire war."[4] The Allied air offensive and the particularly heavy artillery fire had destroyed the bulk of the army vehicles. Lack of fuel and ammunition had already made it imperative for the Germans to destroy many of their guns.[5]

Gersdorff informed General Model that the recent Canadian penetrations into Trun and St. Lambert threatened the northern rim of the gap. British 30 Corps and the 53rd Welsh Division are squeezing us from behind like a limp tube of toothpaste, he told them. To keep the British from baying at our heels we have sown thick minefields and employed other delaying tactics such as booby traps.

The situation was just as bleak on the American front. The enemy had broken through at Chambois, threatening to close the gap from the south.

Gersdorff was in an agitated state when he returned to report to Hausser. He had to dodge intense artillery fire as he stealthily made his way back into the pocket. Gersdorff was shaken to learn that in his absence Welsh troops had attacked Hausser's Seventh Army command post at Nécy (four miles south of Falaise), reportedly wiping out the entire Seventh Army staff. The rumour proved to be untrue, but the Germans had lost most of their vehicles and radio equipment under intense British and Canadian artillery fire.[6]

Later, at an Orders Group with senior commanders, Gersdorff reviewed the bleak facts. It was a sorry handful of men that huddled on two benches around a worn wooden kitchen table. A flickering candle etched the battle weariness of their faces.

Attending the "O" Group were the commanding generals of 84th Infantry Division (Lieutenant-General Elfeldt) and 12th SS Hitler-jugend (Kurt Meyer). As well, there were several senior staff members: Hubert Meyer (12th SS), Major Heinz-Günther Guderian (116th Panzer Division), and Colonel Hans von Kluge (Panzer-gruppe Eberbach). Kluge had just learned of the suicide of his father, disgraced by Hitler.

Major Guderian described the emergency measures he had employed in recent days to try to hold that critical line against the Americans. His 116th Panzer and units from 47 Panzer Corps had rushed whatever battle-fit groups they could muster to that front.

Initially, he told them, his force was so ill equipped that he had not had much hope of success against Patton's powerful forces: "We fought with very few tanks." Luckily, Guderian ran into a detachment of another division, whose commander was a friend. "I told him, you fight here [with me!]"

But when 116th Panzer sent an urgent demand to Army HQ for reinforcements from 1st SS Panzer Division, the Wehrmacht was furious to discover that—without even consulting them—some combat units of the 1st SS had already been moved out of the pocket.

"Probably acting on orders received through SS channels," Gersdorff grumbled.[7] It was this underhanded sort of action that emphasized the debilitating power struggle between the Wehrmacht and the SS that continued unabatedly, despite this crisis.

The German panzers had put up stiff resistance, trying to stem the

American force. Suddenly, Guderian was astonished to find the pressure exerted by the Americans abruptly relaxed.

He couldn't know that Patton's precipitous departure for the Seine on 14 August had left just three unproven divisions holding the southern edge of the pocket, and these had been temporarily halted for lack of a commander.

"If the [Americans] had attacked without stopping, we were blown up," he reported. "There is no doubt. They could have met the English and Canadians coming from the north without difficulty."[8]

The 116th had gained some time, but now the Americans had driven them out of Le Bourg–St. Léonard and had closed on Chambois.

One of Guderian's officers, Walter Kaspers, an adjutant in 116th Anti-tank Division, described his unit's feelings of pending catastrophe: "The British pushed from one side and Patton from the other. We could not hold, and were pushed closer and closer together. This is not a nice feeling, to be so concentrated. The artillery grew more and more intense and we had less and less room."

Kaspers noted that three-quarters of the division was horse drawn. "That was terrible for us. The horse-drawn part could not get away because it moved too slowly. Patton was much faster."[9]

Gersdorff stressed the urgency of coordinating a massed breakout out of the trap. Our strongest combat troops are still caught behind the lines, he told them.

There is one note of hope, he added. Throughout the fighting in Normandy in the past months, Seventh Army strategists have observed that the enemy is most vulnerable at the junction, or "seam" of their lines. Remember Vire, he said. Remember Argentan. Every time the Anglo-Americans try to fight on adjoining battle-lines, they seem to have time-wasting disputes. We capitalized on them then; we will again. "Here again the seam between the 21st Army Group and the Twelfth U.S. Army Group seems to [play] the part of guardian angel to us.

Another encouraging factor is the outside support we can expect. General Model has masterminded a carefully coordinated attack plan to withdraw our units that are still trapped west of the Dives River. The breakout will take place eastward across the Dives between Trun and Chambois."[10]

Escaping the pocket was to be a two-prong operation. Dual forces would attack. One, Hausser's Seventh Army, would break *out* of the encirclement. The other, 2nd SS Panzer Corps, would break *in* to support the escaping troops.

Operating from Army HQ near Paris, Model (who had replaced Kluge) had spirited 2nd SS Panzer Corps out of the pocket two days before. Its orders reflected the desperation of the German plight. The Corps (comprising 9th SS and 2nd SS Panzer Divisions) were "to march during the day regardless of losses . . . from enemy fighter-bombers."[11]

General Bittrich, the commanding general of 2nd SS Panzer Corps, had reassembled the corps near Vimoutiers, a market town five miles north of Maczuga. His job was to launch a major counter-attack back *into* the pocket and hold it open long enough for the armies to escape the trap.

Bittrich had hoped to launch the attack on 18 August. He was getting a lot of pressure from the trapped Seventh Army commanders to move as quickly as possible, before the Allies became aware of the plan: "The withdrawal of the 2nd SS Panzer Corps cannot for long remain concealed," Gersdorff informed him.[12]

However, shortages of fuel and ammunition delayed the assault. General Model was attempting to airlift petrol to troops on both sides of the Allied encirclement. General Bittrich now hoped the expected refuelling would allow him to launch the 2nd SS and 9th SS counter-attack force at 1000 hours Sunday morning.

The job of breaking *out* of the trap was organized in two stages. First was Lieutenant-General Eugen Meindl's advance force of two thousand paratroopers and infantry.

"The entire movement is to be conducted as a surprise attack," they were told. This was laid out as a precise—but wildly unorthodox—military operation. The breakout itself was "only men."

No artillery pieces could be taken other than the few self-propelled or mobile anti-tank guns they still possessed. All troops had been ordered to expend ammunition the day before the breakout and then destroy their guns. They would have to take advantage of any small undefended gap in the four-mile stretch of river for their flight. The 21st Panzer Division's reconnaissance units patrolling the enemy positions along the Dives had identified these soft spots.

General Gersdorff shocked the Orders Group by declaring that the only support for the paratroopers would be the headquarters staff of 84 Infantry—staff officers acting as support troops? Unheard of!

Meindl's paratroopers would advance stealthily on foot through the night to St. Lambert. Their orders were to steal through the Allied lines in a wedge formation, "using Indian tactics," without firing. They would set their course by compass and regroup at Coudehard, near Mont Ormel, linking up with 2nd SS Corps. Food and water would await them. They were then to wheel in their tracks and attack back against the Canadians and Poles they had just eluded.

Next, with the paratroopers safely out, Kurt Meyer and his 12th SS Hitlerjugend would follow in the breakout. The Hitler's Youth division was now a sorry lot, virtually dissolved as a fighting force. Of the *ten thousand* teenage fanatics who had marched into Normandy at the onset of the invasion, only *one hundred* were left.[13] Their last two Tigers were committed for the expected fighting after dawn.[14]

Then, at 0800 hours, the main German force would launch a massive breakout, with tanks, vehicles, and the majority of the besieged German troops. By sheer weight of numbers, screaming *Seig Heil* and brandishing revolvers, tens of thousands of the desperate infantry would surge in a mad charge across the Dives and on to Hill 262, at Coudehard.

Battlegruppe Eberbach, along with Lieutenant-General Heinrich von Lüttwitz's 2nd Panzer Division, would lead this attack. Lüttwitz, a rotund, monocled Silesian officer of stern Wehrmacht tradition, insisted that he was taking no chances with his fifteen remaining tanks. They were all he had left of the 120 with which he had arrived in Normandy. He told his panzer commanders that the tanks and armoured vehicles had no chance of getting through roads clogged with corpses in the dark: "On the route leading into St. Lambert-sur-Dives from Bailleul where my division was collected, a colossal number of shot-up horses and vehicles lay mixed together with dead soldiers in large heaps which hourly [grow] higher and higher."[15]

The two forces—one attacking out and the other attacking in—would link up in the high ground at Coudehard, a village in the hills of Maczuga, where the paratroopers would join in the battle to save their comrades.

Many of the Wehrmacht troops waiting to lay on the attack despaired of ever escaping; a great many were ready to surrender. Filthy, starved, and half-crazed by the incessant shelling and strafing by the dreaded Jabos, one corporal wrote to his family: "Nothing to eat for two days . . . . There is no leadership left. I don't want to fight anymore, it is so useless . . . . Our future looks hopeless . . . most likely we will be taken prisoner."[16]

Some of them were forced to continue with a pistol to their heads—an SS pistol.

Not so for Hitler's tough and dedicated Nazi paratroopers under Meindl's command: "Their mood was excellent; I had seen nothing but glowing eyes the whole day through."[17]

The paratroop commander was contemptuous of those German soldiers who had given up hope. The first thing he had done had been to establish a circle with a radius of 1,000 metres around his command post "so as not be betrayed by the troops gone completely wild." It was only in such a situation, he said bitterly, that "one finds out who is really the soldier and who is only a military, *who belongs to the brave and who to the bosses and cowards and even traitors*!"[his emphasis].

He deeply resented the favouritism shown the SS divisions of 2nd SS Panzer Corps. Why had *they* been sent ahead out of the encirclement? Clearly the army thought so little of the élite paratroopers that they left them in the trap to face possible annihilation: "*We* were good enough to be left inside the ring!" he said sarcastically. "I put a black mark in my mind against the commander-in-chief."[18]

There were only three bridges across the Dives that could handle the weight of tanks, General Von Gersdorff reminded them: at Trun, Chambois, and St. Lambert. "A rumour reached us that Trun had been cut off by British troops," he said, piling on the harsh news. "Chambois [is] impassable because of the heavy enemy artillery fire."[19]

Of the three, only one—the bridge by the church at St. Lambert—was still open. St. Lambert, Hausser believed, was ideal for the breakthrough. "The commander-in-chief has therefore decided to order a breakthrough from the pocket at the weakest spot in the enemy's enveloping ring, namely on both sides of St. Lambert-sur-Dives."

"Our crossing stands or falls at St. Lambert."[20]

The Poles at Maczuga, the Americans and Poles at Chambois, and the meagre force of Canadians at Trun and St. Lambert were directly in the path of this desperate enemy.

THE BREAKOUT

Dawn, Sunday, 20 August 1944
"At 2230 hours the first patrols glided forward like shadows into the dark night."[1]

Thus began the Seventh Army's mass breakout, an attempt to funnel some 65,000 men through a six-mile-wide corridor of the Dives Valley.

At 2315 hours, Lieutenant-General Eugen Meindl led two thousand paratroopers as spearhead units in the escape. Almost immediately Meindl's group came under direct fire from Allied tanks. "We lost time whenever a star shell lit up the landscape," he noted. "We had to lie low until it got dark again." The group soon fragmented into handfuls of combat units.

"They crept through innumerable hawthorn hedges covered with barbed wire and dodged around some tanks at the roadside, arriving at the river Dives about 0030 hours . . . looking for a fordable spot . . . south of the mill."[2]

The troops were ordered to maintain strict silence. No cigarettes, no torches, and no firing unless fired upon. When the Canadian artillery opened up, the Germans dived into ditches. Slowly, sometimes crawling, sometimes sprinting from cover to cover, they neared the Dives River.

"It was a nasty job getting the whole crew across the stream without lights, noiselessly . . . The eastern bank was covered with blackberry trailers and was steep into the bargain and the enemy tanks were standing just behind the bushes."[3]

As the Germans edged closer to the enemy tank positions, they felt safer. They won't fire on their own comrades, Meindl whispered to his men.

By now the intensity of the Canadian fire had caused a number of casualties. Meindl's band—reduced to just fifteen men and a first lieutenant—was crawling cautiously around Hill 117 where Wotherspoon's South Alberta RHQ tanks were massed. So fluid were the Canadian and German lines that when the paratroopers heard an enemy tank rolling towards them they turned to Meindl in confusion.

"A German tank?" his first lieutenant whispered hopefully.

"That's no German tank!" [Meindl] snapped back.[4]

Suddenly, other tanks opened fire. The Germans froze; they were so close they could hear the Canadian crews talking by radio to one another.

> *"There was no time to be lost if we hoped to get past the tanks while it was still dark. I stole around three tanks ... but suddenly we were discovered by one that we hadn't seen in front of us. Its crew opened fire at us at a distance of thirty metres.*
>
> *"I threw myself flat on my face with a few of the others in a potato field. As the tank fire flew about a metre over my head I crept and crept along with my people, centimetre by centimetre along a deeper furrow in the field—eastward."[5]*

Cautiously bypassing that hazard, Meindl and his band clambered over a fence into a garden. "The buildings had a deserted look ... only a dog barked ... a tank was firing away."

> *"We had no time to lose. It was now about four o'clock in the morning and a glimmer of dawn was to be seen in the east. It would soon be light enough for the enemy to take potshots at us. Forward then ... east and northeast.*
>
> *"We had to plunge up to the neck for the second time in that cursed stream again. We were covered with scratches and our clothing was torn to ribbons. At about 0430 hours I heard the sound of tanks again. A soft light rain began to fall and enveloped us in its folds. It was very welcome to us."[6]*

Meindl's objective was the little village of Coudehard on the slopes of Hill 262, the southern head of the Polish Maczuga. Food would be waiting at the rallying point. Here they could regroup and rearm the men. Here, too, on this high point, they expected to rendezvous with 2nd SS Panzer Corps, breaking in that morning from the east to launch an attack.

To their bitter disappointment, enemy tanks had taken over this vital tactical position: "In a minute we made out that the tank crews were talking Polish to one another. Now we had to lie low without a sound. I gave a sign to this effect. We lay there for at least an hour and a half under the eyes of the British tanks with Polish crews, not daring to move a finger. By this time it was at least 0730 hours."

Meindl, peering ahead, anxiously watched for tanks from the 2nd SS Panzer Corps rescuers that were coming "from outside."[7]

Back in the woods, at the Seventh Army's command post, Kurt Meyer paced anxiously by the stony quarry. His 12th SS Hitlerjugend was still deep in enemy territory behind the Dives. Meyer's assignment was to stay put until he received word of the paratroopers' breakout. The distant roar of battle sounds gave them no clue. Had Meindl got through?

Finally at 0200 hours the Hitler Youth decided to strike out on their own.

There was a "solemn farewell" to their comrades in the division they were leaving. These would break out later with the motorized group; their last two Tigers were committed for the expected fighting after dawn. Each man wondered, "Would we ever see each other again?"[8]

In single file the small group filed down the footpath leading east. Trailing behind General Meyer was the unfortunate Lieutenant-General Otto Elfeldt—the corps commander (84th) without a corps—soon to be separated from the group and captured by the Poles at Chambois. Meyer and his chief of staff, Hubert Meyer, pressed on until they spied the village sign poking up from the rubble: "St. Lambert."

At last! They crept along the far banks of the Dives, crossing at the Château de Quantité. Enemy tanks and artillery fired at them fitfully.

They heard soldiers speaking English. This was the enemy—Canadian infantry—with whom they had been in almost continuous direct confrontation since the first day of the invasion. It galled them not to attack their arch foe.

On the far side of the Dives they still had three miles to go to reach the heights of Coudehard. Stragglers, most without weapons, wanted to join them: "Panzermeyer accepted only those who were still armed or managed to find weapons," his chief of staff recorded.

Pistol in hand, blood oozing from a head wound, Kurt Meyer led his group, now swollen to two hundred men, across the fire-swept country. He had been stationed in the area before the invasion. "I know every tree and bush," he reassured them.[9] They advanced from hedge to hedge . . . sometimes crawling stealthily, sometimes running, leaping over ditches filled with their own dead. "Out!" That was their one thought. "Out of this inferno."[10]

On the pastures and in the ditches thousands of dead and wounded Germans lay abandoned, caught by enemy fire. They also saw groups of soldiers who had thrown away their weapons and were waving white flags attached to sticks, indicating their willingness to surrender: "A disgraceful, never-before-seen picture."[11]

Completely worn out, the men had still to clamber up the wooded trails of the steeply ascending hill to reach their designated rallying point. Here they would regroup their own forces and rendezvous with 2nd SS Panzer Corps, now supposedly attacking from outside.

A third unit, General Mahlmann's 353rd Infantry Division, had forded the river at Moissy and also escaped in the direction of Hill 262 at Mont Ormel.

There were many other isolated bands of soldiers stumbling about in the dark, body-strewn no-man's-land that was once a tranquil Norman valley. The hills were alive with such Germans—many exhausted, disoriented, and weak with wounds. "You wouldn't know the name of the man next you; you might not even know what regiment he was from," one German survivor later remembered.[12]

Some were determined to escape; others were recruited into a counter-attack force, sometimes at gunpoint. A few—Meindl's paratroopers and Meyer's Hitlerjugend—continued to fight hard.

In the confusion of the breakout, anti-tank officer Walter Kaspers had the frightening experience of being left behind by his unit. He made his way out alone:

> I knew the direction to go in because I carried a small compass. This helped me—as well as the hedges which gave me cover. One could only see about fifty meters. So I made my way like an Indian through the hedges. It is no fine feeling if you are alone and on foot. There were many wounded and quite a few dead. One of my good friends lay there, as well as other fine men.
>
> I wandered into a wood and watched an SS division launch a counter-attack. Then I became dog tired. I came to a small farmhouse. I asked the girl if I could sleep in the barn. I pointed to the east and said that I was heading that way. She told me not to worry about the Resistance and allowed me to stay and even brought me a jug of milk and a few pieces of white bread.[13]

Dr. Walter Padberg, staff officer of Grenadier Regiment 959, recalled the total confusion as he struggled out of the trap: "There was no battle-line anymore, everything was mixed up. Communication had ended; I did not know where the regimental commander was; I did not know any of the people around me. Everything was chaos. Allied artillery and airplanes were everywhere."

Lieutenant Padberg with a group of twenty or thirty men, found an armoured assault vehicle. It had gasoline, but no munitions. They drove through the Polish position on the hills, luckily escaping being mortared.

"When we made it out of the pocket," Padberg said, "we were of the opinion that we had left hell behind us. We climbed out of the armoured car. There stood a colonel. 'Line up!' he began to bellow. 'Everyone is now under my command! We are going to launch a counter-attack!' We were a pile of twenty or thirty men. I had a pistol and nothing else. Unfortunately, I had to go behind a bush to relieve myself and missed joining the group behind the colonel."[14]

Günter Materne, a battery officer with the 363rd Artillery Regiment, recalled the difficulties of the retreat. "Sometimes we had to go to farmhouses, many of which were abandoned; sometimes we ran across trucks whose contents were spread out over the ground.

Everything was in chaos from the bombing attacks: burned-out vehicles, dead horses. We were living off the land.

"We helped the wounded as much as we could, as did the medics. But it was terrible for those lying there in pain. It was terrible to see men lying there in the throes of death, screaming. They cried 'Mama! Take me with you, don't leave me here! I have a wife and child at home. I'm bleeding to death!' "[15]

Not five miles away, at Vimoutiers, 2nd SS Panzer Corps finally received the air drop of petrol that would allow them to launch their counter-attack into the Canadian lines.

Trapped between the German rescuers outside and the escaping Germans now clambering up the rough Auge hills towards them were two Polish armoured regiments, frantically digging in at Château Boisjois on Maczuga.

In the darkness of that long night Lieutenant-Colonel Swatty Wotherspoon—and certainly David Currie and his men—could hear and even sometimes glimpse shadowy bands of Germans crossing the river and heading north through the town.

With fewer than one hundred infantrymen to cover this broad stretch of infiltrated country where thousands of Germans were slipping past them, there was little they could do except wait: wait for reinforcements and wait for dawn.

27

BLACK SUNDAY

Sunday, 20 August 1944

At 0800 hours, as the fog lifted on a brilliant Sunday morning, warriors from six nations joined battle at the Dives River.

The Poles—expatriates like Michael Gutowski, still anguishing for their Warsaw brothers in arms—arrived with hate in their hearts for the Nazis.

Canadians such as David Currie came sustained by the physical strength of the hard life faced by a prairie lad, and the deep confidence of a man who had just the previous day found his answer. He truly *had* measured up.

The Texas-Oklahomans of the U.S. 90th Division, fresh from their victories at Le Bourg–St. Léonard and Chambois, reached the Dives with a growing sense of pride in the transformation of their unit. The division had not only been given back its soul by General McLain, but it also had found leaders at all levels. Could they finally live up to their division's proud nickname: "tough 'ombres" of World War I?

The British and Scottish troops who had seen so many thousands of their men fall in the sixty-five days of unrelenting and deadly fighting to reach this last battle of Normandy, could now only look on, their numbers so sadly depleted.

Bemused by the magnitude of their artillery fire, and by the uniqueness of it—when had the artillery ever fired in two opposite directions at once?—Allied gunners began to realize that this was essentially a fire war and their contributions would be the decisive factors.

So, too, did American, British and Canadian airmen, taking off from bases just minutes away from the battlefield, swooping again and again across the Dives Valley, have the certain knowledge that their skills were key factors in the coming battle.

The French? With what emotion did they watch their country being torn apart, their countrymen mowed down by shells and bombs, while they dreamed only of Paris?

And the Class of '26? Could they, and the thousands of other tattered but still proud remnants of Hitler's élite SS—could they still believe in their destiny?

The Germans descended like a tidal wave—huge, unstoppable rollers of desperate men. Earlier, the paratroopers had crept by in darkness, small handfuls at a time, crawling on their bellies past blinded Canadian tanks. Now this second force descended by the thousands in strident fury.

"As they marched out, the men were singing," Lieutenant-Colonel Max Anger, a member of the SS Panzer Kampfgruppen, remembered of the start-line. "The mood was good. It was a rare picture." The unit ran into a huge traffic jam at Tournai-sur-Dives, just west of St. Lambert. Colonel Anger felt that the Wehrmacht was for once showing real respect. "For the first time, after all these many campaigns (he said with pride) I heard the call, 'SS to the front!' "[1]

Elsewhere, Lüttwitz's 2nd Panzer Division, with fifteen tanks and various armoured and horse-drawn vehicles, led the charge across the stone bridge at St. Lambert. Screaming their *Sieg Heils* and brandishing fists, they stormed the Dives. Infantry and columns of vehicles followed in their wake.

As the fog lifted, Allied artillery opened up in "a storm such as I had never before experienced," Lüttwitz would long remember. Many of the horses pulling vehicles balked under the hail of fire, wheeling in frantic circles until they were shot up and blocked the narrow roads. "Towering pillars of smoke rose incessantly from petrol tanks as they were hit," he wrote. "Ammunition exploded, riderless horses stampeded, some of them badly wounded." Men, horses, and vehicles tumbled from the bridge and lay "jumbled together in grotesque heaps."[2]

What started out as an orderly attack collapsed into a confused shambles. Success in escaping the closing Allied ring now depended on the individual initiative of each unit commander, on unit morale and the will to fight, and on pure chance—the good fortune, for example, of finding an undefended crossing or a shallow ford.[3]

In the next five hours of "embittered close-in fighting," the battle for St. Lambert raged as wave after wave of Germans battered the defenders.[4]

Currie's small force, now down to 120 troopers and infantrymen, with just five tanks, fought desperately to hold off another huge swarm of thousands of enemy infantry. Lieutenant Jake Summers of "B" Squadron said it was "like trying to stop a buffalo stampede. They went around us, they went over us and they went under us."[5] Currie was forced to pull back from the south end of the village, consolidating his slender resources at the eastern segment to avoid being totally wiped out.

General von Lüttwitz managed to establish a command post of sorts in the village church and round up a few "energetic officers" who kept a narrow escape hatch open for a few hours. Panicky troops, banded into individual, fragmented combat groups, fought their way through the town.

Back at Quantité, Lieutenant Don Stewart was just starting to shave behind his tank when someone yelled that the Germans were attacking.[6] Two platoons of infantry—one Argyll and one Lincoln—dug in at the mill with two South Alberta tanks in support. The small band of thirty men was dead in the path of one massed attack.

Lieutenant "Junior" Arkle Dunlop and his platoon of sixteen Lincoln and Wellands at the mill, facing overwhelming odds, had three of their number killed by the onslaught. Private Stan "Red" Roberts, so named for his blaze of hair, had been guarding a number of prisoners at the river. He was shot through the head by a German soldier who suddenly appeared at the top of the bank on the enemy side.[7]

"We've got orders to pull out or we were going to get slaughtered!" Lieutenant Dunlop yelled to his platoon. They started backing out, herding the prisoners before them. With their two tanks shielding them, they headed across the open fields to St. Lambert.

"Lieutenant Stewart reversed his tank all the way so he could use his firepower on the Germans who were coming up over the hills at us," Dunlop recalled. "He accidentally backed over one of my guys who had been hit. Seeing a fellow backed over lengthways by a tank is terrible."[8]

German troops set up a machine gun on the top of a knoll with a full sweep of the area the Lincs had to cross. "We began playing the old game of 'leapfrog' by which each of us would run perhaps twenty or thirty yards, then dive flat on the ground. Someone in a different sector would then get up and run his stretch and do the same thing. By doing this we were fortunate in getting out with a minimum number of casualties."

When Lieutenant Stewart's guns jammed, he started firing his pistol at the Germans. "He actually got one in the head before being wounded himself."[9]

The situation at regimental headquarters was getting out of hand. Wotherspoon moved his tanks to better fire positions and they began to mow down the advancing enemy. But there were just not enough infantrymen.

Wotherspoon had radioed the 4th Armoured Brigade for more infantry backup four times in the early hours of the morning. Now he sent a final warning: *"Unless support arrives [we] may be pushed out of position."*[10]

Even this dire forecast did not result in any additional manpower being sent forward. Brigadier Booth's death on 14 August, and the subsequent temporary changes of command of two different men while waiting for the arrival of a third, Brigadier Bob Moncel, meant that essentially there was no single brigade commander to take hold during the crisis.

Meanwhile, Major Darby Nash and his South Alberta "B" Squadron had dug in on their hilltop position. They were surrounded. The enemy was fairly swarming under the cover of the thick woods on all sides. They had no infantry support at all. "[They] were all around us and we kept up random fire and threw hand grenades into the hedges and ditches in an effort to drive them off," Trooper John Neff recalls.[11]

The chatter they could hear on the wireless from the Americans, a few miles to the south, frustrated the crews. Nash felt like cutting in and yelling for help, "When are you coming over, Yanks?" but he had to maintain wireless silence.[12]

John Neff remembers the viciousness of one close attack: "I was standing on the back deck of our tank with a Sten gun and George Evans' tank was no more than twenty feet away from mine. I could hear movement about his tank and it sounded to me as if someone was pouring petrol over it. Suddenly, there was the flash of a grenade explosion and George's tank just went up in a sheet of flame. I could see a couple of Jerries duck under the major's tank."[13]

The assault had been coordinated to hit the Allied "soft spots" along the river, pre-identified by German recce patrols: Trun, Chambois, Moissy, St. Lambert. By sheer weight of numbers they punched isolated holes through the fragile Allied lines, sweeping aside determined units posted at the crossings.

At Chambois, startled Americans from 90th Infantry Division and their Polish allies were momentarily overrun by a horde. "The Americans . . . defending the crossroads were to experience the most agonizing hours of the war that night," wrote Major Zgorzelski.[14] In fact, the Germans had no time or inclination for prisoners; they disarmed them and continued on their way. "We did not even know what to do with them," recalled General Gersdorff.[15]

The 359th Infantry Regiment history relates the outcome of the lives of eighty men from the U.S. 80th Infantry Division, who had been captured while attacking Argentan on 17 August. Thirty managed to get free:

> For three days, they had lived as best they could on shrubs and roots. They said that was about most of the German troops who had taken them prisoner had to eat. But when the German force attempted to escape to the east they forced the remaining fifty Americans to ride on the German tanks in the hope that seeing these American, our forces in Chambois would hold their fire. Most of the men lost in this action were killed by fire from our own weapons when the men of the 359th refused to take the bait. Under the constant confusion of this chaotic battle, it is very doubtful that the troops in Chambois were able to spot or to recognize the American prisoners in German vehicles.[16]

At Trun, infantry from the Lincoln and Wellands and gunners from the New Brunswick Rangers (M.G.) staved off successive assaults by frenzied attackers.

David Currie was grimly hanging onto his squadron position, assaulted now from two sides. At one point he used his command tank to knock out a Tiger and his rifle to deal with snipers who had infiltrated so close to his headquarters that they were "pinging bullets off the top of the tank."

The day took its terrible toll on South Alberta officers. "In the early hours, two tank commanding officers were wounded in the head by small-arms fire," Currie recalls. "A little later one of my tank officers was on the ground when he was wounded by shellfire . . . he died from his wounds."

Only a quirk of fate kept Currie from being the next officer killed. He and Major Ivan Martin, who had been a dynamo throughout the battle, were talking to a German doctor who was trying to get help for his wounded. Lieutenant Al Dalphe was translating. Currie was called to his tank to speak to Wotherspoon on the radio. "I had just climbed into the tank when in came an 88mm HE shell . . . both officers [were] killed by the shell." This meant that at this stage, all the South Alberta officers were out of action—five wounded and two killed.[17]

Currie made a point of visiting the men often; he was on his feet most of the time during the three days and nights of battle. This boosted their morale more than anything, giving them "the feeling of being a part of a team that could accomplish anything." His gunner, Lance-Sergeant Reg Campbell, remembers that "he kept us in the picture at all times."[18]

"After his visits to our weapon pits, my men felt that nothing would force them off the position," recalls Lincoln and Welland Captain R.F. Dickie, whose four men stalked and destroyed a German Panther.

Currie's command style was low key; he never seemed ruffled. Trooper Ed Davies recalls, "He would come over, very calm, and say hello to us and ask how it was going."

"Just to go up and talk to him was enough to give us confidence," Sergeant John Gunderson said. "Without his example I do not believe we could have held out. He didn't give a damn how close the Jerries were, and he always had the same every-day expression, just as if we were on a scheme."

To Trooper Ron Virtue, things looked pretty hopeless. "We didn't think we were going to live." A visit and a few words from Dave became a lifeline to his crews.[19]

Currie's soldiers had been collecting several thousand prisoners during the battle, some of whom were wounded. During a lull in the fighting, a young Lincoln and Welland private soldier, who himself *had been taken prisoner* the previous day, amazingly turned up with two medical half-tracks and about seventy-five enemy walking-wounded whom he had captured. In a stone barn used as a temporary medical aid post, wounded Germans and Canadians groaned, tended by a captured English-speaking German doctor and two German soldiers who had been born in America.[20]

The gunners and fighter-bombers, meanwhile, were playing key roles in the battle.

On the hill north of St. Lambert, "B" Squadron and the 15th Canadian Field Regiment joined in the battle. Long lines of enemy trucks, tanks, wagons, carts, and other vehicles could be seen approaching from the west. The tank gunners would pick off the lead and tail vehicle and then systematically shoot up the whole convoy.[21]

"The fighting had reached a very dramatic stage," 13th Canadian Field Regiment noted. "Enemy targets involved switches of over 300 degrees. It was not uncommon to see the regiment engaging targets in one direction, with medium artillery nearby, firing in the opposite direction."[22]

One last, large attack was broken up by artillery at dusk on 20 August. The remaining German troops lacked the will to continue and thousands surrendered. The fight had gone out of the enemy.

St. Lambert was in flames. Nine Shermans were still smouldering. The blazing trucks lit up the ruins where the enemy soldiers "fired, crawled, set fires, and crawled," in the words of Herbert Fairlie Wood. "The flames were so intense that the night was as hot as the midday August sun."[23]

One of Currie's men asked permission to go to the Dives Valley where hundreds of wounded horses were thrashing about in agony. It took over a thousand rounds to put the wretched animals out of their misery.

The battle of St. Lambert had been, as Currie had prophesied from the beginning, "a fight to the finish." The obstinate stand of this handful of men from three Canadian units, the South Albertas, the

Argylls and the Lincs, funnelled the enemy into a corridor of death.

Alan Moorehead cabled to the London *Daily Express*: "If I were to be allowed just one more dispatch from this front, this would be it . . . . We have begun to see the end of Germany here in this village of St. Lambert today."[24]

28

MACZUGA: THE POLISH AGONY

Sunday, 20 August 1944

Dawn broke over the troubled hills of Maczuga. General Meindl and his band of paratroopers had crouched, motionless, waiting for a Polish patrol to move on. The voices faded. An armoured reconnaissance battalion, a panzer rear guard, loomed up, passed, and reported: "Nothing behind us." Meindl woke the men of his escort, commandeered two tanks, and set out along the Vimoutiers road. It was 0500 hours.

Two hours later, the parachute commander entered the lines of 2nd SS Panzer Corps near Vimoutiers as it was assembling troops to mount the rescue attack westward from outside the gap. Nearly three thousand of Meindl's men had managed to reach the rallying point. General Mahlmann's 353rd Infantry Division arrived at about the same time.

At 1000 hours Sunday morning, General Eberbach's break-in force at Vimoutiers of two panzer divisions, the 2nd and 9th SS, attacked Maczuga from the east. For once, the weather favoured the German attack. Allied planes were grounded for most of the day.

"Both divisions had together twenty tanks," General Eberbach recorded. "One of the divisions possessed only one battalion of infantry, the other had two. At first, the advance made good progress. It came, however, to a stop at a range of hills. In the afternoon, the range of hills was taken. After that the advance made practically no more progress."[1]

Meanwhile, Lüttwitz's 2nd Panzer Division was spearheading the avalanche that swept through St. Lambert, leaving in its wake thousands of shattered German bodies and vehicles. It picked up new impetus as it plunged headlong eastward towards the Polish hilltop fortress at Boisjois.

The tenth-century manor stood 262 metres high atop the eastern rise of the Polish "mace"—Maczuga. From its turret, the entire Dives River valley could be seen, now a ghastly panorama of smoke and fire and death. Corporal Edward Podyma of the 1st Polish Armoured Division marvelled that "from Trun, stretching before us in a cloud of dust in the midst of the explosions, we saw thousands and thousands of Germans. It was such an extraordinary sight. We didn't realize there were so many Germans in Normandy."[2]

Boisjois had become a fortress for the beleaguered Polish—two thousand men and eighty-seven tanks holding out against the combined strengths of a German SS Corps and two thousand paratroopers.

It was clear to the Germans escaping from the west, as well as those attacking from the east, that the Poles on Maczuga held the critical position astride the main roads eastward from the Dives. They blocked the exit routes. The Poles were surrounded by the German forces and subjected to constant German artillery shelling and armoured attack for twenty-four hours.

At Coudehard hill, the southern Maczuga, Lüttwitz's 2nd Panzer Division was regrouping. There the division encountered the 1st Polish Armoured Regiment and Lieutenant-Colonel Szdlowski's 9th Infantry Battalion. There was bloody hand-to-hand fighting throughout the night. The only option for the Poles was to consolidate with Koszutski's 2nd Armoured forces at Boisjois. This opened a passage for some of the Germans escaping across the Coudehard hills, but strengthened the Polish position at the château.

The Poles were isolated on their hilltop fortress, with no hope of outside help. The nearest Allied unit that could have intervened was the one with secret orders to stay uninvolved. Colonel de Langlade's tactical group, on loan to 90th Division by General Leclerc's 2ème Division Blindée, was at Ommeél, only two miles south of Maczuga on the Vimoutiers road—one of the German escape routes. He had eighty Sherman tanks—and strict orders from General Leclerc to remain in a passive role and keep his unit free to proceed to Paris. The political imperative overcame the military one: it was essential that Paris be liberated by the Free French forces rather than by the communist partisans.

Even the Poles' comrades—10th Dragoons and 24th Lancers

now fighting in Chambois—were cut off and unable to help. The Canadians in the 4th Armoured and 3rd Infantry divisions had their hands full at St. Lambert and Trun; the Canadian Corps reconnaissance unit, 12th Manitoba Dragoons, was nearby, but was essential as protection for the northeast flank and could not be moved. The Typhoons that had governed the skies through the turmoil of the past three days were grounded by bad weather.

Artillery support, then, was all the Poles had—all there was to prevent them from being overrun and massacred. This became the task of Captain Pierre Sévigny, the French Canadian artillery captain with 4th Canadian Medium Regiment who was attached to the Polish Armoured as forward observation officer. Sévigny had his driver, Corporal Podyma, position his observation post—a Sherman tank—on the perimeter of Hill 262.

Equipped with two radio sets, he and the other Polish FOOs had been able to call down artillery fire from Polish and Canadian divisional and regimental guns to ward off enemy infiltration. His firepower was enormous.

"I had four medium regiments, two hundred guns at least. Their 100-pound shells were very effective. There was the one time I fired a Victor target with all available guns and also I fired all sorts of Mike targets (employing all sixteen regimental guns)."[3]

All the Polish defences were pointed towards the west where the enemy was escaping across the Dives. Eberbach's SS attack from the east took them completely by surprise. All day, the SS and Meindl's paratroopers kept up relentless pressure from two directions. They killed and wounded almost a third of the defending Polish forces and knocked out dozens of their Sherman tanks.

"They were coming wave after wave," Captain Ted Walewicz recalled. "Our machine guns were so hot, they were just exploding. It was a very vicious fight. I lost my tank—I think it was an 88mm gun. The Germans tried everything they could to break through. There were many occasions of hand-to-hand fighting. Hill 262 had a lot of shrubs and trees, so the Germans could come quite close."[4]

Lieutenant-Colonel Koszutski, the "happy wanderer" of Les Champeaux, assembled his officers from 2nd Polish Armoured Regiment and their supporting 8th Light Infantry and stressed the seriousness of their position. We are entirely cut off, he told them.

With this new assault by 2nd SS Panzer from outside the gap, we are surrounded by enemy attacking simultaneously from all sides. Our Canadian, American, and Polish allies at St. Lambert and Chambois are fighting for their lives on the Dives. Supplies of ammunition and petrol are dwindling. No supply trucks have managed to break through the encircling German line.

Sévigny recalls: "[The CO] said to me in French, 'Can you surround the hill with fire from your guns?' I replied in the affirmative. We shook hands and each went back to his post. I directed my guns on four targets where I expected an enemy attack. In this way they could fire later as required and with accuracy."[5]

That night, Saturday, there was little sleep for the exhausted Poles. "Everyone was on the alert. Our tank crews had been in action for over seventy hours and hardly left their vehicles. The fatigue element was beginning to create a serious problem," Commander Czarnecki, chief of staff, Polish 10th Armed Cavalry Brigade, reported.

German infiltration was unnerving. The Polish troopers remember "the ground swarming with shadows emerging from in front of our posts and disappearing into the moonless night."[6] Sévigny recalls, "That was the worst part."

Pierre Grandvalet, a Norman farmer living in the manor with his pregnant wife and two young children, six and eight years of age, spent that long night huddled on some hay in the basement. Sleep was impossible. "The wounded kept pouring in. Everyone was in anguish." As day broke they heard machine gun and submachine gun fire which seemed heavier than the previous day.

A soldier ran in. "Fire! Everyone to the caves!"

Grandvalet and his wife ran upstairs to get necessities to keep the children warm in the cold underground passages. When they returned the children—left for a moment in the care of their work-man—had vanished. They rushed outside to the courtyard in panic.

"The yard was a raging inferno," Grandvalet recalled. "Amid all this fire there were Bren carriers coming and going at top speed. There were bullets ricocheting all over the place on the walls."

As Pierre and his wife tore across the courtyard towards the barn—where the underground passages were concealed—their Flanders sheepdog tried to follow them. Pierre remembered how upset the children had been the day before, when the dog had been wounded. Then, the medics had taken a minute from tending the wounded to bandage him up. Now he turned to warn the animal again, but the terrified dog, clinging two paces behind his masters, was killed.

The Polish troops had set up a command post in the barn. Desperate, Pierre asked a soldier there to take his wife to cover while he tried to locate their children. They've disappeared! he cried. They're not in the underground passage!

"My wife was [talking] with this soldier. He told her he was a Catholic priest, that the children were surely in heaven, and that she must be strong and resigned. She kept crying, 'Let me go! I want to find my children!' In the end, I came up to my wife and the soldier who was still holding her behind a wall, to tell her I had found the children sheltering in the underground passage.

"We both went off to join them, accompanied by unceasing machine gun fire. We went past the body of a German soldier who had just been killed and whose head had been run over by a vehicle which had flattened it in an awful way."[7]

As Sunday morning broke, the attacks on the Poles at Maczuga intensified. "Fortunately, our dominating position ruled out any surprise attack," Sévigny said. "We kept firing without stopping til the machine guns and rifles were red hot! In the end the enemy retreated. But now he was threatening [from] the right: Careful! I gave hurried orders to my signaller. The shells fell; the Huns retreated in disarray."

Conditions at the Boisjois fortress were becoming grim. The commander had been hit in the chest by shrapnel. Their rations were used up; there was barely a half a bottle of water left per man; ammunition was running low. The men had been fighting for seventy-two hours without respite. They had some three hundred German prisoners, and almost no manpower to guard them. They disarmed them, sat them in a field, and assigned a sergeant, Frank Lisowski, to guard them. Lisowski couldn't help but wonder what would happen if the POWs decided to overrun him and take off.[8]

They had sent an urgent appeal for supplies. A flight of American Dakotas flew over, dropping their load of ammunition, food, and water. Stricken, the Poles watched the planes overshoot by five miles. Captain Walewicz has never understood why the Germans didn't catch on to the desperate plight of the Poles: "What surprises me is that the Germans never figured out that because they were dropping ammunition and food we were in a bad way. We had nothing to defend ourselves."[9]

That Sunday night, the Grandvalet family was reunited but still in great danger. From their shelter they could see the soldiers seven or eight metres away, hurling grenades and firing at the Germans infiltrating through the trees in the thicket that encircled Boisjois on that side.

"Seeing the state of my wife, who was expecting a baby, a soldier took off his helmet, put a biscuit in it, and it was passed on from hand-to-hand to her. Being unable to eat anything, she wanted to refuse it, but the soldier next to her told her: 'Take it to please the soldier over there who is waiting for his helmet, and is at extra risk of getting wounded.'"

At dusk, the order came to return to the manor as the Germans might come and throw grenades down into the underground passages. They heard someone using a pickaxe close by; German soldiers were digging foxholes, preparing to attack the next morning.

"We saw on the faces of these brave Poles an immense fatigue and an immense determination. I asked one of these men, who spoke French, whether the Germans would manage to gain a foothold on Boisjois; he told me that as long as there was one Pole still alive, no Hun would set foot in the place, but he also told me that they were down to mere rifles for fighting against tanks."

That night, he recalls, was one of the most disturbed. Nobody could even think of sleep; fear and dread had taken complete control.

"In the yard, everywhere, there were German prisoners who this time had lost their arrogance," Grandvalet said. "The house and the buildings were full of wounded Poles and Germans, nearly three hundred of them. They were being attended to and operated on all over the place. There was a Polish soldier standing leaning against the wall, who had had his jaw shot off. It was frightening; you could see the suffering in the way he looked at you.

"On the threshold of my home, they cut off a Pole's leg without an anaesthetic; in his pain, the man bit into the blanket on which he was lying. He was then carried into the kitchen.

"My wife, who was beside the wounded man, and seeing him in such a bad way, went to fetch the surgeon and told him how the wounded man was. 'I know,' he answered her helplessly, his medical supplies long gone. 'He's going to bleed to death.' My wife offered to give some blood. 'You cannot give blood, Madam, in your condition.' So she said, 'My husband will be willing to give some then.'

"'So would I, Madam, but I have nothing to do it with.' And the wounded man died a few hours later."

In the yard the Poles were treating an SS soldier with a broken leg. When they finished they ripped off his decorations, including the Iron Cross, and threw them in his face saying "Dirty SS!"

A German prisoner looked on. He was thirteen years old.[10]

"By nightfall, on the Sunday evening," Sévigny recollects, "the commander assembled his officers: out of sixty, only four were still in a condition to fight, three lieutenants and myself. The others, including the commander, had been more or less seriously wounded.

"Stretched out on a pallet and suffering terribly, the Polish major found enough strength to sit up and give us his instructions. I shall never forget his words: 'Gentlemen,' he said, 'everything is lost. I do not think the Canadians can come to our rescue. We are down to one hundred and ten fit men. No more supplies, very little ammunition, five shells per gun, and fifty rounds per man! That's not very much ... Still, you must fight all the same! As you know, it is useless surrendering to the SS! I thank you: you have fought a good fight! Good luck, gentlemen, tonight we shall die for Poland and for civilization!'"[11]

With these words he handed over his command to Captain Sévigny.

Closing the Gap: 21 August

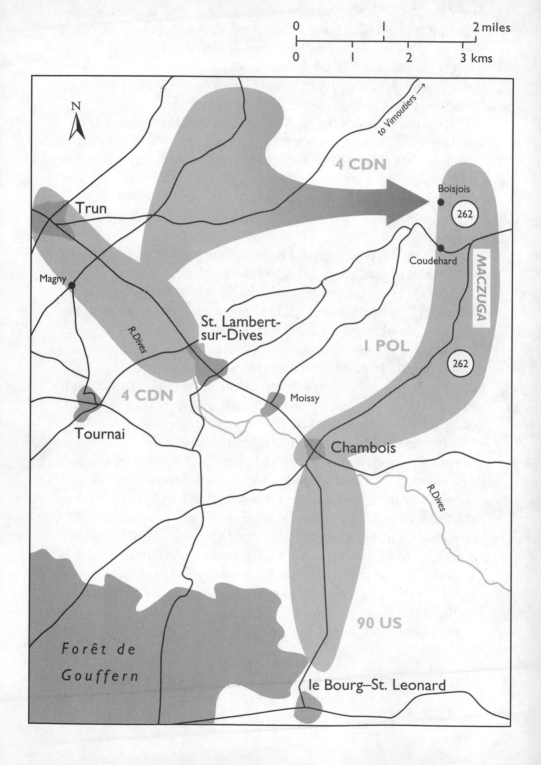

N

to Vimoutiers →

4 CDN

Boisjois
262

Trun

Coudehard

MACZUGA

Magny

R.Dives

St. Lambert-
sur-Dives

I POL

262

4 CDN

Moissy

Tournai

Chambois

R.Dives

90 US

Forêt de
Gouffern

le Bourg–St. Leonard

0   1   2 miles
0   1   2   3 kms

29

THE CORRIDOR
OF DEATH

Monday, 21 August 1944

A cold, steady drizzle fell on the men of the Dives Valley on Monday morning.

At Maczuga, Captain Pierre Sévigny awoke around 0400. He turned on his radio and some Strauss waltzes, played by a London orchestra, drifted softly in the pre-dawn quiet. With a sudden pang he listened to the voices and laughter of the dancers. "Over there, a whole world is enjoying itself!" he mused. "I thought back to the days when I too had no experience of war. . . . I saw my parents again . . . so worried since they had known me to be on the continent . . . feelings shared by thousands of families throughout the world, whose prayers all had a single purpose: to ask God to protect their sons who were in the furnace."

At dawn the shelling started up again with great violence. On the slope of Boisjois a terrible hand-to-hand battle was raging. Soldiers used whatever weapons fell to hand: rifles, machine guns, knives. Pierre Sévigny remembers, "Amidst all the noise and shouts, we thought we could hear men calling 'Mother!' before they died."

The Germans tried one, last, desperate suicidal counter-attack.

"Suddenly to our left we heard the noise of numerous tanks on the move. The Canadians at last!" Sévigny thought. The Poles sent up identifying green flares. Nothing! They suddenly realized that the tanks were German tanks and heading straight towards them. Sévigny relates what happened next:

> The commander decided on a daring move. The best defence was still to attack. And so we headed off to meet the enemy with twelve tanks! Soon sixteen enormous German Tiger-type tanks

appeared; the battle commenced and straightaway within three minutes, six of our tanks were destroyed for just one of theirs!

Only the artillery could save us. Crouching in a foxhole, I gave my signaller orders over a portable radio for him to pass on to the guns. I waited. Had I studied my map properly? Did I indicate the place correctly? Would the guns be able to fire in time? The steel monsters were still moving forward, with all their guns firing. I could see their machine guns blazing: their 88s were whistling over my head. But what were the artillery-men up to? The first tank was only 500 hundred metres away. . . . 400, 300, 250, 200! It was all over: I couldn't look any more. And yet I was still looking: 150 metres, 100 metres. I jumped into the bottom of the hole, and with my face to the ground, I did not make a move; in a second death would come, of that I was certain . . . .

Instinctively, I murmured a prayer. . . . All of a sudden, a hurricane, the noise of thunder, the earth was quaking! Was this death? Was it possible? It was reinforcements. *Our* guns were firing! What I could hear was *our* shells!

And there, in my foxhole, I laughed and cried! Crazily, I raised my head, but only for an instant! We were saved! Like never before, with prodigious accuracy and speed, a cloud of shells poured down on the enemy. The Hun hesitated. Five tanks were burning like haystacks. My gunners received orders to fire all their ammunition! The attack was broken: the Germans retreated, pursued by the Poles who destroyed another three tanks!

Meanwhile, another drama was unfolding in the Boisjois yard: "A German tank had taken up position beside the tower and was firing at the Canadians who were coming to our rescue. The Canadians fired at the manor, believing it to be in German hands. A medic took a sheet and, with a red curtain, placed a large cross on the sheet which he promptly exhibited at a first-floor window, facing the Canadians, which had the effect of stopping them shelling us.

"With the Canadian response, the German tank left the yard and went about sixty metres down the road where it came face to face with a Polish tank. Each of them fired their gun once and came to a halt on the road. The Germans were burnt to death inside their tank, whilst the Poles were taken to Boisjois, some of them in a bad way."

A soldier came to see the Grandvalet family and told them that there was very little ammunition left. Would this so long-awaited Canadian column arrive in time to save us, they wondered?

Sévigny was literally asleep on his feet. "I thought everything was over. I suddenly heard something, not far away: the sound of my armour. My signaller woke me up with a start: 'Sir, I can hear our tanks!' There was no mistaking them. They were Canadian tanks, less than half a mile away."

Sévigny worried that their rescuers would fire on them, thinking they were the enemy. "We decided to go and meet them. They couldn't be far off, maybe six hundred metres to the west, and I could clearly make out the two green flares. What scared us was that they might start firing at us thinking we were Germans."

"Between the Poles and the Canadians, on the hillside, there was a small thicket where the Germans were still entrenched. I assembled my men. We have to attack, I told them, to join up with our saviours. The Polish lieutenant went ahead of me; I saw him fall after being hit by a bullet in the forehead. We came out at the bottom of the hill. Six Shermans were firing at us. We were able to identify ourselves; it was the Grenadier Guards of the Fourth Canadian Armoured Division."[1]

Major Ned Amy, Grenadier Guards squadron commander, recounts the harrowing battle to reach the Poles:

> Brigadier Moncel tasked our regiment to break through. I was given a company of the Lake Superior Regiment and told to get on with it as soon as possible after daylight. The Lake Sups Company was superb and, recognizing its task, went about its business aggressively and professionally. We tankers relaxed when they were present since we knew that no German infantry-man was going to get at us with a panzerfaust. They had many casualties that day and lost several carriers and half-tracks.
>
> I couldn't raise my leading troop leader on the radio so I

walked up and found he was having wireless trouble. I got him to change tanks and within minutes of getting back to my tank, he was hit in the new tank and killed. Shortly thereafter I had a fleeting glance of a tank going hell-bent through the orchard on our left but in the opposite direction. He was within fifty yards of us but out of sight before we could fire a shot.

We came to a couple of farm buildings which had been gutted and nearby was an open vehicle with two incinerated passengers, one a German officer. While the Lake Sups were busy clearing the area, I had three pistol shots at a German who was loping along on the other side of a line of trees at about thirty-five yards and he didn't even speed up.

Major H. A. "Snuffy" Smith had arrived with his squadron and we felt the battle was nearly over as we were within a few hundred yards of where we expected to make contact with the Poles. We were discussing our next move when a Lake Sup sergeant came up and asked if someone would look at a tank up ahead to see if it was one of ours. I went with him and we kept in tight to the trees on the right. As we approached a bend in the road he crouched down and pointed out a bit of the tank's outside track which was visible. The tank itself was parked just around the bend and in close to the trees. It was German. He took off to get a PIAT and I took off to get my tank. I gave my gunner a seemingly crazy fire order. He said, "I can't see anything." My reply convinced him to pull the trigger and down came a tree. I made a correction to shorten the arc and dropped the gun muzzle a bit and he fired again and we had a flamer. It was a *Panzer* Mark IV, but I never did find out if the crew escaped because following this a Stuart light tank, with Polish soldiers hanging on, broke cover at the far end of the field on our right. We had made contact with the Poles.

Snuffy and I walked up the hill to meet their commander. The carnage was incredible with a mélange of bodies, dead animals and burned-out vehicles. The Poles had been cut off for several days from supplies with the tragic inability to evacuate their great number of wounded. They had suffered heavy casualties and their plight seemed hopeless.[2]

Sévigny recalls the meeting. "When we arrived at the command post, the Polish commander received us, vibrant with emotion, and I was witness to scenes of delirious joy. There was laughter, tears, embraces. The soldiers told long stories in Polish to the Canadians who couldn't understand a word, but nevertheless laughed heartily!"[3]

Major Ned Amy remembers one less pleasant encounter: "While we were there they brought in a German soldier in camouflage clothing who apparently had been in a tree sniping at them for some time. He was being questioned and suddenly there was a shot and the questioning was over. Not pleasant to witness but one had to realize that they had been a defenseless shooting gallery for several days without mercy and with little hope."[4]

German prisoners were treated humanely by their Polish captors—up to the moment that they checked the German pay books, which gave the records of their military actions. In their struggle for freedom the Polish survivors had little mercy for the SS that had raped their country in 1939, and again in 1944.

Krzysztof (Chris) Szydlowski, vice-president of the 1st Polish Armoured Association of Canada, is the son of Lieutenant-Colonel Szydlowski, commander of 9th Infantry Battalion. "My father, who finally was in command at Maczuga, told me of the feelings of the men. They were not beaten, but they were in a serious position. I have the impression that General Maczek was surprised they hung on, but they would not give up. The Polish soldiers were happy to meet the Canadians on that hill. The biggest emotion was relief and also it was pride that the 'cork' stayed. That was the impact of the whole action. Pride overruled fear."[5]

Pride had its price. The statistics were grim for a division that had few resources for future reinforcements. One-third of the Polish fighting strength was casualties at Maczuga: 325 men died on the Maczuga hills, including 21 officers; 1,002 were wounded.[6]

Meanwhile, remnants of the German Seventh Army trapped west of the Dives were being taken prisoner in wholesale lots. One corporal, amazed at the huge numbers, said that they "looked like hedgerows . . . but were moving." Stragglers "who had been living in holes in the ground in the forest since separating from their units" were gathered up. It was not uncommon for an Allied division to collect prisoners from as many as twenty different divisional units in a single day.[7]

Perhaps the most rewarding was the bagging of German senior commanders. In Chambois, Captain Gutowski, now second-in-command of 10th Polish Mounted Rifles when his commander was shot, recounts the drama of the surrender of Lieutenant-General Otto Elfeldt. This Wehrmacht commander of 84th Corps had originally set out on his escape with Kurt Meyer. Disagreeing with "Panzer-meyer's" tactics, he then struck off on his own in the pre-dawn hours with a small combat force of two hundred men. They launched an attack near St. Lambert, but were forced to capitulate to the Poles when their ammunition gave out: "A single, powerful attack would have had more success than several smaller ones," he said bitterly to his captors.[8]

Gutowski recalls,

> In the early morning of the twenty-first we were fighting like hell. The enemy came to within three hundred meters and then we opened fire. Everywhere was covered with bodies. We had a loudspeaker and I gave orders in English and in German: "Get your hands up." They brought General Elfeldt straight to me. Still in his general's uniform, with some officers, he stopped and saluted me.
>
> He said, "In whose hands am I, American or British?" I said, "Neither. You are a prisoner of the Polish." Then I asked if he spoke French. So from morning until late in the afternoon he sat by my tank and we were speaking French. Then another enemy attack came in. He said to me in French, "At the present moment I am your prisoner. But you know how it is in the war. Maybe in half an hour you will be my prisoner."
>
> I looked at him scornfully. "*I* do not surrender to Germans."[9]

Elfeldt remembers Captain Gutowski as "a handsome man and a gentleman [who] offered me his last cigarette."[10]

The men of 2nd Battalion, U.S. 90th Division, combed the area for miles around Chambois to be sure that they collected up all the wounded: "Our medical personnel attempted to make use of the many German medics [to care for] their own wounded," a staff officer recalled. This backfired. The enemy medical personnel were unable to read English and therefore did not understand instructions and dosages on bottles. The evacuation of the German wounded went on all day.[11]

A German lieutenant, Hans-Heinrich Dibbern from the Panzer Lehr, had an amazing experience on the Argentan road. "From the direction of the American line came an ambulance driving toward us; he was obviously lost. When he noticed that he was behind the German lines, he slammed on the brakes. We went over. His face was completely white, thinking that he had seen his last hour. But we told him, 'Please climb back into your truck and get out of here—you're Red Cross.' He quickly disappeared. About half an hour later, *it happened again*. Here comes another Red Cross truck! It pulled up right in front of us. The driver got out, opened the back and took a crate out. He left it on the street and disappeared. We remained in our places as if he had left a bomb. But nothing happened, and after a while we became curious. We went over and saw that it was filled with Chesterfield cigarettes."[12]

The Chambois scene was a turmoil of thousands of troops from six nations milling around. But the Americans welcomed one special new arrival: "At 1930 hours Major Markiewicz reported that he was called upon to deliver a baby girl to a French family in the neighbourhood of our CP."[13]

When the Glens (Stormont, Dundas and Glengarry Regiment) arrived to take up a position at Trun, at the northern edge of the Falaise Gap, they found what their intelligence officer Reg Dixon described as a "confused donnybrook." The town was teeming with POWs, German wounded, and civilian refugees: "A sharp German counter-attack by five tanks and two hundred panzergrenadier infantry succeeded in entering the village of Magny-sur-Dives, a nearby village."[14]

Lieutenant Colonel Roger Rowley recalls a desperate moment: "The tanks overran my left-hand forward company, Major Gordon

Clark's—he had five wound stripes and a DSO and was one really wild guy. Gordy was wounded and taken prisoner. We then counter-attacked. The machine-gunners from the Cameron Highlanders of Ottawa MG were on the high ground and they brought down a great deal of fire with their Vickers machine guns."

One of the German tanks became firmly jammed in the sunken track leading from Magny to the Trun-Chambois road: "A couple of my guys jumped up on top of the tank and threw a smoke grenade down, which was pretty quick thinking, and who should pop out but a lieutenant-general, Erwin Menny, commander of 84 Division."[15]

Shortly after this, another of the fleeing German half-tracks came roaring through the town. One of the passengers was Major Gordy Clark, who was being held prisoner. It pulled up at the hospital. The Germans were dumfounded to discover that they had stumbled on Colonel Rowley's command post. Clark coolly jumped out and captured his captors.

General Menny's arrival caused some excitement with the Glens: "When his tank was searched it was found to be well stocked with silk stockings, underwear and perfume, and other French luxuries," Captain Dixon noted. "Most of it found its way eventually to wives and girlfriends of the Glens."[16]

Rowley still recoils at the encounter. "He was in my command post for the next three days. A real son of a bitch. He was a senior general in the Seventh German Army—a nasty bastard; he wouldn't take any food. They'd give him a can of rations and he would just kick it over."[17]

In the early hours of 21 August, the wretched villagers of Tournai believed that their end had come. Relentless pounding by artillery from both sides had reduced the town to rubble. Only eight of the village's sixty-six houses stood undamaged. In a cramped wine cellar, a group of twenty-three civilians, several wounded German soldiers and their major huddled in terror. Outside, in the courtyard, lay the corpses of thirty-eight horses, piled in grotesque heaps.

Five or six hundred civilian refugees and two thousand German soldiers were clinging to whatever shelter they could find in the village. Abbé Marcel Launay approached the Wehrmacht officer. You must surrender, or we will all be killed, he pleaded. "To save your men, run up a white flag on the church."

The German hesitated. "Only the red one," he finally agreed, indicating the Red Cross. The padre protested that the white flag of capitulation was all that could save the survivors of the village. Finally, the major agreed, and a torn white flag knotted to a scythe was carried up to the steeple. To make it more visible, a white surplice and a large cloth were added on the end of a broomstick.

"The tower was full of soldiers," the padre recalled. "Impossible to climb up. We tried to pass up the flag, but no one would take it. A row broke out between the army and the SS under the eaves of the besieged village steeple.

"The SS refused to hang up the flag. The civilians appealed to the major. The major said the SS would not obey his orders: 'Those SS swine!'" The officers parleyed. The discussion was long and drawn out. In a rage, another officer, revolver in hand, cleared the steeple; the SS were lined up against the walls. The white flag was hoisted on the tower.

The padre's drastic appeal for help failed. The rain had grounded Allied support planes. And the American and Canadian artillery, perhaps not spotting the flag amid the smoke and carnage, continued to plaster the village with shells.

Just then a German Red Cross car appeared on the scene. Two orderlies and a sergeant got out.

"Monsieur, are you the one that wants to sue for peace?"

"Yes, mein Herr. You have men here and I have civilians. This evening we shall have no one."

"Monsieur, be kind enough to take us to the enemy lines to sue for peace."

The padre clambered aboard and the vehicle took off. The Germans pleaded with the padre not to surrender to Polish troops. "No! Never! The Poles have the reputation of never taking prisoners!"

They headed for St. Lambert, frantically waving a white flag, but the shells continued to explode around them and the route was almost unrecognizable with wreckage and dead bodies. It was impossible to get through. Turning back to Tournai they encountered a band of twelve French soldiers who had been taken prisoner and were now escaping. One of the soldiers volunteered to accompany them back to Allied lines as interpreter.

This improbable delegation—a distraught 31-year-old Norman

clergyman, an escaping French soldier, and a German Red Cross sergeant and his corporal frantically waving a white flag of surrender—struggled back towards St. Lambert. They approached the Canadians. The first, who had just witnessed the murder of his comrades by Germans approaching under the guise of a white flag, gave a curt refusal. Finally, one Canadian agreed to accompany them back to accept the surrender.

At 1400 hours on 21 August, through the persistent efforts of a village clergyman, a single Canadian with only a submachine gun accepted the surrender of two thousand German soldiers at Tournai-sur-Dives.[18]

SS Colonel General Paul Hausser—now an army commander without an army—was leading a small Seventh Army group towards Vimoutiers. As they plodded wearily eastward, a shell exploded beside them. Hausser, who had already lost an eye in Russia, went down, his jaw shot out, his face a bloody mess. He was carried out on an armoured personnel carrier by one of his senior artillery officers, Colonel Kurzbein.

"Where am I?" Hausser moaned, regaining consciousness. Kurzbein identified himself and reassured the army chief that he was safely out of the encirclement.

"I will bring you before a court martial," Hausser retorted, anger overcoming his pain. "How could you transport a supreme commander from the field of battle without his agreement?"[19]

General Eugen Meindl stood deep in thought on the Maczuga hills in those pre-dawn hours of 21 August. Earlier, Meindl had sent officers on bicycles back into the ring to let those inside know that there was a way out through Coudehard. The news had spread like wildfire. Streams of stragglers swept through the gap all night. "In a short time there was a good collection of men who set some value on an orderly retreat," he remembered. Then "the traffic had dried completely."

It was time now to waken the lads and leave—disappear before it got light. They had been so exhausted they had fallen asleep the moment they sat down. Meindl had forced himself to stay awake by running around in circles from midnight until two o'clock in the morning, afraid he might oversleep the hour for action.

Meindl gazed at the sleeping paratroopers. My boys might look like a pack of ragged tinkers, he mused, but their glance was bright and proud, despite their exhaustion. Not like the majority of men—even the officers—who declined to get out of the trap, believing it to be a hopeless cause.

It started to rain heavily. Good, Meindl thought. This will favour our plans.

Eyes misting, he walked over to one young soldier and gently shook him awake. "Happy birthday, my son," he said gently. "Now we must wake the others and get ready to march again." Father and son quickly roused the others. Meindl smiled inwardly: Imagine, the commanding general himself going around waking his men![20]

At St. Lambert, the battered South Albertas were recovering from the ordeal of the past two days. "There was some shelling but it was rather sporadic," David Currie noted. "Prisoners started rolling in, in a never-ending stream. In mid-morning, a convoy of ambulance vehicles . . . demanded that we let them through in the name of mercy. I took a look in the ambulances and the wounded were piled like cordwood. I told the doctor that if he were really interested in saving lives, he had better go to our lines and to our hospital. He didn't have enough gas in the ambulances to go anywhere else. He finally decided that we were right and took off for our hospital."[21]

Lieutenant Danny McLeod attests to the terrible enemy casualties in the St. Lambert battle: 2,000 killed, 3,000 wounded, and 7,000 taken prisoner.[22]

That night, David Currie slept for the first time in three days: "I slept like the dead for about eight hours and woke up to another beautiful morning. The birds were singing and all shellfire had ceased; it was so peaceful.

"When we came to St. Lambert, it was a neat, small, quiet French village, and when we left, it was a fantastic mess. The clutter of equipment, dead horses, wounded, dying and dead Germans had turned it into a hellhole. It seems incredible that such devastation could be wrought in such a short space of time."[23]

Shortly afterwards, Currie was awarded the Victoria Cross.

Of the 200,000 German troops virtually encircled by the Allies on 12 August, General Eberbach estimated (in a postwar interrogation) that only 20,000 escaped and the same number were killed.[24] Most of the escapees were without weapons or armoured vehicles. Many had been evacuated before the gap was sealed. Kluge should have been honoured instead of disgraced by his countrymen. In his last act before committing suicide, Kluge had indeed been "Clever Hans." By personally ordering all noncombat units out of the encirclement without waiting for Hitler's permission, he saved approximately 30 per cent of the strength of each division. These early evacuees included a sizeable number of troopers without tanks and artillery, men without guns as well as soldiers only involved in administration.

In addition, General Hausser's decision to launch an attack from outside the ring moved to safety 2nd SS Panzer Corps with 9th SS and 2nd SS Panzer divisions. These boosted the numbers of Germans who escaped well before the Allies tried to close the gap.

Despite this, the German force in Normandy had been savaged. The average combat strength of German divisions now numbered only a few hundred men.[25] The 12th SS, with a strength of 20,000 men and 159 tanks on D-Day, now had 100 men, ten tanks and no artillery.[26]

Historian John Keegan described it as "the biggest disaster to hit the German army in the course of World War II, surpassing Stalingrad, Tunisia, or the destruction of Army Group Center. Twenty-seven infantry divisions were completely destroyed and the twelve armored divisions reduced from 1,800 tanks to only 120. Over half a million casualties were incurred and Germany's most lucrative vassal, France, was lost for the Reich."[27]

The Allied armies took some 45,000 prisoners. U.S. 90th Division recorded 4,054 prisoners taken on 21 August alone, and there were still hundreds unprocessed. The total POWs evacuated by the division were 14,183.[28]

The Allies' 206,703 casualties in the Normandy fighting were less than half that of the Germans.[29]

Lieutenant Colonel Rowley remembers being "just swamped" with the hundreds of prisoners. More macabre were the number of German corpses still lying in grotesque piles, and the bloated cattle and horses, all killed by shelling, some still burning. The roads were literally impassable. Finally, Rowley had to get a company of engineers to clear them.

"What we had to do with the German dead, we had a cable with a rope at the end attached to our carriers and we were hooking it over their trousers to haul them away. Then we took mortar bombs and blew graves for them. That was almost the worst part of it."[30]

The soft green hills and shaded glens of the Valley of the Dives had become a giant, five-mile-long coffin, filled with rotting corpses. As many as ten thousand German soldiers lay in obscene heaps, the pile of dead so thick that bulldozers were used to clear a passage. Eisenhower wrote, "It was literally possible to walk for hundreds of yards at a time stepping on nothing but dead and decaying flesh."[31]

There were many other victims of the bitter fighting in the battle of Normandy. Over 20,000 civilians were killed. Out of 763 towns in the Department of Calvados, only two survived intact. Falaise was so smashed that it was difficult to even see where the roads once led. Argentan was equally annihilated.[32]

Another casualty was the commander of 4th Canadian Armoured Division, Major-General George Kitching. He was a professional and astute officer who led his division in its first ever combat on 7 August and was fired on 21 August—a victim of General Guy Simonds' ruthlessness. Now meant now.

"On the morning of Tuesday, August 22nd," Eddie Florentin wrote, "the plain was silent. Stunned and decimated, the living counted their dead, discovering corpses in the meadows, the roads, the cellar, and the trenches. The stench was so appalling that Prince Jean of Luxembourg in the cockpit of his Piper Cub flying over the Trun–Chambois road was forced to gain altitude to avoid the discomfort.

"People emerged from shelters, exhausted, haggard, filthy, and half-bemused. No cattle in the meadows, no leaves on the trees, the grass itself had disappeared beneath a layer of dust, no birds to gladden the sky. There was no life left."[33]

A LAST WORD

Terry Copp
Co-Director, Laurier Centre for Military, Strategic and Disarmament
Studies, Sir Wilfrid Laurier University, Waterloo, Ontario

Victory at Falaise: The Soldiers' Story is a major contribution to an important historical debate. Denis and Shelagh Whitaker have set out to restore the reputation of the Allied soldier and overthrow fifty years of revisionist history on the battle of Normandy. Their previous books have challenged conventional ideas about the Dieppe Raid and the battles of the Scheldt and Rhineland, and now they are redefining our understanding of the summer of 1944.

They join historians such as Stephen Ambrose in questioning the stereotype of the cautious, ineffective Allied soldier versus the resolute and skilled panzergrenadier. The task will not be easy; the discipline of military history in Britain, Canada, and the United States is dominated by men who insist that the Allies overcame their enemies only by the application of overwhelming "brute force" by soldiers who were no match for the Wehrmacht and the SS.

The revisionist consensus on the poor performance of the Allied soldier developed immediately after VE day, when the British military historian Basil Liddell Hart began to cultivate the myth that the German army had revolutionized warfare with Blitzkrieg tactics learned from his books. In interviews with captured generals, Liddell Hart popularized the notion that if it were not for Hitler's interventions, the Germans might well have won the war. His admiration for the men who had organized the conquest of Europe seemed to know no bounds, while Allied generals and their men were portrayed as stodgy and incompetent.[1]

Liddell Hart had an enormous influence in the United States, where his views seemed to explain the "research" reported by an officially accredited U.S. historian-journalist, S.L.A. "Slam" Marshall, who claimed to have pioneered the technique of mass interviews of soldiers. Marshall's 1947 book *Men against Fire* argued that, in the American army, "not more than 15 percent of the men had actually fired at enemy positions or at personnel . . . during combat . . . . The best showing . . . by the most spirited and aggressive companies was that one man in four had made at least some use of his fire power."[2]

Marshall described this phenomenon as the "ratio of fire" and claimed it provided a new way of understanding what happened when citizen soldiers gripped by "fear and inertia" enter combat. The ratio of fire and Marshall's explanation of it were readily accepted by historians who lacked any experience of combat and who were anxious to distinguish their history from mere narrative. It was not until the 1980s, when combat veterans began to retire and learned what the experts were saying, that Marshall's evidence was challenged.

When Harold Leinbaugh and John Campbell began the research for their historical memoir *The Men of Company K*[3] they encountered books like John Keegan's *The Face of Battle*,[4] which relied on Marshall's statistics to argue that poorly motivated combat soldiers avoided action. They found that Weigley, an influential American military historian, accepted the validity of the ratio of fire and used it to bolster his argument that Allied infantry were overcautious and could not be relied upon to attack the enemy.[5]

Harold Leinbaugh knew from experience that Marshall was wrong and the historians who relied upon him had been misled, but it was not until Dr. Roger Spiller, founder of the Combat Studies Institute at Fort Leavenworth, Kansas, re-examined Marshall's evidence that the case for the ratio of fire fell apart. It turned out that the mass interviews of men fresh from combat had never taken place and Marshall's notebooks recording occasional interviews made no reference to how many men fired their weapons. Marshall had made it all up.[6]

There were, however, other pseudo-scientific arguments for veterans to contend with. Colonel Trevor N. Dupuy interviewed *seven* World War II veterans "who had combat experience . . . to quantify the effects and effectiveness of weapons" and then used this "historical data" on eighty-one battles between U.S. and German forces to develop a model of combat effectiveness.[7] Dupuy ignored the detailed reports of operational research scientists who had direct knowledge of these matters and constructed mathematical equations based on weightings that exaggerated the effect of Allied air power and artillery while understating the advantage held by the defender.[8]

Dupuy insisted he had proven that the Germans "consistently, if not uniformly, outfought us on a unit-to-unit basis because of their greater professional skill."[9] Professional historians bought into this approach and in 1983 the Israeli historian Martin Van Crevald produced a study for the Pentagon which relied on Dupuy's statistics to establish the superiority of the German army.[10] Van Crevald argued that their greater fighting power was due to better "morale, elan, unit cohesion and resilience." The GI, and by extension the British "Tommy" and "Johnny Canuck," were the "tired, the poor, the huddled masses" commanded by officers who were "less than mediocre."[11]

Canadian military history was strongly influenced by these ideas. C.P. Stacey, Canadian military historian, and the author of the official history of the campaign in North-west Europe, espoused the view that the Allies had won because of "numerical and material superiority" and the "paralyzing effects" of air power.[12] The Canadians, like their comrades in the American and British armies, were, he suggested, "overcautious"—they failed to maintain the momentum of the attack and were "too easily satisfied."[13] The army as a whole, Stacey claimed, failed to make the most of its opportunities, especially in August, when the capture of Falaise was "long delayed."[14]

Other historians took a different approach, blaming the Allied failure on the commanders. Martin Blumenson's *The Battle of the Generals* is subtitled "The Untold Story of the Falaise Pocket—The Campaign that Should Have Won the War." It is one of a number of books which insist that "Eisenhower, Montgomery and Bradley cared little whether the Germans escaped" and concentrated on future plans, thus failing to "properly finish the invasion."[15] This argument suggests that Bradley should have ignored evidence about the threat to Patton's flank at Argentan and allowed the U.S. Third Army to advance north to Falaise. Other historians blame Montgomery, arguing that he should have intervened, changing the army group boundaries to place Falaise in Bradley's sector. This kind of armchair generalship fascinates readers and historians alike because counterfactual, or "what if," history allows free rein to the imagination.

Counter-factual history can be a valuable exercise if it is used to promote clear thinking about alternative courses of action, but there is no justification for believing that different choices *necessarily* produce better results. If Patton had been permitted to continue north towards Falaise, his two armoured divisions would surely have been engaged in a pitched battle with most of the German armour and a number of infantry divisions. Could two U.S. and one French division have closed the Falaise Gap and kept it closed when attacked from three directions? Would all the combat and rear-echelon troops west of Falaise–Argentan have been unable to escape? The probabilities are that the German army, still an organized force with an equivalent strength of eight to ten divisions, would have fought its way east just as it did a week later at the Trun–Chambois gap. Armies surrender when their will to resist is broken, not when "encirclement" is marked on a large-scale map.

The debate over the "stop order" at Argentan is part of a larger dispute over Allied generalship in Normandy. Most British and Canadian historians praise Montgomery's leadership, a view shared by few Americans then or since. Perhaps the most fulsome praise comes from C.P. Stacey, who accepts Montgomery's claim that his "master plan" called for the Germans to concentrate the bulk of their armour in the Caen sector, while the breakout was planned for the American flank of the bridgehead. There is, Stacey wrote, "no doubt as to the credit for the Normandy victory"—it is Montgomery's. His "grip on operations was firm and effective . . . he conducted them in accordance with a pattern laid down before the landings."[16]

Few American historians would accept this view. Carlo D'Este, whose 1983 book *Decision in Normandy*[17] best encapsulates the American position, dismisses the "master plan" as a myth and argues that Montgomery lost the initiative early in the campaign and was gradually forced to accept the reality of attritional warfare. There was no decision to break out on the right until *Cobra* succeeded, and only then was it reinforced.

A great deal of the controversy about strategic decision-making in Normandy arises out of an unwillingness to admit that the German response dictated the shape of the campaign. Hitler's decision to try to contain the Allied bridgehead without transferring additional infantry divisions from the north of the Seine forced Rommel to keep the panzer divisions well forward in the open country around Caen. There was no role for such divisions in the *bocage* until a major operation such as the Mortain offensive was planned. So long as Montgomery kept attacking, the panzer divisions could not disengage and the battle for Normandy developed into a slugging match reminiscent of the western front in the Great War.

Denis Whitaker, like others who actually fought the Germans in Italy or North-west Europe, agrees that in some situations specific German units were highly effective in stopping Allied advances. Many German soldiers were brave and resolute in battle. But the same was true of the Allies, who had to bear the burden of constantly attacking the enemy. Like other veterans, he also wondered how historians came to emphasize failure when writing about Normandy. Denis Whitaker was one of those who attended Montgomery's famous conference at St. Paul's School in London on Good Friday, April 1944, where the assembled officers were told that by D-plus-90, 6 September, the Allies hoped to occupy an area bounded by the Seine and the Loire and would then have to pause before mounting new operations to overwhelm the enemy before advancing to Germany.[18] No one even suggested that the battle of France might end in August with the total defeat of two German armies *and* the liberation of both France and Belgium. A victory on such a scale was beyond the wildest dreams of the men preparing to invade France.

Readers who really wish to understand what happened in Normandy and why it happened that way will want to know more about the way the Allies and their enemy fought the campaign. A good place to begin is on D-Day when the Allies stormed ashore in one of the most successful military operations in all of history. Those who have seen Steven Spielberg's twenty-minute opening segment in *Saving Private Ryan* know that it is an extraordinary cinematic achievement, but viewers are less certain about the events portrayed. Did men really land in front of such obstacles, suffer such casualties, and keep fighting until they won? The answer is yes. Similar situations developed all along Omaha and on beaches in the British and Canadian sectors.[19]

Success on D-Day depended upon soldiers like the ones portrayed by Tom Hanks and his fellow actors because virtually every part of the plan to overwhelm the German defences with fire-power failed. The Allies tried to apply "brute force," but the weather and the limitations of their weapons meant that the assault troops had to overcome most of the resistance themselves.

Careful studies by operational research teams determined that the elaborate bombing program carried out by RAF Bomber Command and the U.S. Eighth Army Air Force caused little damage to the defences because "most bombs fell some distance back from the beaches."[20] Heavy cloud cover limited the efforts of tactical air force fighter-bombers, and these aircraft played no role in overcoming the beach defences. Naval fire, thought to be one of the keys to the success of the assault landing, did "no serious damage to the defences"[21] and there was little evidence that the massive fire-power directed at the beaches "had any significant neutralizing effect . . . when the infantry touched down, the enemy were able to deliver lethal fire in great quantity."[22] The Atlantic Wall of the Normandy beaches was breached by those "unaggressive, overcautious soldiers who hesitated to fire their weapons."

In the first few days after the landings, the Allies were able to link up their beachheads and establish a substantial bridgehead in Normandy. The confusion in the enemy's command structure, and *Fortitude*, the British deception scheme that persuaded the Germans that a second landing was imminent, helped the Allies, but the enemy was able to bring substantial reinforcements to Normandy before the Allies were strong enough to break out. Much has been made of the role of air power in delaying the arrival of German forces, largely because Rommel and other German commanders reported that the Allied air forces made the "movement of major formations impossible, both at the front and behind it, by day and night." This and other comments on the "dreaded fighter bombers" or Jabos that "paralyzed every movement" have been endlessly quoted by historians unwilling to examine what actually happened in Normandy.[23]

The reality is that every German division ordered to move to the battle front in early June reached its destination without suffering serious losses and major delays. The divisions of II Parachute Corps, stationed in Brittany, moved to the American landing area without serious difficulty and 346 Division, transferred from Fifteenth Army, crossed the Seine on D-plus-1 in daylight. Its lead elements cycled south joining in counter-attacks against British and Canadian airborne troops within forty-eight hours of the landings. The panzer divisions were delayed by Hitler's indecision, but once the order to move was given, the tactical air forces still based in Britain could do little more than harass the columns which were in position to counter-attack on 7 or 8 June. II SS Panzer Corps travelled all the way from Poland between 11 and 28 June, and arrived without significant losses in transit.[24] Air power played a major role in the Allied triumph in Normandy, especially in hampering German movement, but it was never the decisive factor the German generals, seeking to explain their defeat, have claimed.

Again, it is the evidence from operational research, not the self-serving testimony of German generals, that must be reviewed. Experiments with fighter-bombers in England had repeatedly demonstrated that average pilots "given a six-figure map reference were unable to spot well-camouflaged guns even when the guns were firing."[25] When practice targets were recognizable, few hits could be obtained by either fighter-bombers or rocket-equipped aircraft. The tactical air forces were best employed behind enemy lines, seeking targets of opportunity.

As reinforcements arrived, the Germans, in accordance with their doctrine that emphasized decisive action through immediate counter-attacks, struck hard at the bridgehead, especially in the Canadian sector, where the 12th SS Hitler Youth Division mounted a series of attacks intended to secure a start-line for an advance to the beaches. The terrain, natural and man-made, favoured the Canadians, who used their artillery and anti-tank guns to crush the attacker. The historian of the 12th SS, Normandy veteran Hubert Meyer, noted that "the tactic of surprise, using fast mobile infantry and panzers even in small, numerically inferior Kampfgruppen (battle groups), had often been practised and proven in Russia," but in Normandy "against a courageous and determined enemy who was ready for the defence and well equipped" these tactics "had not resulted in the expected success."[26]

Similar attacks upon British and American troops who had time to prepare and tie in their positions with the artillery and other support troops were equally unsuccessful, and the German commanders were forced to dig in and develop a new defensive perimeter. Rommel wanted this line to be withdrawn out of range of naval gunfire, but Hitler refused. Instead, a defence-in-depth was established and the Germans settled in to fight a defensive battle sealing off Normandy from the rest of France.

By the middle of June, the battle had become a company commander and section leader's war. Generals on both sides talk about strategy, but reality was to be found in the hedgerows and stone-walled villages of Normandy. Men had to dig or die, and when they emerged from their slit trenches to carry out an attack they would be wounded and killed in large numbers. Since it was up to the Allies to liberate France, it was they who would have to pay the heaviest price.

Unfortunately, the Allies were equipped with weapons that were distinctly inferior to those employed by their enemy. Attacks on fortified villages such as those around Caen ought to have been carried out by battle groups built around tanks or self-propelled assault guns. Combined with medium artillery to isolate the area and field artillery to shoot the combined-arms teams onto their objectives, such tactics would have improved the effectiveness of the Allies and brought victory at a considerably reduced cost. However, the Allies did not possess armoured fighting vehicles capable of carrying out such a role and Allied battle doctrine reflected this reality. The leading operational research expert on armoured warfare, Tony Sargeaunt, helped to devise the pre-invasion armoured doctrine, which called for indirect support of the infantry. Sargeaunt knew, from the detailed testing done in England, that Allied armour was highly vulnerable at ranges well in excess of 1,000 yards. Tanks could only contribute to success in an attack if they survived and survival depended on using dead ground, offering fire support from the flank or finding other ways of staying alive in battle.[27] When Sargeaunt carried out an investigation of Allied and German tanks casualties in Normandy, he confirmed the most pessimistic views about Allied armour.

The statistics were stunning. Sixty per cent of Allied tank losses were due to a single round from a 75mm or 88mm gun, and two-thirds of all tanks brewed up when hit. German armour-piercing shells almost always penetrated and disabled a tank; the armour offered so little protection that the only way to survive was to avoid being targeted. The contrast with German tank casualties was especially striking. Only 38 per cent of hits from Sherman 75mm shells or 6-pounder anti-tank shells penetrated German armour, and both the Panther and Tiger often survived one or two penetrations. The sloping front armour of the Panther and the German self-propelled assault and anti-tank guns prevented penetration of three-quarters of all direct hits.[28]

Sargeaunt accepted anecdotal evidence that spare tank tracks welded onto the front of Shermans might deflect some shots but the main impact was on morale. Tank crews believed it worked and this helped sustain them in battle. Sargeaunt recommended that the army concentrate on "providing a better gun to make German tanks more vulnerable,"[29] but as the man who had supervised the testing of the 17-pounder he was well aware of its limitations when mounted in a Sherman. For all practical purposes the gun could only fire armour-piercing shells and was therefore only useful as an anti-tank weapon. The ratio of one Sherman Firefly to three Sherman 75s per troop was about right, but it frequently meant that the troop concentrated on manoeuvres designed to position the Firefly for defensive fire in the event German AFVs appeared.

The Americans had not received any of the 17-pounder Fireflies, and tanks equipped with a 76mm gun provided only marginally better performance than the Sherman 75mm. The extent of the problems encountered in fighting German armour was indicated in a letter Eisenhower wrote to General Marshall on 5 July 1944:

I have just returned from a visit to First Army where I found them deeply concerned over the inability of our present tank guns and anti-tank weapons to cope successfully with the German Panther and Tiger tanks. None of our present ammunition . . . can penetrate the front armour . . . and due to the restricted terrain and narrow roads in which we are fighting we are unable consistently to attack these tanks from a favourable angle. Moreover, even from the flanks our present weapons and ammunition are not adequately effective.[30]

The Americans were never able to solve this problem, nor to address the equally serious weakness in tank armour. One history of the 3rd U.S. Armoured Division, titled appropriately *Death Traps*, reports that, during the European campaign, the division, which entered combat in Normandy with 232 M4 Sherman tanks, "had 648 tanks completely destroyed in combat . . . and 700 knocked out, repaired and put back into action. This was a loss rate of 580 per cent."[31] The experience of all Allied armoured units was similar.

Seven long agonizing weeks were to pass before the new German defensive perimeter in Normandy could be broken. During that period, the Allies enjoyed some local success, the fall of Cherbourg on 24 June and of Caen on 8 July, but the price of these and other offensive operations was high. The Allies had trained their infantry divisions to rely on the artillery to support every aspect of combat. The battle for Caen, *Operation Charnwood*, provides an illustration of this, and while the details and some of the terminology would be different in a description of the attack on Cherbourg, the principles and the problems are very similar.

The operation was based upon an elaborate fire plan which included the first attempt to use heavy bombers in direct support of an attacking army. In addition to the field regiments of four divisions, the medium guns of two Army Groups Royal Artillery (AGRAs), plus the fire power of the battleship *Rodney*, the monitor *Roberts*, and the cruisers *Belfast* and *Emerald*, were available. With 656 artillery pieces and the navy ready to assist, many thought *Charnwood* would break the defenders without too much difficulty. Instead, the operation cost the British and Canadians almost as many casualties as they suffered on D-Day.[32]

The fire plan called for the navy and the mediums to concentrate on counter-battery work and the destruction of targets beyond the defensive perimeter. A great deal of attention was paid to rear areas to prevent reinforcements from arriving. The field artillery, still employing self-propelled 105mm guns, had the primary responsibility for firing the infantry onto its objectives with a timed barrage that lifted at a fast walking pace. It would then respond to requests from forward observation officers, providing their radio sets worked and they were still alive.

The capacity to neutralize hostile gun batteries, anti-tank positions, mortar and Nebelwerfer sites depended on two variables: intelligence, based almost exclusively on photo-reconnaissance, and the accuracy of the artillery fire brought to bear on the target area. Good photo-reconnaissance could locate most of the larger enemy installations, though it was seldom possible to distinguish between dummy positions and ones which were occupied. The small mortar pits and machine gun posts and the low-profile anti-tank guns camouflaged in hedges and in other infantry positions were another matter, although in the case of *Charnwood*, patrolling and observation of fire over a four-week period helped.

Once the known positions were plotted, a fire plan, based on the premise that half of the rounds would be concentrated in a "50 per cent zone" that would be centred on the target, was prepared. Unfortunately, accuracy depended on a host of variables which meant that unobserved and therefore uncorrected fire was frequently plus or minus 100 to 300 yards for both range and line. To achieve neutralization under such conditions required a very large number of guns firing many shells so that the overlap would ensure that the target *area* was struck.

"Neutralizing the target areas" did not mean destruction. This required even larger numbers of guns and shells because the 105mm or 25-pounder was not powerful enough to inflict casualties on dug-in troops or weapons unless it scored a direct hit. Tests had demonstrated that a shell had to land within three feet, six inches of a slit trench to transmit a shock wave through the earth, never mind inflict casualties. Medium guns fired a heavier shell with a slightly increased zone of lethality, but a bigger crater is only significant if it is in the right place.[33]

Operation Charnwood was the first major set-piece battle of the campaign, and it is clear that the gunners had a great deal to learn. The attack on 8 July by the Highland Light Infantry on Buron, the single most costly engagement of the operation, is exceptionally well documented and it is possible to learn a good deal about what actually took place.[34]

The Germans had dug a long V-shaped anti-tank ditch in front of Buron. They hoped to channel the Allied armour into carefully constructed killing zones. The barrage got the infantry to this obstacle easily enough, but it quickly became evident that few of the

German positions had been destroyed. The infantry, assisted by the 105mm guns of the field regiment firing on the village, got into Buron and began to clean out the enemy positions. The armour, which had circled west to try to provide support from the flank, ran into a minefield, suffered losses and was effectively out of action during the advance on the village.

The struggle to win Buron lasted until late afternoon. As enemy shelling and mortar fire took its toll the 12th SS attempted to recapture the village employing a battle group of Panther and Mark IV tanks. This counter-attack was quickly dealt with by a self-propelled battery of the corps' anti-tank regiment, mounting 17-pounder anti-tank guns, which destroyed thirteen tanks at the cost of three of its own SPs.[35]

The final phase of *Charnwood* required an assault on the inner defensive ring, including the Abbaye d'Ardenne. That battle lasted well into the night, but as dawn broke it was evident the surviving Germans were gone.[36] Rommel was unwilling to sacrifice more men in counter-attacks and ordered a withdrawal across the River Orne, abandoning the ruins of Caen to the Allies.

There were many lessons to be learned from the battle for Caen. The gunners, particularly the medium regiments, needed air ops— pilots flying light, single-engine planes to observe and correct fire— to be effective. The RAF had bombed accurately, but fears of short bombing had led to a decision to concentrate on rear areas, including the northern part of the city, rather than risk targeting the ring of defended villages closer to Allied positions. The bombers boosted Allied morale and impressed the enemy but did no damage to the defences. The next time the planners would take greater risks and use the bombers more effectively.

Another problem of enormous importance was the development of an effective counter-mortar doctrine. Everyone in the front lines knew that the enemy employed virtually unlimited amounts of mortar fire, but it was not until operational research scientists analysed the impact of enemy mortars and Nebelwerfers across the battlefield that systematic action was undertaken. Michael Swann, who had carried out extensive work on mortars at Barnard Castle, the British advanced infantry training school, prepared a report that defined the extent of the problem in early July:

The German army uses mortars and Nebelwerfers in large numbers. These weapons are small and difficult to detect from the air; their trajectories make it possible to conceal them completely from ground observation, particularly in close country. The small noise of discharge of the mortar and the ripple fire of the Nebelwerfer make sound ranging difficult, while the flash and smoke from the mortar is slight and hard to spot. In defence the casualties from mortars and Nebelwerfers may be considerable, while the strain of holding a position and being mortared for days on end is intense. In attack the casualties in forming up areas and on the objective may be very heavy indeed, and are often decisive in throwing back an attack. In either attack or defences, mortars can make movement in forward areas difficult.

So much has long been realized. In the present campaign, however, casualties from mortars have been particularly heavy and have contributed as much as anything else to making advances slow and costly. The enemy's mortars are as much a weapon to be defeated as his tanks. This will continue as long as fighting goes on in undulating and cultivated country. Even on the plains of Picardy and Flanders, there is enough cover to conceal mortars, and although their importance may decline, they are still likely to prove a great source of trouble.[37]

Swann interviewed battalion medical officers from four different divisions and found that all agreed in placing the proportion of mortar casualties at above 70 per cent of total casualties. He found that divisional counter-mortar staffs tended to underestimate the number of mortars and Nebelwerfers opposite them, noting that a German infantry division possessed as many as fifty-seven 81mm mortars plus between twelve and twenty of the 120mm type. Panzer divisions were equipped with about half these numbers. In Normandy, the German army had also provided a regiment composed of fifty-four six-barrel Nebelwerfers on the scale of one per division. Swann estimated that to bring the problem under control, divisions might need to obtain between sixty and eighty hostile mortar locations a day.

Every division in the Allied armies developed its own methods of dealing with enemy mortars. Most relied on sound bearings and flash spotting with dedicated signals equipment which permitted rapid response from howitzers or heavy mortars. The best solution, radar sets that could track the arc of the mortar bomb and provide an instant location, were not available until the fall of 1944—an oversight that was to cost many lives.[38]

Efforts to improve the accuracy of artillery and to develop better counter-battery and counter-mortar techniques began to pay dividends but the war could not wait. On 18 July, Montgomery and Dempsey, his army commander, launched *Operation Goodwood*, an attempt to stage an armoured Blitzkrieg employing all three British armoured divisions. The gently rolling countryside south of Caen, with its network of fortified villages, was the worst possible country for Allied armour. It was actually flatter than the desert in that "there were few bumps or depressions where a tank could take a hull down position and provide covering fire."[39]

The planners of *Goodwood* were aware of the problems the tanks would encounter if the enemy was able to direct long-range anti-tank fire at them in this wide-open country, and they proposed to use heavy bombers and medium artillery to neutralize or destroy the fortified village network, which was the key to the German defences. The plan worked in the sense that those villages which were accurately bombed were neutralized and the armour was able to advance beyond them. The difficulty was that a number of villages were left untouched, as were the 88mm guns of the flak corps positioned on Bourguebus–Verrières ridge. The British lost more than two hundred tanks in just two days.[40]

While the British and Canadians were learning how to deal with mortars, Nebelwerfers and long-range anti-tank guns in the Caen sector, the U.S. army was coping with the problem of the *bocage*. The American army had underestimated the problems of fighting in this close, hostile terrain that gave every advantage to the defender. The Germans could take the risk of keeping their armoured divisions in the Caen sector because platoon-sized battle groups, backed up by one or two self-propelled guns, were able to hold off repeated attacks. If the GIs ignored their casualties and pressed forward, the Germans could yield one enclosed field and get ready to defend the next one.

Much attention has been focused on the innovations in tactics and equipment that helped the Americans overcome the *bocage*:

The most effective method of attack proved to be a combined action of infantry, artillery and tanks with some of the tanks equipped with dozer blades or large steel teeth in front to punch holes through the hedgerows. It was found necessary to assign frontages according to specific fields and hedgerows instead of by yardage and to reduce the distances or intervals between tactical formations.[41]

These methods certainly helped in the advance to St-Lô, but such tactics worked far better after six weeks of steady combat had worn down German resistance, reducing the fighting power of their divisions to a small fraction of their original strength. Russell Weigley, who insists that "aggressive American infantry fighting was rare," admits that the Germans found the American pressure in July "unrelenting" and called in vain for reinforcements. Weigley also recognizes that, when the Germans mounted major attacks such as Panzer Lehr's thrust along the Vire River on 11 July, GIs taking advantage of the terrain inflicted enormous casualties on their enemy.[42]

The U.S. Army's steep learning curve was also evident in the changes introduced by Major-General Pete Quesada's 9th Tactical Air Force. The U.S. Army Air Force went to war in 1944 with a system of air support adapted from the British experience in North Africa. This doctrine called for centralized control of all aircraft, with daily conferences deciding upon the missions that would be flown in direct or close support of the ground troops. These tasks, in turn, had to compete against the air force's favoured roles, the maintenance of air superiority, and armed reconnaissance, both of which permitted the pilot freedom to choose his targets.

Ninth Tac modified the British system, introducing greater flexibility, but it was not until the results of air support in the battle for Cherbourg were studied that Quesada revolutionized tactical air doctrine. The first step was to arrange for pilots to be briefed by an Air Support Party Officer (ASPO) working beside the forward troops. One of the first experiments resulted in a devastating attack by Thunderbolts which broke up a German counter-attack without inflicting any casualties through "friendly fire." Quesada built up ground-to-air communication capability, creating a system known as Armoured Column Cover that provided a VHF radio link between an ASPO in a Sherman tank and pilots in the air over the column.[43]

The RAF were much less successful in establishing a workable close-support system, though the introduction of "Cab Rank," in which a forward controller directed aircraft onto a selected target, was an improvement on previous methods.[44] Cab Rank was, however, rarely employed in Normandy, whereas Armoured Column Cover became the norm in the U.S. Army.

Armoured Column Cover could not be fully exploited until the breakout that followed *Operation Cobra* began, but that story has already been told in the preceding pages. The purpose of this epilogue is to link the events of the last month of the Normandy battle with the entire campaign, reminding the reader that it took almost two months of attritional warfare to set the stage for the breakout, encirclement, and destruction of the German armies in France—two months of fighting that fully paralleled the horrors of the western front in World War I.

Modern memory has a firm image of "suicide battalions" and futile battles in the Great War, but we are not accustomed to thinking of Normandy in these terms. Perhaps a single crude comparison will help to make the point. During a single 105-day period in 1917, British and Canadian soldiers fought the battle of Third Ypres, which included the struggle for Passchendaele. General Haig employed forces equivalent to those Eisenhower commanded in Normandy. When it was over, Haig's armies had suffered 244,000 casualties, or 2,121 a day. Normandy cost the Allies close to 2,500 casualties a day, 75 per cent of them among the combat troops at the sharp end who had to carry the battle to the enemy. It was their valour, their endurance, and their ability to adapt that won the battle of Normandy and launched the liberation of Western Europe.

POSTSCRIPTS

Major David Currie

Two months after his fight to the finish in the hell of sweltering St. Lambert, Major David Currie was again facing crack German troops in the frigid polder warfare in the battle of the Scheldt. He received an order from South Alberta regimental headquarters: You're to go to London—on the double.

Still wearing his oil-stained and muddy tanker's overalls over the battle dress that he'd had on for weeks, Currie rushed across the Channel in a motor torpedo boat. A car hurried him along to Buckingham Palace. He doffed the coveralls in a palace anteroom, quaffed a drink of water proffered by a court attendant and walked along the carpeted dais to be presented to his king. George VI was about to honour him with the Victoria Cross.

The morning-coated Lord Chamberlain read the citation of David Currie's gallantry:

> There can be no doubt that the success of the attack on and stand against the enemy at St. Lambert-sur-Dives can largely be attributed to this officer's coolness, inspired leadership and skilful use of the limited weapons at his disposal. The courage and devotion to duty shown by Major Currie during a prolonged period of heavy fighting were outstanding and had a far-reaching effect on the successful outcome of the battle.

The King picked up the Cross from a velvet cushion held by a brigadier and pinned it on Currie's battle dress tunic. His Majesty, dressed in the naval uniform of admiral of the fleet, smiled and chatted with the Canadian major for a minute or so and then shook his hand in congratulations as the khaki-clad orchestra struck up "God Save the King."

The investiture over, Currie donned his coveralls and stepped out in the rain to the palace courtyard to face a photographic barrage by a surprised international and Canadian media. His was the first of three VCs awarded to Canada's military in the North-west Europe campaign.

Within a few days, he was on his way home to Canada. His wife Isabel and their nine-year-old son, David Junior, were living with her parents in Owen Sound, Ontario. Isabel was facing another bleak Christmas without her husband and was recuperating from an appendectomy. The family knew nothing about the award.

"There was a knock at the door and there were some army people," Isabel said. "In those days we lived from day to day and feared anyone coming to the door." Then she got the great news: "Davie was coming home."

As a fitting tribute to Currie's outstanding efforts towards stopping the German army at St. Lambert, Prime Minister John Diefenbaker appointed Lieutenant-Colonel David Vivian Currie, VC, as Sergeant-at-Arms of the Canadian House of Commons, a position he held for seventeen years. Known as "The Colonel," he led the parade of House of Commons officers through the Hall of Honour into the chamber during sittings, ceremoniously shouldering the heavy gold-gilded mace, the symbol of parliamentary government.

Currie died in 1986 at the age of 73.[1]

The Spitfire Twins: Duke Mk1 and Duke Mk2
The Western Canadian Warren twins, Spitfire aces over Normandy, survived the war and returned home to Canada. Wing Commander Duke Mk2 writes: "In January 1949 my twin and I were sent overseas again as members of the Regular RCAF. Duke was sent to the Test Pilot School at Farmborough and I was sent to the Fighter Leaders School at West Raynham. My career was basically as a fighter pilot. I was in charge of a group of Canadians training the new fighter arm of the re-armed Germany.

"We knew our careers were moving apart, for the RCAF at that time only planned on 12,000 personnel all ranks and we were senior F/Ls (Flight Lieutenants). They wouldn't put two senior people in the same slot. But we were pleased to have been selected for these prestigious schools.

"The trip over was wonderful, first class, but we had to pay for our wives, about 50 British pounds. England was still cold and bleak, and Melba says had we the money she would have turned around and gone home. I don't believe this, for we had only been married three years and Melba was crazy about me.

"Duke MkI was killed flying as a test pilot while on loan to AV Roe from the RCAF to test the CF-100 prototype. It was 5 April 1951. Never a day goes by but what I think of him. When I lecture at schools about Remembrance Day, I am doing what we both would be doing if he were alive. When I act as Padre of the Legion, I feel I am representing both of us, as we grew up in Western Canada in a small town where the Legion was important."

Duke Mk2 retired with the rank of Wing Commander, and he and his (still) adoring Melba moved back to Comax, BC.

"I started helping an ordained padre here in 1977 who was our Legion Padre. When he left, he insisted I become the Padre for Branch 160 RCL [Royal Canadian Legion] Comox. I guess I am a lay minister, now in my 20th year. I do funeral and memorial services for Legion members, as well as others who like my way of doing the service. One of my Legion comrades describes it as 'a short service, and no bible thumping.'

"When proper ministers ask me where I was ordained (a common question), I tell them I learned to pray in the cockpit of a Spitfire. Quite often they say 'that was probably better training than what I received.'"[2]

"Snuffy" Smith

Anecdotes about "Snuffy" Smith are legion with the Canadian Grenadier Guards. Lieutenant-Colonel H.A. Smith was a squadron commander of the Guards in Normandy, and went on to command the regiment in December 1944. During the Rhineland battle in February 1945, he lost his leg when his command tank was holed by a German 88mm.

After the war, he returned to his west coast home. "'Snuffy' was a speedster in a car and kept losing his license," his second-in-command, Major-General Ned Amy remembers. "So finally, everywhere he went, he took his bicycle. One night—it was in Victoria, very dark, back in the '80s—he was cycling along the road and he was hit by a car.

"His wooden leg flew off. A woman nearby passed out when she saw the leg—complete with shoe—sailing past her. Later, in the hospital, the admitting nurse was quizzing him about his religion, marital status etc. 'Snuffy,' now in great pain, yelled, 'For Christ sake, don't ask me. Ask my wife!'"

Major-General Kurt Meyer, 12 SS Hitlerjugend

Panzermeyer was captured by Belgian partisans who found him hiding in a barn and handed him over to the Americans on 6 September 1944. He had discarded his SS uniform, but was identified later when his SS tattoo gave him away.

In 1945, in the first war crimes trial ever held in Canada, Meyer was charged with the murder of forty-one Canadians in cold blood, all prisoners of war far behind the lines. Wehrmacht General Heinrich Eberbach was the first witness. He was Meyer's senior commanding general in July and August 1944, with Commander Panzer Group West, and was with him for three months in a prisoner of war camp. General Geyr von Schweppenburg and Meyer's wife, Kate, were also character witnesses.

Meyer was found guilty and at the age of thirty-five was sentenced to death. The sentence was later commuted to life imprisonment by Major-General Chris Vokes. Meyer was imprisoned in Canada, and his wife, Kate, four daughters and ten-month-old son, Kurt, Jr., were allowed to visit him at Christmas in 1945.

After ten years in jail, the latter time spent in Germany, he was released from captivity in September 1954. One of Meyer's first jobs after his release was to work for a German brewery. "Ironically," his biographer Howard Margolian said, "he sold beer to Canadians at NATO headquarters, and would socialize with them in their mess after deliveries. He was very popular with Canadians."

His son, Kurt, Jr., said in a recent interview that Meyer never stopped believing in and promoting the principals of Nazi socialism. "Long after the war, my father attended Nazi rallies with Waffen SS officers and spoke at countless meetings and gatherings, once again the Panzermeyer.

"He was no hero; he was a tragic figure in German history. He never distanced himself from Hitler."

In 1959 Meyer published his memoirs, as arrogant of the Hitler-jugend and as disdainful of his enemies as he had been during the war. Like most Nazi and Wehrmacht officers, he disclaimed any knowledge of the Jewish extermination camps. "In my father's case, the German excuse, 'I knew nothing because I wanted to know nothing,' was valid," Kurt Meyer, Jr., said.

In 1961, on his 51st birthday, Meyer died of a heart attack.[3]

Michael Gutowski: The Polish Warrior

When the war ended, Captain Michael Gutowski, one of the liberators of Chambois, was, like all of his Polish compatriots, facing the bitter fact that the country they had fought for so fervently for six years was still denied them.

Polish suffering in the war was almost unparalleled. In Warsaw, more than 20,000 Polish soldiers were killed, as were hundreds of thousands of civilians, murdered by the Germans during the uprising or shipped to concentration camps after the garrison surrendered. The Germans destroyed most of the city during the fighting, and later burned whatever buildings were still standing.

But in the immediate postwar years, historians tended to ignore the contributions in the North-west European campaign by 1st Polish Armoured Division. The Sikorski Institute in London, whose aim is to fully document Poland's history, became a gathering place for Gutowski and his compatriots. They returned on a number of occasions to the battlefields and to the Polish Cemetery in Normandy to honour the 1,100 graves of Polish soldiers. "They were all volunteers, who came from around the world to fight for the freedom of our country," he said with pride.

The freedom they had fought so savagely for still eluded them. Following Germany's defeat, Poland's borders were redefined by the Potsdam Conference of 1945, and Russia gained control of a nation that despised it. The Polish patriots who had struggled so hard to escape one tyranny now faced another. They could not go back.

Resolutely, they became new immigrants in corners of the world where freedom was still fostered. In those early days, physicians ploughed fields and scientists dug ditches; it was a small price to pay to escape the Nazis and the communists. Historian John Keegan wrote that the Poles became "the most successful immigrant community ever absorbed into British life." There isn't a country that wouldn't endorse that sentiment.

Michael Gutowski tucked his Polish war decorations—the highly respected Virtuti Militari and the American Legion of Merit—and his pre-war Olympic equestrian medals into the bottom of his tack box and embarked on a new life in Canada with his wife and children.

He felt lucky to land a job so soon after his arrival in Canada, working in the sport he loved, for a horse trainer. It didn't take long for him to realize that his pre-war skills as an Olympic show jumper, bought for eighty dollars a month, would barely pay the rent. Like his countrymen in dozens of other countries, he adjusted resignedly to his new life and patiently forged ahead to establish himself all over again in his equestrian career. Ultimately, Gutowski became a renowned coach of Canada's Olympic Three-Day Event Equestrian Team.

In 1998, Captain Gutowski finally returned to Poland, with the sad mission of burying his wife of more than fifty years, as he had always promised her. To his surprise, he was met at the airport by a government official in a gleaming limousine. He learned then that he had been promoted to rank of Brigadier-General by a grateful Polish government.[4]

Patton, Bradley and Monty: The Outcome

On 8 December 1945, just two days before he was due to leave his European command and fly home, Lieutenant-General George Patton was involved in a car accident. His neck was broken. He remained alive, in traction in a hospital in Heidelberg, but died of complications on 21 December and was buried in the American Cemetery at Hamm in Luxembourg.

The man who was most outspoken in his criticism of Field-Marshal Sir Bernard Montgomery, accusing him repeatedly in post-war articles and interviews for not ordering Patton to close the Falaise Gap, was General Omar Bradley.

Lieutenant-Colonel Trumbull Warren was Montgomery's PA—the only Canadian of Monty's twelve liaison officers. When Monty died in 1976, Warren was invited to the state funeral at Windsor. He recounts the moment when General Bradley—long identified as a bitter enemy of Montgomery's—laid a wreath at the coffin.

"Brad said just one word: 'Thanks.'"

The Windhunds

Lieutenant-General Gerhard Graf von Schwerin was one of the few German generals who openly defied Hitler's orders—not once but twice—and survived to become a hero to his people.

In August 1944, Schwerin was fired by SS General von Funck when he refused to commit his division, 116th Panzer, to the Mortain counter-attack. He was convinced that Hitler's attack would fail; why throw his good troops into the disaster. Schwerin assumed he was fired in order to shift the responsibility for eventual failures entirely on his division. His unfortunate replacement, General Reinhard, was wounded and taken prisoner at Falaise. Shortly afterwards, General Sepp Dietrich insisted on the return of General von Schwerin as commander of 116 Division after the Seine crossing.

Three months later, Schwerin again defied the SS, who were defending the German city of Aachan. They were determined to hold out, although American artillery would have destroyed the old city. Schwerin intervened at great personal risk, ordering the city abandoned without a fight. Today, a street in Aachan is named "von Schwerin Strasse." Postwar, he was "one of the fathers of the postwar Bundeswehr."

His staff officer, Lieutenant-Colonel Heinz Günther Guderian (later, Major-General) was one of the last German officers to escape the Falaise pocket on 21 August, and, by his account to the authors, he was also the last German officer to escape across the Rhine ahead of the Allied armies on 10 March 1945.

"As a member of the German General Staff, I was on the list of war criminals. I was sent to a special camp. Later I came into the historical camp, to help prepare a history of the war. My father [General Guderian] arrived soon after," Guderian said. "It was the first time I had seen him since October 1944, when he brought me the Iron Cross direct from Hitler.

"I was released in October, 1947 but my father remained there. They let my mother and her dog go and live with him. On the 60th birthday of my father, he was released.[5]

Stephen Campbell's Quest

In the course of pursuing his lifelong fascination with the events of St. Lambert-sur-Dives, Stephen Campbell, CA, an amateur historian from Manotick, Ontario, spent several years amassing a visual record of the battle where Major David Currie won his VC from 19 to 21 August 1944.

As part of his research he sought out original negatives and cine film taken in that historic time by Lieutenant Donald Grant, MC (35mm 3-¼" × 4-¼" Speed Graphic still photographs) and Sergeant Jack Stollery MM (cine film) of the Canadian Army Film and Photographic unit.

"Playing detective," Campbell finally tracked Grant down in a small seaside village in England and discovered the sorry account of the postwar fate of our wartime photographers—and their work.

Although Lieutenant Grant had risked his life photographing Canadian soldiers in action, and had sent many thousands of negatives back from the front lines to the war office in England, he had rarely seen any of the developed photographs.

In 1992, Donald Grant decided to do something about it. He drove to the Canadian National Archives in Ottawa and spent several hours trying to find copies of some of his wartime work. Finding hundreds of his photographs in the cardex files, many of which he was seeing for the first time, he selected a small sample, including the now familiar St. Lambert sequence of Major Currie arresting a German convoy of troops, and ordered enlargements. Then he got the bill. You've got to pay for these, he was told.

"*Odd* reaction paying for personally exposed pix," he noted wryly.

In a taped report in 1988, Grant is highly critical of some of the "published offal"—the distorted and sometimes fictional interpretations—of his visit to St. Lambert. "Memories of the valiant," he says sarcastically of some of the authors. "I'll stick to my photos."

He especially scoffs at the implications that he prophesied at the moment of snapping the shutter that his photograph of Major Currie, revolver in hand capturing Germans, would become world famous. "The photo probably is the most published of Canadians at war, but as the photographer, it is not the greatest or best. A good news pix at the rite time/place/subject [sic] to fit a media headline ... LUCK!"

Stephen Campbell then embarked on a years-long search for the originals of Jack Stollery's cine footage of St. Lambert. Examining the photos carefully, he deduced that "from Lieutenant Grant's still photographs, Sergeant Stollery can be seen filming a variety of scenes. "

Campbell tracked down items of this footage in army newsreels and other documentary videos, and deduced that a fair portion of the footage was still outstanding.

Then began his search for the original unedited reel. He traced the procedure of filing photographs and cine film: "The exposed film was sent from France to London by plane where it was developed at army studios. Newsreels were prepared from copies of the original, the original being archived in the studio library in London."

But the originals, he discovered, had disappeared. His search led him to the Imperial War Museum and thence, still following the trail, he found that the reels were transferred in 1946 or 1947 to Canada to the National Film Board.

The mystery, however, was still not solved. The catalogued collection of the National Archives and the National Film Board only listed the same footage already seen in army newsreels and videos. The residue was still missing. Returning to Ottawa he then discovered, to his horror, that original out-takes of the cine footage taken by Stollery and his ilk from the Canadian Army Film and Photographic unit had been stored in a wooden building outside of Ottawa, with none of the humidity control necessary to preserve old film. He later learned that the building had burned down. "A fire at the NFB nitrate storage warehouse (somewhere near Ottawa) in 1967 might have consumed some or all of the collection," he noted.[6]

But Stephen Campbell has not given up. He wonders if by chance any reels were salvaged from that fire. Or he puzzles whether the burned photographs were only copies. Perhaps, somewhere in a London archive, the originals lie collecting dust, waiting for a keen young amateur historian to uncover them.

NOTES

The following archival sources frequently referred to in this book have been abbreviated as follows:

EC: Eisenhower Center for American Studies, Metropolitan College, University of New Orleans

NAC: National Archives of Canada, Ottawa

NA: National Archives, Washington, DC

LCMSDS: Laurier Centre for Military Strategic and Disarmament Studies, Wilfrid Laurier University

IWM: Imperial War Museum, London, England

WD: War Diary

RG: Record Group

Chapter 1: The Class of '26

1. Craig W.H. Luther, *Blood and Honor: The History of the 12th SS Panzer Division "Hitler Youth," 1943–1945* (San Jose, CA: Bender, 1987), 13.

2. Ibid., 18.

3. Ibid., 84.

4. Col. Charles C.P. Stacey, *The Victory Campaign: The Operations in North-West Europe, 1944–1945, Vol. III* (Ottawa: Queen's Printer, 1960), 221. Col. Stacey writes that Meyer did not learn of his promotion from SS Colonel to SS Major General until after he became a prisoner of war.

5. Luther, 244.

6. Howard Margolian, *Conduct Unbecoming: The Story of the Murder of Canadian Prisoners of War in Normandy* (Toronto: University of Toronto Press, 1998).

7. EC, Oral History: Maj. Gerhard Lemcke, 12th SS Panzer Div.

8. EC, Oral History: 2nd Lt. Hans-Heinrich Dibbern, Panzer Grenadier Regt. 902, Panzer Lehr Division.

9. Eversley Belfield and H. Essame, *The Battle for Normandy* (London: Pan, 1967), 73.

10. EC, Oral History: 2nd Lt. Wenzel Borgert, Anti-tank Batt. 228, 116 Div.

11. EC, Oral History: 2nd Lt. Dibbern.

12. EC, Oral History: Cpl. Friedrich Bertenrath, Radioman/Reconnaissance Batt., 2nd Panzer Div.

13. Ibid.

14. EC, Oral History: Pte. Adolf Rogosch, Pfc. 1st Class, Grenadier Regt. 942, 353 Infantry Div.

15. Dr. Paul German, *100 Days of War for Peace* (Condé-sur-Noireau, France: Charles Corlet, 1998), 23.

16. John Keegan, *Six Armies in Normandy* (London: Jonathan Cape, 1982), 320.

17. EC, Oral History: Cpl. Bertenrath.

18. Milton Shulman, *Defeat in the West* (London: Secker & Warburg, 1963), 116.

19. EC, Oral History: 2nd Lt. Borgert.

20. Max Hastings, *Overlord: D-Day and the Battle for Normandy 1944* (London: Pan, 1985), 327.

21. EC, Oral History: 2nd Lt. Dibbern.

22. EC, Oral History: Lt. Günther Materne, Battery Officer, Artillery Regt. 363.

23. EC, Oral History: Dr. Walter Padberg, staff of Grenadier Regt. 959.

24. EC, Oral History: Maj. Helmut Ritgen, Commander, 2nd Batt., Panzer Lehr Regt. 130.

25. EC, Oral History: Maj. Lemcke.

26. Martin Lindsay, *So Few Got Through: The Personal Diary of Lt-Col Martin Lindsay* (London: Collins, 1946), 49.

27. EC, Oral History: Capt. Walter Kaspers, Adj., Anti-tank Unit 228, 116 Panzer Div.

28. Walter Warlimont, *Inside Hitler's Headquarters, 1939–1945* (London: Weidenfeld & Nicolson, 1964), 440.

29. EC, Oral History: Pte. Herbert Meier, Radioman, Tank-Artillery-Training Regt. 130, Panzer Lehr Div.

30. EC, Oral History: Cpl. Bertenrath.

31. J.J. How, *Normandy: The British Breakout* (London: Kimber, 1981), 28.

32. Carlo D'Este, *Decision in Normandy* (New York: Dutton, 1983), 181.

33. Hubert Meyer, *The History of the 12th SS Panzer Division Hitlerjugend* (Winnipeg: J.J. Fedorowicz, 1992), 161.

34. EC, Oral History: Pte. Meier.

35. EC, Oral History: Lt. Materne.

36. EC, Oral History: Maj. Helmut Ritgen.

37. Mitcham, Samuel W., *Hitler's Field Marshals and Their Battles* (Chelson, MI: Scarborough House, 1990) 291.

38. LCMSDS, German Army Sit Reps [situation reports], Normandy.

39. EC, Oral History: 2nd Lt. Borgert.

Chapter 2: Operation Fortitude

1. William Breuer, *Death of a Nazi Army: The Falaise Pocket* (New York: Scarborough House, 1985), 29.
2. Russell F. Weigley, *Eisenhower's Lieutenants: The Campaigns of France and Germany, 1944–1945* (Bloomington: Indiana University Press, 1981), 232.
3. Gen. Dwight D. Eisenhower, *Crusade in Europe* (New York: Doubleday, 1948), 224.
4. Michael Howard, *British Intelligence in the Second World War*, Vol. V: *Strategic Deception* (London: Her Majesty's Stationery Office, 1990), 18.
5. Ibid., 100, 120.
6. Ibid., 121.
7. Ibid., 185.
8. Ibid., 185.
9. NA, "Moving, Commitment and Fighting of the 116 Pz Div in France, 6 Jun–12 Aug/4." Box 736, MSB-017. In J.J. How, *Hill 112* (London: Kimber, 1984), 42.
10. D'Este, 201.
11. Breuer, 38.
12. Howard, 235.

Chapter 3: The Bocage: A Land So Evil

1. B.J. Danson, "A Personal Essay: Being Hit, Normandy, August 1944," 28 February 1994. Kindly lent to the authors.
2. Ernie Pyle with 4th Division: http://eb.com/normandy/pri/Q00237.html.
3. Weigley, 186.
4. Ken Tout, *A Fine Night for Tanks: The Road to Falaise* (Phoenix Mill, Gloucestershire: Sutton, 1988), 150.
5. Sydney Jary, *18 Platoon* (Surrey: Self-published, 1987), 20.
6. EC, Oral History: Pte. Rogosch.
7. Ibid.
8. Jary, 20–1.
9. Tout, *A Fine Night for Tanks,* 134.
10. Ibid., 142.
11. Ibid., 102.
12. Ibid., 8.
13. Jary, 20–1.
14. Eisenhower, 224, 269.
15. NA Hospital Files, RG407 E427. ML Series (hereinafter cited as NA Hospital Files): Interview with 2nd Lt. Kussman, 3rd Batt., 115 Inf., 29 Div.

16. Belfield and Essame, 172.

17. Nigel Hamilton, *Monty: Master of the Battlefield, 1942–1944* (New York: Hodder & Stoughton, 1983), 751.

18. Stephen E. Ambrose, *The Victors: Eisenhower and His Boys: The Men of World War II* (New York: Simon & Schuster, 1998), 210.

19. Denis Whitaker and Shelagh Whitaker, *Tug of War: The Allied Victory that Opened Antwerp Harbour* (Toronto: Stoddart, 1984, 2000), 256. Nearly 20 per cent of the Canloans were killed; total casualties, including killed or wounded, were 438, or 70 per cent. Many won decorations, some more than once. There were 41 MCs, 1 DSO, 1 MBE, 1 U.S. Silver Star, 4 Croix de Guerre, and 1 Order of Bronze Lion. This effort, both brave and brilliant, had a significant effect on the war's outcome.

20. William B. Folkestad, *The View from the Turret: The 743rd Tank Battalion During World War II* (Shippensburg, PA: Burd Street Press, 1996), 29–30.

21. Stephen E. Ambrose, *Citizen Soldiers: The U.S. Army from the Normandy Beaches to the Bulge to the Surrender of Germany* (New York: Simon & Schuster, 1997), 63.

22. Lindsay, 48.

23. Hastings, 230.

24. Alan Moorehead, *Eclipse* (London: Hamish Hamilton, 1967), 110.

25. Eisenhower, 269; Ambrose, *Citizen Soldiers*, 67.

26. Ibid., 67.

27. How, 203.

28. Ibid.

29. Moorehead, 113.

30. Ken Tout, *Tanks, Advance! Normandy to the Netherlands, 1944* (London: Grafton Books, 1987), 87.

31. Corp. J.A. Womack, *Summon Up the Blood: A Unique Record of D-Day and Its Aftermath.* Ed. by Celia Wolfe (London: Leo Cooper, 1997), 65.

32. Lindsay, 40.

33. Womack, 66.

34. Ambrose, *Citizen Soldiers*, 66, 73.

35. NA, 21 Army Group intelligence summary No. 154, Part One, 10 August 1944.

36. EC, Oral History: Dr. Walter Padberg. See Ch. 23.

37. EC, Oral History: Pte. Kenneth Russell, 82nd Airborne.

38. Ernie Pyle with 4th Division: http://eb.com/normandy/pri/Q00237.html.

39. Michael Reynolds, *Steel Inferno: 1 SS Panzer Corps in Normandy* (New York: Spellmount, 1997), 208.

40. Shulman, 144.

41. H. Essame, *Patton: A Study in Command* (New York: Scribner's, 1974), 142.
42. Ambrose, *Citizen Soldiers*, 74.
43. EC, Oral History: Pte. Rogosch.

Chapter 4: Bless 'em All

1. Ken Tout, quoted in Terry Copp and Bill McAndrew, *Battle Exhaustion* (Montreal and Kingston: McGill-Queen's University Press, 1990), 149.
2. Author interview with Padre Jock Anderson, MC and Bar, 28 July 1998.
3. W.R. Feasby, *Official History of the Canadian Medical Services, 1939–1945*. (Ottawa: Queen's Printer and Controller of Stationery, 1953), 211.
4. Whitaker and Whitaker, *Tug of War*, 251–2; author interview with Corp. Wes Burrows, 6 May 1983.
5. Capt. Cliff Chadderton, *Caen to Calais: July-August-September 1944*.
6. NAC, RG24, WD of 11th Canadian Field Ambulance.
7. Author interview with Dr. Art Stevenson, RCAMC, 20 July 1998.
8. Ibid.
9. Statement by John Redden as dictated to his son, 7 February 1996: Steven Campbell collection.
10. Folkestad, 46.
11. Author interview with Maj. Donald Campbell, MD.
12. Col. G.W.L. Nicholson, CD, *Seventy Years of Service: A History of a Royal Canadian Army Medical Corps* (Ottawa: Borealis, 1977), 226.
13. J.B. Hillsman, *Eleven Men and a Scalpel* (Winnipeg: Columbia, 1948), 7.
14. Tout, *A Fine Night for Tanks*, 85.
15. Brenda McBryde, *A Nurse's War* (London: Chatto & Windus, 1979), 84–96.
16. Hillsman, 76.
17. B.J. Danson, "A Personal Essay: Being Hit, Normandy, August 1944."
18. Maj. John J.M. Connors, *The Story of an Unremarkable Canadian* (London, Ont.: Published by the author, 1981).
19. Author interview with Dr. Art Stevenson, RCAMC, 20 July 1998.
20. Connors.
21. Feasby, 204.
22. Ambrose, *Citizen Soldiers*, 322–23.
23. Feasby, 203.
24. Ambrose, 323.

Chapter 5: It All Seemed So Hopeless—And Then . . .

1. Hamilton, 754.

2. IWM, Bernard Law Montgomery Papers, BLM 126/16.

3. Hamilton, 746.

4. Hastings, 300–301.

5. LCMSDS, WD, 2nd Canadian Field Historical Section, 16 August 1944.

6. Hastings, 293.

7. Henry Maule, *Normandy Breakout* (New York: Quadrangle/New York Times Book Co., 1977), 66.

8. Ibid., 67.

9. A.J. Liebling, *The Road from Saint-Lo*: http://eb.com/normandy/pri/Q00237.html.

10. Essame, 144.

Chapter 6: The British Breakout

1. How, 19–20.

2. G.P.B. Roberts, *From the Desert to the Baltic* (London: Kimber, 1987), 168.

3. Ibid., 185–9.

4. IWM, 84/50/1: diary of Trooper John Thorpe, 2nd Fife and Forfar Yeomanry.

5. Ibid.

6. How, *Normandy*, 54.

7. Roberts, 189.

8. How, *Normandy*, 54.

9. Ibid.

10. Roberts, 185–9.

11. How, *Normandy*, 59.

12. Ibid., 68.

13. Ibid., 218.

14. Roberts, 193.

15. How, *Normandy*, 208.

16. IWM, Bernard Law Montgomery's Signal to CIGS, BLM 119/3 Aug. 44.

17. IWM, BLM 119/2 Aug. 44.

18. Maj.-Gen. Sir Francis Guingand, KBE, CB, DSO, *Operation Victory* (London: Hodder & Stoughon, 1947), 399.

19. IWM, BLM 94/8.

20. Sir Brian Horrocks, with Eversley Belfield and Maj.-Gen. H. Essame, *Corps Commander* (Toronto: Griffin House, 1977), 28.

21. Jary, 22.

22. Ibid.

23. Tout, *A Fine Night for Tanks*, 30.

24. Horrocks, *Corps Commander*, 28; Sir Brian Horrocks, with Eversley Belfield and Maj.-Gen. H. Essame, *A Full Life* (London: Collins, 1960), 188.

25. Hastings, 343.

26. Patrick Delaforce, *Churchill's Desert Rats: From Normandy to Berlin with the 7th Armoured Division* (London: Alan Sutton, 1994), 70.

27. Jary, 8.

28. Horrocks, *Corps Commander*, 35; Horrocks, *A Full Life*, 90.

29. Thomas J. Bates, *Normandy: The Search for Sydney* (Berkeley: Bayes, 1999), vii, 91, 94.

30. IWM, 84/50/1: diary of Trooper John Thorpe.

31. Ibid., 60; Delaforce, 60.

Chapter 7: Hitler's Gamble

1. NA, German Army Sit Reps. Weekly Review, 24–30 July 1944.

2. Tout, *A Fine Night for Tanks*, 126.

3. NA, "Moving, Commitment and Fighting of the 116 Pz Div in France, 6 June–12 Aug/4." Box 736, MSB-017.

4. NA, RG94, German Intelligence Section: Special Interrogation Series No. 11, 14 June 1945: SS-General Sepp Dietrich.

5. NA, "Moving, Commitment and Fighting of the 116 Pz Div in France, 6 June–12 Aug/4," Box 736.

6. NA, Army Gp Intelligence Summary #155. Part II. 15 Aug/44.

7. NA, 116 Pz Div.

8. Ibid.

10. Alwyn Featherston, *Battle for Mortain: The 30th Infantry Division Saves the Breakout, August 7–31* (Novato, CA: Presidio, 1993), 71–2, 144.

11. LCMSDS, German Army Sit Reps. A Gp B Sitrep.

12. F.H. Hinsley, *British Intelligence in the Second World War, Vol. III*. London, HMSO, 1981, Pt. 2: 245–6.

13. Featherston, 71–2.

14. Paul Carell, *Invasion: They're Coming* (New York: Bantam, 1964), 249.

Chapter 8: The Battle of Mortain

1. NA, RG94, Combat Interviews, 24038.96: Interview of Co. "F", 119th Infantry, via Bruyelles, Belgium, 5 September 1944.

2. René Langlois, *1944: Les Douets in Torment: A Memoir*. Trans. by Joyce Carter. (Mortain: self-published, 1996), 17.

3. Ibid.

4. NA, RG94 WWII. Operations Reports, 1940–8 ,Combat Interviews: Folders 95–7, 5CI 96: Activities of the 120th Regt., 30 Inf. Div.: The Counterattack at Mortain, 6–12 Aug. 1944.

5. NA, RG94, Combat interviews: The counter-attack against the 120th Inf at Mortain; The L'Abbaye-Blanche Roadblock.

6. Featherston, 62.

7. Ibid., 64.

8. NA, RG44, Combat interview: Activities of the 120th Regiment, 30 Inf. Div., 6–12 Aug. 1944.

9. Featherston, 62.

10. Langlois, 21.

11. Featherston, 74.

12. Langlois, 23.

13. Featherston, 79.

14. Breuer, 113.

15. Ibid., 113.

16. Langlois, 24.

17. NA, RG94, Combat interview: Co A's Action in the Mortain counterattack; B Company Account.

18. NA, RG94, Combat interview with Sgts Grady & Workman, 117 Infantry at St-Barthélmy.

19. Featherston, 128.

20. NA, RG94, Combat interview: WWII Operations Reports 1940–48. 117 Infantry at St-Barthélmy.

Chapter 9: Mortain's Lost Battalion

1. Featherston, 115.

2. "Chronology of the actions of Second SS Panzer Division Das Reich at Mortain" by Mark Reardon (Mark Yerger's Books). Email the Webmaster, WW2 Website Association.

3. NA, RG94, Combat interviews: The counter-attack against the 120th Inf. at Mortain. The L'Abbaye-Blanche Roadblock.

4. NA, RG94, Repulse of German Counterattack at Avranches. Comments by Brig.-Gen. James Lewis.

5. Reynolds, 218.

6. Featherston, 129–30.

7. Charles Demoulin, *Firebirds! Flying a Typhoon in Action* (Washington, D.C.: Smithsonian Institution Press, 1986), 186.

8. Hugh A. Halliday, *Typhoon and Tempest: The Canadian Story* (Toronto: CANAV, 1992), 163.

9. Author interview with F/L William Baggs, 164 Squad., 84 gGroup, RCAF, 11 October 1998.

10. Ibid.

11. Featherston, 134–5.

12. Reynolds, 220; PAC, RG24, Vol. 20518, File 981 (D117), Seventh Army.

13. Christopher Evans, "The Fighter-Bomber in the Normandy Campaign: The Role of 83 Group," *Canadian Military History* 8/1 (Winter 1999): 26; Terry Copp, "TAF Over Normandy," *Legion Magazine*, January/February 1999: 38.

14. Author interview with F/L William Baggs, 21 August 1999.

15. Ibid. F/L Baggs noted in an interview that, while 151 Typhoon pilots were killed in Normandy, a total of 656 were killed in the course of the war. "I knew the losses were high," he recalled, "but I did not realize they were *that* high" (12 June 1999). Baggs completed a tour of ninety-two sorties in the war.

16. NA, RG 24. File 981 (D117) Vol 20518: Report by Gen. von Gersdorff, Chief of Staff, on the activities of Seventh Army.

17. Reynolds, 219.

18. Martin Blumenson, *Breakout and Pursuit* (Washington, D.C.: Center of Military History, 1961), 474.

19. NA, "Moving, Commitment and Fighting of the 116 Pz Div in France, 6 June–12 Aug/44."

20. Ibid.

21. Ibid.

22. EC, Oral History: Maj.-Gen. Heinz Günther Guderian.

23. NA, MS B840. 981SOM (D123). Eberbach: Panzer Group Eberbach and the Falaise Encirclement, 1 February 1946.

24. Shulman, 148.

25. Blumenson, *Breakout and Pursuit*, 481.

26. Featherston, xi.

27. NA, RG94, Combat interviews: The counter-attack against 120th Inf. at Mortain.

28. NA, RG94, Combat interviews: The counter-attack against 120th Inf. at Mortain; the L'Abbaye-Blanche Roadblock.

29. Langlois, 25.

30. NA, RG94, Combat interviews: The counter-attack against 120th Inf. at Mortain; the L'Abbaye-Blanche Roadblock.

Chapter 10: Everybody Breaks . . . Sometime . . .

1. Copp and McAndrew, 110.

2. Author interview with Padre H/Capt. Jock Anderson, HLI, 29 July 1983.

3. Alan Wood, *The Falaise Road* (Toronto: Macmillan, 1944), 37.

4. David French, "Morale of Second British Army 1944," *Journal of Strategic Studies* 19/4 (December 1996): 113, 100, 171.

5. Belfield and Essame, 184–6.

6. EC, Oral History: Pte. Rogosch.

7. Author interview with Corp. Art Kelly, 6 June 1981; Whitaker and Whitaker, *Tug of War*, 184, 188.

8. Author interview with Capt. Charles Mackay, carrier platoon, RHLI, 23 October 1999.

9. Chadderton, 5.

10. LCMSDS: Censorship Report for period 1–15 Aug. 1944, Canadian Army Overseas.

11. Ibid.

12. George Blackburn, *The Guns of Normandy: A Soldier's Eye View, France, 1944* (Toronto: McClelland & Stewart, 1995), 383.

13. Maj. D.J. Goodspeed, *Battle Royal: A History of the Royal Regiment of Canada, 1862–1962.* (Toronto: Royal Regiment of Canada, 1962), 22.

14. IWM, 84/50/1. Trooper John M. Thorpe, 2nd Fife & Forfar Yeomanry, 11 Armoured Division.

15. Chadderton, 5.

16. Tout, *Tanks, Advance!*, 209.

17. IWM, 84/50/1, Trooper John M. Thorpe, 2nd Fife & Forfar Yeomanry, 11 AD.

18. Chadderton, 7

19. Delaforce, 69.

20. Author interview with F/L Warren, 15 January 2000.

21. Martin Blumenson, ed., *The Patton Papers* (Boston: Houghton Mifflin, 1972), 511.

22. Carlo D'Este, interviewed on his book *Patton: A Genius for War,* 28 January 1996: http:// www.booknotes.org/transcripts/10088.htm.

23. NA, Combat Exhaustion Cases: Maj. N.L. Weintrop, 29 Div.

24. Ambrose, *Citizen Soldiers*, 329.

25. Copp and McAndrew, 127.

26. Author interview with Padre II/Capt. Jock Anderson, 28 July 1983.

27. Letter to the authors from Capt. Cliff Chadderton, 20 October 1998.

28. Tout, *Tanks, Advance!*, 93.

Chapter 11: Operation Totalize

1. Terry Copp, "The Canadians in Normandy: A Reassessment" (Unpublished paper, Wilfrid Laurier University, April 1998), 12.
2. Author interview with Richard Malone, Sept. 16, 1981.
3. NAC, RG 24, 2 Br. Army Intel. Rep. No. 32, 1 July 1944.
4. Stacey, 212–13.
5. Wood, 33.
6. Murray Johnston, ed., *Canada's Craftsmen at 50: The Story of Electrical and Mechanical Engineers in the Canadian Forces* (Borden, ON: EME Officers' Fund, 1997), 88.
7. Keegan, 253. The casualty figures prove the success, as Mr. Keegan points out: four infantry battalions on foot lost sixty-eight; the three mounted lost only seven.
8. Delaforce, 68.
9. Author interview with Brig. J.M. Rockingham, November 10, 1983.
10. Elliot Rodger, quoted by Dominick Graham in *The Price of Command: A Biography of General Guy Simonds* (Toronto: Stoddart, 1993), 148.
11. IWM, BLM 72/174.
12. Author interview with Maj. David Russell, 5 Black Watch, St. Andrews, Scotland, 17 September 1986.
13. Denis Whitaker and Shelagh Whitaker, *Rhineland: The Battle to End the War* (Toronto: Stoddart, 1989, 2000), 98.
14. Author interview with Maj. Sidney Radley-Walters, Sherbrooke Fusiliers, 7 Sept. 1998.
15. Keegan, 254.
16. J. B. Salmond, *History 51st Highland Division* (Edinburgh: Blackwood, 1953), 5.
17. Shulman, 149.
18. Reynolds, 234.
19. NA, Report No. 65. Historical Section (G.S.) Army Headquarters.
20. Roman Jarymowycz, *The Quest for Operational Maneuvre* (Unpublished doctoral dissertation, McGill University, 1997), 82.
21. Ernie Pyle, *In Normandy, August 8, 1944.* http://eb.com/normandy/pri/Q00237.html.
22. G. L. Cassidy, *Warpath: The Story of the Algonquin Regiment, 1939–1945* (Markham: Paperjacks, 1980), 97.
23. Tout, *Tanks, Advance!*, 96.

24. Ibid., 112.
25. Ibid., 95–6.
26. Jarymowycz, 89.
27. Author interview with Maj.-Gen. Radley-Walters, 7 September 1998.
28. Jarymowycz, 93. Wittmann's body was found in 1982 and identified by the German War Graves Commission, who examined his ID disc, fragments of a leather jacket, and his pistol. He was finally buried with his crew in the German War Cemetery at La Cambe. His grave was 500 yards from Walters' position, and some 1,700 yards from the British guns. General Walters notes that "the Brits were about 1,700 yards on the opposite side and probably took the tanks closest to them out" (author interview with Gen. Radley-Walters).
29. Tout, *A Fine Night for Tanks*, 54.

Chapter 12: Hill 195
1. Terry Copp, *The Canadians in Normandy*, 14.
2. Cassidy, 107–8.
3. Stacey, 228.
4. Ibid.
5. LCMSDS, "An Account of Battle Experiences of 'D' Company, Algonquin Regiment," by Maj. Keith Stirling.
6. Author interview with Capt. Bill Whiteside, 10 October 1989.
7. Author interview with Capt. Bob Patterson, 12 October 1989.
8. Author interviews with Capt. Bob Patterson and Bill Whiteside, Argyll & Sutherland Highlanders.

Chapter 13: Patton: Farther and Faster
1. Essame, *Patton*, 157.
2. NA, ETHINT 67. Notes from an interview with Lieutenant General Fritz Bayerlein. Critique of the Normandy breakthrough. Panzer Lehr division from St-Lô to the Ruhr, 15 August 1945.
3. Essame, 157.
4. George Patton, *War As I Knew It* (Boston: Houghton Mifflin, 1947).
5. IWM, Montgomery Papers: Signal to CIGS from General Montgomery, 7 August 1944.
6. Essame, 163; Ambrose, *Citizen Soldiers*, 89.
7. Ladislas Farago, *Patton: Ordeal and Triumph* (New York: Astor-Honour, 1964), 527; Featherston, 157.
8. Omar N. Bradley and Blair Clay, *A General's Life: An Autobiography by*

General of the Army Omar N. Bradley (New York: Simon & Schuster, 1983), 296; Featherston, 158.

9. Maule, 132.

10. Ibid. Quote by Thomas E. Cassidy from Illinois, Captain U.S. 3rd Armored Div.

11. Robert A. Miller, *August 1944* (Novato, CA: Presidio, 1988), 19.

12. NA, ETHINT 67: Report by Maj.-Gen. Bayerlein.

13. Ibid.

14. NA, 981SOM (D118): Maj.-Gen. Gersdorff. Comments in the Seventh Army's War Diary.

15. NA, ETHINT 67: Report by Maj.-Gen. Bayerlein.

16. NA, 981SOM (D123-4): Report on the fighting of panzergruppe West from 3 July–9 August 1944, by Field Marshal Eberbach. MS #B-840.

17. Shulman, 152.

18. NA, Report of Field Marshal Eberbach.

19. Patton, 104.

20. Eddy Florentin, *Battle of the Falaise Gap* (London: Elek, 1965), 107.

21. Breuer, 231.

22. Martin Blumenson, *Breakout and Pursuit*, 504.

23. Omar Bradley, *A Soldier's Story* (New York: Henry Holt, 1952), 376.

24. Terry Copp, "Closing the Gap," *Legion Magazine*, Oct. 1999: 28.

25. Martin Blumenson, "General Bradley's Decision at Argentan," in Kent Roberts Greenfield, *Command Decisions* (Washington: Office of the Chief of Military History, 1960), 409.

26. Eisenhower, 278.

27. Essame, 163.

28. Blumenson, *Breakout and Pursuit*, 509.

29. Copp, "Closing the Gap"; Featherston, 215.

30. Blumenson, *Breakout and Pursuit*, 505.

31. Patton, 510.

32. Ibid., 511.

Chapter 14: The Scapegoat

1. NA, Microfiche. "Panzer Group Eberbach at Alençon its breakthrough the encirclement of Falaise," report by General Hans Eberbach. MS B840.

2. Ibid.

3. Ibid.

4. Ibid.

5. Ibid.

6. Ibid.

7. Ibid.; Warlimont, 151.

Chapter 15: Barbery Cross

1. Author interview with Judge Wm Parker, Adj., RHLI, 14 October 1998.

2. Goodspeed, 445.

3. Charles Martin, with Roy Whitstead, *Battle Diary* (Toronto: Dundurn, 1994), 31–4.

4. Author interview with Cpl. Doug Shaughnessy, RHLI, 10 September 1998; Cpl. Doug Shaughnessy Wartime Diary, unpublished, kindly loaned to the authors.

5. Brereton Greenhous (ed), *Semper Paratus* (Hamilton, ON: The Royal Hamilton Light Infantry Historical Association, 1977), 260.

6. Author interview with Cpl. Doug Shaughnessy, 10 September 1998.

7. Whitaker and Whitaker, *Tug of War,* 184; John Ellis, *Sharp End of War: The Fighting Men in World War II* (Newton Abbot, Devon: David & Charles, 1980), 46.

8. Arthur Kelly, *There's a Goddamn Bullet for Everyone* (Paris, ON: Arts and Publishing, 1979), 59.

9. Author interview with Col. John Williamson and Cpl. Doug Shaughnessy, RHLI, 10 November 1999.

10. Ibid., 60.

11. Author interview with Lt. Colin Gibson, RHLI, 6 December 1998.

12. NAC, RG 24, WD RHLI, 12 Aug/44.

13. Greenhous, 260–1.

14. Author interview with Maj. J. Pigott, 23 September 1998; Greenhous, 258–260.

15. Blackburn, 371.

16. David Bercuson, *Battalion of Heroes: History of the Calgary Highlanders* (Calgary: Calgary Highlanders Regimental Funds Foundation, 1994), 99.

17. Blackburn, 381–2.

18. NA, Historical Section (G.S.) Army Headquarters. Report No. 65, Para. 119. DHist/Heritage DND.

19. Author correspondence with Lt. Charles Forbes, 18 January 1999.

20. NA, Historical Section (G.S.) Army Headquarters: Report No. 65, Para. 176.

Chapter 16: Operation Tractable

1. Author interview with Lt.-Col. Mowbray Alway, CO 8th Recce Regt., 26 September 1998.

2. Author interview with Lt.-Col. Mowbray Alway; Report No. 65, Historical Section

(G.S.) Army Headquarters: "Canadian Participation in the Operations in North-West Europe, 1944."

3. Essame and Bellfield, 29–30.

4. Report No. 65, Historical Section (G.S.) Army Headquarters; Report No. 50: "The Campaign in NW Europe from German Sources." DHist/Heritage DND.

5. Whitaker and Whitaker, *Tug of War*, 284–5.

6. *The History of the First Hussars, 1856–1980*, 91; an Account of Ops by 2 Cdn Armd Bde in France, 14 to 16 August 1944.

7. NAC, RG 24, WD, 1 Cdn Scot Regt., 14 August 1944.

8. Author interview with Maj. John Munro, Canadian Grenadier Guards, 1988; Whitaker and Whitaker, *Rhineland*, 232.

9. Report No. 65, Historical Section (G.S.) Army Headquarters.

10. *The History of the Corps of Royal Canadian Engineers,* Vol. II (Ottawa: The Corps, 1966), 290.

11. Report No. 65, Historical Section (G.S.) Army Headquarters.

12. NAC, RG 24, Vol. 20519, File 981, Som (D133).

13. *The History of the Corps of Royal Canadian Engineers, Vol. II,* 290.

14. NAC, RG 24, WD, Governor General's Foot Guards.

15. Author interview with Cpl. Adam Kreuter, July 1999.

Chapter 17: "My God! We're Bombing Short!"

1. "Report on the Bombing of our own Troops during *Operation Tractable*." Air Chief-Marshal Arthur Harris; CP, vol. 5, Memo COS to GOC-in-C Regarding the Report of the AOC in C Bomber Command, 25 August 1944. Kindly lent by Wing Commander (later Lt.-Gen.) A. Chester Hull.

2. CP, Vol. 5, Memo COS to GOC-in-C. Regarding the Report of the AOC in C Bomber Command, 28 August 1944, LCMSDS.

3. Bomber Command report, 11/26/97. Kindly lent by Wing Commander (later Lt.-Gen.) A. Chester Hull. Of the volunteers who flew, almost 60 per cent (more than 55,000 men) were killed, 10,000 of them Canadians. It was a loss rate comparable only to the worst slaughter of World War I trenches. LCMSDS.

4. Ibid.; Murray Peden, *A Thousand Shall Fall* (Toronto: Stoddart, 1988), v; author interview with F/L (later Squadron Leader) John Turnbull, DFC, CM, 12 October and 2 November 1998. Squadron Leader Turnbull's statistics pertain to 1943–4, when bombing was most intensive.

5. "Report on the Bombing of our own Troops during *Operation Tractable*"; CP, vol.

5, Memo COS to GOC-in-C Regarding the Report of the AOC in C Bomber Command, 25 August 1944, LCMSDS.

6. Author interview with Flt. Sgt. Roy Clarke, 20 November 1998.

7. Author interview with F/L Jim Llewellen, Mooloolaba, Australia, 15 March 1998.

8. Flight log of F/O Ken Fulton, 14 August 1944.

9. Ibid.

10. Author interview with Lt. (later Capt.) Ken Turnbull, Toronto Scottish Regiment (M.G.), 10 March 2000.

11. Belfield and Essame, 230.

12. "Report on the Bombing of our own Troops during *Operation Tractable.*"

13. Author interview with Wing Commander (later Lt.-Gen.) A. Chester Hull, DFC, Croix de Guerre Silver Star, CMM, 12 October 1999.

14. Author interview with Capt. Ken Turnbull.

15. Lindsay, 52.

16. NAC, RG24 Vol 10499, WD, Royal Regiment of Canada 14/44.

17. Author interview with Cpl. John Angus McDonald, Stormont, Dundas and Glengarry Highlanders, 18 May 1998.

18. IWM, Diary of Padre N.J. Jones, 2nd Derbyshire Yeomanry.

19. IWM, Diary of Sgt. J.G. Perry, 15th Med. Regt., RA.

20. Terry Copp, "Allied Bombing in Normandy," *Legion Magazine*, Nov./Dec. 1998: 19–21; CP, vol. 5, Memo COS to GOC-in-C. LCMSDS.

21. NAC, RG24, Vol 10797, WD, 2 Canadian Corps. File 225C2.008D4: GOC's Activities.

22. Author interview with F/L (later Squadron Leader) John Turnbull, DFC, CM, 12 October and 2 November 1998.

23. Ibid.

24. Author interview with F/O Ken Fulton, DFC, 10 October 1998.

25. IWM, 95/19/1: Personal diary of Serg. R.T. Greenwood, 9th Royal Tank Reg, August 1944.

26. Blackburn, 418.

27. Author interview with F/O Ken Fulton.

28. Author interview with Wing Commander (later Lt.-Gen.) A. Chester Hull.

Chapter 18: Just One Gutsy Leader

1. Terry Copp, *A Canadian's Guide to the Battlefields of Normandy,* (Waterloo, Ont.: LCMSDS, 1994), 135.

2. LCMSDS. Historical Records of the Queen's Own Cameron Highlanders, 111.

3. EC, Oral History: Maj. Helmut Ritgen, Panzer Regt. 130.

4. Author interview with Lt.-Col. (later Maj.-Gen.) Roger Rowley, DSO, ED, CD, GCLS, 6 October 1998.

5. Ibid.

6. Reynolds, 250.

7. Ibid., 254.

8. NAC, Op Tractable: An Account of Ops by 2 Cdn Armd Brigade in France, 14 to 16 Aug. 1944. RG24; vol. 10992; file 275C2.013(D1).

9. NAC, RG 24, WD, 1 Cdn Scot, 15 August.

10. Ibid.

11. Stacey, 249.

12. NAC, RG 24, WD, 1 Cdn Scot, 15 August.

13. Chadderton.

14. Tout, *Tanks, Advance!*, 106.

15. IWM, Highland Padre N.F. Jones.

16. Ambrose, *Citizen Soldiers*, 67–8.

17. Wilfred I. Smith, *Code Word Canloan* (Toronto: Dundurn, 1992), 46.

18. Lindsay, 51.

19. Author interview with Maj.-Gen. Radley-Walters, 15 November 1998.

20. Author interview with Brig.-Gen. Fredrick Clift, 16 November 1998.

Chapter 19: The Typhies and Their Lovable Erks

1. Charles Bowyer, "The Main Role and Achievements of the Typhoon during the Preparation and Invasion of Europe: Summary of Losses May–August 1944," LCMSDS.

2. Christopher Evans, "The Fighter-Bomber in the Normandy Campaign: The Role of 83 Group," *Canadian Military History,* Vol 8, Number 1 (Winter 1999): 21.

3. Charles Demoulin, ed., *Firebirds! Flying a Typhoon in Action* (Washington, D.C.: Smithsonian Institution Press, 1986), 222.

4. Halliday, *The Tumbling Sky* (Ottawa: Canada's Wings, 1978), 21.

5. Halliday, *Typhoon and Tempest*, 66.

6. Author interview with F/L Bill Baggs, 1 October 1999.

7. Author correspondence with Dr. Jonathan E.C. Tan, Munaster, England, 1 February 2000.

8. Ibid.

9. Author interview with Wing Commander Russell Bannock, DSO, DFC, 10 January 2000.

10. Author interview and correspondence with Wing Commander (then F/L) Duke Warren, 1 November 1999.

11. Personal papers of F/L Bill Baggs: Report by F/L Roy A. Crane, 182 Squadron and then 181, both in 124 Wing, to WWII Typhoon Pilots' Memorial, Noyers Bocage, France. "This document is the result of a suggestion made in a letter to the writer from Air Commodore C.D. 'Kit' North-Lewis DSO, DFC and Bar, Commanding Officer Flying, 124 Typhoon Wing, 83 Group, 2nd Tactical Air Force. He suggested: "A record should be made of all historical aspects of the Noyers Bocage Memorial for the benefit of future generations," adding "before we have all gone.""

12. Halliday, *Typhoon and Tempest*, 70.

13. Author interview and correspondence with Wing Commander Duke Warren.

14. Stacey, 257.

15. Author interview with F/L Cecil Brown, 9 February 2000.

Chapter 20: Cheers!

1. Blackburn, 48.

2. Dr. W.G. Grant, *Did I Ever Tell You about the War?* (Hampton, ON: Self-published, 1990), 34. Kindly lent to the authors.

3. Author interview with Padre H/Capt. Jock Anderson, 22 May 1998.

4. Author interview with Maj. Ray Hodgins, 1982; Whitaker and Whitaker, *Tug of War*, 295.

5. IWM, 91/13/1, Maj. A.J. Forrest, OC, 272 Battery, 90 Middlesex HA.

6. Author interview with Padre H/Capt. Jock Anderson.

7. Horrocks, *Corps Commander*, 33.

8. LCMSDS, 1st Canadian Army Censorship Report, 16–31 August 1944.

9. IWM, 81/13/1: W.E. Mason.

10. Folkestad, 48–9.

11. Danson, 6.

12. IWM, 94/34/1: Lt.-Col. M. Crawford, CO, 8 Middlesex Reg, 43rd Div.

13. NAC, WD, Royal Regt. of Canada, August/44.

14. Jary, 71.

15. Censorship Report.

16. Grant, 38.

17. Censorship Report.

18. Ibid.

19. NA 02406, History 305 Engineer Combat Bn.

20. Tout, *Tanks Advance!*, 99.

21. Censorship Report.

22. Author interview with Col. Richard Malone, 21 September 1981; Richard Malone, *A World in Flames, 1944–1945* (Toronto: Collins, 1984), 49.

23. NAC, WD, Canadian Army Film Unit. See "Postscripts" for the sorry tale of their demise.

24. NAC, RG24, 12330, 88/3; *Time* magazine, 4 September 1944. Stephen Campbell collection.

Chapter 21: "Bloody Warsaw"

1. Stacey, 252.

2. Author interview with Capt. (now Brig.-Gen.) Michael Gutowski, Virtuti Militari, 18 May 1998. For general information on the Polish campaign, see Jozef Garlinski, *Poland in the Second World War* (New York: Macmillan, 1985).

3. *For Your Freedom and Ours, 1944–1994.* Published by the Polish Combatants of Canada, Toronto, 1994.

4. Keegan, 268–9.

5. K. Jamar, *With the Tanks of the 1st Polish Armoured Division* (Hengelo: H.L. Smit & Son, 1946), 160.

6. Stacey, 243, 257.

7. Jamar, 116.

8. Ibid.

9. Author interview with Krzysztof Szdlowski, Vice President, 1st Polish Armoured Division Association in Canada, 15 July 1999.

10. Stacey, 252.

11. Jamar, 104.

12. Author interview with Krzysztof Szdlowski.

13. Author interview with Capt. Ted Walewicz, 2nd Polish Armored Regt., 7 June 1999.

14. Author interview with Capt. (now Brig.-Gen.) Gutowski, 4 April 1998.

15. Author interview with Capt. Walewicz.

16. Jamar, 107; Marle, 162.

17. Stacey, 252.

18. Author interview with M. Grandvalet, 5 June 1998, Boisjois, Normandy.

19. Author interview with Col. (then Capt.) Pierre Sevigny, 4 Cdn Medium Regt., RCA, 6 May 1999.

20. Author interview with Robert Chombart, Chambois, Normandy, 9 June 1998.

21. *Boisjois Hill 262.* Published by Montormel Memorial Committee, 1961.

Chapter 22: David Currie's Destiny

1. Donald E. Graves, *South Albertas: A Canadian Regiment at War* (Toronto: Robin Brass Studio, 1998), 163.

2. Ibid., 131.

3. Ibid., 131.

4. Maj. David D. Currie, *Story in His Words*. Taken from *After the Battle: The Battle of the Falaise Pocket, Number 8*. Winston G. Ramsey, ed. (London: Battle of Britain Prints International, 1982). Stephen Campbell collection.

5. NAC, RG24, 4 CAB Battle Log, 18 Aug 1944.

6. Currie, 17.

7. Graves, 163.

8. Currie, 19.

9. Ibid.

10. Graves, 163.

11. Robert Fraser, *Black Yesterdays: the Argylls' War* (Hamilton: Argyll Regimental Foundation, 1996), 237.

12. Graves, 138.

13. Ibid.

14. Currie, 138.

15. Stephen Campbell collection, Capt. John Redden interview, 9 February 1996.

16. Graves, 139.

17. Stacey, 258.

18. The above paragraphs are based on Graves, 141–159.

19. NA, WD, South Alberta Regiment, 18 August 1944.

20. Graves, 164.

Chapter 23: Bravery at St. Lambert

1. Hastings, 223.

2. Graves, 142.

3. Fraser, 239.

4. Graves, 144.

5. Stephen Campbell collection: Capt. John Redden interview, 9 February 1992; Graves, 144.

6. Currie, 19.

7. NAC, RG24, WD, No. 3 P.R. Group, Canadian Army Film Unit, 19 August 1944.

8. Graves, 179.

9. Stacey, 260.

10. NAC, RG24, WD, CAFU, 19 August 1944.

11. Letter from Donald Grant to Stephen Campbell, April/95, Poole England. Donald Grant tape, dictated by Donald Grant, Windsor, Ont., and addressed to George Ronald, 1988. Stephen Campbell collection.

12. Currie, 19.

13. Stacey, 260.

14. Author interview with Lt. (later Maj.) Danny McLeod MC, 29 July 1998.

15. Currie, 20.

16. Graves, 149.

17. Copp and Vogel, 124.

18. "St. Lambert-sur-Dives, August 19 to 21, 1944: A memoir" by Lt. Arkle Dunlop, Canadian Argyll Regt. (written c. 1980).

19. Fraser, 239.

20. Geoffrey Hayes, *The Lincs: A History of the Lincoln and Welland Regiment at War* (Alma, ON: Maple Leaf Route, 1986), 38.

21. Graves, 150.

22. Florentin, 251.

23. Fraser, 240.

24. Author interview with Pte. Art Bridge, 24 January 2000.

25. Ibid.

Chapter 24: Polish Vodka at Chambois

1. Featherston, 159.

2. Blumenson, 427.

3. NA, The Gap at Chambois, 15–22 August 1944.

4. Weigley, 310.

5. NA, The Gap at Chambois, 15–22 August 1944.

6. Florentin, 234.

7. NA, 2nd Battalion Action at Chambois. Interview with Maj. L.C. Dull, 27 August 1944.

8. Author interview with Capt. (now Brig.-Gen.) Michael Gutowski, 4 April 1999.

9. Jamar, 141.

10. Keegan, 274–5.

11. NA, The Gap at Chambois, 15–22 August 1944.

12. Georges Bernage and Ronald McNair, *Falaise–Argentan: Le Couloir de la Mort* (Bayeux: Éditions Heimdal, 1944), 35.

13. NA, The Gap at Chambois, 15–22 August 1944.

14. Author interview with Capt. (now Brig.-Gen.) Michael Gutowski, 15 July 1998.

15. NA, 2nd Battalion Action at Chambois. Interview with Maj. L.C. Dull, 27 August 1944. (Information on the supplies taken from Corps G-4 report.)

16. NAC, RG24, 1st Polish Armoured Division.

17. The story of the villagers is based on Abbé Marcel Launay's book, *Dans la*

Tourmente de la Guerre (Tournai-sur-Dives, 1985); on an author interview with the Abbé, 12 June 1998; on Florentin, 110, 146, 171, 196; and on an author interview with Col. Jacques van Dijke, 5 June 1998.

Chapter 25: Trapped!

1. Meyer, 197.
2. NA, 90 Div in Action. US troops captured a German bearing a document showing one of the actual escape routes.
3. NA, RG24, Vol. 20519.981 Som (D132). History of 21 Pz Div Normandy Campaign. Part II.
4. NA, RG24. Vol 20519.981 Som (D118) Seventh Army. Interview with Gen. von Gersdorff.
5. Ibid.
6. Ibid.
7. Ibid.
8. EC, Oral History: Maj. Heinz Günther Guderian, 116 Panzer Div. Staff Officer.
9. EC, Oral History: Capt. Walter Kaspers, Adj., Anti-tank Unit 228, 116 (Pz) Div.
10. NA, MS #B727.The Campaign in Northern France. Vol VI, Ch. 6: The Battle of the Falaise–Argentan Pocket. Interview with Freiherr Oberst Freiherr von Gersdorff, September 1946.
11. 21 Army Group Intelligence Summary, No. 154, LCMSDS, 131.
12. NA, MS #B727.The Campaign in Northern France. Vol VI, Ch. 6: The Battle of the Falaise–Argentan Pocket. Interview with Freiherr Oberst Freiherr von Gersdorff, September 1946.
13. D'Este, 438.
14. Meyer, 197.
15. Shulman, 158.
16. Ibid., 160–161.
17. NA, RG24, Vol. 20522. Report by Lt.-Gen. Eugen Meindl, 2 Parachute Corps, 3 May 1946.
18. Ibid.
19. 21 Army Group Intelligence Summary, No. 154, LCMSDS, 131.
20. Graves, 152.

Chapter 26: The Breakout

1. NA, RG24, Vol. 20522; report by Lt.-Gen. Eugen Meindl, 2 Parachute Corps, 3 May 1946.
2. Ibid.

3. Ibid.

4. Ibid.

5. Ibid.

6. Ibid.

7. Ibid.

8. Meyer, 198.

9. Kurt Meyer, *Grenadiers* (Winnipeg: J.J. Fedorowicz, 1994), 170.

10. Belfield and Essame, 232.

11. Meyer, 199.

12. "The Last Battle of Normandy: The Corridor of Death." Montormel videotape produced by the Montormel Memorial Committee, (date unknown): statement by Gen. Heinz Guderian.

13. EC, Oral History: Capt. Walter Kaspers, Adj., Anti-tank Unit 228, 116 (Pz) Div.

14. EC, Oral History: Lt. Walter Padberg, Grenadier Regt. 959.

15. EC, Oral History: Günter Materne, Battery Off., Artillery Regt. 363.

Chapter 27: Black Sunday

1. EC, Oral History, Col Max Anger.

2. Shulman, 160.

3. Martin Blumenson, Office of the Chief of Military History (now US Army Center of Military History), Internet Centre Military History, Washington, "Examples of employment of tanks in night fighting on the European land mass during world war." 2 June 1966. (The original manuscript is on file in the Historical Manuscripts Collection (HMC) under file number 2-3.7 AC.Y.)

4. NA, Army Gp B, Daily Sitreps, 20 August 1944.

5. Graves, 176.

6. Graves, 155.

7. Speech given by Maj. Arkle Dunlop, Royal Canadian Legion dinner, 13 November 1985. (Major Dunlop was awarded the Croix de Guerre avec Étoile de Vermeil for this action; the footbridge was renamed "Dunlop Bridge.")

8. Author interview with Maj. Arkle Dunlop, 4 August 1998.

9. Dunlop, Royal Canadian Legion dinner.

10. Graves, 155.

11. Ibid., 168.

12. Ibid., 162.

13. Ibid., 168.

14. Florentin, 285.

15. NA, RG24, Vol 20510. 981 Som (D117) Seventh Army.
16. NA, 2nd Bn Action at Chambois, RG 407, Folder 24065, 90 Infantry Div., 359 Inf. Regt.
17. Currie, *After the Battle*. Maj. Martin was awarded the American DSC for his bravery.
18. Graves, 162.
19. Ibid., 163.
20. Maj. R. L. Rogers, *History of the Lincoln and Welland Regiment*, 1954, 158.
21. Terry Copp, "Closing the Falaise Pocket," *Legion Magazine*. August 1994: 42–3.
22. W.W. Barrett, *The History of the 13th Canadian Field Regiment, Royal Canadian Artillery, 1940–1945*, (Collection of R.K. Mackenzie), 60.
23. Florentin, 277.
24. Ibid., 27

Chapter 28: Maczuga: The Polish Agony

1. NA, Microfiche MSB840: Interview with General Eberbach.
2. *"The Last Battle of Normandy: The Corridor of Death."* Montormel videotape produced by the Montormel Memorial Committee, (date unknown): statement by Cpl. E. Podyma.
3. Author interview with Capt Pierre Sévigny, 12 November 1999.
4. Author interview with Capt. Ted Walewicz, 8 June 1999.
5. *Boisjois: Hill 262*. Published by Montormel Memorial Committee, 1961. Statements by: Commander Czarnecki, chief of staff, Polish 10th Armoured Brigade; Capt Sévigny; Pierre Grandvalet.
6. Ibid.
7. Ibid.
8. Author interview with Sgt. Frank Lisowski, 8 June 1999.
9. Author interview with Capt. Ted Walewicz.
10. *Boisjois: Hill 262:* Pierre Grandvalet account.
11. Author interview with Pierre Sévigny.

Chapter 29: The Corridor of Death

1. *Boisjois: Hill 262:* Sévigny and Grandvalet accounts.
2. Author interview with Maj. (now Brig.-Gen.) Ned Amy, 9 September 1999.
3. *Boisjois: Hill 262:* Sévigny account.
4. Author interview with Brig.-Gen. Amy.
5. Author interview with Krzysztof (Chris) Szydlowski, 10 August 1999.

N O T E S

6. Jozef Garlinski, *Poland in the Second World War* (New York: Macmillan, 1985), 260–1.

7. Blumenson, 554.

8. Florentin, 257.

9. Author interview with Brig.-Gen. Gutowski, 12 May 1998.

10. Florentin, 257.

11. NA, RG407, Folder 24065, The Gap at Chambois, 2 Bn, 359 Inf. Regt., 90th Inf. Div.

12. EC, Oral History: 2nd Lt. Dibbern.

13. NA, The Gap at Chambois, 90th Infantry Div.

14. Author interview with Capt. R.R. Dixon, 6 October 1998.

15. Author interview with Lt.-Col. (now Maj.-Gen.) Roger Rowley, 6 October 1998.

16. Author interview with Capt. Dixon.

17. NA, account by Lt.-Col. R. Rowley, OC. SD&G Highrs, given to historical officer, 22 August 1944; author interview with Lt.-Col. (now Maj.-Gen.) Roger Rowley.

18. Launay, 70–80.

19. Hubert Meyer, 201.

20. NAC, RG24, Vol. 20522. Report by Lt.-Gen. Eugen Meindl, 2 Parachute Corps, 3 May 1946.

21. Currie, 19.

22. Author interview with Maj. Danny McLeod MC, 29 July 1998.

23. Currie, 21.

24. NAC, RG24, Vol. 20522. Report by Lt.-Gen. Eugen Meindl, 2 Parachute Corps, 3 May 1946.

25. Weigley, 314.

26. Stacey, 271.

27. Keegan, http://www.angelfire.com/tn/ww2essays/keegan.html

28. NA, RG94, 24065, The Gap at Chambois, 90 Inf. Div., 15–22 August 1944.

29. Stacey, 270–271.

30. Author interview with Lt.-Col. (now Maj.-Gen.) Roger Rowley.

31. Florentin, 320.

32. Department of Calvados tourism information bulletin.

33. Florentin, 320.

A Last Word

1. B.H. Liddell Hart, *The German Generals Speak* (London: Cassell, 1951).

2. S.L.A. Marshall, *Men against Fire* (New York: William Morrow, 1947), 54–7.

3. Harold P. Leinbaugh and John D. Campbell, *The Men of Company K* (New York: William Morrow, 1985).

4. John Keegan, *Face of Battle* (London: Penguin, 1976).

5. Weigley, *Eisenhower's Lieutenants: The Campaigns of France and Germany, 1944–1945.*

6. Roger S. Spiller, "S.L.A. Marshall and the Ratio of Fire," *RUSI Journal* 133/4 (Winter 1988): 68–71. For an overview see Fredric Smoler, "The Secret of the Soldier Who Didn't Shoot," *American Heritage*, March 1989: 37–45.

7. Trevor N. Dupuy, *Numbers, Predictions and War* (Fairfax, VA: Hero Books, 1979).

8. See John Sloan Brown, "Colonel Trevor N. Dupuy and the Mythos of Wehrmacht Superiority: A Reconsideration," *Military Affairs*, January 1985: 16.

9. Trevor N. Dupuy, "Mythos or Verity? The Quantified Judgment Model and German Combat Effectiveness," *Military Affairs*, October 1986: 210.

10. Martin Van Crevald, *Fighting Power: German and U.S. Army Performance, 1939–1943* (London: Arms and Armour Press, 1983).

11. Ibid., 168.

12. Stacey, 271.

13. Ibid., 118–19.

14. Ibid., 276.

15. Martin Blumenson, *The Battle of the Generals* (New York: Morrow, 1993).

16. Stacey, 272–3.

17. D'Este.

18. Ibid., 82–6.

19. For an account of one Canadian's D-Day see Charlie Martin, *Battle Diary* (Toronto: Dundurn, 1994).

20. Headquarters, United States Strategic Air Forces in Europe, "Survey of Effectiveness of Bombing of Invasion Coast Defenses, 7 July 1944" (United States Military History Institute, Carlisle, PA), 2.

21. NAC, RG24, Vol. 10673: Combined Operations Headquarters, Bulletin Y/37: Naval Fire Support in Operation Overlord, November 1944.

22. Terry Copp, ed., *Montgomery's Scientists: Operational Research in Northwest Europe, 1944–1945* (Waterloo, ON: LCMSDS, 2000).

23. John Ellis, *Brute Force* (London: Viking, 1990), 364.

24. Robert Vogel, "Tactical Air Power in Normandy: Some Thoughts on the Interdiction Plan," *Canadian Military History*, 3/1 (Spring 1994): 37–47.

25. Fighter Command Tactical Memorandum No. 30, 14 March 1943, DND Directorate of History and Heritage Ottawa, 79/32.

26. Hubert Meyer, 61.

27. Terry Copp interview with Tony Sargeaunt, 1991.
28. Copp, ed., *Montgomery's Scientists*, 405.
29. Ibid.
30. Alfred D. Chandler, ed., *The Papers of Dwight D. Eisenhower*, Vol. III (Baltimore: Johns Hopkins, 1970).
31. Belton Y. Cooper, *Death Traps* (Novato, CA: Presidio, 1998), viii.
32. L.F. Ellis, *Victory in the West*, Vol. I (London: HMSO, 1962), 308–16.
33. Blackburn, *The Guns of Normandy*, offers a non-technical account of Canadian artillery operations in Normandy. See Copp, ed., *Montgomery's Scientists*, for a scientific evaluation of artillery in Normandy and Northwest Europe.
34. Allan Snowie, *Bloody Buron* (Erin, ON: Boston Mills, 1984).
35. Tony Foulds, "In Support of the Canadians: A British Anti-tank Regiment's First Five Weeks in Normandy," *Canadian Military History,* 7/2 (Spring 1998): 78.
36. Gordon Brown, "The Attack on the Abbaye d'Ardenne," *Canadian Military History*, 4/1 (Spring 1995): 91–99.
37. Copp, ed., *Montgomery's Scientists*, 431.
38. Terry Copp, "Counter Mortar and Operational Research in 21 Army Group," *Canadian Military History*, 3/2 (Autumn 1994): 45–52.
39. Terry Copp interview with Tony Sargeaunt.
40. Stacey, 228.
41. Weigley, 127.
42. Ibid., 128.
43. How, *Normandy*, 221.
44. Copp, ed., *Montgomery's Scientists*, introduction and 22–23.
45. EC, Oral History: Maj. Joachim Barth.
46. B. Michael Bechthold, "The Development of an Unbeatable Combination: US Close Air Support in Normandy," *Canadian Military History*, 8/1 (Winter 1999): 15–17.
47. Christopher Evans, "The Fighter Bomber in the Normandy Campaign: The Role of 83 Group," *Canadian Military History*, 8/1 (Winter 1999): 21.

Postscripts

1. The postwar account of David Currie is based on notes from Donald Graves' excellent history *South Albertas: A Canadian Regiment at War* (Toronto: Robin Brass Studio, 1998); *Major David D. Currie: Story in His Own Words*; Winston G. Ramsey, ed., *After the Battle: The Battle of the Falaise Pocket* (London: Battle of Britain Prints International, Number 8, 1982); Herbert Fairlie Wood, *Encounter at St. Lambert* (*The Legionary*, January 1964); Arthur Bishop, *Our Bravest and Our*

Best: The Stories of Canada's Victoria Cross Winners (Toronto: McGraw-Hill Ryerson, 1995).

2. Wing Commander Duke Warren's story was based on correspondence and conversation with the authors in 1999 and 2000.

3. The Kurt Meyer story is based on the following books and documentaries: Howard Margolian, *Conduct Unbecoming: The Story of the Murder of Canadian Prisoners of War in Normandy* (Toronto: University of Toronto Press, 1998); David Paperny Films Ltd., "Murder in Normandy," 1999; Lt. Col. B.J.S. Macdonald, *The Trial of Kurt Meyer* (Toronto: Clarke Irwin, 1954), 79; author interview with Lt.-Col. Trumbull Warren, 14 September 1998.

4. For the Polish story, the authors are indebted to Capt. (now Brig.-Gen.) Michael Gutowski, Virtui Militari, and to Krzysztof Szdlowski, Vice-President, 1st Polish Armoured Division Association in Canada, for their cooperation and interest in telling the story of Polish patriots in the Second World War. Other readings included Jozef Garlinski, *Poland in the Second World War*; Polish Combatants of Canada, *For Your Freedom and Ours, 1944–1994*; John Keegan, *Six Armies in Normandy*; and K. Jamar, *With the Tanks of the 1st Polish Armoured Division*.

5. Notes on the General Guderian story were based on personal correspondence with the authors, 1988; Charles B. MacDonald, *The Mighty Endeavour: The American War in Europe*. New York: Morrow, 1969, 1986.

6. Stephen Campbell's search is documented in personal letters and in a meeting with Donald Grant in April 1995.

BIBLIOGRAPHY

Ambrose, Stephen E. *Citizen Soldiers: The U.S. Army from the Normandy Beaches to the Bulge to the Surrender of Germany.* New York: Simon & Schuster, 1997.

————. *The Victors: Eisenhower and His Boys: The Men of World War II.* New York: Simon & Schuster, 1998.

Bates, Thomas J. *Normandy: The Search for Sydney.* Berkeley, CA: Bayes, 1999.

Bechthold, B. Michael. "The Development of an Unbeatable Combination: U.S. Close Air Support in Normandy," *Canadian Military History*, 8/1 (Winter 1999).

Belfield, Eversley, and H. Essame. *The Battle for Normandy.* London: Pan, 1967.

Bercuson, David. *Battalion of Heroes: History of the Calgary Highlanders.* Calgary: Calgary Highlanders Regimental Funds Foundation, 1994.

Bernage, Georges, and Ronald McNair. *Falaise–Argentan: Le Couloir de la Mort.* Bayeux: Éditions Heimdal, 1944.

Bhenamou, Jean-Pierre. *Normandy 1944: An Illustrated Field-Guide, June 7–August 22 1944.* Bayeux: Éditions Heimdal, 1982.

Bishop, Arthur. *Our Bravest and Our Best: The Stories of Canada's Victoria Cross Winners.* Toronto: McGraw-Hill Ryerson, 1995.

Blackburn, George. *The Guns of Normandy: A Soldier's Eye View, France, 1944.* Toronto: McClelland & Stewart, 1995.

Blumenson, Martin. *The Battle of the Generals.* New York: Morrow, 1993.

———. *Breakout and Pursuit.* Washington, D.C.: Center of Military History, 1961.

———. *Patton. The Man Behind the Legend.* New York: Morrow, 1985.

———, ed. *The Patton Papers.* Boston: Houghton Mifflin, 1972.

Bradley, Omar. *A Soldier's Story.* New York: Henry Holt, 1952.

Bradley, Omar N., and Blair Clay. *A General's Life: An Autobiography by General of the Army Omar N. Bradley.* New York: Simon & Schuster, 1983.

Breuer, William B. *Death of a Nazi Army: The Falaise Pocket.* New York: Scarborough House, 1985.

Brown, Gordon. "The Attack on the Abbaye d'Ardenne," *Canadian Military History* 4/1 (Spring 1995).

Buisson, Gilles. *Mortain 44: Objectif Avranches.* Mortain: Éditions OCEP, 1984.

Carell, Paul. *Invasion: They're Coming.* New York: Bantam, 1964.

Cassidy, G.L. *Warpath: The Story of the Algonquin Regiment, 1939–1945.* Toronto: Ryerson, 1948; Markham, ON: Paperjacks, 1980.

Chandler, Alfred D., ed. *The Papers of Dwight D. Eisenhower*, Vol. III. Baltimore: Johns Hopkins, 1970.

Colby, John. *War from the Ground Up: The 90th Division in WWII.* Austin, TX: Nortex, 1991.

Cooper, Belton Y. *Death Traps.* Novato, CA: Presidio, 1998.

Copp, Terry. "Allied Bombing in Normandy," *Legion Magazine* Nov./Dec. 1998.

———. *A Canadian's Guide to the Battlefields of Normandy.* Waterloo, ON: Laurier Centre for Military Strategic and Disarmament Studies, Wilfrid Laurier University, 1994.

———. "Closing the Gap," *Legion Magazine* Oct. 1999.

———. "Counter Mortar and Operational Research in 21 Army Group," *Canadian Military History*, 3/2 (Autumn 1994).

———. "The Canadians in Normandy: A Reassessment." Unpublished paper: Wilfrid Laurier University, April 1998.

———, ed. *Montgomery's Scientists: Operational Research in Northwest Europe.* Waterloo, ON: LCMSDS, Wilfrid Laurier University, 2000.

———. "TAF Over Normandy," *Legion Magazine* Jan./Feb. 1999.

Copp, Terry, and Bill McAndrew. *Battle Exhaustion.* Montreal and Kingston: McGill-Queen's University Press, 1990.

Copp, Terry, and Robert Vogel. *Maple Leaf Route: Falaise.* Alma, ON: MLR, 1983.

Currie, Maj. David D. "Story in His Own Words," in *After the Battle: The Battle of the Falaise Pocket, Number 8.* Winston G. Ramsey, ed. London: Battle of Britain Prints International, 1982.

De Guingand, Maj.-Gen. Sir Francis, KBE, CB, DSO. *Operation Victory.* London: Hodder & Stoughton, 1947.

Delaforce, Patrick. *Churchill's Desert Rats: From Normandy to Berlin with the 7th Armoured Division.* London: Alan Sutton, 1994.

Demoulin, Charles. *Firebirds! Flying a Typhoon in Action.* Washington, D.C.: Smithsonian Institution Press, 1986.

D'Este, Carlo. *Decision in Normandy.* New York: Dutton, 1983.

Dupuy, Trevor N., "Mythos or Verity? The Quantified Judgment Model and German Combat Effectiveness," *Military Affairs*, October 1986.

———. *Numbers, Predictions and War.* Fairfax, VA: Hero Books, 1979.

Eisenhower, Gen. Dwight D. *Crusade in Europe.* New York: Doubleday, 1948.

Ellis, John. *Brute Force.* London: Viking, 1990.

———. *Sharp End of War: The Fighting Men in World War II.* Newton Abbott, Devon: David & Charles, 1980.

Ellis, L.F., CVO, CBE, DSO, MC. *History of the Second World War.* Vol. II: *Victory in the West.* London: HMSO, 1962.

English, Jack. *The Canadian Army and the Normandy Campaign: A Study of Failure in High Command.* New York: Praeger, 1991.

Erbes, John, MD. *Hell-on-Wheels Surgeon.* New York: Vintage, 1995.

Essame, H. *Patton: A Study in Command.* New York: Scribner's, 1974.

Evans, Christopher. "The Fighter Bomber in the Normandy Campaign: The Role of 83 Group." *Canadian Military History* 8/1 (Winter 1999).

Farago, Ladislas. *Patton: Ordeal and Triumph*. New York: Astor-Honour, 1964.

Feasby, W.R. *Official History of the Canadian Medical Services, 1939–1945*. Vol. 1: *Organization and Campaigns*. Vol. 2: *Clinical Subjects*. Ottawa: Queen's Printer and Controller of Stationery, 1953.

Featherston, Alwyn. *Battle for Mortain: The 30th Infantry Division Saves the Breakout, August 7–21*. Novato, CA: Presidio, 1993.

Florentin, Eddy. *Battle of the Falaise Gap*. London: Elek, 1965.

Folkestad, William B. *The View from the Turret: The 743rd Tank Battalion During World War II*. Shippensburg, PA: Burd Street Press, 1996.

Foulds, Tony. "In Support of the Canadians: A British Anti-tank Regiment's First Five Weeks in Normandy," *Canadian Military History*, 7/2 (Spring 1998).

Fraser, Robert. *Black Yesterdays: The Argylls' War*. Hamilton: Argyll Regimental Foundation, 1996.

French, David. "Colossal Cracks . . . Morale of Second British Army 1944," *Journal of Strategic Studies* 19/4 (Dec. 1996).

Garlinski, Jozef. *Poland in the Second World War*. New York: Macmillan, 1985.

German, Dr. Paul. *100 Days of War for Peace*: Condé-sur-Noireau, France: Charles Corlet, 1998.

Goodman, Eddie. *Life of the Party*. Toronto: Key Porter, 1988.

Goodspeed, Maj. D.J. *Battle Royal: A History of the Royal Regiment of Canada, 1862–1962*. Toronto: Royal Regiment of Canada, 1962.

Graham, Dominick. *The Price of Command. A Biography of General Guy Simonds*. Toronto: Stoddart, 1993.

Grant, Dr. W.G. *Did I Ever Tell You about the War?* Hampton, ON: Published by the author, March 1990.

Graves, Donald E. *South Albertas: A Canadian Regiment at War*. Toronto: Robin Brass Studio, 1998.

Greenfield, Kent Roberts, ed. *Command Decisions*. Washington, D.C.: Office of the Chief of Military History, United States Army, 1960.

Greenhous, Brereton; Kingsley Brown, Sr., and Kingsley Brown, Jr., eds. *Semper Paratus*. Hamilton, ON: Royal Hamilton Light Infantry Historical Association, 1977.

Guingand, Maj.-Gen. Sir Francis, KBE, CB, DSO. *Operation Victory*. London: Hodder & Stoughton, 1947.

Halliday, Hugh A. *The Tumbling Sky*. Ottawa: Canada's Wing, 1978.

————. *Typhoon and Tempest: The Canadian Story*. Toronto: CANAV, 1992.

Hamilton, Nigel. *Monty: Master of the Battlefield, 1942–1944*. New York: Hodder & Stoughton, 1983.

Hastings, Max. *Overlord: D-Day and the Battle for Normandy, 1944*. London: Pan, 1985.

Hayes, Geoffrey. *The Lincs: A History of the Lincoln and Welland Regiment at War*. Alma, ON: Maple Leaf Route, 1986.

Hillsman, J.B. *Eleven Men and a Scalpel*. Winnipeg: Columbia, 1948.

Hinsley, F.H. *British Intelligence in the Second World War*, Vol. III. London: HMSO, 1981.

Horrocks, Sir Brian, with Eversley Belfield and Maj.-Gen. H. Essame. *Corps Commander*. Toronto: Griffin House, 1977.

———. *A Full Life*. London: Collins, 1960.

How, J.J., MC. *Hill 112*. London: Kimber, 1984.

———. *Normandy: The British Breakout*. London: Kimber, 1981.

Howard, Michael Eliot. *British Intelligence in the Second World War*, Vol 5: *Strategic Deception*. London: HMSO, 1990.

Jamar, K. *With the Tanks of the 1st Polish Armoured Division*. Hengelo: H.L. Smit & Son, 1946.

James, F.A. *Nos Plus Longs Mois (D + 76)*. Falaise: Jean James, 1994.

Jary, Sydney. *18 Platoon*. Surrey: self-published, 1987.

Jarymowycz, Roman. *The Quest for Operational Maneuvre*. Unpublished doctoral dissertation, McGill University, 1997.

Johnston, Murray, ed. *Canada's Craftsmen at 50: The Story of Electrical and Mechanical Engineers in the Canadian Forces*. Borden, ON: EME Officers' Fund, 1997.

Keegan, John. *Six Armies in Normandy*. London: Jonathan Cape, 1982.

———. *Face of Battle*. London: Penguin, 1976.

Kelly, Arthur. *There's a Goddamn Bullet for Everyone*. Paris, ON: Arts and Publishing, 1979.

Kitching, George. *Mud and Green Fields*. Vancouver: Battleline, 1986.

Langlois, René. *1944: Les Douets in Torment: A Memoir*. Trans. by Joyce Carter. Mortain: self-published, 1996.

Launay, Abbé Marcel. *Dans la Tourmente de la Guerre*. Normandy: Self-published, 1985.

Leinbaugh, Harold P. and John D. Campbell. *The Men of Company K*. New York: William Morrow, 1985.

Liddell Hart, B.H. *The German Generals Speak*. London: Cassell, 1951.

Liebling, A.J. *The Road from Saint-Lo*. http://eb.com/normandy/pri/Q00237.html

Lindsay, Martin. *So Few Got Through: The Personal Diary of Lt.-Col. Martin Lindsay*. London: Collins, 1946.

Luther, Craig W. H. *Blood and Honor: The History of the 12th SS Panzer Division "Hitler Youth," 1943–1945*. San Jose, CA: Bender, 1987.

MacDonald, Charles B. *The Mighty Endeavour: The American War in Europe*. New York: Morrow, 1969, 1986.

Malone, Col. Richard Sankey, OBE. *Missing from the Record*. Toronto: Collins, 1946.

———. *A World in Flames, 1944–1945*. Toronto: Collins, 1984.

Margolian, Howard. *Conduct Unbecoming: The Story of the Murder of Canadian Prisoners of War in Normandy*. Toronto: University of Toronto Press, 1998.

Marshall, S.L.A., *Men against Fire*. New York: William Morrow, 1947.

Martin, Charles, with Roy Whitstead. *Battle Diary*. Toronto: Dundurn Press, 1994.

Maule, Henry. *Normandy Breakout*. New York: Quadrangle/New York Times Book Co., 1977.

McBryde, Brenda. *A Nurse's War*. London: Chatto & Windus, 1979.

McKee, Alexander. *Caen: Anvil of Victory*. London: Souvenir, 1964.

McNeil, Bill, ed. *Voices of a War Remembered: An Oral History of Canadians in World War Two*. Toronto: Doubleday, 1991.

Meyer, Hubert. *The History of the 12th SS Panzer Division Hitlerjugend*. Winnipeg: J.J. Fedorowicz, 1992.

Meyer, Kurt. *Grenadiers*. Winnipeg: J.J. Fedorowicz, 1994.

Miller, Robert A. *August 1944*. Novato, CA: Presidio, 1988.

Milner, Marc. *Canadian Military History*. Toronto: Copp Clark Pitman, 1993.

Mansoor, Peter. *The GI Offensive in Europe*. Kansas City: University Press of Kansas, 1999.

Mitcham, Samuel W. *Hitler's Field Marshals and Their Battles*. Chelson, MI: Scarborough House, 1990.

Moorehead, Alan. *Eclipse*. London: Hamish Hamilton, 1967.

Nicholson, Col G.W.L., C.D. *Seventy Years of Service: A History of a Royal Canadian Army Medical Corps*. Ottawa: Borealis, 1977.

Patton, George. *War As I Knew It.* Boston: Houghton Mifflin, 1947.

Peden, Murray. *A Thousand Shall Fall.* Toronto: Stoddart, 1988.

Ramsey, Winston G., ed. *After the Battle: The Battle of the Falaise Pocket, Number 8.* London: Battle of Britain Prints International, 1982.

Reynolds, Michael. *Steel Inferno: 1 SS Panzer Corps in Normandy.* New York: Spellmount, 1997.

Roberts, G.P.B. *From the Desert to the Baltic.* London: Kimber, 1987.

Rogers, Major R. L. *History of the Lincoln and Welland Regiment.* St. Catharines, ON: The Regiment, 1954.

Roy, Reg. *1944: The Canadians in Normandy.* Ottawa: Canadian War Museum, 1984.

Salmond, J.B. *History 51st Highland Division.* Edinburgh: Blackwood, 1953.

Shulman, Milton. *Defeat in the West.* London: Secker & Warburg, 1963.

Sloan Brown, John, "Colonel Trevor N. Dupuy and the Mythos of Wehrmacht Superiority: A Reconsideration," *Military Affairs,* January 1985.

Snowie, Allan. *Bloody Buron.* Erin, ON: Boston Mills, 1984.

Smith, Wilfred I. *Code Word Canloan.* Toronto: Dundurn, 1992.

Spiller, Roger S. "S.L.A. Marshall and the Ratio of Fire," *RUSI Journal* 133/4 (Winter 1988).

Stacey, Col. Charles C.P. *The Victory Campaign: The Operations in North-West Europe, 1944–1945. Vol III.* Ottawa: Queen's Printer, 1960.

Szygowski, Ludwik J. *Seven Days and Seven Nights in Normandy.* London: self-published, 1976.

Tout, Ken. *A Fine Night for Tanks: The Road to Falaise.* Phoenix Mill, Gloucestershire: Sutton, 1988.

———. *Tanks, Advance! Normandy to the Netherlands, 1944.* London: Grafton Books, 1987.

Van Crevald, Martin. *Fighting Power: German and U.S. Army Performance, 1939–1943.* London: Arms and Armour Press, 1983.

Vogel, Robert. "Tactical Air Power in Normandy: Some Thoughts on the Interdiction Plan," *Canadian Military History* 3/1 (Spring 1994).

Warlimont, Walter. *Inside Hitler's Headquarters, 1939–1945.* London: Weidenfeld & Nicolson, 1964.

Warner, Philip. *Horrocks: The General Who Led from the Front.* London: Hamish Hamilton, 1984.

Weigley, Russell F. *Eisenhower's Lieutenants: The Campaigns of France and Germany, 1944–1945.* Bloomington: Indiana University Press, 1981.

Whitaker, Denis, and Shelagh Whitaker. *Rhineland: The Battle to End the War.* Toronto: Stoddart, 1989, 2000.

———. *Tug of War: The Allied Victory that Opened Antwerp Harbour.* Toronto: Stoddart, 1984, 2000.

Wilmot, Chester. *The Struggle for Europe.* London: Collins, 1952.

Winterbotham, F.W., CBE. *The Ultra Secret.* New York: Harper & Row, 1974.

Womack, J.A. *Summon Up the Blood: A Unique Record of D-Day and Its Aftermath.* Ed. by Celia Wolfe. London: Leo Cooper, 1997.

Wood, Alan. *The Falaise Road.* Toronto: Macmillan, 1944.

Regimental Histories
Barrett, W.W. *The History of the 13th Canadian Field Regiment, Royal Canadian Artillery, 1940–1945.* (Collection of R.K. Mackenzie.)

History of the Corps of Royal Canadian Engineers, Vol. II. Ottawa: The Corps, 1966.

The History of the First Hussars, 1856–1980. Published by the Regiment, 1981.

The Regimental History of the Governor General's Foot Guards. Ottawa: The Regiment, 1948.

Personal Memoirs and Private Collections
Chadderton, Captain Cliff: *Caen to Calais: July-August-September 1944.*

Connors, Major John J.M. *The Story of an Unremarkable Canadian.* London, ON: self-published, 1981.

Danson, B.J. *"A Personal Essay: Being Hit, Normandy, August 1944."* 28 Feb. 1994. Kindly lent to the authors.

Dunlop, Lt. Arkle. "St. Lambert-sur-Dives, August 19 to 21, 1944. A memoir." Canadian Argyll Regiment (written c. 1980).

Boisjois: Hill 262. Montormel Memorial Committee, 1961.

Polish Combatants of Canada. *For Your Freedom and Ours, 1944–1994*.

van Dijke, Jacques. *L'Effondrement du front allemand en Normandie*. Rotterdam: 1995.

CREDITS

Victory at Falaise: The Soldiers' Story mirrors the thoughts and deeds of the warriors of Normandy. Scores of veterans of the armies and airforces of six nations were generous in sharing with us their personal experiences, their diaries, letters and photographs. The many references in our endnotes at the back of this book to these interviews and personal archives are a reflection of their value. We are very grateful for the confidence and support of these veterans. Without their input there would be no "soldiers' story."

We acknowledge and thank the Ontario Arts Council for its generous support. The Laurier Centre for Military Strategic and Disarmament Studies at Wilfrid Laurier University offered invaluable help in giving research assistance and retrieving archival data maps and photographs. We especially thank staff members Mike Bechthold, Chris Evans, Allan Thurrot and Ian Miller.

Our U.S. research was greatly assisted by the assistant director, Annie Wedekind, and the staff of the Eisenhower Center for American Studies, Metropolitan College, University of New Orleans: Kevin Willey, Michael Edwards and Matthew Ellefson. We are indebted to the research staff at the National Archives at College Park, Maryland, for guiding us through their vast reservoir of material.

We walked the battlefields of Normandy with much help and encouragement. Of great value – and fun – were the days we spent clambering over battle sites with the fine young scholarship students of the Canadian Battle of Normandy Foundation and their director, Professor Terry Copp. We had a fascinating day reliving the St. Lambert battle through the eyes of men who grew up in that area, assembled and coordinated through the kindness of a scholar of the battle, Colonel Jacques van Dijke of Rotterdam. We thank Ms. Pierre Grandvalet, Fank, Margerie, Madeleine, Huille and Masson for their *témoinages* and hospitality.

In Argentan we met M. Poulain; in Chambois, M. Chambart; in Thury Harcourt, Abbé Launay (formerly padre of Tournai-sur-Dives); in Falaise, M. Digueres and M. James; in Mortain, M. Langlois and M. Buisson; in Paris, M. Eddy Florintin.

Our Canadian research was greatly assisted by a number of associations, with the Royal Canadian Military Institute being, as ever, of unfailing co-operation and help. Krzysztof (Chris) Szydlowski, vice president of the 1st Polish Armoured Association of Canada, provided insight to the Polish battle and introduced us to veterans of those days. We thank two young scholars who assisted us: Patrice Collin of Ottawa (translations) and Thomas McDermott of Hamilton.

We appreciate the thoughtfulness and professionalism of all the staff at HarperCollins, and of our good friend and editor, Don Loney. The excellent maps are the work of Paul Kelly, gecko graphics inc. Kirsten Sheffield created the wonderful portraits of the soldiers of Normandy.

We are grateful for the input from the readers of our manuscript, whose critiques were invaluable: Linda Copp, Professor Ian Shaw and, as ever, our daughter Martie Hooker. During the lengthy process of producing our four books of military history, our families have stood by us with unwavering love and loyalty. To them, we say a special thank you.

INDEX

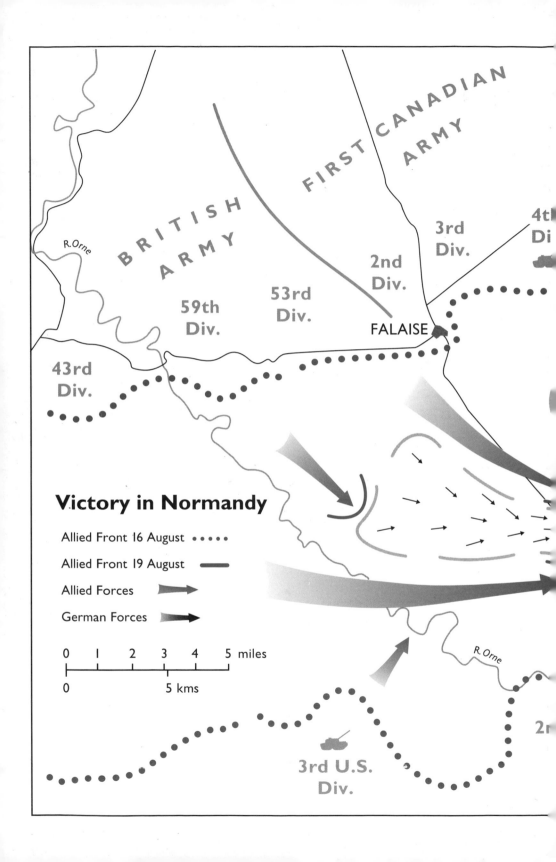

R. Orne

BRITISH ARMY

FIRST CANADIAN ARMY

4th Di

3rd Div.

2nd Div.

59th Div.

53rd Div.

FALAISE

43rd Div.

Victory in Normandy

Allied Front 16 August ·····

Allied Front 19 August ——

Allied Forces ➔

German Forces ➔

| 0 | 1 | 2 | 3 | 4 | 5 miles |

0   5 kms

R. Orne

3rd U.S. Div.

2r